A SOURCEBO
AMERICA
LITERARY JOURI

A SOURCEBOOK OF AMERICAN LITERARY JOURNALISM

Representative Writers in an Emerging Genre

Edited by THOMAS B. CONNERY

GREENWOOD PRESS
New York • Westport, Connecticut • London

Library of Congress Cataloging-in-Publication Data

A Sourcebook of American literary journalism : representative writers
in an emerging genre / edited by Thomas B. Connery.
    p.   cm.
  Includes bibliographical references and index.
  ISBN 0–313–26594–1 (alk. paper)
  1. Reportage literature, American—History and criticism.
2. American prose literature—History and criticism. 3. Nonfiction
novel—History and criticism. 4. Journalism—United States—
History. I. Connery, Thomas Bernard.
PS366.R44S68 1992
818'.08—dc20   91–17127

British Library Cataloguing in Publication Data is available.

Library of Congress Catalog Card Number: 91–17127
ISBN: 0–313–26594–1

First published in 1992

Greenwood Press, 88 Post Road West, Westport, CT 06881
An imprint of Greenwood Publishing Group, Inc.

Printed in the United States of America

The paper used in this book complies with the
Permanent Paper Standard issued by the National
Information Standards Organization (Z39.48–1984).

10 9 8 7 6 5 4 3 2 1

CONTENTS

PREFACE

It has been almost twenty years since Tom Wolfe attempted to define what came to be called "new journalism," a type of writing that he said combined the information-gathering methods of journalistic reporting with the narrative techniques of realistic fiction. In Wolfe's self-serving discussion of the new journalism, he grudgingly agreed that there were probably a few precursors to the form (Wolfe 1973, 45–46). But Wolfe refused to acknowledge the possibility that the form he described had a history or tradition, or that it was less restrictive in style and function than he claimed.

Since then, most critics who have analyzed the style and impact of the new journalism have at least mentioned precursors, and some have even suggested the possibility of a tradition. But a larger context has been either ignored or explored only fleetingly. No one has attempted to show that over time a body of writing exists that does not neatly conform to our common literary taxonomy, a body of writing that shares enough significant characteristics that it can be treated as a distinct form or genre.

This book brings together for the first time discussion of a wide range of writers who are treated as part of an ongoing, largely unrecognized American prose tradition, that of literary journalism of the nineteenth and twentieth centuries. Such writing is not "new" journalism, therefore simply a type of journalism, nor is it "factual" fiction, merely a type of realistic fiction. Rather, it is a distinct literary form, a type of cultural expression that can be defined and characterized. The new journalism is treated here as a part of that tradition and not as literary expression particular to a time.

The literary journalism considered in this book covers a period that begins with Mark Twain and concludes with the present day. This should not imply that literary journalism was suddenly born with Twain. Generally, however, when critics cite antecedents for new journalism before Twain, they provide British examples and specifically writing by Daniel Defoe,

William Hazlitt, and Charles Dickens, and various selections from the British press. Defoe's *Journal of the Plague Year* receives frequent mention, and in 1905 Hutchins Hapgood mentioned Defoe's *Moll Flanders* as an example of the creative nonfiction he was espousing. Although Defoe cleverly mixed fact and fiction and wanted his readers to think that he was telling a *true* story, both these books are works of fiction.

Examples of dramatic storytelling similar to literary journalism appeared in American newspapers prior to when Twain worked for newspapers in Nevada and San Francisco. One might argue, for example, that the reporting of James Gordon Bennett in his *New York Herald* contains elements of literary journalism.

For instance, when Bennett covered the murder of a young prostitute, he visited the scene of the crime and described the woman's room and her burned body. Bennett's article centers on the undeveloped theme of innocence violated. The article tells of a visit to the crime scene, but it is also about romantic notions gone astray, which Bennett conveys through his selection of detail. For example, when he describes the woman's room, he says, "It was elegant, but wild and extravagant in its ornaments." He notes the "light novels, poetry and monthly periodicals" on a shelf, and hanging on a wall is "a beautiful print of Lord Byron as the presiding genius of the place." Bennett's response to and description of the body bear a striking resemblance in tone to Poe's fiction, specifically his "Ligeia":

He half uncovered the ghastly corpse. I could scarcely look at it for a second or two. Slowly I began to discover the lineaments of the corpse as one would the beauties of a statute of marble. It was the most remarkable sight I ever beheld—I never have, and never expect to see such another. "My God," exclaimed I, "how like a statue! I can scarcely conceive that form to be a corpse." Not a vein was to be seen. The body looked as white, as full, as polished as the purest Parian marble. The perfect figure, the exquisite limbs, the fine face, the full arms, the beautiful bust, all, all surpassed in every respect the Venus de Medici. (Carlson 1942, 150)

But while such examples of descriptive narrative might be pulled from various newspapers or magazines from the 1840s on—and further investigation into mid-nineteenth-century publications is needed—no American writer produced either the quantity or quality of literary journalism of Twain until the 1890s, which is the first of three periods in which a significant amount of literary journalism can be identified.

Richard Harding Davis, George Ade, Abraham Cahan, Julian Ralph, Stephen Crane, Theodore Dreiser, Hutchins Hapgood, Lincoln Steffens, and William Hard all wrote literary journalism in the first period, around the turn of the century. Articles by Davis and Ralph that might be classified as literary journalism occasionally ran in *Harper's*; Crane's important piece of literary journalism, "The Men in the Storm," ran in *Arena*; and two of

Hapgood's attempts at extended literary journalism were book-length. But at this time, newspapers were as likely as magazines to contain literary journalism, in contrast to the later two periods.

By the 1930s, newspapers were solidly entrenched in the information model of reporting, to use Michael Schudson's terms, and a story model that might contain and be more conducive to literary journalism was generally shunned by newspapers. Consequently, literary journalism during this period primarily appeared in magazines and books, and includes work by James Agee, Joseph Mitchell, John Hersey, Ernest Hemingway, John Steinbeck, Ernie Pyle, and A. J. Liebling. John Dos Passos and John O'Hara also did some writing that could be treated as literary journalism, and as we move out of the forties and into the fifties, the work of Lillian Ross and Truman Capote appears in the *New Yorker*, where the literary journalism of Mitchell, Liebling, and Hersey had already been published.

Literary journalism of the third period begins in magazines and books but is carried over to newspapers. Of the writers covered in this most recent period, only Richard Ben Cramer and Bob Greene wrote significant amounts of literary journalism for newspapers. R. Thomas Berner, however, has documented the existence of literary journalism on the news pages (rather than on feature pages or in columns). Nevertheless, the major figures of this period include several writers who no longer write literary journalism, such as Norman Mailer, Gay Talese, and Tom Wolfe, as well as two who do, Joan Didion and John McPhee. Some would add Tracy Kidder to that list.

Despite the delineation of three periods when literary journalism seemed more abundant and more important, the line from the nineteenth through the twentieth century is continuous. Between the first and second periods appeared writing by John Reed, Ben Hecht, Ring Lardner, and Damon Runyon. While Capote and Ross wrote for the *New Yorker* in the 1950s, *Esquire* regularly published literary journalism as well, and occasional examples can be found in the *Saturday Evening Post*, *Collier's*, and *Life*.

The reader will find here discussions of most of the writers just mentioned, including the major new journalists such as Tom Wolfe, Gay Talese, Truman Capote, and Norman Mailer. But this chronological review also will include discussions of seemingly dissimilar writers, such as Mark Twain and John McPhee, or James Agee and Bob Greene.

Would Twain, McPhee, Agee, and Greene call themselves literary journalists? Probably not. They all are best known according to more traditional categories of writing: Twain, the fiction and humor writer; McPhee, the magazine journalist (or a specific subcategory, a *New Yorker* writer); Agee, the playwright, poet, film critic, and magazine journalist; Greene, the newspaper and magazine columnist.

Yet the central contention of this book is that a certain amount of the work of these writers, while often containing similar narrative approaches and literary techniques, is distinguishable from most mainstream journalism by virtue of *what* was conveyed, not just by *how* it was conveyed. It is distinguishable from fiction by virtue of its actuality. Although these concepts will be explored fully in the Introduction, literary journalism can briefly be defined as nonfiction printed prose whose verifiable content is shaped and transformed into a story or sketch by use of narrative and rhetorical techniques generally associated with fiction. The themes that then emerge make a statement, or provide an interpretation, about the people and culture depicted.

In his book *The Literature of Fact*, Ronald Weber declined to define what he meant by "literary nonfiction," his term for literary journalism, describing it as a "hazy and perhaps puzzling form" (1980, 3). But his analysis of a number of literary journalists, from Agee and John Hersey to Joseph Wambaugh and C.D.B. Bryan, did clear away some of the haze. Ultimately, this book attempts to push away some more of that haze and tries to clarify and simplify what we know about this nonfiction genre, and thereby make it easier for both students and scholars to explore literary journalism.

The book has two parts. Part One, the Introduction, serves several purposes. It notes writers and critics from the 1890s who have acknowledged the existence of a type of writing that falls between journalism and fiction, and establishes a historical context. It also provides a justification for using the term "literary journalism" and defines literary journalism, a definition derived from carefully considering the work of its practitioners. Finally, the Introduction will serve as a bibliographical discussion, noting the limited amount of scholarship and research conducted on literary journalism written before the 1960s, and mentioning all the major criticism and research on the new journalists.

Part Two, the bulk of the book, consists of essays by thirty-two different contributors on thirty-five writers who have produced either a significant amount of literary journalism or a particularly important work of literary journalism. For the most part, the essays are not merely reviews of the writer's literary journalism, but are critical essays that try to demonstrate exactly why the work of a writer is literary journalism and to what extent the writing succeeds. Sometimes that is done by a close reading of several pieces of a writer's work, while other essays take a broader thematic approach. For instance, Patricia Bradley's discussion of Richard Harding Davis takes a chronological approach to Davis's work, but she analyzes in some detail Davis's "The Death of Rodriguez," one of his more accomplished pieces of literary journalism; Paul Ashdown considers Agee's *Let Us Now Praise Famous Men* in relation to a Keats poem; Arthur Kaul sees Hunter Thompson's work as the embodiment of an American Jeremiah; and Jack Lule analyzes Joe Eszterhas's literary journalism as a form of political expression or discourse.

For readers already well acquainted with literary journalism, and particularly the better-known new journalists, the content and point of view of some of the essays will be familiar. However, even those conversant with the form will find fresh, original, and challenging discussions of literary journalists who have not received much critical attention. This is true of the Davis and Eszterhas pieces but especially applies to the contributions on George Ade, Theodore Dreiser, Stephen Crane, William Hard, Damon Runyon, Dorothy Day, Lillian Ross, Gay Talese, and Michael Herr.

I make no claim that the Introduction stands as the final word on literary journalism, and I certainly make no claim that this book's list of literary journalists is complete. To a degree, the writers included here are representative. A number of writers not included are discussed briefly near the end of the Introduction.

At the very least, this book intends to provide readers with a better grasp of the idea of literary journalism as a literary form and as a cultural way of knowing. It also serves as a call to assess literary journalism by its own standards and not those of either conventional journalism or realistic fiction. The essays and bibliographies should provide a place to begin additional investigations of literary journalism and literary journalists from a variety of critical approaches.

PART ONE

INTRODUCTION

DISCOVERING A LITERARY FORM

Thomas B. Connery

DEFINING AND NAMING

Although much has been written about a type of writing that contains elements of journalism and fiction, consensus has not emerged as to what to call it or how to define it. Some diehards still insist on using the term "new journalism," but literary nonfiction, artistic nonfiction, the nonfiction novel, the nonfiction story, and new reportage are a few of the names used to describe what is here being called literary journalism. Jon Franklin, a literary journalist and a teacher, has called the form literary journalism (1987), but also has described it as "true short stories" (1986, 6). But before explaining why literary journalism seems the most appropriate terminology, it is necessary to explain more specifically the nature and boundaries of the form by looking at a few of the definitions that have emerged, particularly regarding new journalism, and by presenting a definition that can be applied to works from various time periods.

Most of the critics who were responding to what was being called new journalism essentially accepted Tom Wolfe's definition, with some modification. Wolfe very basically described new journalism as reporting that read like fiction. More specifically, he described new journalism as "intense" and "detailed" reporting presented "with techniques usually associated with novels and short stories" (Wolfe 1973, 15). Four techniques or narrative devices are common to the new journalists and connect them to fictional realism, according to Wolfe: (1) scene-by-scene construction, or depicting people in dramatic scenes as in traditional storytelling; (2) complete dialogue as recorded and remembered rather than journalism's selective quotations; (3) varying the point of view, and even using third-person point of view; and (4) "status" details" or the habits, mannerisms, gestures, and so forth that distinguish people, societies, and subcultures (31–33).

For the most part, those who attempted to analyze the new journalism after Wolfe generally used Wolfe's ideas either as a basis or as a point of departure. James E. Murphy, for instance, tries to clarify Wolfe's definition by simplifying the form's characteristics. He describes new journalism as "an artistic, creative, literary reporting form with three basic traits: dramatic literary techniques; intensive reporting; and reporting of generally acknowledged subjectivity" (1974, 16). That definition includes Wolfe's requirement of thorough, detailed reporting, while "dramatic literary techniques" is broad enough to include Wolfe's criteria and those of others as well.

John Hollowell refines Wolfe's definition but adds little to it, while Ronald Weber expands the definition through analysis of specific writers ignored or dismissed by Wolfe. Both agree with Wolfe, however, in saying that new journalism is more artistic than conventional journalism and contains, in Hollowell's terms, the "intuitive insights of the novelist" (1977, ix). Most critics contradict Wolfe's contention that literary journalism, or new journalism, must include dialogue.

Writing more than ten years after Wolfe's declarations, Norman Sims both expands and revises Wolfe's definition in the introduction to *The Literary Journalists*. Sims describes the work of literary journalists as follows:

Reporting on the lives of people at work, in love, going about the normal rounds of life, they confirm that the crucial moments of everyday life contain great drama and substance. Rather than hanging around the edges of powerful institutions, literary journalists attempt to penetrate the cultures that make institutions work. (1984, 3)

Although that does not exactly indicate how literary journalism differs from conventional journalism. Sims goes on to say that literary journalists "view cultural understanding as an end" and present that understanding by letting "dramatic action speak for itself" (6). As an illustration, Sims refers to one of the writers included in his collection:

Bill Barich takes us to the horse races and brings alive the gambler's desire to control the seemingly magical forces of modern life; he aims to find the essences and mythologies of the track. By contrast, standard reporting presupposes less subtle cause and effect, built upon the events reported rather than on an understanding of everyday life. (6)

Sims interviewed at least six literary journalists, and from those interviews he came up with several characteristics of literary journalism, or, as he puts it, "the boundaries of the form": (1) immersion, or what Wolfe calls "saturation" reporting; (2) structure (each piece has its own dynamic and structure and does not conform to a journalistic formula); (3) accuracy; (4) voice (noninstitutional, personal); (5) responsibility (to the writers' subjects); (6) underlying meaning or symbolism (8).

More recently, in *The Art of Fact: Contemporary Artists of Nonfiction*, Barbara Lounsberry identifies four features of literary or artistic nonfiction: (1) documentable subject matter; (2) exhaustive research (immersion, saturation); (3) the scene; and (4) fine writing. The fourth feature is the most crucial for Lounsberry. She writes: "Verifiable subject matter and exhaustive research guarantee the nonfiction side of literary nonfiction; the narrative form and structure disclose the writer's artistry; and finally, its polished language reveals that the goal all along has been literature" (1990, xv).

In discussing "underlying meaning," Sims seems rather vague, perhaps because he based his discussion on interviews with literary journalists who themselves were rather vague and evasive on the matter of symbolism. Lounsberry, on the other hand, clearly emphasizes the importance of theme and symbolism to literary journalism as a distinguishing characteristic. She states that a major purpose of her book is "to indicate the importance of this genre in addressing many of the persistent themes of the American imagination," including conflicts between the individual and society and "the continued efficacy of the 'American Dream' " (xvi).

PATTERNS OF REALITY

If one reads the writing over the past hundred years that falls between traditional categories of fiction and journalism, and not just the core of writers identified with the new journalism, characteristics of the genre emerge, many of them similar to the defining elements identified by Sims and Lounsberry.

For instance, rather than just relating the informational who, what, or where, literary journalism depicts and conveys moments in time, behavior in society and culture. It broadly and subjectively explores how and why, reaching beyond the institutional parameters of those categories to produce prose characterized by, to use Alan Trachtenberg's phrase, "a rendering of felt detail" (1974a, 278). When it succeeds, literary journalism incorporates "the mythmaking power of fiction and the credibility of reportage" (Goldstein 1989, xvii). As Edwin Ford explains in "The Art and Craft of the Literary Journalist," "If the news reporter writes a record of reality, the literary journalist may be said to give a pattern to reality through the medium of his imagination" (1950, 309). Similarly, Jon Franklin says that "literary journalism does more than shovel data at readers. Instead, it uses carefully selected data from which it constructs patterns" (1987, 10).

Consider, for example, the following three works of literary journalism:

• In "The Broken-Down Van," which ran in the *New York Tribune* in 1892 under the standing head "Travels in New York," Stephen Crane takes a minor news item, a horse-drawn furniture van breaking down and causing a traffic jam, and transforms it into a local color piece that is almost out of control in throwing up a tumultuous flush of images, sounds, and people.

- In "Havana Cruise," which ran in *Fortune* in 1937, James Agee takes a relatively routine magazine assignment—what it is like to take a typical sea cruise on an ocean liner—and tells a bitter tale of American middle-class types behaving boorishly as they chase false dreams.

- In "How Can I Tell Them There's Nothing Left," which ran in the *Saturday Evening Post* in 1967 and was later reprinted as "Some Dreamers of the Golden Dream," Joan Didion takes a sensational California murder and retells it, suffusing her account with imagery that says more about illusion and reality, and confusion over values and the American dream, than it does about crime and punishment.

In writing these articles, Crane, Agee, and Didion were, to use David Eason's terms, trying to make sense of culture by telling stories. All three articles are works of literary journalism because they deal with actuality, with observed life, but inform at a level common to fiction or poetry rather than journalism.

By actuality I mean that the people, places, and events in these articles are not products of the writers' imaginations; they are not concocted. All three articles involved the use of the traditional journalistic function of recording information through observation, interviews, and reviewing documents.

Verifiable detail is essential to the literary journalist. Most literary journalists could identify with Didion's fascination with "physical fact" and Tracy Kidder's "close attachment to the particular" (Didion 1984, 5–6; Sims 1984, 24). Perhaps Agee said it best in *Let Us Now Praise Famous Men* when he explained that products of the imagination were not necessarily superior to observed detail, and declared that "there is quite as considerable value (to say nothing of joy) in the attempt to see or to convey even some single thing as nearly as possible as that thing is" (Agee and Evans 1939, 232).

But literary journalism informs at a level common to fiction. This means that it conveys impressions, ideas, and emotions and draws upon themes and motifs identified by the writer and revealed in the details of an event or in the manners, morals, and actions of people. Here is where Ford's "patterns" come into play, as well as Lounsberry's "themes of literature." Because literary journalists have a different purpose than mainstream journalists, the facts and particulars they gather are largely different from those found in mainstream journalism.

Many literary journalists would agree with Agee, who said that "who, what, where, when and why (or how) is the primal cliché and complacency of journalism." For Agee, and other literary journalists, the typical facts of a journalistic account simply do not provide enough detail, context, or interpretation to depict reality adequately. Essentially declaring conventional journalism a failure at accomplishing its purpose, Agee said:

I have never yet seen a piece of journalism which conveyed more than the slightest fraction of what any even moderately reflective and sensitive person would mean and intend by those achievable words, and that fraction itself I have never seen clean of one or another degree of patent, to say nothing of essential, falsehood. (Agee and Evans 1939, 234)[1]

Crane revealed the same sensibility as Agee when, in a newspaper piece, he implied that the kind of facts valued in much conventional news reporting might even be irrelevant. In that account, a man falls to the street in a seizure as he is walking home with his son from work, and a crowd forms around the two. Crane sarcastically writes: "Meanwhile others with magnificent passions for abstract statistical information were questioning the boy. 'What's his name?' 'Where does he live?' " (1973b, 347).

Such information might sometimes be useful and necessary, but Crane was more interested in what the incident revealed about people and urban life. The information of primary interest to the literary journalist is not whatever fits current concepts of news or the latest magazine conventions but whatever will depict human behavior.[2] As Bob Greene explains it, his topics "are the kinds of things that don't really qualify as 'news,' but that seem to me to have as much to do with the way we live as most of the events that warrant bold banner headlines" (1983, 15–16). This means that what is on the periphery of a subject for the conventional journalist may be of central interest to the literary journalist.

When William Dean Howells, for instance, reviewed Mark Twain's *Innocents Abroad*, he noted that the book "taught him nothing about the population of the cities and the character of the rocks in different localities," the kind of facts and description common in such accounts. Howells said that, instead, Twain's book was about "the realities of human life everywhere" (F. Anderson 1971, 28, 29).

Crane also was interested in depicting human life and said that in his writing he wanted "to give readers a slice of life" (1960, 158). Crane's contemporary, George Ade, who wrote for Chicago newspapers, expressed the same sensibility when he said:

My ambition . . . was to report people as they really were, as I saw them in their everyday life, and as I know them to be. Consequently, I avoided exaggeration, burlesque, and crude caricature; and I did not try to fictionalize or to embroider fancy situations, as was common in the fiction of that day. (1941, xxiii)

When Hutchins Hapgood in 1905 called for "a new form of literature" that would combine the reporting skills of the journalist with those of the literary artist, he emphasized that such a form of writing would allow for "a section of life" to be portrayed "and a human story told" (424). When Agee's article appeared in *Fortune*, the magazine's editor called "Havana Cruise" a "human document." Similarly, when Ford defined literary journalism, he emphasized its "human quality" and the fact that it consists of "showing people in the midst of life" (310).

This same desire to capture people as they really are was also crucial to the new journalists of the 1960s and 1970s. According to Wolfe, the new journalists were motivated by "that rather elementary and joyous ambition to show the reader *real life*—'Come here! Look! This is the way people live these days! These are the things they do!' " (Wolfe 1973, 33). New journalism critic Hollowell said that the form consists of works preoccupied with "the nature of man and his power to shape solutions . . . to the difficulties that confront him" (1977, 16).

To say that depicting observed life in printed prose is a primary goal of literary journalism is not to suggest that conventional journalism tells us nothing about reality, or life, or human behavior. Despite Agee's rather strong indictment, journalism's information does indeed often reveal "human life." But that occurrence is secondary, and often accidental, to its primary function as it has been defined by the industry and the profession in the twentieth century.

Even in the late nineteenth century what we now recognize as standard journalistic form and content were becoming established and well defined. That is why Hapgood was looking for a form that would have the actuality of journalism but the look and feel of fiction. That is at least one reason why articles like Crane's were labeled "studies" or "travels" or "stories" or "scenes" when they appeared in newspapers: such prose no longer fit the content requirements of conventional newspaper accounts.[3] That is also why much of what fills Julian Ralph's book of literary journalism, *People We Pass*, appeared first under a standing head in *Harper's Monthly* and then in book form as fictional stories. Ralph's accounts of tenement and immigrant life were from his reporter's notebook but did not fit the newspaper's emerging formula.

Of course, if literary journalistic content is different from that of conventional journalism, structure and style will be different as well. The literary journalist makes judgments and interprets by showing and dramatizing, as the fiction writer does, and by selection and arrangement of detail and imagery. Tone and theme are crucial to the literary journalist. This means that what the literary journalist has learned or observed is communicated by using whatever literary techniques and narrative forms work, rather than through the use of conventional journalistic news and feature forms. The Crane, Agee, and Didion articles demonstrate specifically how literary journalism is distinguished by both its form and content.

In Crane's "The Broken-Down Van," what occurs on the periphery is as important as the fact that generates the specific incident, a nut coming off a wagon wheel, or the consequences of that fact, a congested street and the inconvenience to other travelers. Crane's article teems with as much detail as the busy city street it depicts, and that detail is structured—with a clear beginning, middle, and end—to reveal aspects of human nature and characteristics of urban life. Thus the reader learns something about Howell's "human life," but in New York City instead of abroad.

The reader sees the reactions of various city types to the accident and hears bits of conversation among the wagon drivers and onlookers, between a barber and a sixteen-year-old girl. In one section, words and sentences run together as Crane tries to capture a moment's swirl of images and sounds. Through such a technique, and through description and use of dialogue, ironic contrasting, and literary allusion, Crane presents one of his recurring themes: the city as threatening and chaotic, cruel and indifferent. As Michael Robertson points out in his essay on Crane in this book, Crane's version of urban living is full of "poverty, vice, and petty crime."

Crane showed his readers working-class city types in the "Broken-Down Van"; in "Havana Cruise" Agee introduces readers to middle-class types. Agee's article appeared in an issue of *Fortune* devoted to the American shipping industry. The articles primarily dealt with the business and economics of the American merchant marine, and looked at the role and impact of American foreign policy on American shipping, as well as the role of unions and government economic policy. The foreword was written by Joseph P. Kennedy, chairman of the U.S. Maritime Commission, and a flattering profile of Kennedy was included as one of the articles on the industry. Agee's article seems totally out of place, contrasting with the tone and intent of the issue. As an introduction to Agee's unsigned article, the editor even acknowledged that it "has little to do with the profound economic problems of the merchant marine."

Agee obviously was sent on a cruise to get a different side of shipping, to provide a first-hand report on the pleasures of vacationing at sea. It was a perfect opportunity for a punchy, upbeat magazine feature. But what he brought back was not an article filled with shipboard facts and descriptions of the delights and joys of an ocean voyage. Although Agee did depict some happy moments, readers found writing that looked much like a short story, with the ship's journey nicely providing narrative unity. Through descriptive scene-setting and bits and pieces of conversation, Agee depicted the typical cruise ship tourist as someone rather sad and deluded, full of insecurities and false hopes and dreams. As one critic has observed:

All the experiences and emotions of a pleasure cruise...are captured in the course of the narrative. And Agee raises his piece to the level of profound social criticism when he describes the tourist as the helpless, anonymous, middle-class victim of the unscrupulous tourist industry, whose main motive, of course, is profit. It is the essential emptiness of middle-class life that makes the exploitation possible. (Quoted in Ashdown 1985, xxxvi)

Although Agee's journalistic assignment had a typical pleasure cruise as its subject, the cruise became a vehicle for his critique of his real subject, American character and culture.

Similarly, when Didion decided to look closely at a wife's murder of her husband in an affluent California suburb, her topic was not crime but the people involved and the culture that produced them. Her article contains facts (actual names, places, trial testimony) and concrete details, but they are placed within a carefully structured five-part narrative that begins with Didion saying that she is going to tell a "story about love and death," two of life and literature's greatest themes, and it is all going to take place in a metaphorical "golden land" (1968, 3).

In her account, Didion does not develop characters any more than Agee does in "Cruise." But she places the principal players in the drama within a context of mistaken notions of love and consumer-driven dreams. Didion's "information" in this article is not that a woman has been convicted of murdering her husband; nor does her article simply go beyond the basic facts to provide authoritative comments from police, psychologists, social workers, and so forth about why this woman might have killed her husband, or what kinds of forces are at work, according to the experts, to make such an event possible. Instead, Didion provides us with her subjective, artistic interpretation and shares her discovery, which is "that the dream was teaching the dreamers how to live" (17). Didion shows us a curious picture of people who have abandoned their roots to live parched lives devoid of spirituality and driven by material acquisition.

Crane, Agee, and Didion took what they had witnessed or learned, and they used whatever literary techniques were appropriate to communicate their versions of reality. Those literary techniques are commonly used by fiction writers but rarely used in conventional journalism. The versions of reality they produced ultimately are three distinct cultural interpretations in a literary form that goes beyond conventional journalism's facts but stops short of fiction's inventions.

Archibald MacLeish has said that "the recognition that the newspaper story or the magazine article is capable of a form comparable to the great form of fiction is as just as it is belated" (1958, 5). MacLeish obviously was echoing Ford as well as several late nineteenth-century commentators who will be discussed later, but MacLeish added a twist, denying that even the most basic journalism was less "creative" than literature (fiction or poetry).

In comparing poetry and journalism, MacLeish called both "recreations" rather than one being a "creation" and the other not, because both are "derived from the common human reality" (10–11). He also declared that the "purpose of both is the reordering of the fragments selected in a sequence that makes sense" (7–8). What finally separates poetry and journalism, MacLeish argued, is that the imagination "transforms" that material of human reality. This happens because of the separate purposes of the two kinds of writing:

Journalism is concerned with events, poetry with feelings. Journalism is concerned with the look of the world: poetry with the feel of the world. Journalism wishes to tell what it is that has happened everywhere as though the same things had happened for every man. Poetry wishes to say what it is like to any man to be *himself* in the presence of a particular occurrence as though only he were alone there. (13)

What should be clear at this point is that literary journalism merges these concerns and purposes. Literary journalism deals with both the "look" and the "feel" of the world. Although the Crane and Agee articles both depicted types, point of view, theme, and a specific cultural context distinguish the depiction. Literary journalism has, as Paul Ashdown puts it, "a quality of extrapolating universal significance from isolated experience" (1985, xxx).

Didion has referred to writing as the attempt to impose a narrative "upon disparate images . . . to freeze the shifting phantasmagoria which is our actual experience" (1979, 11). That is the goal of the literary journalist: to attempt to "freeze" life so that reality can be depicted, not by creating, but by attempting to recreate the feel and look of life and experience from a single, subjective point of view. Many literary journalists would probably agree with Bob Greene, who says he makes his living by "seeing things. Then I write stories about what I saw." Greene calls himself a "storyteller" who tries to give the reader "some sense of what it was like to have been there" (1983, 15).

But some literary journalists and critics question whether it is even possible to "freeze" life, whether printed prose can adequately make reality comprehensible. According to David Eason, that awareness that narratives no longer allow us to know has led to two distinct types of literary journalism, realist and modernist. Eason writes: "While realism assures its readers that traditional ways of making sense still apply in society, modernist texts describe the inability of traditional cultural distinctions to order experience" ("The New Journalism and the Image-World," 194). Wolfe, Talese, and Capote are realists, Eason says, while Didion, Mailer, and Hunter Thompson are modernists.

Although Eason's theory makes an important distinction among works of new journalism, it is not clear whether this type of characterization can be applied to literary journalism that precedes the new journalism. Agee's *Let Us Now Praise Famous Men*, for instance, reflects a struggle on Agee's part to make reality comprehensible. Agee even declares the impossibility of ever reproducing life in prose, as he explains in *Let Us Now Praise Famous Men* when talking about George Grudner:

He is in those terms living, right now, in flesh and blood and breathing, in an actual part of a world in which also, quite as irrelevant to imagination, you and I are living. Granted that beside that fact it is a small thing, and granted also that it is essentially and finally a hopeless one, to try merely to reproduce and communicate his living as nearly exactly as possible, nevertheless I can think of no worthier and many worse subjects to attempt. (Agee and Evans 1939, 233)

Similarly, Crane acknowledged the unlikelihood of ever providing a mirror image of reality. He wrote: "But to get the real thing! It seems impossible! It is because war is neither magnificent nor squalid; it is simply life, and an expression of life can always evade us. We can never tell life, one to another, although sometimes we think we can" (1970, 222). But whether a piece of literary journalism can depict life is irrelevant to the fact of its existence as a distinct literary form, as a means of cultural expression. The point is that literary journalism attempts to show readers life and human behavior, even if what actually emerges is life's incomprehensibility and the inexplicability of human behavior.

TWO TYPES

This definition obviously shares much with previous definitions and does not specifically contradict those definitions. However, it includes no reference to immersion (saturation reporting or exhaustive research). Immersion may or may not be an element of literary journalism; its use is *not* necessary for a work to be classified as literary journalism. Making immersion optional allows for a broader, yet legitimate, application of the definition, as well as the identification of two categories of literary journalism.

By insisting on immersion as an identifying trait, a host of works that are shorter and impressionistic, but clearly both literary and journalistic, would be excluded. Yet these works would still fall outside the realm of conventional journalism or realistic fiction. These works make up one category of literary journalism. Crane's "The Broken-Down Van" falls into this category, as does Davis's "The Death of Rodriguez," Hemingway's "A New Kind of War," Wolfe's "The Girl Who Has Everything," and a considerable amount of writing by George Ade, Abraham Cahan, Damon Runyon, Ernie Pyle, Jimmy Breslin, and Bob Greene.

Although these writers did not spend days or weeks or months observing their subjects or researching, their works are about actual people and events and inform at a level common to fiction. Although they depict human behavior as it occurs over a much shorter time, they still rely on a variety of literary techniques to communicate what has been witnessed and learned. They also principally rely on showing readers scenes from life; they attempt to freeze actuality. And the scenes contain "the subtle lights and shadings of the author's vision" (Lounsberry 1990, xv).

The incident in Crane's "Broken-Down Van" occurs as people are completing the workday and ends a short time later. Yet, as has been shown, Crane's account is extensively detailed and intensely focused and has a literary purpose. When Bob Greene tells of a paralyzed sixteen-year-old testifying against the two young men who shot him while trying to rob him of ice cream money, he focuses sharply but briefly on the boy's court appearance. His short story is about a spark of courage and faith in a bleak, incomprehensible urban existence marked by ruthless violence. Greene tells his tale by providing background, relating the court testimony, and using concrete description that reinforces his theme and sets the tone. That neither Crane nor Greene gave up huge chunks of their lives to get the information for these two articles, but only observed a single scene for a short time, does not negate the articles' pedigrees as literary journalism.

Both Crane and Greene could have provided longer and more complex works whose characters were well developed individuals rather than types, works whose themes were more richly interpretive and grander. Crane could have taken us into the lives of those in his story, the wagon drivers, the barber, or a young girl carrying beer. He could have shown us how they live day to day. Similarly, Greene could have taken us inside the poverty-stricken lives of the young people involved in the shooting. Both could have integrated into their pieces the demographic and sociological facts of urban existence, information about wages, violence, family size, and so forth. This would have required days, weeks, and perhaps months of immersing themselves in the subject.

Had Greene or Crane done this, their work would fall into the second category of literary journalism, with Greene's book-length *Billion Dollar Baby*, Agee's *Let Us Now Praise Famous Men*, Hersey's *Hiroshima*, Ross's *Picture*, and much of the work of Talese, Wolfe, Mailer, Didion, Kidder, and McPhee. Even some shorter works, such as Agee's "Havana Cruise," Ross's "The Yellow Bus," Wolfe's "Las Vegas (What?) Las Vegas (Can't Hear You! Too Noisy) Las Vegas!!!!," and McPhee's "In Search of Marvin Gardens," involved spending a considerable amount of time observing people and digging for information. Immersion is crucial to writing longer, more complex articles or book-length works. But whether immersion is used or not, whether the piece is long or short, works from both categories consist of interpretive scenes from life that reveal aspects of human nature and American culture.

NAMING A GENRE

Weber, Sims, and Lounsberry all called this type of writing that contains elements of journalism and fiction by different names, which reflects the difficulty in coming up with a term that adequately and specifically identifies it.

While Weber's important book uses "literary nonfiction" to describe the form, a 1989 collection, *Representing Reality: Readings in Literary Non-fiction*, edited by John Warnock, includes a separate section called Literary Journalism and another called Literary Documentary, as well as sections on Travel Writing, Biography, History, Autobiography, Writing about Nature, and Writing about Culture. Four of the writers included in this book appear under Literary Journalism, three more are under Literary Documentary, and another is under Travel Writing. The Warnock collection suggests some ambiguity over the meaning of literary journalism, but it also demonstrates that literary nonfiction is an extremely broad category that might include a Eudora Welty essay or a John McPhee magazine article, a reflection by St. Augustine, or history by Thucydides. A collection of essays, *Literary Nonfiction: Theory, Criticism, Pedagogy* (Chris Anderson, ed., 1989), reflects the same meaning of literary nonfiction. It includes discussions of essays and journalism by such writers as George Orwell, John McPhee, Richard Selzer, Annie Dillard, and Lewis Thomas.

Lounsberry provides one of the most useful discussions of terminology, although primarily from the perspective of the literary critic. In part, Lounsberry perceptively places her discussion within the context of the news/novel discourse identified by Lennard Davis in *Factual Fictions*. In doing so, she points to the inadequacy of categorizing prose narrative as *either* fiction or nonfiction, with fiction being artistic and imaginative and nonfiction being nonartistic and unimaginative. In effect, Lounsberry builds on Mas'ud Zavarzadeh's contention in *The Mythopoeic Reality* that "theories of prose narrative suffer from a restrictive taxonomy" (1976, 50).

Nevertheless, although Lounsberry ultimately seems to suggest that it is best to study this type of discourse without using any terminology, she chooses to use either literary nonfiction or artistic nonfiction in her discussion. Interestingly, however, her book provides a close reading of five writers—Talese, Wolfe, Didion, Mailer, and McPhee—whom she calls "the Realtors," terminology first used, as she notes, by Barbara Tuchman (1990, xii). Lounsberry specifically defines what she means by this difficult-to-name discourse or genre, but in the end, "artistic" as a descriptive term still does not adequately suggest the boundaries she sets with some thought and care (xiii–xv).

Literary journalism is no more an ideal phrase than Lounsberry's artistic nonfiction, but I contend that it is the terminology that best fits the nature of the works under consideration. On the one hand, the term has occasionally been used over time to identify this form of writing. Hutchins Hapgood used the term early in the century, and Ford used it in the 1930s. But Wolfe also used "literary journalist" in his discussion of new journalism (Wolfe 1973, 8), and Charles C. Flippen, one of the early commentators on the new journalism, identified the writing of Wolfe, Talese, and others as literary journalism (1974). Significantly, Harold Hayes, editor of *Esquire* when much of this kind of writing was being published in that magazine, also called it literary journalism (1972). Norman Sims gave the term greater prominence with the publication of *The Literary Journalists* in 1984, and Sims's 1990 collection of essays also uses the term (*Literary Journalism in the Twentieth Century*).

The occasional use of the term, however, is not the primary justification for using it here. The two words, literary journalism, simply seem to best identify the printed prose under consideration.

Use of the word "journalism" is preferred over "nonfiction" because the works assigned to this literary form are neither essays nor commentary. It also is preferred because much of the content of the works comes from traditional means of news gathering or reporting, including interviews, document review, and observation. Finally, journalism implies an immediacy, as well as a sense that what is being written about has a relevance peculiar to its time and place.

Use of the word "literary" is more problematic than the use of "journalism." The word "literary" is not meant to suggest that journalism is not a part of literature, or that literary journalism is literature and most daily journalism and magazine journalism is not. Nor should it be thought of as an attempt to categorize a specific kind of journalistic writing as more artistic, and perhaps elite, although occasionally that may be the case. "Literary" is used because it says that while the work considered is journalistic, for the reasons just cited, its purpose is not just informational. A purely journalistic work is structured to convey information, primarily facts and authoritative viewpoints, clearly and efficiently. In a literary work, and in literary journalism, style becomes part of the meaning conveyed; the structure and organization of language interpret and inform.

While the journalistic aspect of literary journalism solidly grounds the writing in a specific time, with actual people and places, the literary aspect makes the work less ephemeral and allows it to become writing that is more likely than conventional mainstream journalism to stand up over time.

SEARCHING FOR ROOTS

The possibility of a nonfiction prose form that has elements of journalism and fiction was recognized long before the new journalists of the 1960s and 1970s, and particularly in the late nineteenth and early twentieth centuries. For instance, Lincoln Steffens tried to practice what he called "descriptive narrative" when he was a New York City reporter and then tried to implement that style of reporting and writing when he was editor of the *Commercial Advertiser* newspaper (1931, 242, 317).

About the same time that Steffens was experimenting at the *Advertiser*, a writer declared in the *Atlantic* that while most daily journalism had no life beyond the immediate facts reported, occasionally there emerged a "poet reporter" whose writing had the power to "make a day last forever" (Lee 1900, 232). This "transfigured reporter," said the writer, is "a journalist who is more of an artist than the artists, an artist who is more of a journalist than the journalists" (237).

Another *Atlantic* writer said that most of life's material can be reproduced as *either* journalism *or* literary art, but occasionally a reporter ceases to be a "machine or a mouthpiece" and uses "extra-journalistic skill in the portrayal of experience or character." When that happens, the article "asserts its right to be considered not as journalism, but as literature" (Boynton 1904, 848).

However, the most detailed early consideration of a form of writing that merged aspects of journalism and fiction was that of Hutchins Hapgood, who worked for Steffens at the *Advertiser*. In a 1905 article in *Bookman*, Hapgood called for a type of writing in which the writer would "be both interviewer and literary artist" (425). Newspaper interviews were "necessarily limited to facts," wrote Hapgood, while the fictional imagination of his day seemed limited in force and vitality. Why not use the interview and "look for a real tale?" he asked, and "instead of imagining a character, why not go forth and discover one?" (424). Like the new journalists years later, Hapgood even suggested immersion or saturation reporting, which he described as becoming totally involved with the lives of subjects (425).

Hapgood later said in his autobiography that when he joined the *Commercial Advertiser*, he fit in well with others who believed in "Steffens's idea of a literary journalism" (1939, 140). In 1937, Edwin H. Ford tried to give that term and the topic further currency and definition. In "The Art and Craft of the Literary Journalist," Ford made a distinction between a news report, or "a simple record of routine events of everyday life," "interpreting" the news in editorials and columns, and writing articles of "literary insight" in which the newspaper writer tries to "make the reader hear, feel, and see" by using "an approach somewhat similar to that of the novelist, short-story writer, and the poet" (1950, 305). Ford's literary journalists included Richard Harding Davis, Lafcadio Hearn, Ben Hecht, John Dos Passos, and Ben Field, as well as the humor writing of Ben Franklin and Mark Twain, among others.

Ford also explored the literature-journalism connection in another 1937 publication, *A Bibliography of Literary Journalism*. Ford listed a number of articles that had been written from the 1890s on in which the artistic possibilities of journalism were discussed, in which journalism with a literary purpose rather than an informational purpose was identified, including the Lee and Boynton articles. But he also described literary journalism as "writing that falls within the twilight zone that divides literature from journalism," and as "writing which has the interpretive caste [*sic*] of literature as well as the contemporary interest of journalism" (i).

But most of Ford's writers were overlooked by the critics of the new journalism. These critics usually included some of the writers Wolfe mentioned in passing, such as Stephen Crane, John Hersey, George Orwell, Lillian Ross, and A. J. Liebling, and often noted other "early" new journalists as well, including Mark Twain, James Agee, Jimmy Cannon, and James Baldwin. Typical was Nicolaus Mills's introduction to his *The New Journalism: A Historical Anthology*. Mills states, "The new journalism has never been so new that it was without precedent." He then quotes Jack Newfield's contention that Defoe, Addison and Steele, Crane, and Twain were new journalists and spends a sentence or two on Defoe, Twain, Orwell, and John Hersey as new journalists (1974, xvi–xvii).[4] Mills does add James Agee's *Let Us Now Praise Famous Men* to the list. Wolfe had called Agee's work "a great disappointment" and denied that it could be considered new journalism (Wolfe 1973, 44).

Some discussions of new journalism's roots, however, have been a bit more developed and thoughtful than either Wolfe's or Mills's. For instance, *Journalism History* tried to bring a historical perspective to the new journalism discussion in its Summer 1974 issue with three articles devoted to, as the publication said, "Tracing the Roots of the New Journalism."

In one of the articles, Warren T. Francke makes a case for British journalist W. T. Stead being the first new journalist. Francke looks closely at Stead's writing, suggesting that Stead's "well-fleshed narrative scenes" and the way he "immersed himself in the story" made his work very much like that of Wolfe, Talese, and the other new journalists.

In the second article, "The New Journalism in Historical Perspective," Jay Jensen acknowledges that new journalism is "tied to a history and to a very long tradition," but does not really establish a tradition as much as simply state that some of the techniques of the new journalists can be traced as far back as the ancient Greeks. Jensen contends that the new journalism is part of "a historical pattern of appearance and re-appearance of different types of writings ... content ... and different approaches to journalism that occur again and again in American history" (1974, 37).[5]

The third article, "Historical Perspective on the New Journalism" by Joseph Webb, ambitiously tries to lay the groundwork for others to explore new journalism's historical roots. Webb complains that Wolfe's description of new journalism as "social realism" gives the form a "literary context and perspective," but it needs a "journalistic context and perspective" (1974, 38). Webb then argues that new journalism is a rejection of a rationalist epistemology that underlies modern journalism with its notions of objectivity and faith in external facts. The new journalist operates on the romantic philosophy and is, in fact, a Romantic Reporter, someone who assumes that

reality is to be found by focusing on internal, rather than external, human processes and movements; that feeling and emotion are more essential to understanding human life and activity than ideas; that a particular, unique perspective is to be sought in reporting more than the consensual one; and that human experience must be approached as a dynamic, organic phenomenon rather than as something which can be compartmentalized. (43)

With those assumptions, Webb then shows how one can work back through history and identify other Romantic Reporters, including Daniel Defoe, Mark Twain, George Orwell, and John Hersey. But he stops short of claiming a tradition. Rather, he concludes by stating that the term "Romantic Reporter" "places the emphasis . . . on the philosophical structure of the reportorial process, and it places those who do this kind of reporting in a specific historical perspective—and in what may turn out to be a specific historical *tradition* in journalistic writing" (60). As far as I know, neither Webb nor any other scholar has tried to apply Webb's definition and framework over time so as to establish the frequency and extent of his version of literary journalism, Romantic Reporting.

Journalism History's three articles did not confirm that the new journalism was part of a genre with a past or tradition, but they did make clear the possibilities for further exploration.

Some writers were not concerned with demonstrating that new journalism had a separate history, but rather wanted to argue that the style had *always* been a part of the journalistic tradition.[6] George A. Hough III wrote one of the more thoughtful articles in this vein, describing new journalism as "evolutionary" rather than "revolutionary." He says that rather than the new journalism being the "sudden arrival of a new style," as Wolfe maintained, "it is another stage in a long and gradual evolution of journalistic techniques. It is an honest journalistic genre—not just a borrowing from writers of fiction—which can be traced backward generation by generation through recognizable journalistic forbears" (1975, 115).

Hough notes the usual list of "forbears" and suggests a number of other contenders, although he does not demonstrate specifically that they did indeed consistently produce writing similar to new journalism. Among those named by Hough are several big names from "the golden age of the reporter," the late nineteenth century, including Julian Ralph, Winifred Black (Annie Laurie), Elizabeth Cochrane (Nellie Bly), and James Morgan. In this century, he mentions the *New Yorker*'s Joseph Mitchell, and specifically his collected magazine pieces, *McSorley's Wonderful Saloon*; John Bartlow Martin, and particularly an article he wrote for the April 5, 1952 *Saturday Evening Post*, "Death on M-24"; and *New York Times* reporter Meyer Berger.

If the new journalism seemed more stylish than earlier versions of the writing, Hough said, that was because contemporary writers had more freedom, which came from new technology and the economics of the journalism industry. Publications needed "new writers and new material," wrote

Hough, just as the publications in the late nineteenth century needed "new" writing (120).

To a certain extent, Hough and Jensen were claiming that new journalism was not new but rather a new stage of development for an old form. That was also the stand of James Murphy, who declared: "It is clear that New Journalism is not new. What is now billed as a literary genre is the product of gradual development and a reflection of the times more than it is a radical innovation" (1974, 34).[7]

In one of the first critical books that attempted an extended analysis of the new journalism as a literary form, *Fact and Fiction: The New Journalism and the Nonfiction Novel*, Hollowell, in what was becoming a familiar refrain, cautiously declared that "the historical roots of the present reporting are probably centuries old" (1977, 33). Hollowell echoed Ford and Hough when he said that "in America a reciprocal relationship has always existed between our literary and journalistic traditions," and mentioned how many American fiction writers had been journalists (34), which Ford had noted as well. But although Hollowell made connections and suggested possibilities that had not yet been explored, he used only four pages of his 152-page book on consideration of antecedents and did not attempt to establish a history of the form.

Weber did little to verify a genre over time, but in *The Literature of Fact: Literary Nonfiction in American Writing*, he greatly extended the range of the form's history by closely analyzing the work of Agee and Hersey.

DOING RESEARCH: A REVIEW OF THE LITERATURE

If there had been limited acknowledgment of the existence of literary journalism over time and limited exploration of it outside of the new journalism period, then it only follows that scholarly research and criticism have been relatively limited as well. Of the three major periods of literary journalism—late nineteenth and early twentieth century, the thirties and forties, and the sixties to the present—only the most recent period has generated a significant body of criticism and commentary. Consequently, those wishing to do research into literary journalists and literary journalism prior to the 1960s must, for the most part, cut new paths of investigation and interpretation by relying almost solely on the original works of the writers under consideration. Secondary sources are few, and a number of those have already been cited.

The new journalism has been the spark for the recent discussion, as has scholarly interest in nonfiction and acknowledgment of the importance of nonfiction and popular writing in contemporary society. Research into the previous periods has been hampered by any type of general agreement or acknowledgment that literary journalism exists prior to the 1960s except in certain isolated instances, such as in the writing of Agee or Hersey, and by the belief that what might be called literary journalism really belongs to another genre or is a longstanding journalistic form.

A review of the literature before the 1970s would vary, depending on the author and period, as well as the research focus. For instance, a general investigation into the literary journalism of a Crane, Hemingway, Agee, or Capote is considerably easier than an investigation into Lafcadio Hearn, George Ade, or Richard Ben Cramer, because much of the literary journalism of Crane, Hemingway, Agee, and Capote has been collected and published. Much of the work of Hearn, Ade, and Cramer would have to be pulled from newspaper microfilm, magazines, and obscure volumes that are difficult to find and seldom appear in bibliographies. But whether or not the writer's nonfiction has been collected, the researcher's first task might be to identify the writings that can be considered as literary journalism. Obviously, this requires establishing a definition of literary journalism.

The researcher also would want to place the writer under consideration within a literary and journalistic context. That might involve comparing the writer's literary journalism to the conventional journalism of the time, and therefore reviewing the period's newspapers and magazines, or reading various histories of journalism. It also could involve comparing the writer's work to the fiction of the period and to the prevailing narrative styles.

Secondary sources that have an acknowledged connection to literary journalism should not be ignored. For example, Shelley Fisher Fishkin's *From Fact to Fiction* carefully looks at how the journalism of Twain, Walt Whitman, Theodore Dreiser, Hemingway, and John Dos Passos influenced, and even defined, their poetry and fiction. Fishkin's book is indispensable in any consideration of the relationship between journalism and literary art. But the journalistic style she identifies in much of the work of her five writers has more in common with literary journalism than with conventional journalism. That is, it is not clear that the journalism of these writers had a strictly informational purpose. When she says that in his newspaper sketches Whitman "probes pockets and polite exchanges for motives and meanings," and that he "projects his imagination behind the surface of the scene he witnesses," the same could be said of the journalism of any of these writers, and of literary journalists as well (1985, 18).

Similarly, William Stott's *Documentary Expression and Thirties America* is not intended as an interpretation of literary journalism, but one can find many connections between his categories of thirties documentary prose and literary journalism. He does not identify the nonfiction he discusses as a distinct literary form; rather, he considers the nonfiction of the period that might be treated as literary journalism as just one aspect of a natural movement to document actuality in culture, to capture not facts but "the feeling of lived experience" (1973, 11).

Stott, for example, identifies the work he discusses as being part of "the genre of actuality" that has as its essence "the communication ... of real things" (xi). Depicting the human condition vividly and personally lies at the center of Stott's documentary expression, and that applies to literary journalism as well. He specifically makes the connection to literary journalism when he says that his discussion of the period's "documentary nonfiction" illustrates the "various ways the literate have found to approach and describe actuality and their fellow man" (144). Stott's documentary aims "to make real to us another person's experience, make us see what he sees and feel what he feels" (191).[8]

Although research into the new journalists and the more recent literary journalists may begin in a similar fashion and rely on similar general secondary sources, far more criticism and analysis exist. Much of the new journalism discussion, however, pertains to issues that emerged with the new journalism. For instance, whether the new journalism was actually "new," whether it was legitimate nonfiction or journalism, whether it could be trusted, are some of the issues that concerned critics in the 1970s. Such topics have more of a historical interest today, but have limited value in a consideration of such writing as a literary form or cultural expression, unless one's concern is the relationship between fact and fiction.

Nevertheless, a sense of the debate and controversy over the new journalism can be obtained from Weber's *The Reporter as Artist: A Look at the New Journalism Controversy* (1974), Flippen's *Liberating the Media* (1974), and a special section of the *Journal of Popular Culture* called "New Journalism" (1975). Flippen's book, however, like the Dennis and Rivers book, *Other Voices: The New Journalism in America* (1974), considers new journalism as a number of new or rediscovered approaches to journalism. Flippen's book, for instance, contains essays on the underground press, television, and film, while the Dennis and Rivers book identifies six types of new journalism, including literary journalism or what they call "the new nonfiction." Similarly, Michael L. Johnson's *The New Journalism* treats new journalism as part of larger countercultural changes in journalism. He devotes a chapter to "three major stylists," Capote, Wolfe, and Mailer, and another chapter is titled "New Journalists Writing on the General Scene and the Race and War Scene."

Weber's book might be the most useful of these because it contains articles that go beyond the bickering over the form's newness or its journalistic and artistic validity. Weber's introduction provides a critical perspective, and he discusses new journalism as "a new form of popular literature" that goes after a distinct part of the culture's mass audience. The book's articles are placed under four topics: Personal Journalism, The Article as Art, Fact in the Fiction Void, and Dissent and Qualification. The last section contains perspectives that many researchers exploring literary journalism as a cultural expression or literary form would find almost irrelevant, although it does contain literary critic Dwight Macdonald's attack on Wolfe and new journalism, which he calls "parajournalism." Authors included in the other sections are Tom Wolfe and Gay Talese (excerpts from introductions), Nat Hentoff, Dan Wakefield, Norman Podhoretz, Brock Brower, Herbert Gold, Harold Hayes, Seymour Krim, George Plimpton, and Donald Pizer. Also included are interviews with Talese and Capote.

The *Journal of Popular Culture* section begins with Marshall Fishwick's discussion of new journalism as a form of popular culture, and Richard Kallan provides an overview of commentary on new journalism to that point. Hough's article, discussed earlier, appears here. Many of the essays relate a work of new journalism to some aspect of popular culture. For instance, Ronald Weber takes the notion of space exploration and the space program and briefly discusses Wolfe's *The Right Stuff* and Mailer's *Of Fire on the Moon*, noting parallels in theme and perspective to fiction and reality. Elizabeth Landreth discusses the idea of Las Vegas and all that it symbolizes and represents in American culture, but ties her observations to brief analyses of works on Las Vegas by Wolfe, Hunter Thompson, and John Gregory Dunne. The special section also includes brief samplings of what a number of professional writers and editors think of new journalism, and a put-down by Robert J. Van Dellen, who describes new journalism as sensational ego-art and concludes that it is both "dishonest art and dishonest journalism" because it confuses fact and fiction, illusion and reality.[9]

Of particular interest, however, is Michael Johnson's essay "Wherein Lies the Value?" Johnson provides a perceptive literary and cultural interpretation of the new journalism, relating it to the fiction of the time, describing it as "an extremely rich and wide view of the world seen through the media of sensibilities intent on transforming our culture's awareness of itself, making it mythically self-conscious, making it see itself as its own work of art" (1975, 140).

As previously suggested, Hollowell in *Fact and Fiction* and Weber in *The Literature of Fact* offer an overview of the new journalism discussion, but both books are intended as literary studies. Hollowell's study deals with "the nonfiction novel's place in contemporary writing and the changes in the writer's relationship to history that it reflects" (1977, xi). Weber's concern is "journalism as literature," a "higher journalism" that has a "self-conscious literary purpose" (1980, 2–3).

In exploring new journalism or literary nonfiction, Hollowell and Weber rely on close readings of texts. The selection of writers and texts, however, reflects a limitation of the research into the new journalism. Much of the critical discussion evolves around a handful of writers. Norman Mailer, Truman Capote, and Tom Wolfe get most of the attention, with Gay Talese and Joan Didion appearing frequently; Hollowell analyzes works by Mailer, Capote, and Wolfe, as does Weber.

Weber, however, also looks at Talese, and specifically *Honor Thy Father.* But, more important, Weber considers works by Hersey, Agee, Jane Kramer, John McPhee, a trio of books on crimes (*Blood and Money* by Thomas

Thompson, *The Onion Field* by Joseph Wambaugh, and *The Michigan Murders* by Edward Keyes), and Tom Wicker's *A Time to Die*. He also very briefly discusses *Black Mountain: An Exploration in Community* by Martin Duberman, *John Brown's Journey* by Albert Fried, *Heroes* by Joe McGinniss, *Who Killed George Jackson* by Jo Durden-Smith, and *Friendly Fire* by C.D.B. Bryan. Thomas Thompson's *Serpentine*, Mailer's *The Executioner's Song*, and Wolfe's *The Right Stuff* are summarized and highlighted as recent works worth noting. Thus Weber's discussion shows the range of literary journalism and demonstrates that accomplished literary journalism is not necessarily confined to writing by literary stars and effective self-promoters.

In *The Mythopoeic Reality*, Zavarzadeh discusses "nonfiction novels" by Wolfe, Capote, Mailer, and Hersey, but also includes Oscar Lewis's *La Vida*. But what distinguishes Zavarzadeh's book from other works of literary journalistic criticism is its postmodernist critical perspective.

For Zavarzadeh "nonfiction novelists . . . have captured the fictive nature of technetronic culture" because the nonfiction novel by its nature rejects interpretation and any attempt to make reality coherent and meaningful. The nonfiction novel, says Zavarzadeh, has a bi-referential narrative mode, "simultaneously self-referential and out-referential, factual and fictional" (1976, 57). Zavarzadeh writes that the meaning in nonfiction novels lies "in the fictuality which emerges out of the counterpointing of fact and fiction through their bi-referential mode: an acting out of the contemporary experience which defies being labeled as fact or fiction and interpreted in terms of any single metaphysical framework" (57). The nonfiction novelist is, according to Zavarzadeh, "the mythographer of contemporary consciousness" (67).

Most critics have rejected Zavarzadeh's "zero interpretation" thesis, and would agree with Weber, who acknowledges that Zavarzadeh's ideas "draw on the significant critical current of the time," but "fail to conform to a close reading of some of the central works of literary nonfiction" (1980, 46). For Weber and others, Zavarzadeh's theory can be applied to *some* works of literary journalism, but not to all.

David Eason's categorization of new journalism into two distinct ways of responding to reality, one of which basically resembles Zavarzadeh's, provides a more workable model ("The New Journalism and the Image-World"). Eason's work is best understood, however, by reading three of his articles as though they are part of a single work. In those articles, Eason undertakes a highly perceptive inquiry into new journalism as a cultural and literary phenomenon, and specifically into the limitations and possibilities of new journalism as new language for depicting reality.

In "Telling Stories and Making Sense" (1981), Eason explores "the process of reporting as a literary act" and emphasizes how new journalism "called attention to the numerous realities which constituted society" (125,

129). Eason continues his exploration in "New Journalism, Metaphor and Culture" (1982), where he raises questions regarding "the relationship of narrative technique to empirical validity" (142) and examines how new journalism is a "metalanguage" and a competing discourse that challenges the assumptions of routine journalism.

But Eason's third article, "The New Journalism and the Image-World: Two Modes of Organizing Experience" (1984), recently revised as "The New Journalism and the Image-World" (Sims 1990), is generally considered his most significant contribution to the literary journalism discussion. Eason, like other critics, uses works by new journalism's stars—Wolfe, Capote, Mailer, Talese, Didion, Hunter Thompson—but his theory can be applied to literary journalism over time.

Eason builds on the ideas represented in his two previous articles, presenting new journalism as a cultural means of knowing, with two distinguishing views of society, "two different ways of responding to the problem of social and cultural diversity and of locating the reporter in regard to the traditions of journalism and the broader history of American society." Works by Wolfe, Talese, and Capote, according to Eason, are grounded in a belief in reality's comprehensibility. This type of new journalism "assures readers that traditional ways of making sense still apply in society." Eason calls works grounded in this belief *ethnographic realism* in the first version, and *realism* in the second.

Works by Didion, Mailer, and Thompson, on the other hand, are based on a belief that reality is incomprehensible. This type of new journalism describes "the inability of traditional cultural distinctions to order experience," and exists "in the space between realism and relativism." In his first version such works were called *cultural phenomenology*, but in the revision he calls them *modernist*. Eason concludes that these "diverse realist and modernist texts share a common identity . . . in the spirit of experimentalism which . . . pushed the conventions of realism to order emerging forms of subjectivity, and . . . dramatized the gaps between those very conventions and forms of subjectivity they seemed incapable of containing."

Another literary interpreter of the new journalism, John Hellman, also rejected Zavarzadeh's idea that new journalism was a form of pure transcription. But Hellman accepted Zavarzadeh's contention that contemporary experience had an absurd fictive quality that called for an experimental literary form. For Hellman, the new journalism is not literary nonfiction, but a "genre of new fiction."

Hellman bases his argument on Northrop Frye's contention that fiction is "a work of art in prose." New journalism's final direction, like fiction's, is inward (ultimately concerned with interior consciousness rather than external actuality); journalism, on the other hand, is descriptive and assertive, and its final direction is outward. Hellman rejects the claims of Wolfe, Hollowell, and Weber that new journalism is a new nonfiction realism. New journalism, says Hellman, shares roots with fabulist fiction, with works by John Barth, Thomas Pynchon, Donald Barthelme, and Kurt Vonnegut.

Like the fabulists, the new journalists find "a fragmented reality . . . avoid representations and seek construction" (1981, 17). The new journalist and the fabulist assert "the necessity of an imaginative pattern-making consciousness," and they use imagination to "create a meaningful design" from personal experience (12). For instance, according to Hellman, Mailer creates a mock-heroic epic in *Armies of the Night*, and Wolfe creates a tragic quest in *The Electric Kool-Aid Acid Test*. Both works, and works by Thompson and Herr also analyzed by Hellman, are not objective representations of the actual world but the personal constructs "of a shaping, selecting, interpretive mind" (34).

Two book-length critical studies published in the late 1980s again focus on new journalism's stars. Anderson's *Style as Argument* analyzes the work of Didion, Wolfe, and Mailer, while Lounsberry's *The Art of Fact* looks at those writers plus Talese and McPhee, who has never been considered a new journalist but was included in Sims's 1984 anthology. Anderson and Lounsberry approach their analyses from very different perspectives.

Anderson contends that "a pure rhetorical motive" underlies the work of the new journalists. He describes new journalism as one of "the principal rhetorical genres of the age" and says that it "is inextricably connected with the effort to express the force and magnitude and sheer overpowering energy of the American experience" (1987, 2). As the new journalists attempt to capture that experience, however, they employ rhetorical strategies that are "shaping readers' attitudes and perspectives" (2). Anderson examines how each writer does this by establishing a unique voice that becomes part of a "metadiscursive" writing.

Lounsberry's perspective already has been discussed. Once she defines artistic nonfiction, Lounsberry turns to her five writers to demonstrate the artistry of their nonfiction through close readings. Unlike previous studies of these writers, however, Lounsberry provides a comprehensive rather than selective exploration of their nonfiction. She says that her goal "has been to describe themes and rhetorical strategies which unfold across the writer's whole body of nonfiction to date, and even to project likely future directions for their work, given current artistic trajectories." Furthermore, she says, she has tried "to demonstrate that the artistry of literary nonfiction can be equal to that of fiction, poetry, and drama" (xvi).

In the course of her analyses, she makes more striking observations: that Talese is "an American historian, crafting 'stories with real names' " in the tradition of Howells, Dreiser, Sinclair Lewis, and Fitzgerald; that Wolfe, hiding behind "mock sophistication and satire," is "carrying on the tradition of Jonathan Edwards and his 'new light' revivalism"; that Thoreau is McPhee's closest literary parent, and his work "preserves and extends the ideals of the nineteenth-century transcendentalists." Lounsberry's book does more to place the new journalists, and literary journalism, within the established literary tradition, with its traditional canon and themes, than any other critical study to this point.

Most of the writing identified as literary journalism from the 1930s to the present has appeared in either magazines or books, and consequently literary journalism in those publications has drawn just about all of the critical attention, with a few exceptions. Berner's *Literary Newswriting: The Death of an Oxymoron*, for instance, deals with an analysis of eight page-one articles from seven different newspapers that he monitored over a three-month period.

Berner's short work expands on the central thesis of a special issue of *Style* (1982), which was called "Newspaper Writing as Art." That issue contains articles on Ellen Goodman and Red Smith and two on Richard Ben Cramer, who was then writing for the *Philadelphia Inquirer*; Berner's article, "Literary Notions and Utilitarian Reality," in which he argues against newspaper writing as "art"; and an essay by Donald M. Murray in which he discusses "The Changing Style of Newswriting." Murray concludes that newspaper style is becoming more literary, moving "toward a new style that will not only inform about events, but about the human condition; that will not only sell papers, but will approach and sometimes become literature" (451). The back of the volume contains a bibliography broken into three categories: historical studies of individual writers, journalism as literary art, and journalistic style. The entries were taken from several indexes and journalistic bibliographies as well as thirty journals, most of which deal with journalism and communication.

Berner's discussion in *Literary Newswriting* stays close to the ideas of Weber and Hollowell, but his concern is newspaper writing. Berner defines literary newswriting as "the marriage of depth reporting and literary techniques in newspaper writing," and his essay explores those techniques and the significance of that definition to newswriting and reporting. Like the new journalists and realistic novelists, Berner says, the literary newswriter attempts to "replicate reality," tries to bring the reader as close as possible to what has occurred or has been witnessed by using techniques commonly employed by realistic fiction writers.

Perhaps the most significant aspect of Berner's essay, other than the fact that he is the first researcher to concentrate on literary journalism in newspapers, is that his examples of literary journalism are from big *and* small newspapers. Berner's examples come from the *New York Times*, *Washington Post*, and *Philadelphia Inquirer*, but also from the *Finger Lakes Times*, *Pottsville* (Pa.) *Republican*, and *Stockton* (Calif.) *Record*.

Tracking literary journalism in newspapers makes research especially difficult. About 1,600 daily newspapers are published in the United States, so reviewing a significant number of dailies of various sizes would be a far more tedious and complex exercise than reviewing literary journalism in books or magazines, and could be expensive and extremely time-consuming as well. Reviewing bound volumes of monthlies such as *Esquire*, *Rolling Stone*, *New York*, or the *New Yorker* in search of literary journalism simply requires time and access to a library. Furthermore, the work of established literary journalists is regularly published in books. But if one intends to look at a newspaper journalist, it is easier to seek out the work of a writer who already has been recognized as doing literary journalism, such as Richard Ben Cramer, or to focus on a columnist whose work has been collected, such as Bob Greene.

Berner focused his review on thirty non-Pennsylvania metropolitan newspapers and thirty Pennsylvania newspapers that the Pennsylvania State University library subscribes to. Although that is a significant number, it leaves out nonmetropolitan dailies in forty-nine other states. A friend provided Berner with one of his examples, and he discovered another reading Gannett's corporate magazine.[10]

The annual collection *Best Newspaper Writing*, which contains outstanding newspaper writing as judged by a committee of the American Society of Newspaper Editors, published by the Poynter Institute for Media Studies, sometimes contains writing that can be classified as literary journalism, beginning with the work of Cramer and Mary Ellen Corbett in the first volume, 1979. Other strong examples of literary journalism from the *Best Newspaper Writing* books include articles by H. G. Bissinger in 1982, David Zucchino and James Kindall in 1984, John Camp and David Finkel in 1986, and Jimmy Breslin in 1988.

Good samplings of literary journalism, of course, can be found in Wolfe and Johnson's *New Journalism* and Sims's *The Literary Journalists*. Three of the twenty-four selections in Wolfe's collection are from magazines or books, and one is from the *Village Voice*, one from the *New York Herald-Tribune*, and a third from the *London Times*. The only newspaper writing in Sims's collection is from Barry Newman of the *Wall Street Journal*.

Literary journalism also can be found in *Smiling Through the Apocalypse: Esquire's History of the Sixties*, edited by Harold Hayes; *Popular Writing in America* (selections change from edition to edition); Warnock's *Representing Reality*; and *Reporting: The Rolling Stone Style*, edited by Paul Scanlon. Otherwise, the best sources of literary journalism are individual writers' collections or the newspapers and magazines.

Sometimes a book on writing, such as Andre Fontaine's *The Art of Writing Nonfiction*, William Ruehlmann's *Stalking the Feature Story*, or Berner's *Writing Literary Features*, will contain all or part of works of literary journalism, as will collections such as *Eyewitness to History*, edited by John Carey, or *The Pulitzer Prizes* collections.

Fontaine's book is particularly valuable because his purpose is to document how to write literary journalism, or journalism "based on rigorous reportage, which employs the creativity and skills of the fiction writer"

(1974, ix). Similarly, Jon Franklin's *Writing for Story: Craft Secrets of Dramatic Nonfiction by a Two-Time Pulitzer Prize Winner* is a book on writing. But Franklin is an accomplished literary journalist, and his book contains "Mrs. Kelly's Monster" and "The Ballad of Old Man Peters," Pulitzer Prize–winning literary journalism that he wrote for the *Baltimore Sun*. Also worth a look is *Writing Creative Nonfiction* by Theodore A. Rees Cheney (1987). Cheney dedicates his book to Capote, Talese, and Wolfe.

Although *A Treasury of Great Reporting*, edited by Louis L. Snyder and Richard B. Morris, contains examples of outstanding, vivid journalism that often use various literary techniques, it is arguable whether many of the selections are genuinely writing with a literary purpose. It does contain a condensed version of Mark Twain's 1873 coverage for the *New York Herald* of the Shah of Persia's visit to England, and articles by Irvin S. Cobb (1907), Frank Ward O'Malley (1907), Herbert Bayard Swope (1912), and Lee McCardell (1932) are worth a look. *Treasury* also has some British selections that some might treat as early literary journalism, including articles by Defoe and Dickens.

OTHER LITERARY JOURNALISTS

As stated previously, this book makes no claim to being an inclusive review of American literary journalists. Several writers not included in the essays that follow should be mentioned, however briefly.

JULIAN RALPH: Generally acclaimed as one of the great reporters of the late nineteenth century, Julian Ralph covered many of the major events of his time. His newspaper writing was characterized by use of extensive detail, while his magazine articles, particularly those done for *Harper's Magazine*, often contain the scene-setting, dialogue, concrete description, and dramatic recreations designed to depict human behavior and emotion that are associated with literary journalism. Even his newspaper accounts, such as his coverage of the death of Ulysses S. Grant (the *Sun*, 1885), reflect a tone and mood common to storytelling. His ability to use dialogue to capture both a place and a character type can be found in his magazine travel pieces, such as "Where Time Has Slumbered" (*Harper's*, Sept. 1894), but his *People We Pass: Stories of Life Among the Masses of New York City* (1896) perhaps contains his strongest work of literary journalism. Ralph described the book as a "reflection of scenes that have been actually witnessed" when he was a reporter. Some of the book's selections, such as "Cordelia's Night of Romance," may seem more like fiction than literary journalism, but others, such as "The Mother's Song" and "The Lineman's Wedding," are legitimate works of literary journalism. An earlier book by Ralph, *On Canada's Frontier* (1892), contains selections that also might qualify, especially "Dan Dunn's Outfit," "Antoine's Moose-Yard," and "Big Fishing."

LAFCADIO HEARN: Hearn was a prodigious writer in several genres. From 1872 to 1877 he worked for the *Cincinnati Enquirer* and for the *Cincinnati Commercial*; he wrote for New Orleans newspapers from 1877 to 1890. Some of his writing for these papers can be classified as literary journalism. Good bibliographies of Hearn's writing exist, and the Public Library of Cincinnati and Hamilton County contains a Hearn Collection that includes files of his *Enquirer* and *Commercial* articles. Perhaps the best examples of Hearn's literary journalism can be found in *Children of the Levee* (University of Kentucky Press, 1957), which contains sketches of life among the blacks who worked the Cincinnati docks and steamboats. Particularly strong pieces of literary journalism are "Dolly: An Idyl of the Levee," "Pariah People," and "Banjo Jim's Story." *The Selected Writings of Lafcadio Hearn* (Citadel Press, 1949) contains two sections of newspaper writing, one from Cincinnati newspapers, including "Dolly," and the other from New Orleans. Also of interest are *Barbarous Barbers and Other Stories* (Hokuseido Press, 1939) and Jon Christopher Hughes's *The Tanyard Murder: On the Case with Lafcadio Hearn* (University Press of America, 1982), which recounts Hearn's coverage of a grisly murder for the *Enquirer*. Hughes's *Period of the Gruesome: Selected Cincinnati Journalism of Lafcadio Hearn* (University Press of America, 1990) has the most complete collection of Hearn's Cincinnati work, and *Fantastics and Other Fancies* (Houghton Mifflin, 1914) contains New Orleans newspaper articles.

BEN HECHT: Best known for writing *The Front Page*, Hecht worked as a reporter and columnist for the *Chicago Journal*, the *Chicago Daily News*, and *PM* in New York. Of particular interest to literary journalism are collections of his newspaper columns, *1001 Afternoons in Chicago* (1922), *Broken Necks* (1926), and *1001 Afternoons in New York* (1941). Of related, but perhaps limited interest, would be the *Chicago Literary Times*, a tabloid that Hecht founded in 1923 and which died in 1924. Hecht's sketches of urban life lack the subtlety and grace of George Ade's and the detail and precision of Julian Ralph's, but his work is in the same tradition of literary journalism, and comparable in many respects to the work of his contemporary, Damon Runyon, and to the early work of Jimmy Breslin. Also of interest is *Gaily, Gaily* (1963), a collection of Hecht's reminiscences about his days as a youthful reporter. Most of these articles appeared in *Playboy*.

A. J. LIEBLING: Although Liebling began his career in newspapers and is well known for his press criticism, his work that can be treated as literary journalism was done for the *New Yorker* in the late 1930s and 1940s. Liebling's so-called lowlife pieces are collected in *Back Where I Come From* (1938), and his war reportage in *The Road Back to Paris* (1944). *The Earl of Louisiana* (1961), which is about Louisiana Governor Earl Long, merits consideration as an extended work of literary journalism. Liebling's work has become more accessible due to a reissuing by North Point Press of San Francisco. *The Honest Rainmaker: The Life and Times of John R. Stingo*, first published in book form in 1953, was published by North Point in 1989 and includes an introduction by Garrison Keillor and Mark Singer, whose literary journalism is included in Sims's collection (1984). *Rainmaker*, as much as Liebling's other work, deserves treatment as literary journalism. Taken together, these pieces written for the *New Yorker* are unified thematically and inform at a level common to fiction. North Point also published *Back Where I Come From* in 1990. Schocken Books published some of Liebling's best war reportage in *Mollie and Other War Pieces* (1989), including "The Westbound Tanker" from *The Road to Paris* collection. A most useful collection of Liebling's work is *Liebling at Home* (1982), which contains five previously published works, including *Rainmaker* and *The Earl of Louisiana*.

JANET FLANNER: Most of Flanner's smoothly analytical pieces for the *New Yorker*, although providing rich cultural interpretations, are not literary journalism. However, some of the pieces in *An American in Paris* (1940), particularly selections written for *Harper's Bazaar*, such as "Murder Among the Lovebirds," are highly noteworthy. Some of the profiles in this volume, especially "The French Lilly," also deserve a close look and might be classified as literary journalism.

JOHN O'HARA: O'Hara, of course, is best known for his realistic fiction, for being an imaginative recorder of life and human behavior. But Berner demonstrates in an unpublished article, "The Doctor's Son Covers a Euthanasia Trial," how O'Hara applied his literary vision to coverage of a murder trial for the International News Service. O'Hara wrote sixteen articles, with the best collection of the work appearing in the *Boston Daily Record*. As Berner states, O'Hara's coverage is only "a modest piece of literary journalism," but O'Hara clearly mixed fact and fiction in his writing and had a strong influence on one of literary journalism's more important recent writers, Gay Talese.

ERNIE PYLE: Pyle's journalistic reputation lives today primarily because of his war reporting. Many of Pyle's articles (written for the Scripps-Howard Newspaper Alliance) from the World War II battlefields of Europe and the Pacific, and bomb-ravaged London, can be found in *Ernie Pyle in England* (1941), *Here Is Your War* (1943), and *Brave Men* (1944). But an excellent source for Pyle's war pieces is *Ernie's War* (Simon and Schuster, 1986), edited by David Nichols. Nichols also came out with a collection of Pyle's American columns, written while Pyle traveled the country in the 1930s, called *Ernie's America* (Random House, 1989). Both volumes contain writing that can be treated as literary journalism, but a careful reading would be required to identify the pieces that best qualify. Pyle's writing at first glance can seem deceptively simple, and primarily informational. But reading a block of the 500 to 800-word columns reveals a strong point of view, a storytelling sensibility marked not so much by thematic patterns as by depiction of values such as honesty, integrity, generosity, and a belief in simple pleasures, plain language, and faith in common people. In the war dispatches, Pyle turns to ironic contrasting more than in the American pieces (i.e., describing how beautiful London looks as it is being bombed). Also, larger themes emerge as his depictions of wartime conditions for the common foot soldier are transformed into tales about loyalty, resignation, survival, adaptation, loneliness, and, ultimately, endurance.

MEYER BERGER: Mentioned by Hough as one of several "old" new journalists, Berger primarily falls into that category of literary journalism that contains Ade, Runyon, Hecht, Breslin, and Greene. Like them, Berger makes good use of dialect and dialogue, and paints mini-sketches of New York City and its residents. Articles Berger wrote for the *New York Times*, the *New Yorker*, and *Life* are collected in *The Eight Million: Journal of a New York Correspondent* (1949; Columbia University Press, 1983).

JOHN SACK: Sack wrote for *Esquire* when Harold Hayes was editor; his work appears in *Esquire* collections, and a selection appears in the Wolfe anthology as well. Perhaps Sack's finest literary journalism dealt with the Vietnam War, especially "When Demirgian Comes Marching Home Again (Hurrah? Hurrah?)," which ran in *Esquire* in January 1968. It is included in *Smiling Through the Apocalypse* and in Sack's book, *The Man-Eating Machine* (Farrar, Straus, 1973). Sack's *M* (New American Library, 1967) is his insider's look at an Army company from training camp to Vietnam in 1965–66. When parts of *M* were first submitted to *Esquire*, Sack's use of interior monologues was challenged, but Sack tracked down M Company soldiers all over the country and had each one verify the veracity of his version of their thoughts and experiences. *Esquire* then ran Sack's article.

JOHN GREGORY DUNNE: Dunne's reputation lies with his novels, particularly *True Confessions* and *Dutch Shea Jr.*, but the former *Time* magazine writer was a freelance magazine writer in the 1960s and produced two book-length works of nonfiction, *Delano: The Story of the California Grape Strike* (Farrar, Straus, 1967), an expanded version of an article he did for the *Saturday Evening Post*, and *The Studio* (Farrar, Straus, 1969), his inside look at the operation of Twentieth Century Fox. *Delano* is more of an example of good first-person, in-depth reporting than literary journalism, but *The Studio* is a polished work of literary journalism that contains wonderful dialogue and scenes made possible by Dunne's listening to and watching his characters for almost a year. A chapter from *The Studio* appears in Wolfe's anthology. Dunne's *Vegas: A Memoir of a Dark Season* (Random House, 1974) was supposed to be similar to *The Studio*, but Dunne found the reporting and writing of *The Studio* depressing drudgery and could not bring himself to do the same thing to capture Las Vegas. So he wrote a more imaginative work, part fiction and part fact, and ultimately more of an autobiographical novel rather than literary journalism. Nevertheless, *Vegas* is often treated as a work of literary journalism, comparable to Hunter Thompson's work. Dunne's declaration a few pages before the book begins is often quoted: "This is a fiction which recalls a time both real and imagined. There are, for example, comics, prostitutes and private detectives in Las Vegas; there is no Jackie Kasey, no Artha Ging, no Buster Mano. I am more or less 'I,' he and she less than more he and she." Some of Dunne's sixties articles can be found in *Quintana and Friends* (1968), and essays, observations, and reflections he wrote for magazines such as the *New York Review of Books* and *Esquire* can be found in *Crooning: A Collection* (Simon and Schuster, 1990).

HARRY CREWS: Best known as a fiction writer, Crews also has written literary journalism, primarily for *Esquire* and *Playboy*. *Blood and Grits* (Harper and Row, 1979) is a collection of these articles, and includes "L. L. Bean Has Your Number, America!," "Going Down in Valdeez," "Tuesday Night with Cody, Jimbo and a Fish of Some Proportion," and "Carny." Many of the pieces in *Blood and Grits* also are included in *Florida Frenzy* (University of Florida Press, 1982). Crews's pieces are personal, and he is the narrator and principal character encountering other distinctly American characters and their institutions.

JOSEPH WAMBAUGH: *The Onion Field* (William Morrow, 1973) was Wambaugh's first attempt at literary journalism and followed on his success as a best-selling novelist. Wambaugh, a former police officer, focuses on crime and police life. He wrote *The Onion Field* with Truman Capote's encouragement. Like Capote's *In Cold Blood*, *The Onion Field* attempts to go beneath the surface of a crime; it involved reviewing 65,000 pages of court records and conducting more than sixty interviews. The book takes the reader inside the judicial system, but also attempts a psychological portrait of two killers and one of their victims who survived. Wambaugh's more recent works of literary journalism include *Lines and Shadows* (William Morrow, 1984), which is about the work and lives of members of a special squad of San Diego police officers who patrol the border with Mexico, and *Echoes in the Darkness* (1987), the story of Philadelphia's "Main Line Murder Case," which Wambaugh presents as a contemporary nonfiction Gothic tale. Like *The Onion Field*, these books are novelistic in structure and are keen depictions of human behavior, interpretations of segments of American culture. Wambaugh's account of how authorities in England captured a rapist and killer by using genetic fingerprinting, called *The Blooding*, also is novelistic, but character development seems less important than the tension created by the search for the killer using a new scientific process that will identify him.

CHILTON WILLIAMSON, JR.: Williamson merits mention on the strength of a single book: *Roughnecking It* (Simon and Schuster, 1982). Williamson, a former back-of-the-book editor for *National Review*, moved to the western oil boomtown of Kemmerer, Wyoming, and worked and lived there as a roughneck (oilfield worker) for a year. The book, his account of the people and the land, is chock full of vivid description, lively scenes, and memorable characters that all reflect a modern western sensibility that has distinct roots in its western past. An earlier effort at journalistic immersion by Williamson, *Saltbound: A Block Island Winter* (Methuen, 1980), also deserves consideration as literary journalism, although at times it reads more like a personal and reflective journal. Nevertheless, Williamson's account of joining the close-knit permanent residents of Block Island, Rhode Island, richly portrays human behavior and the tension and struggle that come when rural ways resist modern development.

JIMMY BRESLIN: Breslin's reporting and writing style were noted by Wolfe in *The New Journalism*, although Breslin's writing was not included in that collection. As previously noted, Breslin's work lies within the literary journalistic tradition of Ade, Runyon, Hecht, and Meyer, and the persona he has created might be described as Runyonesque. His columns for the *New York Herald-Tribune* are collected in *The World of Jimmy Breslin* (Viking, 1967) and his work for the *Daily News* in *The World According to Jimmy Breslin* (Ticknor and Fields, 1984). Several of his 1987 columns are in *Best Newspaper Writing 1988*. His earlier work, although suffused with a subjective point of view distinctly Breslin's, primarily consists of sketches of types that rely on dialogue and concrete detail to depict a single evocative scene. His more recent work, while still full of detail and dialogue, scene-setting, and typical characters, contains openly stated judgments and commentary by Breslin.

RICHARD GOLDSTEIN: Goldstein's "Gear," one of several pieces he did for the *Village Voice*, is included in Wolfe's anthology. Articles Goldstein wrote from 1966 to 1970 primarily for the *Voice*, but also for *New York*, *Eye*, and the *New York World Journal Tribune*, are collected in *Reporting the Counterculture* (1989), one of the books in Hyman's Media and Popular Culture series. The series editor describes Goldstein's work as "fragmentary and intuitive" and both a "commentary" on and an "expression of" the late sixties. Goldstein's introduction is particularly useful because he places himself within the new journalism movement and discusses his work in relation to other new journalists, pointing out that new journalism was "a movement with many narrative stances" (1989, xvi).

FRANCIS X. CLINES: Like a number of other literary journalists, Clines was allowed to roam New York City and bring back brief tales of what he witnessed and heard. His "narrative story" of the city can be found in the columns he wrote for the *New York Times* from 1976 to 1979 and collected in *About New York: Sketches of the City* (McGraw-Hill, 1980).

CALVIN TRILLIN: One of many *New Yorker* writers who have produced works of literary journalism, Trillin writes nonfiction that falls into several categories, including political commentary and food page criticism. But examples of his literary journalism can be found in his *U.S. Journal* (Dutton, 1971) collection and in *Killings* (Ticknor and Fields, 1984), Trillin's *New Yorker* "U.S. Journal" pieces that deal with murders in small towns and cities all over America. The book is dedicated "to the *New Yorker* reporter who set the standard—Joseph Mitchell." In the book's introduction, Trillin attempts to explain how what he has done differs from typical newspaper or magazine journalism. The reference to Mitchell and this discussion, in which Trillin describes his work as "stories...about how Americans live" (xix), places Trillin within the literary journalistic tradition. "Stranger in Town" in the February 1, 1988, *New Yorker* is a more recent example of Trillin's literary journalism of this type.

J. ANTHONY LUKAS: Lukas won a Pulitzer for *Common Ground: A Turbulent Decade in the Lives of Three American Families* (Knopf, 1985; Vintage, 1986), which is an accomplished work of literary journalism. Critics have noted the book's novelistic structure and detail, as well as the richly developed characters, who, Lukas explains in an author's note, "are real, as are their names, the places where they live, the details of their personal lives." The book also has been compared to works by Capote, Mailer, and Agee. But although *Common Ground* attempts to show the effect of American culture on specific Americans, like works by these three writers, Lukas's book is less literary and more documentary. Nevertheless, Lukas's book contains the recurring imagery and themes, the revealing details and scenes, that provide a narrative interpretation of American culture. Lukas's first booklength work of literary journalism is *Don't Shoot—We Are Your Children!* (Random House, 1971). It largely was prompted by an article Lukas wrote for *The New York Times* on October 16, 1967, "The Two Worlds of Linda Fitzpatrick," written after Lukas's return from five years abroad as a foreign correspondent for the *Times*. That piece is expanded and modified for the book, which essentially contains profiles of ten young people who loosely "represent a broad spectrum of youthful disaffection." Through the profiles, Lukas investigates relationships between generations. But his reluctance to allow his narrative to interpret is evident in the book's final chapter, in which Lukas cautiously speculates about what it all might mean. In this sense, Lukas is more in the literary journalistic tradition of Hutchins Hapgood than that of Mailer, Capote, or Agee.

RICHARD RHODES: Rhodes's "Death All Day," an account of chasing and killing coyotes during the day and watching cockfights at night in Kansas, can be found in Sims's *The Literary Journalists*. It first appeared in *Esquire* and also was included in Rhodes's collection of pieces about the midwest, *The Inland Ground* (Atheneum, 1970), which also contains at least one other example of literary journalism, "The Community of True Inspiration." Although Rhodes's much acclaimed, Pulitzer Prize-winning *The Making of the Atomic Bomb* contains elements of literary journalism, it is more of a narrative history. The work that pushes Rhodes to the forefront of literary journalism, however, is *Farm: A Year in the Life of an American Farmer* (Simon and Schuster, 1989), which is similar in approach and achievement to Tracy Kidder's *Among School Children*. Rhodes's book documents the life of a Missouri farm family, but the telling of the story of Tom Bauer and his family becomes a tale of a struggle over a way of life. Although the book's extensive detail regarding the workings of farm machinery and the farming process seem excessive at times, it only lends authenticity to the depiction of certain traditional values that are part of American myth and reality—independence, hard work, self-reliance, the importance of family—which seem to be the real focus of the book. In trying to classify what he does, Rhodes has called himself "a veritist," or someone who captures what is real and true.

Early newspapers in colonial America often left a page blank so that as the paper lay in the tavern, coffee house, or post office, others might provide their own additional news. Similarly, it would be appropriate for this book to have such a page so that others might add their own examples of literary journalism. Many more newspaper and magazine writers from the late nineteenth century merit further consideration as literary journalists, including Josiah Flynt and Jack London, as do twentieth-century writers, including John Dos Passos and Meridel Le Sueur from the 1920s and 1930s, Thomas Morgan and Terry Southern from the late 1950s and early 1960s, or more recently Mark Singer and Sara Davidson. In fact, in more recent years literary journalism has become so common that it is difficult to track work being done for newspapers, regional and city magazines, and small presses, as well as the traditional major sources, such as the *New Yorker* or *Esquire*.[11]

The essays that follow will demonstrate just how broad literary journalism's umbrella is. When combined with the Introduction's discussion, the essays should provide a strong sense of an elusive tradition as well as the possibility for further definition and exploration.

NOTES

1. Agee claimed that it just was not the nature of journalism to be any different. "Journalism is not to be blamed for this; no more than a cow is to be blamed for not being a horse" (Agee and Evans 1939, 234–35).

2. Agee used the term "journalism" and did not distinguish between newspapers and magazines, and it would be wrong to think that magazines in general would be exempt from such criticism. Although newspapers in the twentieth century have tended to stick closely to the so-called inverted pyramid formula, magazines have subscribed to formula writing as well. As Harold Hayes once explained: "The magazine article was a form very largely taken for granted among editors and writers. They knew precisely what we required of the writer on any given assignment. The magazine article was a convention of writing, and those who were successful at it

were those who understood the convention in the same way that a reporter under-stands the demands of a news story. There was an anecdotal lead opening into the general theme of the piece; then some explanation, followed by anecdotes or ex-amples. If a single individual was important to the story, some biographical material was included. Then there would be a further rendering of the subject, and the article would close with an anecdote" (from "The New Journalism: A Panel Discussion," in Weber, *The Reporter as Artist*, 67). Hayes cited the *New Yorker* as an exception to magazine formula writing and occasionally *Esquire, Harper's*, and *Atlantic*. An-other time, Hayes acknowledged that throughout magazine history one could find examples of literary journalism. "The wealth to be found from mining magazine journalism somewhat prior to the day before yesterday is embarrassing—or should be to historians of the New Journalism and others who persist with the term" (1972).

3. For example, when Richard Harding Davis told an interviewer that in looking for the dramatic, pathetic, and human he always tells the thing that most "interests me" and "impressed me," the author points out that Davis's approach "requires an abrupt breaking away from journalistic formula and precedent" (Allen Sangree, 1901, Feb. 7, "Richard Harding Davis," *Ainslee's Magazine*), 4.

4. Although Mills's book contains pieces by some notable literary journalists, including Wolfe, Hunter Thompson, Richard Goldstein, and Norman Mailer, most of the articles are *not* literary journalism. Rather, the book contains articles that deal with coverage of the major issues and events of the sixties written in a variety of genres and styles.

5. Jensen's article is drawn from a longer piece that appeared in Flippen's *Lib-erating the Media*.

6. Some of the discussion over the "newness" of new journalism appears in Weber's *The Reporter as Artist*. Often the challenges to the claims of Wolfe for the new journalism occurred in book reviews. See, for example, Trachtenberg's "What's New" in *Partisan Review* 41 (1974). Trachtenberg says that some of what was being called new journalism "belongs to an older practice of picking up stories in the press and *imagining* them into novel form" (299). He places other examples of new journalism in other traditional categories, including political reporting, inter-views with celebrities, in-depth stories, and human interest accounts, in effect de-clining to acknowledge the possibility of a distinct form. There is, he wrote, "nothing new in writing narratives of firsthand experiences in contemporary society with dialogue, scene, dramatization" (299), which, of course, this book contends as well. Wolfe's new journalism, Trachtenberg says, "is full of half-baked versions of ideas in currency" (302).

7. John Pauly maintains that today's literary and cultural critics tend to ignore that the new journalism was a call to "symbolic conflict" and a challenge to "the authority of Journalism's empire of facts, and the sanctity of Literature's garden of imagination." Pauly says that historians and critics have "forged it [new journalism] into a literary canon and, in the process, disarmed its politics." "The Politics of the New Journalism," in *Literary Journalism in the Twentieth Century*, ed. Norman Sims (New York: Oxford University Press, 1990).

8. Although it would be difficult to find two books as directly related to the purpose and execution of literary journalism as those by Fishkin and Stott, various cultural-literary studies might prove useful to investigating literary journalism. A few examples include Larzer Ziff's *The American 1890s* (New York: Viking Press,

1966); Christopher P. Wilson's *The Labor of Words* (Athens: University of Georgia Press, 1985); Alfred Kazin's *On Native Grounds* (New York: Harcourt, Brace, 1942 [reissued with a new preface in 1982]); and Edmund Wilson's *Shores of Light*, first published in 1952 and reissued in 1985 by Northeastern University Press. Studies on literary realism also apply.

9. The fact-fiction tension is evident in any discussion of literary journalism. And the divergence in views is great, running from one extreme to another, as in, for instance, the Hollowell and Lounsberry studies. Theoretical discussions that apply to the literary journalism context can be found in various studies of literary realism, including Warner Berthoff's *The Ferment of Realism* (New York: The Free Press, 1965), Berthoff's *Fictions and Events* (New York: Dutton, 1971), Harold H. Kolb's *The Illusion of Life: American Realism as a Literary Form* (Charlottesville: University of Virginia Press, 1969), and Everett Carter's *Howells and the Age of Realism* (Philadelphia: Lippincott, 1954). Davis's *Factual Fictions* is particularly useful and interesting because Davis challenges traditional categories of literature and makes a case for the existence of what he calls a news-novel discourse. For a modest application of Davis's ideas to Hutchins Hapgood and literary journalism, see Connery, "Hutchins Hapgood and the Search for a 'New Form of Literature,' " *Journalism History* 13 (Spring 1986): 2–9. See also Hayden White, "The Fictions of Factual Representation," in *The Literature of Fact* (New York: Columbia University Press, 1976); Lionel Gossman's "History and Literature," in *The Writing of History*, ed. Robert H. Canary and Henry Kozicki (Madison: University of Wisconsin Press, 1978); E. L. Doctorow, "False Documents," *American Review* 26 (Nov. 1977): 215–32; Louis Mink, "History and Fiction as Modes of Comprehension," *New Literary History* 1 (1970): 541–58; Eric Heyne, "Toward a Theory of Literary Nonfiction," *Modern Fiction Studies* 33 (Autumn 1987): 479–90; and Angus Fletcher, ed., *The Literature of Fact* (New York: Columbia University Press, 1976). Also worthwhile is Phyllis Frus's discussion of fact and fiction, and of journalism as literature in regard to Crane's shipwreck experience, in "Two Tales 'Intended to Be After the Fact' " in Anderson's *Literary Nonfiction* (1989).

10. Although it may be unlikely that a great deal of literary journalism is being written at small dailies, the nation's best small dailies do occasionally encourage nontraditional writing and reporting. For instance, the *Columbia Tribune* allowed a reporter to spend an immense amount of time trying to discover why and how a bright, talented, self-made woman holding public office faced public disgrace and charges of felony theft. Jeff Truesdell's article took up three complete pages of the Sunday newspaper on May 25, 1986. The piece, "Stolen Dreams, Secret Guilt: The Rise and Fall of Barbara McDonald," is the story of a woman's search for esteem and an expression of her pain and anxiety at failing.

11. For example, William Finnegan's literary journalism for the *New Yorker* is worthy of note (see "A Street Kid in the Drug Trade," Sept. 10 and 17, 1990; see also Finnegan, *Crossing the Line: A Year in the Land of Apartheid* [Harper and Row, 1986]), as is Verlyn Klinkenborg's account of Midwest farming, *Making Hay* (Vintage, 1986), and H. G. Bissinger's story of misplaced values and high school football in Texas, *Friday Night Lights* (Addison-Wesley, 1990).

PART TWO

THE WRITERS

EDITOR'S NOTE

Essays follow on thirty-five major representatives of literary journalism presented in roughly chronological order, from Mark Twain to Tracy Kidder. The lists of sources cited at the conclusion of each essay are not intended to be complete bibliographies for each writer. Primary sources list the literary journalism of the writer as well as other writing discussed in the essay. The secondary sources include any works mentioned in the essay or used to write the essay, as well as works that directly apply to the author's literary journalism.

MARK TWAIN

Jack A. Nelson

When Samuel L. Clemens walked through the door of the *Territorial Enterprise* in Nevada on a September day in 1862, the lanky young Missourian was about to launch a career as America's foremost humorist, novelist, and social satirist. In addition, if we define journalism as an account of events and conditions in the reporters' world, there is little trouble in identifying Mark Twain—as Samuel L. Clemens was known almost universally by the time he left the West—as an early and noteworthy practitioner of what we call literary journalism, writing that endures and remains of interest.

Although Twain's reputation as the preeminent American writer of the nineteenth century rests mostly on his fiction, it is fair to say that his nonfiction work alone merits him a foremost place with so-called New Journalists of the twentieth century like Norman Mailer, Tom Wolfe, and Hunter Thompson. Among his contemporaries, Twain's wit, his style, his pithy observations and mordant insights, along with his frontier-honed skill at cutting through sham, hypocrisy, pretense, and show to get at the bare-boned reality of a thing, made his work sought after then and makes it readable and pertinent yet.

In his travel books especially—in a world where readers relied on the written work to bring the world to their doorsteps—Twain reflects on scenes that were fascinating because they were exotic, far removed, and often idealized. His accounts of the Far West in *Roughing It* and of Europe and the Holy Land in *Innocents Abroad* particularly show these lands in a different light than the glorified accounts readers were accustomed to. As Rodman Paul says of *Roughing It*:

There exist accounts of this era that are more detailed, more complete, more factually accurate than *Roughing It*, but there are none that give a greater insight into the psychology of prospectors and would-be millionaires, into the prejudices and habits of a new western community, and into the folklore of frontier America. (1953, vii)

One reason Twain succeeds in these works is because of the roles he allows himself as participant. At varying times he is an exuberant greenhorn and bungler, an innocent apt to be put upon by bamboozlers, a true believer who finds the reality a disenchantment after what he has been led to expect by other published accounts, a cynic—and yet over all a traveler in tune with the marvels and adventures offered by these new places and people.

In a real sense this involvement of the writer, this straining of the scene through the journalist's psyche with little attempt at objectivity, paved the way for the so-called New Journalists of this century. There is a relationship with writers such as Mailer in *Armies of the Night* and Hunter Thompson in *Fear and Loathing in Las Vegas*. After all, Thompson, in what he called "Gonzo journalism," lived and ran for eighteen months with the famed motorcycle gang of California to write *Hell's Angels: The Strange and Terrible Saga of the Outlaw Motorcycle Gang*. In his manic, half-psychotic, highly adrenal style of portraying himself as a frantic loser, he sounds strange modern echoes of Twain. For instance, in the cajoling put-on to get press passes at the race track in "The Kentucky Derby Is Decadent and Depraved," Thompson is reminiscent of Twain wandering through the bazaars of Turkey or Florence.

In addition, Twain's travel accounts offer such a panorama of unforgettable characters, zestful narrative, yarn-spinning and humorous exaggeration, unbridled optimism, striking observation, wry comment, and richness of imagery and metaphor that they stand as hallmarks of participatory journalism even today.

If we grant that Twain's native genius was fashioned and honed by his experiences in Nevada and California, it is useful to look at his early newspaper work there as a prime ingredient of the writing skills that later burst full bloom upon the world. Yet in many ways Twain was a reluctant journalist, forced into the business more than once when down on his luck.

For instance, in the very beginning, before strolling into the *Enterprise* offices, Twain had been in Nevada fifteen months, prospecting, doing hard manual labor to get along, living in any handy shelter, and enduring assorted miseries with the aim of ending up rich. He owed $50 and wondered how he was going to survive until fall. "The fact is, I must have something to do, and that shortly too," he wrote his brother Orion (1917, 82). Declining to return home to Missouri with his tail between his legs, he instead turned to newspaper work. After struggling with the erratic fortunes of mining, he had begun in April 1862 to send in facetious letters to the *Territorial Enterprise* of Virginia City, the premier newspaper of the mining camps of

Nevada and much of California. Editor Joe Goodman recognized the talent of this correspondent, who signed himself "Josh." Fortunately for Twain and for the world, the *Enterprise*'s local reporter, well-known humorist and mining specialist Dan De Quille (William L. Wright), was planning to return to Iowa to visit his family, leaving a temporary opening. In July Goodman offered Sam Clemens a job as a local reporter at $25 a week.

Already Twain had spent several years in the Midwest and the East as a printer, a Mississippi river pilot, and a Confederate soldier. But here in the free-wheeling society of the Comstock mines and San Francisco, observing and recording grand events and human nature at work, he was what Henry Nash Smith called "a frontier Bohemian . . . an enchanted spectator" (1957, 16).

It did not take long for Twain to begin attracting notice. Hoaxes, exaggerated burlesque, and mock feuds with other reporters were standard fare in the uninhibited journalism of Washoe, as most inhabitants called Nevada then. After only a month on the *Enterprise* Twain produced one of his most memorable pieces, his "Petrified Man" hoax, which was reprinted October 15, 1862, in the San Francisco *Daily Evening Bulletin*.

Newspapers across the country reprinted the story, and according to Twain it even crossed the Atlantic to run in the London *Lancet*, a scientific journal. For readers accustomed to news in their newspapers, there was a plausibility and matter-of-factness about the story that gave it credibility— even though the description left the petrified man thumbing his nose and winking at the corner. For Twain and the staff of the *Enterprise*, this satire was made all the better by people's believing it.

In his early journalism, Twain is remembered as much as anything else for such outrageous hoaxes, but the young writer soon outgrew the genre. As a reporter during his eighteen months on the *Enterprise*, he developed a split personality. In February 1863 he began to use the pseudonym "Mark Twain" for personal and humorous journalism, although routine news items still bore the byline Samuel L. Clemens.

The asides and whimsy in his political dispatches were not universally admired. One contemporary, an editor of the Virginia City *Daily Union*, called his legislative reports "contemptible in the literary sense" and "scandaling to the reportorial profession and public journalism" (30 Jan. 1894). Nevertheless, Twain's letters from out of town were forerunners of modern humor columns. Gossipy and full of fancy, they offered fertile ground for his talents and his tongue-in-cheek approach to life.

Dan De Quille, who roomed with Twain on his return from Iowa, said that Twain as a reporter was

earnest and enthusiastic in such work as suited him—really industrious—but when it came to "cast-iron" items, he gave them a "lick and a promise." He hated to have to do with figures, measurements and solid facts, such as were called for in matters pertaining to mines and machinery. (Wright 1893, 170–71)

By May 1863 Twain had gained a following in Nevada and California, partly because of the custom of editors of reprinting particularly interesting articles from the exchange papers of other locales. This example from the *Territorial Enterprise* of a letter from San Francisco, under the headline "Letter from Mark Twain," testifies to his growing reputation. It also exhibits his developing abilities in telling a story with wit and style, and deals with his supposed journalistic enemy Clement T. Rice of the *Daily Union* in Virginia City, whom he called "The Unreliable." It is notable that Twain was in San Francisco from early May 1863 until early July. Such an extended visit was surely a sign of the leeway he was given by his employers.

The content shows the increasing use of his imagination and the reproduction of scenes to engross the readers, rather than the summary used by most reporters—all playing on Rice's naïveté in seeing his big-city experiences in mining-town vernacular, perfectly suited to the audience of Virginia City and the Pacific slope.

Eds. Enterprise: The Unreliable, since he has been here, has conducted himself in such a reckless and unprincipled manner that he has brought the whole territory into disrepute and made its name a reproach, and its visiting citizens objects of suspicion. He has been a perfect nightmare to the officers of the Occidental Hotel. They give him an excellent room, but if, in prowling about the house, he finds another that suits him better, he "locates" it (that is his way of expressing it). Judging by his appearance what manner of man he was, the hotel clerk at first gave him a room immediately under the shingles—but it was found impossible to keep him there. He said he could not stand it, because spinning round and round, up that spiral staircase, caused his beer to ferment, and made him foam at the mouth like a soda fountain; wherefore, he descended at the dead of night and "jumped" a room on the second floor (the very language he used in boasting of the exploit). He said they served an injunction on him there, "and," says he, "if Bill Stewart had been down here, Mark, I'd have sued to quit title, and I'd have held that ground, don't you know it?" And he sighed; and after ruminating a moment, he added, in a tone of withering contempt: "But these lawyers won't touch a case unless a man has some rights; humph! They haven't any more strategy into 'em than a clam. But Bill Stewart—thunder! Now, you just take that Ophir suit that's coming off in Virginia, for instance—why, God bless you, Bill Stewart'll worry the witnesses, and bullyrag the Judge, and buy up the jury and pay for 'em; and he'll prove things that never existed—hell! What won't he prove? That's the idea—what won't he prove, you know? Why, Mark, I'll tell you what he done when— ...

"This hotel ain't incorporated under the laws of the Territory, and they can't collect—they are only a lot of blasted tenants in common! O, certainly," (with bitter scorn), "they'll get rich playing *me* for a Chinaman, you know." I forbear to describe how he reveled in the prospect of swindling the Occidental out of his hotel bill— it is too much humiliation even to think of it. (13 May 1863)

Rice's reaction tells more about customs in Virginia City than those in San Francisco, for the Bill Stewart mentioned was a prominent mining attorney in Virginia City and later represented the state for many years as a U.S. senator. In this and later works, Twain's insightful social satire sets his writing apart from that of his fellows and helps his accounts to remain readable. Although Twain began with the customary fare of Comstock journalism, such as the petrified man hoax, he soon deserted the traditional devices to develop his own peculiar style and wry approach. For instance, the humor of tortured spellings as then practiced by Artemus Ward, Josh Billings, Petroleum V. Nasby, and Bill Arp was rejected by Twain. He had tried it when he had dabbled in journalism before coming to Nevada, in his "Thomas Jefferson Snodgrass Letters" written for the Keokuk *Saturday Post*. Fortunately he gave up such artificialities, learning instead to lean upon character and situation for humor.

Always one with itchy feet, Twain had a special affinity for bringing the experiences of travel alive for the reader by focusing on eccentricities of both people and places he visited. This report in the *Enterprise* of sitting by the driver on a treacherous stage trip over the Sierra Nevada in the dead of night gives a sample of the skills that later blossomed in *Innocents Abroad* and *Roughing It*:

Whenever I stopped coughing, and went to nodding...he would stir me up and inquire if I were asleep. If I said "No" (and I was apt to do that), he always said, "it was a bully good thing for me that I warn't, you know," and then went on to relate cheerful anecdotes of people who had got to nodding by his side when he wasn't noticing, and had fallen off and had broken their necks. He said he could see those fellows before him now, all jammed and bloody and quivering in death's agony—"G'lang! d——n that horse, he knows there's a parson and an old maid inside, and that's what makes him cut up so; I've saw him act jes' so more'n a thousand times!" The driver always lent an additional charm to his conversation by mixing his horrors and his general information together in this way. "Now," said he, after urging his team at a furious speed down the grade for a while, plunging into deep bends in the road brimming with a thick darkness almost palpable to the touch..."Now I seen a poor cuss—but you're asleep again, you know...As I was sayin', I see a poor cuss tumble off along here one night—he was monstrous drowsy, and went to sleep. I'd took my eye off him for a moment—and he fetched up agin a boulder, and in a second there wasn't anything left of him but a promiscus pile of hash! It was moonlight, and when I got down and looked at him he was quivering like jelly, and sorter moaning to himself, like, and the bones of his legs was sticking out through his pantaloons every which way, like that." (Here the driver mixed his fingers up after the manner of a stack of muskets, and illuminated them with the ghostly light of his cigar.) "He warn't in misery long though. In a minute and a half he was deader'n a smelt. Bob! I say I'll cut that horse's throat if he stays on this route another week." In this way the genial driver caused the long hours to pass sleeplessly away. (13 Sept. 1863).

By that time Twain had achieved a modest fame in Nevada and California. He was not only young but brash and arrogant. He wrote his mother and sister: "Everybody knows me, and I fare like a prince wherever I go, be it on this side of the mountains or the other. And I am proud to say I am the most conceited ass in the Territory" (1917, 92).

Only twenty-nine when he left Virginia City, Twain seemed younger. Growing restless, as he explains in *Roughing It*, and spurred by facing a dueling charge and considerable rancor on the part of some citizens for his charges against the Ladies Sanitary Commission, he headed for San Francisco to look for fortune.

After the bare hills, sagebrush, and alkali flats of Nevada, Twain fell in love with the green hills of San Francisco. Following a time of unemployment, out of necessity he found a position with probably the worst possible newspaper for him, the San Francisco *Morning Call*. In contrast to the *Enterprise*, here the editors invited no frills or literary contributions, nor did they allow any signed articles, thus imposing a certain damper on the young writer's natural inclinations. Looking back in 1906, Twain reminisced:

I felt a deep shame in being situated as I was—a slave of such a journal as the *Morning Call*. After having been hard at work from nine or ten in the morning until eleven at night scraping material together, I took the pen and spread this muck out in words and phrases and made it cover as much acreage as I could. It was fearful drudgery, soulless drudgery, and almost destitute of interest. . . . I got to neglecting it. . . . Mr. Barnes discharged me. It was the only time in my life that I have ever been discharged, and it hurts yet. (DeVoto 1940, 254–60)

Given the conditions, it is probably a wonder that Twain lasted the four months he did on the *Call*. Interestingly, however, researchers have identified dozens of articles, though unsigned, that they feel sure came from the pen of the former *Enterprise* reporter.

Indeed, some critics dismiss Twain's journalism in California as insignificant (Cox 1966, 24). Yet in his humorous work there is the spark, the insightful color and tongue-in-cheek approach that still makes it engrossing today. Even in his routine stories, his talent often shines through. For instance, the hand of Twain is evident in this follow-up item, appearing in the *Morning Call* on September 24, 1864, about two Chinese men who had got into an altercation in a butcher shop that resulted in the surgically precise carving of one of them:

Ah, Sow, the mathematical Chinaman, who stabbed Ah Wong "not too litty, not too much," but just exactly enough to make him uncomfortable, was discharged from custody yesterday, at the request of the grateful creature who was indebted for his life to his spirit of forbearance and the exercise of his extraordinary anatomical judgment.

Likewise, this comment on the frequent earthquakes could have been written by no one else on the staff of the *Call*:

When we contracted to report for this newspaper, the important matter of two earthquakes a month was not considered in the salary. There shall be no mistake of that kind the next contract, though. Last night, at twenty minutes to eleven, the regular semi-monthly earthquake, due the night before, arrived twenty-four hours behind time, but it made up for the delay in uncommon and altogether unnecessary energy and enthusiasm. The first effort was so gentle as to move the inexperienced stranger to the expression of contempt and brave but very bad jokes; but the second was calculated to move him out of his boots, unless they fitted him neatly. (22 July 1864)

After his dismissal from the *Morning Call*, Twain made a living of sorts by what his *Call* editor, George Barnes—reminiscing in his columns in 1867 about Twain's experience on the newspaper—termed "all sorts of literary work whereby he could turn a cent. It was a terrible, uphill business, and a less determined man than himself would have abandoned the struggle and remained at the base" (17 Apr. 1887).

During his two and a half years in San Francisco, Twain was in the center of West Coast journalism, which at that time was to say the literary scene. At various times he wrote for such publications as the *Californian*, the *Dramatic Chronicle*, and especially the *Golden Era*, a literary paper that was attracting the brightest figures in literature on the coast, including, along with Twain, Bret Harte and Joaquin Miller.

During these so-called Bohemian years, Twain left behind such columns as one that dealt with a recent spurt of interest in spiritualism in San Francisco. After investigation, he advises Californians to avoid the new "wildcat" religions and to stick to the old standard ones, such as the Presbyterians practice:

Notice us, and you will see how we do. We get up of a Sunday morning and put on the best harness we have got and trip cheerfully down town; we subside into solemnity and enter the church; we stand up and duck our heads and bear down on a hymn book propped on the pew in front when the minister prays; we stand up again while our hired choir are singing, and look in the hymn book propped on the pew in front when the minister prays; we stand up again while our hired choir are singing, and look in the hymn book and check off the verses to see that they don't shirk any of the stanzas; we sit silent and grave while the minister is preaching, and count the waterfalls and bonnets furtively, and catch flies; we grab our hats and bonnets when the benediction is begun; when it is finished, we shove, so to speak. No frenzy—no fanaticism—no skirmishing; everything perfectly serene. You never see any of us Presbyterians getting in a sweat about religion and trying to massacre our neighbors. Let us all be content with the tried and safe old religions, and take no chances on the wildcat. (*Golden Era*, 4 Mar. 1866)

Like all Twain's pieces, of course, it means considerably more than it says. Twain often found that the most serious things were best suited to humorous treatment. As a reporter both in Virginia City and California, he was exposed to crime, brawls, death, and misery along with the routine events he covered. These experiences forever marked his outlook on life and the human race and obviously provided fodder to chew on in his declining and cynical years. At the same time, during the years he was reporting, such events were spurs to the creative imagination that made Twain much more than a mere reporter of news events.

After languishing in California, Twain saw his fortunes change in 1866 when two things happened to alter the course of his career. First, the noted American humorist Artemus Ward, who got along famously with Twain during a two-week visit to Virginia City in 1863, wrote and asked for a humorous sketch for a book he was printing. Twain's contribution, arriving too late for inclusion in the book, was published in a New York magazine instead, and "The Celebrated Jumping Frog of Calaveras County" brought him instant fame in the East.

At about the same time, Twain cajoled the publishers of the *Sacramento Union* into sending him to the Sandwich (Hawaiian) Islands for a series of letters reporting on life there. Always Twain had a disposition to use the earthy vernacular of the mining camps, which sometimes offended genteel readers, but the habit gave life to his works and enabled him to report the world as he saw it. Besides, he was seldom able to resist such ventures into less-refined passages, as when he told of finding twenty-two of his fellow passengers on the voyage leaning over the bulwarks, with his fictitious friend Brown consoling them while the passengers were

vomiting and remarking, "Oh, my God!" and then vomiting again. Brown was there, ever kind and thoughtful, passing from one to another and saying, "That's all right—that's all right, you know—it'll clean you out like a jug, and then you won't feel so ornery and smell so ridiculous." (*Sacramento Union*, 16 Apr. 1866)

Twain's travel letters provided a forum to wax descriptive on the sights he saw, but he went beyond standard travel fare to offer insights and observations in his typical vivid, frank, and amusing style that makes them still widely read. The success of those letters led Twain to convince the San Francisco *Alta California* that he should be sent around the world in exchange for fifty on-the-scene letters. These were reprinted by James Gordon Bennett's New York *Herald* and Horace Greeley's New York *Tribune*, bringing the writer unprecedented fame. Gathered along with a few other letters and rewritten for a book, they became *The Innocents Abroad*.

In the preface Twain explains:

It has a purpose, which is, to suggest to the reader how he would be likely to see Europe and the East if he looked at them with his own eyes instead of the eyes of those who travelled in those countries before him.... I offer no apologies for any departures from the usual style of travel-writing that may be charged against me. ... I am sure I have written at least honestly, whether wisely or not. (1904, 3)

The book is informative—Twain in fact apologizes profusely for being so informative—but its major attraction remains his *reaction* to the events and sights he experienced. For instance, on being reminded for the umpteenth time of a local legend while climbing the Rock of Gibraltar, he uses dialogue to recount his protest:

While I was resting ever so comfortably on a rampart, and cooling my baking head in the delicious breeze, an officious guide belonging to another party came up and said:
"Senor, that high hill yonder is called the Queen's Chair—"
"Sir, I am a helpless orphan in a foreign land. Have pity on me. Don't—now *don't* inflict that most inFERNAL old legend on me any more today!" (54)

Throughout his travel books Twain fills in any possible gaps in his audience's education by recounting such time-honored history as the story of Abelard and Heloise in France. As always, however, it is Twain's reaction that is of most interest. Rejecting the traditional romanticizing of the affair, he applauds the punishment of Abelard: "Such is the history—not as it is usually told, but as it is when stripped of the nauseous sentimentality that would enshrine for our loving worship a dastardly seducer like Pierre Abelard" (117).

Similarly, Twain brings the same iconoclastic, jaundiced view to bear on many of the hallowed sites held in staunch awe by generations of travelers. With a skepticism that marked his lifetime, for instance, he describes the treasures of the Milan Cathedral in Italy:

The priests showed us two of St. Paul's fingers, and one of St. Peter's; a bone of Judas Iscariot, (it was black) and also bones of all the other disciples; a handkerchief in which the Savior had left the impression of his face. Among the most precious of the relics were a stone from the Holy Sepulchre, part of the crown of thorns, (they have the whole one at the Notre Dame) a fragment of the purple robe worn by the Savior, a nail from the cross ... (142)

Yet his good-natured scorn was generally without rancor and was spread around equally. For instance, mixing his reportage with sardonic observations of people and customs as always, he describes the merchants he found in Turkey this way:

Commercial morals, especially, are bad. There is no gainsaying that. Greek, Turkish, and Armenian morals consist only in attending church regularly on the appointed Sabbaths, and in breaking the ten commandments all the balance of the week. It comes natural to them to lie and cheat in the first place, and then they go on and improve on nature until they arrive at perfection. (291)

It is interesting that even after the astonishing success of *Innocents Abroad*, Twain still saw himself as a journalist rather than a literary figure. In 1871, five years after leaving California, he wrote the story of his earlier sojourns in Nevada, California, and Hawaii. To accomplish this, he dredged up his and his brother's memories, scrapbook, and clippings in delivering by way of reminiscence what may be his finest literary reportage, *Roughing It*.

In this lively account of a midwesterner seeing for the first time the wonders of the American West, Twain sharpens the devices of top-notch participatory journalism that became so prevalent in the 1970s and after. Unlike other contemporary accounts of the West, he uses scenes rather than summaries; he intrudes unabashedly as an innocent greenhorn into the bustling frontier, refuses to be intimidated by the lines between reality and fancy, offers insights and comparisons often startling by their clarity and truth, and at the same time improves on the exaggeration so famous on the frontier and not ignored by later practitioners of the New Journalism.

As in *Innocents Abroad*, in *Roughing It* Twain portrays himself as an eager traveler, a gullible greenhorn who is the butt of numerous jokes, a keen observer, and at the same time a passionate optimist and a romantic disillusioned by what he finds in the reality of the West. Nowhere is this exemplified better than in his regard for the American Indian, often glorified in literature and sociology of the time.

The disgust which the Goshoots gave me, a disciple of Cooper and a worshipper of the Red Man—even of the scholarly savages of *The Last of the Mohicans* who are fittingly associated with the backwoodsmen who divide each sentence into two equal parts, one part critically grammatical, refined and choice of language, and the other part just an attempt to talk like a hunter or a mountaineer, as a Broadway clerk might make after...studying the frontier life at the Bowery Theatre a couple of weeks—I say that the nausea the Goshoots gave me...set me to examining authorities to see if perchance I had been over-estimating the Red Man while viewing him through the mellow moonshine of romance. (1899, 1:157)

As in his other works, Twain's observations provide the flavor of the book. When, on his first silver-hunting venture, he returns gloating to camp to inform the others that he has already struck gold, the experienced miner Ballou shatters his dream, pronouncing his find "nothing but a lot of granite rubbish and nasty glittering mica that isn't worth ten cents an acre." Not only has Twain shown himself the bumbling, arrogant newcomer, but he draws from the incident a lesson that comes home to all of us. "Mr. Ballou said I could...lay it up among my treasures of knowledge that *nothing* that glitters is gold....However, like the rest of the world, I still go on underrating men of gold and glorifying men of mica. Commonplace human nature cannot rise above that" (1899, 1:228).

As with the literary journalists of a later time, Twain displays passion in his interests. He burns with mining fever like the other early prospectors in Nevada; he exults in owning his own timber tract before burning it down out of carelessness; he imbibes the invigorating life of Virginia City and the madness of speculation in mining stocks; he is aghast at territorial government. He is not without opinion on even the most common matter. For instance, of the changing of the name Bigler Lake—where he spent an idyllic time—to the Indian name Lake Tahoe, Twain fumes, denouncing Tahoe as "that spoony, slobbering, summer-complaint of a name" (*Golden Era*, 13 Sept. 1863).

Some of the major incidents in the book can be traced to events he covered for either the *Territorial Enterprise* or the other newspapers he wrote for during the 1860s. Other chapters are based on his general experiences, such as the hilarious lack of communication between the miner Scotty Briggs and the minister when the former comes to make arrangements for Buck Fanshaw's funeral. As usual, in *Roughing It* Twain is rambling and disorganized in his approach, one topic reminding him of another in the fashion of a man spinning yarns around a fire with a friendly audience. This provides a forum for his commentary, opinions formed in his years in the mining camps of Nevada and the hills of California. For instance, Twain's satire on the folly of a jury system that rewards ignorance and rejects anyone who is informed has lost none of its pertinence today. He tells of efforts to empanel a jury in the case of a desperado who wantonly killed a respected citizen. After discussing an intelligent and informed panel of jurors who were dismissed because they had heard of the case, Twain concludes: "But of course such men could not be trusted with the case. Ignoramuses alone could mete out unsullied justice" (2:75).

Of course those comments remind Twain of the case of fearless Captain Ned Blakely, who sailed out of San Francisco. In one of the far islands without law, he tells, ne'er-do-well bully Bill Noakes, mate on another ship, shoots downs in cold blood the Negro mate on Blakely's ship, witnessed by six sea captains. Then Captain Ned marches in with a shotgun, takes Noakes prisoner, and announces that he will hang the man. Twain launches into dialogue—a device that is the hallmark of his literary reporting—to hammer home his point in a delightful way as, aghast, the captains protest that there must be a trial.

> "Trial! What do I want to try him for, if he killed the Nigger?"
> "Oh, Captain Ned, this will *never* do. Think how it will sound."
> "Sound be hanged! Didn't he kill the Nigger?"
> "Certainly, certainly, Captain Ned—nobody denies that—but—."
> "Then I'm going to hang him, that's all.... Mind you, I don't object to trying

him, if it's got to be done to give satisfaction; and I'll be there ... but put it off till afternoon, for I'll have my hands middling full till after the burying—"

"Why, what do you mean? Are you going to hang him *anyhow*—and try him afterward?"

"Didn't I say I was going to hang him? I never saw such people as you." (2:75)

The captains prevail for a trial, but Captain Ned is there waiting with his rope to take care of his business as soon as the trial ends. Twain closes the sketch with this note: "When the history of this affair reached California ... it made a deal of talk, but did not diminish the captain's popularity in any degree. It increased it, indeed." Combined with his lack of regard for the jury system, the chapters make his views on the American system of justice far more powerful than any essay.

In both *Roughing It* and *Innocents*, we see the world—as filtered through Twain—as an astonishingly fascinating, corrupt, pompous, colorful, wonderful, and above all human place. In the juxtaposition of comedy, mundane facts, raucous history, tragedy, and wry analysis he engrosses us and ultimately wins us over to his view.

If there is a theme in Twain, it is that he sets out to enlighten with the unvarnished truth—truth that sometimes is best made clear by exaggeration, by tall tale and anecdote, by whimsical observation, by reaction and debunking and use of sharp, fiction-like scenes to show the sometimes-ridiculous reality beneath the patina of a thing. That is the power of participatory journalism. Because of that unique virtue, it endures.

Even after a century, in the search for truth through the particular colored glasses of the writer, Mark Twain remains the forerunner and blood brother to the best literary journalists of all time.

PRIMARY SOURCES

Twain, Mark (Samuel L. Clemens). 1899. *Roughing It.* 2 vols. New York: Harper and Brothers.

———. 1904. *The Innocents Abroad, or The New Pilgrims' Progress, Being Some Account of the Steamship Quaker City's Pleasure Excursion to Europe and the Holy Land.* New York: Harper and Brothers.

———. 1917. *Mark Twain's Letters.* Vol. 2. Ed. Albert Bigelow Paine. New York: Harper and Brothers.

———. 1924. *Mark Twain's Autobiography.* Vol. 1. Ed. Albert Bigelow Paine. New York: Harper and Brothers.

———. 1953. *Roughing It.* Introduction by Rodman Paul. New York: Rinehart.

SECONDARY SOURCES

Benson, Ivan. 1938. *Mark Twain's Western Years.* Palo Alto: Stanford University Press.

Branch, Edgar M., ed. 1969. *Clemens of the Call: Mark Twain in San Francisco.* Berkeley: University of California Press.

Branch, Edgar M., and Robert H. Hirst, eds. 1979. *The Works of Mark Twain: Early Tales and Sketches.* Vol. 1. 1851–1864. Berkeley: University of California Press.

Brooks, Van Wyck. 1922. *The Ordeal of Mark Twain.* London: William Heinemann.

Cox, James M. 1966. *Mark Twain: The Fate of Humor.* Princeton, N.J.: Princeton University Press.

DeVoto, Bernard, ed. 1940. *Mark Twain in Eruption.* New York: Harper and Brothers.

Fatout, Paul. 1964. *Mark Twain in Virginia City.* Bloomington: Indiana University Press.

Fishkin, Shelley Fisher. 1985. *From Fact to Fiction: Journalism and Imaginative Writing in America.* Baltimore: Johns Hopkins University Press.

Paine, Albert Bigelow, ed. 1912. *Mark Twain: A Biography.* Vol. 4. New York: Harper and Brothers.

Paul, Rodman. 1953. Introduction to *Roughing It,* by Mark Twain (Samuel L. Clemens). New York: Rinehart.

Smith, Henry Nash, ed. 1957. *Mark Twain of the Enterprise.* Berkeley: University of California Press.

Thompson, Hunter S. 1973. "The Kentucky Derby Is Decadent and Depraved." In *The New Journalism,* by Tom Wolfe. With an Anthology by Tom Wolfe and E. W. Johnson. New York: Harper and Row.

Wagenknecht, Edward. 1935. *Mark Twain: The Man and His Work.* New Haven, Conn.: Yale University Press.

Walker, Franklin. 1938. *The Washoe Giant in San Francisco.* San Francisco: George Fields.

Walker, Franklin, and G. Ezra Dane, eds. 1940. *Mark Twain's Travels with Mr. Brown.* New York: Alfred A. Knopf.

Wright, William L. 1893. "Reporting with Mark Twain." *California Illustrated Magazine* 4: 170–71.

RICHARD HARDING DAVIS

Patricia Bradley

Richard Harding Davis was the embodiment of the strenuous decade of the 1890s. He was handsome, physically adept, famous, and well rewarded as a novelist, playwright, writer of travel books and short stories and as the most visible war correspondent of the period. Yet even in his own day, his fame was based not so much on the enduring values ascribed to his work as on his glamorous lifestyle. Although he had been feted early in his career for his first novels and sketches, literary critics grew impatient with what they viewed as the continued immaturity of his novels. By the end of the century, his fiction was considered out of style—likened to waxen fruit by one acid critic. "The perennial charm and youthfulness of his stories appear a little unnatural now and make the critical reader think of waxen cherries and of those curious green palms which have been embalmed to preserve their look of vigor" ("Notes of a Novel Reader" 1900, 29).

Nor did his popular fame as a war correspondent make him a favorite among reporters of the period, who saw him as a poseur, a dandy, and a man whose insistence on a personal point of view put him at variance with a growing sense that a reporter's job was to be a professional observer. Newspaper writers whooped in glee in 1898 when a literary magazine published a picture of him outfitted in his "war kit." "It may be ungracious to criticize such a work of art," wrote a reporter on the Springfield *Republican*, "but it would be interesting to know how Mr. Davis proposed to extract that revolver from under his armpit. And those high shooting-boots! We do hope that he has some easy carpet slippers" ("The Lounger" 1898c, 318).

Nor did his newspaper colleagues give him credibility for accuracy. According to the New York *Evening Sun*, Davis had misinformed readers about U.S. preparedness for war with Cuba by his "erroneous impressions and selections from his surprising private stock of misinformation" (17 Dec. 1898, 6).

But Davis had his defenders, many of them literary critics who, while they often decried his fiction, praised his reportage. The *Critic* reviewed *A Year from a Reporter's Notebook* favorably: "In all truth, Mr. Davis has reason to be proud of his reporter's work, for it is nearly perfect—vivid, clear, full of color, light and atmosphere" ("The Lounger" 1898d, 332). Davis also had a significant supporter in the journalistic community. Talcott Williams was a Philadelphia editor and Davis family friend who became the first dean of the Columbia University School of Journalism. Although Williams was a proponent of journalism as a profession that required religious self-sacrifice and discipline—hardly Davis characteristics—Williams saw the value in Davis's work as an unsurpassed "descriptive writer" (1925, 64). The literary critics and the journalists agreed at least in one area. Davis had an unerring ear and eye for the telling detail, the exact adjective, and the evocative tone. "His description of the entry of the German legions into Brussels, printed in this paper, showed at its best his rare gift of descriptive writing," according to the *New York Tribune* writer at his death. "As a writer of fiction his achievement was of slighter texture" (13 Apr. 1916, 8).

Present-day critics agree with the judgment of his time. Literary critics see the value of his work mainly as representative of a chauvinistic and imperialistic age. His reportage will never be remembered for its investigative qualities. But he continues to hold an important place in literary journalism, and the story quoted by the *Tribune* writer, often known by its famous "river of steel" metaphor, holds a place as one of the benchmarks of the genre.[1]

Even in his earliest writing, Davis's work was imbued with a remarkable sense of observation coupled with a value system that left no room for doubt. From the time he was a young reporter in Philadelphia, Davis saw himself not as a recorder of detail for public evaluation but rather as a collector of the material that provided the evidence for his interpretation. For most of his early career, it was his interpretation that fashioned the material into something worth reporting. Even a routine fire story could become a dramatic aphorism for some aspect of his value system. This egocentricity was undoubtedly fostered by the age, but in Davis's case, it was clearly fostered by his role as favored son and by a childhood in which his artistic expression was encouraged.

Davis was born into a writing family. His mother, Rebecca Harding Davis, whose initials he bore (and which, alone, often served to represent him in newspapers and magazines), is remembered as a precursor of naturalism. Although she continued to write throughout her life, she never fulfilled the promise of her early novels. After her marriage and the birth of Richard, her primary energy seemed to be poured into her elder son. Even after he had left the family home, first to attend college in Lehigh, Pennsylvania, and later when he went to New York as a young reporter, their bond was maintained until her death by a voluminous correspondence that was substantial enough to provide the framework for one full-length Davis biography. Indeed, for more than twenty years, Rebecca Harding Davis poured out thousands of pages of support and advice to her son, letters that not only shaped his works in progress but also served to maintain the values instilled in his childhood.

Although Rebecca Harding Davis was clearly the strongest single influence in Davis's life, that influence did not eclipse the role of his father. L. Clarke Davis was editor of Philadelphia's prestigious *Public Ledger*. Davis's lifelong insistence that he was first and foremost a reporter may be ascribed to the example set by his father and the other major journalistic figures of the period who were guests in the Davis household.

The Davis household, however, not only had a journalistic and literary ambience but also a theatrical bent. L. Clarke Davis was passionate about theater. Young Davis was frequently taken to touring plays, and the Davis circle also included visiting actors and actresses. Like his father, the young man became fascinated with the stage. Later in his career, when his fiction was losing popularity, Davis turned, with success, to playwriting. And his second marriage was to a musical comedy performer half his age whom he had first seen on the stage.

But the influences of the theatrical world of his childhood were evident in less direct ways, from whetting his own appetite for fame to an appreciation of artistry and style in his life and work. Moreover, the visitors from the stage provided Davis with examples of men and women who were risk-takers, freelancers in a sense, who moved from vehicle to vehicle, as Davis was to do in his literary career, never attaching himself to a newspaper, magazine, or publishing house for very long. Davis was always a sharp dealer of his own talents, based on a faith in his own abilities and the value system that shaped them.

Given this literary, journalistic, and theatrical mix early in his life, and supported by adoring parents, it is not surprising that Davis's career was always in the mode of a writer who unabashedly brought literary techniques to his unquestioned interpretations of events. There is little evidence that Davis ever found it necessary to challenge any of the values that had been so early encouraged. The chivalric and idealistic notions of his family were implanted strongly enough that he saw no reason that they should not be the foundation of every word he wrote.

EARLY WORK

After college at Lehigh and Johns Hopkins (although graduating from neither), Davis began his reporting career in Philadelphia, first on the Philadelphia *Record*. He was soon fired from the *Record* for an insouciant attitude and moved to the Philadelphia *Press*. But even in his earliest work on the *Record*, Davis exhibited that he came to the journalistic craft with a philosophy that was to shape his material to produce a particular effect. For example, "Sports in the Rain" reads like the opening of a short story. "Corbin, centre-rush of the Yale team, gazed calmly over his shoulder at his own men, and then as calmly at the other men ... the lines broke, the forward met with a thud and Woodruff disappeared under a mass of mud-covered jackets and trousers" (26 Nov. 1886). Even these lines illustrate the principles of Davis's literary journalism. Imbedded is his value system, which admired bonhomie between men and saw leadership as calmness under crisis. In addition, Davis assumed that his interpretation of the scene was the correct one—Corbin does not simply look around but gazes "calmly." And, finally, there is his use of colorful detail and a structure of combat. The little story foretold Davis's success with football stories. William Randolph Hearst paid him $500 to report the Yale-Harvard game of 1895.

Davis moved to the Philadelphia *Press* with renewed energy "to see"—his phrase for the collection of the kind of detail that would sell his view of what a story was all about. What Davis "saw" in a story that called for the closing of bordellos, for example, was a way to render his disgust with its patrons. He usually saw women as victims in such situations. Thus, the walls were covered with suggestive pictures "in keeping with the thoughts of the dive's habitues." And he concluded that the habitués were "sick and weary with debauchery" (20 Mar. 1887, 6).

Other stories from the *Press* during this period indicate his early attention to visual language. In a nonsentimental story that attacked the Reading Railroad's practice of crossing its gates across Philadelphia's main thoroughfare, a story that would not seem to lend itself to the picturesque, Davis wrote, "The green lanterns of the signalmen made circles of light in the dusk, and the red lanterns on the gates rose and fell like slow-moving rockets" (4 Dec. 1887, 3).

One of his most famous pieces from his Philadelphia period, "Dead with His Dog," was indeed sentimental. It told the story of the son of a Bryn Mawr gardener who had committed suicide because of, in Davis's view, the death of the boy's dog. Davis had no compunctions in supposing the motivations of the dead boy and supported his view of the event with metaphor, descriptive writing, and, one of his favorite and unfortunate techniques, heavy-handed irony.

The boy's only companion had been a beloved Scotch collie whose dumb sympathy the silent, melancholy boy seemed to find all sufficient. When the dog died, the youth shot himself by its grave and, while for contrast, an orchestra in the nearby hotel played a waltz, his mother found him with his body thrown across the newly-made grave. (20 Jul. 1887, 3)

Many of these early stories are newspaper potboilers, but occasionally the writing indicates future promise. A story about Civil War veterans waiting outside a pensioners' office produced the line that, for the men, "the smoke of the battle still hung in the air" (5 Dec. 1887, 3). Once rid of the sentimentality and glib ironies, his descriptive ability was powerful, as in a story about the life of a fisherman:

The night was cold and clear, and down below the lighted windows of the last ferryboat were plainly visible as the black mass surrounding them pushed slowly across the river . . . colored lights at neighboring yardarms showed the massive black balls beneath, as dark and forbidding in the darkness as those of prison ships. (1 May 1887, 10)

By the time Davis took a job as reporter on the New York *Evening Sun*, his skills needed only a range of choices. On the *Sun*, he sought out stories that best suited his storytelling style, events that had elements of the picturesque, the pathetic, the dramatic, the sensational, and his lifelong interest in the ironic—the closest he came to cynicism. Thus, in a story about the death of a bartender in a tenement fire, Davis concluded with the observation that as the firemen extinguished the last embers an alarm clock rang "just a half hour too late" (quoted in Osborn 1953, 168). As the Davis biographer Scott Osborn points out, it was the irony that made the story worthwhile. The death of the bartender was interesting because it could be attached to a shared emotion. Davis was only interested in the particulars of a story when they could be used to illustrate what he considered a universal value. Such an outlook undoubtedly made sense in a city teeming with a million stories and a population threatened by shifting danger. Certainly, a technique that reduces disparate events into a few overarching themes provides readers with a view of the world as stable—comfortably controlled by a few undisputed verities.

One of the themes frequently found in Davis's work was the role of women. In an *Evening Sun* story about an illegal abortion—Davis was not one to shy away from subjects that engendered interest—the villain of the piece was the abortionist, not the "beautiful cigarette girl" who had sought him out. The young woman, perhaps saved by her beauty, may have fallen from grace temporarily, but Davis is not about to expel her from society (22 Jul. 1890, 1).

In another sexually oriented story that called for the closing of a famous whorehouse, recalling the "Dives Will Go" story of his Philadelphia days, Davis still cannot condemn the prostitutes. The closest Davis comes to an admission that all women are not representations of his chivalric notions is to personify the house in terms of a courtesan, "bright and beautiful in a vulgar, wicked, showy way" (*Evening Sun*, 17 Apr. 1890, 2). In "Where Is Mr. Bradley?" a story about a suicide in a "love nest," the same principle seems to be at work. Under the guise of irony, Davis noted that the apartment was furnished quietly and richly with signed etchings and "Baghesta rugs upon the floor" (*Evening Sun*, 29 Sept. 1890, 3). The unexpected twist took the story out of the ordinary and also provided Davis with yet another way to express his notions of women as incorruptible. Shortly after publication of the story, Davis wrote to his brother that the police had refused him entry, which suggests that he had invented the details to sell his version of the story (Langford 1961, 103).

His career at the *Sun* also included sketches of a young man-about-town. The Van Bibber stories were collected and published by Harper and met with critical success. His growing acclaim gave him the boost that freed him from daily journalism. After a short editorship at *Harper's*—at the age of twenty-six—Davis turned to freelance work, as a writer of fiction, travel books and articles, and, eventually, as war correspondent.

It is as a war correspondent that Davis is judged as a literary journalist of merit. Whereas his newspaper work had often shown glimpses of powerful language and interesting insights, too often it was glib, contrived, and immature and sacrificed accuracy in order to make a point.

Similarly, his novels and travel reportage were marred by his inability to extend his perceptions of gender or culture. The women of his fiction were always wooden, and he found little to recommend any culture but his own. But on the large stage of war reportage, the value system that seemed so narrow in the daily grind of the journalistic world grew in stature. Attitudes that appeared increasingly old-fashioned as the new century approached became statements to live by when challenged on a foreign field. His personal voice remained paramount, and he was no great reporter of military matters, but now that personal "I" provided readers with a benchmark of familiarity that could be understood and appreciated.

Also, his skills as a writer were well suited to the drama, the ironies, and the sensational aspects of war. Techniques that often looked ridiculously out of proportion on the tiny canvas of day-to-day reporting, as Davis tried to hook small events into major values, were appropriate when applied to the grand scope of the battlefield.

Davis served as a war correspondent in several conflicts: the Cuban insurrection, the Greek-Turkish War, the Spanish-American War, the South African War, the Japanese-Russian War, and, finally, World War I. Davis never devoted himself entirely to war reportage, but even as he was being assailed for the sentimentality of his writing in other media, his war reportage was greeted warmly. "The Death of Rodriguez," part of his reportage of the Cuban insurrection in 1897, is an example where style and substance come together.

For years RHD had shown himself to be master of the evocative detail, the use of dialogue and setting, but in "The Death of Rodriguez" those tools are put in service of a view of the world that is closer to that of literary contemporaries such as Stephen Crane than to the jingoistic worldview of the mass media. Like Crane's "The Open Boat," "The Death of Rodriguez" occurs on a landscape of indifference. Unlike Crane, however, Davis—through the young Cuban Rodriguez—affirms his belief in idealistic values and holds out some faith that those values will persist as long as they are carried by heroic standard-bearers such as Adolpho Rodriguez. Rodriguez, in facing the firing squad in what Davis would consider a strong and manly way, holds true to chivalric notions of courage when there is no obvious support for them.

There is certainly no life-giving support in the physical setting. The Cuban fields where the Spanish are to execute the young peasant insurgent are portrayed as vast, almost sealike—"on the great plain that stretches from the forts out to the hills" (Davis 1897, 100). It is an inhospitable setting, eerily lit by the moon in the opening narrative. The palms on the far hills show "white in the moonlight, like hundreds of marble columns" (101). If marble columns are meant to suggest the Grecian world of civilization and justice, they are too far away to be effective. Only the line of campfires—a mark of life—burns clearly. But by the time the execution is to take place those campfires have been stamped out: "The moon was a white ball in the sky, without radiance, the fires had sunk to ashes, and the sun had not yet risen" (102). It is as if Davis has portrayed a return to the predawn of history. Not only are the marble columns promising civilization in the future; even fire, the symbol of the first step toward civilization, has been put out.

Davis reinforces this bleak world by language that eschews the ironical tone and sophisticated shared view of the young man-about-town. Sentences have been constructed without convolution, metaphors are rather plain—the moon is a "white ball"—and the narrative moves directly from the dawn of the day to the close of the execution. It is a style that would later be developed by Ernest Hemingway in the promulgation of a philosophy that is not so far from that of this Davis piece.

But most of all there is an inevitability about the tone that prohibits a romantic escape or last-minute pardon and reinforces the title. Davis, indeed, provides the muffled drums for the young man as he is ingloriously led across the stubbly fields.

The condemned man, in fact, is the only life in this ghostly, barren world. Davis describes him as being more like a Neapolitan than a Cuban, perhaps in the belief that to the American mind an emotional, carefree Italian presented a clearer image. "You could imagine him sitting on the quay at Naples or Genoa lolling in the sun and showing his white teeth when he laughed" (104). There is no doubt that the young man takes himself seriously, however. He is wearing a "new scapular" outside his linen blouse (105).

Although Davis skillfully sets a scene in which Rodriguez, so "shockingly young for such a sacrifice" (104), is portrayed as an innocent, his execution, to Davis's mind, is most shocking because it occurs outside any respect for the universal verities that Rodriguez clearly represents. A man who is dying for his cause should be honored, Davis seems to suggest, even by his enemies. But in the death of Rodriguez, the ritual of the execution, designed to imply such respect, borders on foolishness when the firing squad must reposition the young man so as not to shoot any of their own members. It is primarily because of Rodriguez's behavior in the face of such bumbling that the dignity of the occasion is retained. His bravery is evinced by the fact that he must face death without any support for what Davis believes should be universal values that overarch commitments to particular causes.

But Rodriguez is not quite alone. He has Richard Harding Davis at his side to give meaning to his death. On these barbaric plains, Rodriguez is the carrier of nineteenth-century idealism, and the condemned man smoking his last cigarette becomes such an important symbol for Davis's theme that he puts it in a personal voice:

It seems a petty thing to have been pleased with at such a time, but I confess to have felt a thrill of satisfaction when I saw, as the Cuban passed me, that he held a cigarette between his lips, not arrogantly nor with bravado, but with the nonchalance of a man who meets his punishment fearlessly, and who will let his enemies see that they can kill but cannot frighten him. (105)

The cigarette continues its symbolic journey after the young man is felled, finally, by the firing squad. At the side of the body "the cigarette still burned, a tiny ring of living fire, at the place where the figure had first stood" (111). Given the association of the cigarette with Rodriguez as a heroic figure, the living ring of fire is a positive statement. The burning of the dropped cigarette is not the usual Davis irony, as in the alarm clock that goes off a half-hour after the man has burned in his bed. The living ring of fire holds out the possibility that men like Rodriguez, representing universal values by their individual behavior, will not be subsumed into the collectivism of a pre-history landscape. Unlike the campfires, the living ring of the cigarette has not been stamped out.

Interpreted thus, "The Death of Rodriguez" expresses Davis's continuing commitment to the values of his generation, particularly the importance of the individual in representing the values of civilization. There can be no civilization without individual integrity, and thus the onset of impersonality and indifference is a move away from civilization back into a tribal past. He carries this theme into his reportage of World War I when he is repelled by the impersonality of the German war machine. In the face of this unleashed, barbaric power there is no place for individual integrity.

But before reaching the apex of his career as a World War I correspondent, he was to encourage the nationalistic tendencies of his age as a reporter

covering the Spanish-American War. One story Davis filed from Havana
became for a time the center of the yellow-press war between Hearst and
Joseph Pulitzer. Davis had written a story for Hearst that suggested, by
selective omission, that a young Cuban girl was searched by a group of
Spanish officers. In the article, headlined "Does Our Flag Shield Woman?"—
Davis could not have written a better headline—he wrote:

When the young ladies stood at last on the deck of an American vessel, with the
American flag hanging from the stern, the Spanish officers followed them and demanded that a cabin should be furnished them to which the girls might be taken,
and they were again undressed and searched for the [third] time. (*Journal*, 12 Feb.
1897, 1)

Davis did not write that the officers conducted the search. He had written:
"Spanish officers, with red crosses for bravery on their chests and good lace
on their cuffs, strutted (scowlingly) up and down while the search was going
on." Given Davis's view on the appropriate roles for men and women, the
passage seems a clear indictment of the Spanish officers for including a
search of a woman in the manly business of war. But the article was accompanied by a sketch by Frederic Remington, who was not on the scene,
that showed five officers searching a nude young woman. Pulitzer's *World*
was quick to note the mistake in the next day's paper, accompanied by an
explanation written by Davis, who considered that his honor had also been
impugned in the affair. Yet Davis's insistence on writing a story that eschewed preciseness in order to shape his material caused the problem.

Davis was on firmer ground in the actual war zone, where there was less
danger that his view of the manly life could be misinterpreted. In "The
Battle of San Juan Hill," the charging Teddy Roosevelt was the man of the
hour.

Roosevelt, mounted high on horseback, and charging the rifle-pits at a gallop and
quite alone, made you feel that you would like to cheer. He wore on his sombrero
a blue polka-dot handkerchief, a la Havelock, which, as he advanced, floated out
straight behind his head, like a guidon. Afterward, the men of his regiment who
followed this flag, adopted a polka-dot handkerchief as the badge of the Rough
Riders. (Davis 1911, 96)

"The Battle of San Juan Hill" also provided Davis with the opportunity
for novel-like development and dialogue, as in a de rigueur scene of soldiers
settling down to sleep before battle.

As we turned in, there was just a little something in the air which made saying
"good night" a gentle farce, for no one went to sleep immediately, but lay looking
up at the stars, and after a long silence, and much restless turning on the blanket
which we shared together, the second lieutenant said: "So if anything happens to

me, tomorrow, you'll see she gets them, won't you?" Before the moon rose again, every sixth man who had slept in the mist that night was either killed or wounded; but the second lieutenant was sitting on the edge of a Spanish rifle-pit, dirty, sweaty, and weak for food, but victorious, and the unknown she did not get them. (83–84)

"The Battle of San Juan Hill," however, does not succeed as any kind of work beyond a piece of literary history that unwittingly portrayed the na-ïveté of the war. Line by line, Davis's skill with visual description is apparent, but his lack of a critical sense or overarching intelligence that questioned what he "saw" makes it difficult for the piece to escape the confines of jingoistic sentimentality.

Although Davis reported on the Boer War for the London *Daily Mail* and the Japanese-Russian War for *Collier's*, war reportage was only one area of his activities in the first decade of the century. As critics rejected his fiction, Davis turned to playwriting, and he was successful enough to pur-chase a gentleman's farm in Mt. Kisco, New York, and pursue and marry a young stage star, Bessie McCoy. But when World War I broke out it was clear that his reputation as a war correspondent had not faded. He was soon in London as a correspondent for the Wheeler syndicate and *Scribner's* magazine.

Two books resulted from his two European tours: *With the Allies* (1914), which included the account of his being arrested by Germans who mistook him for a British spy, and *With the French in France and Salonika* (1916), published after his death in April of that year. Like other writers and men of the age, Davis was stunned by the destruction of modern warfare. He found no room for the glorification of individual courage in the face of the overwhelming slaughter.

After the Germans were repulsed at Meaux and at Sezanne the dead of both armies were so many that they lay intermingled in layers three and four deep. They were buried in long pits and piled on top of each other like cigars in a box. Lines of fresh earth so long you mistook them for trenches intended to conceal regiments were in reality graves. Some bodies lay for days uncovered until they had lost all human semblance. They were so many you ceased to regard them as corpses. They had become just a part of the waste, a part of the shattered walls, uprooted trees, and fields ploughed by shells. What once had been your fellow men were only bundles of clothes, swollen and shapeless, like scarecrows stuffed with rags, polluting the air. (Davis 1914, 218–19)

His eye for unerring detail is similarly effective in his famous story of the German entry into Belgium. Here it is often his use of domestic rather than dramatic detail that portrays the confidence of the "river of steel."

This army has been on active service three weeks, and so far there is not apparently a chin strap or a horseshoe missing. It came in with the smoke pouring from the cookstoves on wheels, and in an hour had set up post-office wagons, from which mounted messengers galloped along the line of columns, distributing letters, and at which soldiers posted picture postcards. (Quoted in Pickett 1977, 229)

In another dispatch written during the same tour, Davis described the destruction of the French city of Louvain. His chivalric notions of the role of women and children in wartime were challenged, and he was appalled. He had seen good men wasted on both sides in other wars, he wrote in compelling and unsentimental prose, but they were men—presumably individuals who had some chance at survival.

At Louvain it was war upon the defenseless, war upon churches, colleges, shops of milliners and lacemakers; war brought to the bedside and fireside; against women harvesting in the field, against children in wooden shoes at play in the streets.
At Louvain that night the Germans were like men after an orgy. (1914, 92)

It was as if, finally, Davis had grown up. His final work indicated that his assumptions about the world had been shaken. World War I could not be dismissed as a skirmish resulting from the lack of North European virtues. He was seeing civilized nations conduct a war without rules, a war that threatened to overwhelm everything that had gone before. He had to put away the idea of his age that history was the working out of what was best.

The war, however, pushed him to produce his most mature work as a writer, challenging the preconceived notions that had weakened his work for decades. At the same time, his years of writing and "seeing" in his special way gave him the tools to express his new breadth of vision.

Davis died of a heart attack at his desk after he returned from Europe, ready to commit himself to the Allied cause. He was fifty-two and, in the irony he loved so well, he probably was on the brink of the best work in his career.

NOTE

1. The "River of Steel" story was originally published in the London *News Chronicle*, Aug. 23, 1914. Republished in *Voices of the Past*, ed. Calder M. Pickett (Columbus: Grid), 228–30 and *A Treasury of Great Reporting*, ed. Louis L. Snyder and Richard B. Morris (New York: Simon and Schuster), 312–15.

PRIMARY SOURCES

Davis, Richard Harding. 1897. "The Death of Rodriguez." In *A Year from a Reporter's Notebook*. New York: Harper and Brothers.
———. 1911. "The Battle of San Juan Hill." In *The Notes of a War Correspondent*. New York: Charles Scribner's Sons.
———. 1914. *With the Allies*. New York: Charles Scribner's Sons.

SECONDARY SOURCES

Archibald, J.F.J. 1902, Sept. "Localities and Scenes of Richard Harding Davis's Stories." *Book Buyer* 25: 115–21.

Beer, Thomas. 1924, Oct. 11. "Richard Harding Davis." *Liberty* 1: 15–21.

"Briefer Mention." 1897, Oct. 30. *Academy* 52: 349–50.

"Chronicle and Comment, Notes on R. H. Davis." 1916, June. *Bookman* 43: 33–62.

"Crack Reporting." 1898, Feb. *Book Buyer* 16: 65.

Davis, Charles Belmond, ed. 1917. *The Adventures and Letters of Richard Harding Davis*. New York: Charles Scribner's Sons.

Downey, Fairfax. 1917. *Richard Harding Davis: His Day*. New York: Charles Scribner's Sons.

Duffy, James O. G. 1916, Apr. 13. "Harding Davis as Friend Knew Him." *Press* (Philadelphia) 1.

Eichelberger, Clayton L., and Ann M. McDonald. 1971. "Richard Harding Davis 1864–1916: A Check List of Secondary Comment." *American Literary Realism* 4: 313–89.

"Getting Angry at RHD." 1895, Sept. 21. *New York Daily Tribune*: 5.

"How 'Dick' D Got His First Job." 1916, Apr. 23. *Daily Eagle* (Brooklyn): 7.

Langford, Gerald. 1961. *The Richard Harding Davis Years: A Biography of a Mother and Son*. New York: Holt, Rinehart and Winston.

"The Lounger." 1898a, Jan. 8. *Critic* 32: 23–24.

———. 1898b, Apr. 23. *Critic* 32: 283.

———. 1898c, May 7. *Critic* 32: 318–19.

———. 1898d, May 14. *Critic* 32: 332.

"Major Max Is Angry." 1893, Nov. 3. *Sun* (New York): 8.

Maurice, Arthur Bartlett. 1906, Apr. 23. "Representative American Story Tellers." *Bookman* 23: 137–42.

———. 1916, May. "Richard Harding Davis—An Estimate." *Bookman* 43: 329–37.

"Mr. RHD and His Comrades." 1896, Sept. 26. *Critic*: 185–96.

"Mr. RHD and His Comrades." 1896, Nov. 21. *Critic*: 320.

"Notes of a Novel Reader." 1900, Jan. *Critic* 36: 29.

Osborn, Scott C. 1953. "Richard Harding Davis: The Development of a Journalist." Diss., University of Kentucky.

———. 1956. "The Rivalry-Chivalry of Richard Harding Davis and Stephen Crane." *American Literature* 28: 50–61.

———. 1960, Spring. "RHD: Critical Battleground." *American Quarterly* 12: 84–92.

Osborn, Scott C., and Robert L. Phillips. 1978. *Richard Harding Davis*. Boston: Twayne.

Palmer, Frederick. 1926. "Richard Harding Davis." *Scribner's Monthly* 80: 472–77.

Pickett, Calder M. 1977. *Voices of the Past: Key Documents in the History of American Journalism*. Columbus, Ohio: Grid.

Quinby, Henry Cole. 1924. *Richard Harding Davis: A Bibliography*. New York: Dutton.

"A Richard in the Field." 1898, July 14. *Sun* (New York): 6.

Sangree, Allen. 1901. Feb. 7. "Richard Harding Davis." *Ainslee's Magazine*: 2–10.

Solensten, John M. 1971. "The Gibson Boy: A Reassessment." *American Literary Realism* 4: 303–12.

Wheeler, John. 1916, June 18. "RHD as His Friends Knew Him." *Sun* (New York): 3.

"Why He Is Not a War Correspondent." 1894, Sept. 27. *New York Daily Tribune*: 5.

Williams, Talcott. 1925. *The Newspaperman*. New York: Charles Scribner's Sons.

Wisan, Joseph E. 1934. *The Cuban Crisis as Reflected in the New York Press (1895– 1898)*. New York: Columbia University Press.

"With the French in France and Salonika." 1916, Apr. 23. *New York Times Review of Books* 7:1.

STEPHEN CRANE

Michael Robertson

Stephen Crane worked as a journalist from the time he was sixteen until his death at twenty-eight. He began by collecting news at New Jersey shore resorts, went on to write sketches of New York City street life, traveled throughout the West and Mexico for a newspaper syndicate, and served as a war correspondent in Greece and Cuba. Though *The Red Badge of Courage*, which made Crane internationally famous when it was published in 1895, has remained his best-known work, much of his journalism continues to interest readers.

Crane was never a conventional newspaper reporter; throughout his career, he worked as a freelance contributor of feature articles to a wide range of newspapers and magazines. Crane's best articles share the distinctive qualities of his fiction: pervasive irony, a naturalistic view of humans as products of their environment, and, above all, a rejection of any absolute reality or truth in favor of an impressionistic attention to the processes of individual perception.

Crane began his career in journalism by assisting his older brother Townley, who operated an Asbury Park, New Jersey, news bureau that supplied the *New York Tribune* with news from the summer shore resorts. Starting at age sixteen, Stephen gathered news of arriving guests. An editor on the *Tribune* has left a parodic example of the news bureau's typical contributions: "The Flunkey-Smiths of Squedunk are at the Gilded Pazaza Hotel for the season" (Johnson 1926, 290). By 1892, when he was twenty, Crane had left this typical format far behind and was regularly contributing feature articles that, though unsigned, are immediately recognizable as the work of a literary artist.

The most distinctive feature of Crane's Asbury Park articles is their irony. Crane's first novel, *Maggie*, has been described as the first entirely ironic American novel; Crane brought a similar wide-reaching, coruscating irony into his journalism. Son of a Methodist minister, he invariably flaunted his irreverence whenever reporting on the Methodists' summer encampment at Ocean Grove, New Jersey. "The sombre-hued gentlemen who congregate at this place in summer are arriving in solemn procession," he began one article, "with black valises in their hands and rebukes to frivolity in their eyes" (Crane 1973, 508).[1] Crane extended the same irony to the crowds of upper-middle-class vacationers at Asbury Park.

The average summer guest here is a rather portly man, with a good watch-chain and a business suit of clothes, a wife and about three children. He stands in his two shoes with American self-reliance and, playing casually with his watch-chain, looks at the world with a clear eye.... He enjoys himself in a very mild way and dribbles out a lot of money under the impression that he is proceeding cheaply. (516–17)

The staid *New York Tribune* was willing to enliven its lengthy columns of resort news by printing its young correspondent's ironic features. But Crane found himself in hot water when he tackled the taboo subject of class differences.

Crane's most famous Asbury Park article is known variously by its series headline, "On the New-Jersey Coast," or its subhead, "Parades and Entertainments." His subject was a parade of the Junior Order of United American Mechanics, a nativist organization. Crane gave the group's working-class membership the same sharp treatment he extended to all his subjects, describing the parade as "the most awkward, ungainly, uncut and uncarved procession that ever raised clouds of dust on sun-beaten streets" (521). But the article soon makes clear that the real targets of Crane's satire are the natives of Asbury Park. "The bona fide Asbury Parker," he writes, "is a man to whom a dollar, when held close to his eye, often shuts out any impression he may have had that other people possess rights. He is apt to consider that men and women, especially city men and women, were created to be mulcted by him" (522). Crane uses the parade to set up a thematic counterpoint, playing off the ungainly but honest and hard-working Mechanics against the exploitative Asbury Park entrepreneurs. But it was the Mechanics who complained in a letter to the *Tribune*. The newspaper printed a fulsome apology, declaring its abhorrence of the "vain class distinctions" that had been discussed in "a bit of random correspondence" (909). Years later, a *Tribune* editor wrote a memoir of the affair, disputing the legend that Crane was fired as a result of this article. But when the 1892 summer season ended shortly afterwards, Crane left Asbury Park for New York City, where he wrote freelance journalism and worked on his first novel.

Crane completed the novel, *Maggie*, late that same year but was unable to find a publisher for his story of New York slum life; eventually, he published the book himself, selling only a few copies. Crane's experience with *Maggie* was not unique; other writers of the time complained that the major magazine and book publishers were hostile to realistic literary treatment of urban poverty. During the 1890s, newspapers were the major outlet for writing about New York City's slums. Though Crane wrote one other New York City novel after *Maggie*, the vast majority of his writing about the city appeared in the Sunday feature pages of various newspapers.

Yet, while 1890s newspapers frequently printed feature articles on the city's poor, almost invariably these articles treated the poor in condescending, moralistic language. For reforming journalists such as Jacob Riis, the members of "the other half" were pathetic victims dependent on philanthropy to better their lot. Other writers, less progressive in their views than Riis, saw the poor mainly as potential criminals to be guarded against. Whatever their authors' views, newspaper feature articles generally regarded the city's slums from a morally superior middle-class perspective.

In language and narrative technique, Crane's sketches of New York street life differ radically from conventional articles. His earliest identified feature, "Travels in New York/The Broken-Down Van," is notable for the way in which it presents details of poverty, vice, and petty crime without any moralistic commentary. This brief sketch, which appeared unsigned in the *New York Tribune*, is a human-interest piece about the traffic jam that results when a horse-drawn van loses a wheel in the middle of a busy lower Manhattan street. What makes the article remarkable is the way in which the narrative frequently shifts its attention from the comical efforts to repair the van to the street life that swirls around the scene. The sketch includes terse, matter-of-fact descriptions of small children carrying pails of beer, a drunk singing, a "ten-cent barber" trying to pick up girls, a boy writing graffiti on the stalled van while another tries to steal its horses' harness, and children selling newspapers and heading for work in a sweatshop. Crane's narrative includes a wealth of detail about the poverty, vice, and exploitation present in lower New York but rigorously avoids any moralistic commentary on the scene. In place of the moral perspective on the city that readers had come to expect, Crane offers a purely visual perspective and leaves readers to draw their own conclusions.

Crane's goal, however, is not to create an "objective" news article. In the 1890s, the ideal of objectivity that dominates modern journalism was much less important. "The Broken-Down Van," like the rest of Crane's New York journalism, is unconcerned with verifiable facts. The opening sentence of the sketch is typical of his work: "The gas lamps had just been lit and the two great red furniture vans with impossible landscapes on their sides rolled and plunged slowly along the street" (275). The absence of proper nouns—neither the location, the date, nor the participants' names are ever revealed—reflects Crane's lack of interest in conventional reporting. Instead, he plunges his readers into an "impossible" linguistic landscape of hyperbole and extravagant metaphor. His concern is less with factual reporting than with the process of individual perception.

"The Men in the Storm," one of Crane's best-known New York sketches, opens by contrasting differing perceptions of a howling late-afternoon blizzard. Crane writes of the middle-class pedestrians hurrying to their homes that "there was an absolute expression of hot dinners in [their] pace." But to a group of homeless men waiting in the street for a charity shelter to open, "these things were as if they were not" (316). During "an afternoon of incredible length," a constantly growing crowd of men huddle together for warmth and protection from the violent storm. Written during the winter of 1894, when America was undergoing the worst economic depression in its history up to that point, "The Men in the Storm" is in part a work of social protest. But it is also a piece of virtuoso narrative, dense with metaphors and shifts of visual perspective; a study of vernacular language that faithfully transcribes the men's questions, shouts, and curses; a description of the implacable harshness of nature, a theme common in both Crane's journalism and his fiction; and a naturalistic study of the ways in which environment determines human behavior.

The same elements are present in the sketch that many consider to be Crane's journalistic masterpiece, "An Experiment in Misery," as well as in its companion piece, "An Experiment in Luxury." The "experiment," in which a reporter assumes a role in some little-known or exotic social group, was a common journalistic form in the 1890s. Numerous reporters took on temporary identities—as a lion tamer or fire fighter, for example—in order to write articles about their experience. Crane's distinction was to use this conventional newspaper form as the vehicle for experiments in consciousness. In his two experiments, published on successive Sundays in 1894 in the *New York Press*, Crane shows how changes in environment can shape human perception and identity.

"An Experiment in Misery" begins as two middle-class men stand regarding a tramp. One of them, identified only as "the youth," is clearly Crane himself. The youth wonders how the tramp feels and decides to find out by living as one. He borrows a tattered suit and hat from an artist friend and, transformed in appearance, walks toward the poverty-stricken areas of lower Manhattan. Soon he begins to experience an equivalent transformation of consciousness. By the time he is far downtown, the youth is "so completely plastered with yells of 'bum' and 'hobo,' and with various unholy epithets that small boys had applied to him at intervals that he was in a state of profound dejection" (862). The youth has already assumed the tramp's dejected mental state; shortly afterward, he meets a guide who initiates him into tramp society.

Outside a saloon, the youth encounters an unkempt, reeling drunk whom he dubs "the assassin." Serving as a sort of derelict Virgil to the youth's

Dante, the assassin leads the young man into the underworld of a backstreet flophouse, where, for seven cents, each gets a cot for the night in a large room filled with men. Crane's description of the youth's sleepless night is an artistic tour de force, with violent metaphors—the room is "a graveyard, where bodies were merely flung"; the sleepers heave and snore "with tremendous effort, like stabbed fish"—that reflect the youth's disoriented, fearful state (287, 288). By the next day, however, the transformation of the young man's consciousness is complete. As he sits on a park bench, it is the well-dressed passersby who seem alien to him. The sketch ends as the young man "confess[es] himself an outcast." Newly aware—and resentful— of the city's sharp class divisions, he forms convictions that the larger society would consider "criminal" (293). "An Experiment in Misery" rejects all conventional approaches to the poor, whether moralistic, patronizing, or compassionate, and instead uses the journalistic form of the experiment to reveal how the catalyst of poverty alters the consciousness of the experimenter.

"An Experiment in Luxury" describes the youth's dinner at the home of a college friend, son of a Fifth Avenue millionaire. Part of the novelty of the sketch is Crane's decision to subject the wealthy to the same sort of experimental treatment that newspapers usually reserved for exotic or marginalized groups. Newspapers of the era generally reported on New York's upper class in respectful society-page features; in contrast, Crane treats his friend's family with irreverence, describing the mother as "a grim old fighter . . . a type of Zulu chieftainess who scuffled and scrambled for a place before the white altars of social excellence" (299). As in "An Experiment in Misery," the youth undergoes a change of consciousness. But in this case he adopts a facile, snobbish superiority, a pose that is quickly undercut by the narrator's irony. "Presently he began to feel that he was a better man than many—entitled to a great pride," Crane writes of the youth. "He stretched his legs like a man in a garden, and he thought that he belonged to the garden" (297). While "An Experiment in Misery" offers a harrowing plunge into the lives and minds of the oppressed, "Luxury" is an ironic send-up of the wealthy's pretensions to superiority.

Shortly after the publication of the last of his 1894 New York sketches, Crane left the city for a tour of the West and Mexico, sponsored by a newspaper syndicate. He did not return to New York City journalism until two years later, when *The Red Badge of Courage* had made him famous. Aside from a few articles on current fads such as bicycling, most of the 1896 sketches, like his earlier work, focus on the poor and marginalized; he wrote about opium smokers, the slum district known as the Tenderloin, and a crime-ridden African-American ghetto. Though Crane's name was now featured in the headlines of his articles, in general these sketches do not match the level of his earlier work, written when he was twenty-two.

Crane completed only a few articles during his western tour; the best is his description of the severe drought of 1894–95, "Nebraska's Bitter Fight for Life." In this potentially dull story about the weather, Crane found the basis for a lengthy article dealing with one of his central preoccupations, the struggle of the individual against an overwhelmingly powerful nature. In characteristically extravagant metaphors, Crane personifies the wind and sun, casting them as pitiless antagonists of the farmers and their crops. In one of his most memorable sentences, he writes of the farmers, "It was as if upon the massive altar of the earth, their homes and their families were being offered in sacrifice to the wrath of some blind and pitiless deity" (410). With its harsh Old Testament imagery, the line could belong to one of Crane's many poems about humanity's relationship with a distant, implacable god.

None of Crane's other travel writing—he published pieces about Ireland and England as well as Mexico and the West—matches the power of his Nebraska article. Crane acknowledged the difficulty of writing good travel journalism in "The Mexican Lower Classes," an unpublished article that remained in manuscript until 1967. In this fascinating, self-reflective article, Crane announces that "the most worthless literature of the world has been that which has been written by the men of one nation concerning the men of another." The visitor to another country, he writes, can be sure of only two things: "form and color" (436). Of course, Crane's journalism is not limited to the purely visual, but his announced emphasis on sense impressions underscores the distrust of abstract generalization and the corresponding importance of individual perception in all his writing.

This emphasis on individual perception is seen in the best of his extensive war reporting. When he published *The Red Badge of Courage*, Crane had never seen battle. However, newspapers were eager to enlist the acclaimed novelist as a war correspondent, and Crane himself yearned to witness warfare. His chance came in the spring of 1897, when a long-simmering conflict between Greece and Turkey erupted into war. The war lasted just a month, and Crane was present at only one major battle, the three days' campaign at Velestino. Still, he filed a dozen dispatches from Greece, some of them distinctive works of art.

A modern reader is likely to be struck by certain qualities of the war dispatches—such as the liberal use of the first person and the frankly partisan stance in favor of the Greeks—that are not unique to Crane; this personal approach was common among 1890s reporters. What makes Crane's war correspondence unique is, in part, his unabashed love of battle. His dispatch "Crane at Velestino" records an eager young man's romantic view of the glory of battle. He calls the sound of rifle fire "the most beautiful sound of my experience"; it is "more impressive than the roar of Niagara and finer than thunder or avalanche" (Crane 1971, 20).[2]

Yet Crane's view of battle was not one-sidedly romantic; unfailingly, any mention of war's glory is countered with a view of its costs. In a dispatch

written aboard a troop ship carrying wounded soldiers to Athens, he describes how crowds reading a newspaper extra about a Greek victory
shouted "Hurrah for war!" as a seemingly endless procession of wounded
men on stretchers filed from the ship (54). Crane's dispatches are filled with
similar ironic juxtapositions, creating a dialectic between tributes to heroism
on the battlefield and compassionate detailing of the suffering endured by
both soldiers and displaced civilians.

Above all, Crane's war reporting is distinguished by its unconcern with
the results of battle—the easy summary of victory or defeat—and its impressionistic attention to the process of warfare as experienced by the individual. "A Fragment of Velestino," a long article completed and published
after the end of the war, skewers the typical newspaper reader, concerned
solely with who wins and loses. This attention to the rise or fall of "the
mercury of war" is absurd, Crane writes (37). The reality of war, as he
conveys it, is confused and fragmentary. "A Fragment of Velestino," the
finest of Crane's reports from Greece, is a series of brilliant, disconnected
vignettes, alternately absurd and horrifying. He describes how an officer,
irate when a befuddled soldier brings him a bottle of wine instead of the
field glasses he asked for, absentmindedly keeps the bottle in his hands as
he gestures orders to fire. He writes about an observer's certainty that the
brilliant red color on a soldier's face must be paint and the dawning realization that in fact it is blood from a head wound. Throughout "Fragment
of Velestino," Crane jolts readers out of their preconceptions about war.
He parodies conventional heroic descriptions of battle and offers in their
place surprising similes that emphasize visual and aural perception: Turks
at a distance are simply "a dark line"; the recoil of a howitzer is like a child
throwing a tantrum; artillery shells sound alternately like the rapid flapping
of birds' wings or "as if someone had thrown an empty beer-bottle with
marvelous speed at you" (33–45).

Within less than a year after leaving Greece, Crane was again at the
battlefront, reporting on the 1898 Spanish-American War. Even before the
official declaration of war, Crane signed on with Joseph Pulitzer's New
York World as a special correspondent. He spent four weeks aboard the
World's tugboat covering the preliminary naval campaign off the Cuban
coast, was present at the first land battle, and witnessed the storming of
San Juan Hill. After American forces conquered Cuba, Crane switched from
the World to William Randolph Hearst's New York Journal and reported
on the brief Puerto Rican campaign, then slipped illegally into Havana and
stayed there for three months during the peace negotiations. Crane witnessed
every significant aspect of the war, wrote a total of almost fifty dispatches,
and won praise as author of the best accounts of the fighting—a significant
accolade when one considers that some five hundred reporters, photographers, and artists covered the war, including virtually all of the era's most
famous journalists.

Reading over Crane's dispatches, one is likely to be as impressed by his descriptions of battle as his contemporaries were. But the modern reader is also likely to be struck by the xenophobia and racial stereotyping of many of the articles. Crane was not immune to the jingoistic fervor that swept America into its first war outside its borders. However, his articles avoid the worst excesses of the era's yellow journalism, and in a long article published a year after the war ended, he repudiated the jingoism of his earlier dispatches.

The principal connecting link between Crane's war dispatches from Greece and Cuba is their emphasis on the quiet courage of the common soldier. In *The Red Badge of Courage*, written before Crane had witnessed battle, protagonist Henry Fleming swings wildly between extremes of heroism and cowardice. What struck Crane about the soldiers he observed in both Greece and Cuba, however, was their stolid, workmanlike demeanor. He wrote of the Greek troops that they "fought with the steadiness of salaried bookkeepers" (20). In "Marines Signaling Under Fire at Guantanamo," he describes his astonishment at "the absence of excitement, fright, or any emotion at all" on the face of soldiers in an extremely dangerous situation; they looked merely like men "intent upon...business" (Crane 1970, 196).[3]

Treating the soldiers as unfailingly brave under fire, Crane assigns all emotions of fear to himself and other correspondents. After describing the grave serenity of a sergeant under fire in "Marines Signaling," Crane tells how he and his colleagues fled from the signalman: "We gave [the sergeant] sole possession of a particular part of the ridge. We didn't want it. He could have it and welcome. If the young sergeant had had the smallpox, the cholera, and the yellow fever, we could not have slid out with more celerity" (199). Two sketches written aboard the *World*'s dispatch boat, "Narrow Escape of the Three Friends" and "Chased by a Big "Spanish Man-O-War,' " are small comic masterpieces about journalists' fear in a close call.

Like his Greco-Turkish war dispatches, Crane's accounts of battle in Cuba reject summaries of victory and defeat for a focus on the process of battle. The narrative structure of "Stephen Crane's Vivid Story of the Battle of San Juan," one of his best-known dispatches, mimics what Crane perceived to be the structure of battle; the article is long and fragmented, lacking any clear climaxes. Crane graphically portrays the start of the famous charge up San Juan Hill. But his narrative then immediately reminds us of the costs of that heroic venture, shifting to a description of the wounded men straggling back from the battlefront. The actual capture of the hill is never described. The text refuses to offer readers the expected structure of charge followed by victory; instead, it recreates the confusion and complexity of battle.

After an armistice ended the fighting, Crane wrote a number of short stories about the Spanish-American War, which were collected in *Wounds in the Rain*. Also included in that collection is "War Memories," a long nonfiction piece that covers the entire Cuban campaign. Seldom republished in subsequent collections of Crane's work, and given little attention by critics, "War Memories" is a neglected masterpiece, Crane's best work of war journalism and arguably one of the greatest American nonfiction narratives about war.

"War Memories" repeats and elaborates upon many of the incidents Crane described in his dispatches, such as the battle of San Juan Hill. It also emphasizes the central theme of his war reporting, the workmanlike bravery of the regular soldier. But it differs from his earlier reports in its explicit rejection of jingoism. Crane abandons the appeals to patriotism and the righteousness of the American cause that marked his earlier dispatches. Instead, his stated concern is to convey to his readers the reality of war; his principal theme is the impossibility of doing that. "War Memories," Crane's most complex and sophisticated nonfiction narrative, uses a wide variety of innovative techniques that test the limits of narrative and of language itself; repeatedly, the narrator concedes the inadequacy of language to convey experience.

The piece opens with an announcement of its linguistic concerns. "But to get the real thing!" it begins. "It seems impossible! It is because war is neither magnificent nor squalid; it is simply life, and an expression of life can always evade us. We can never tell life, one to another, although sometimes we think we can" (222). Throughout the piece Crane uses startling narrative techniques in the attempt to "tell life," such as digression, repetition, and direct address to the reader—so often does he use the last that, reading "War Memories," we feel as if the narrator is trying to escape the bounds of the text, grab us by the lapels, and shake us into awareness of the message he is trying to convey.

In content as well as narrative technique, "War Memories" draws our attention to the limits of language. The piece is filled with stories of misunderstanding, failures of communication, and silence. Silence is a major theme. The narrator writes movingly about the silence of wounded men, of refugees, of the crowds that greet returning prisoners of war and observe the unloading of a ship filled with casualties. The text itself tries to fight against its own linguistic limits and to achieve the unachievable condition of silence. Writing of the regular soldiers who fought at San Juan, the narrator says: "One cannot speak of it—the spectacle of the common man serenely doing his work. . . . One pays them the tribute of the toast of silence" (249).

"War Memories" concludes in taunting, puzzling fashion: "And you can depend upon it that I have told you nothing at all, nothing at all, nothing at all" (263). In his final sentence the narrator once again pushes up against the limits of language, directly addressing his reader, attempting to engage us in the construction of elusive meaning. And in his triply repeated negative, he reminds us of the impossibility of representing reality. War is, finally, unknowable, and the truest response is a reiterated phrase of denial that trails off into silence.

Six months after he published "War Memories," Crane was dead, of tuberculosis and complications of the malaria that he contracted in Cuba. Despite the brevity of his career, Stephen Crane left behind him a body of nonfiction that places him in the first rank of America's literary journalists.

NOTES

1. All page citations given for the Asbury Park articles, the New York City sketches, and "Nebraska's Bitter Fight for Life" are taken from *Tales, Sketches, and Reports*, vol. 8 of *The University of Virginia Edition of the Works of Stephen Crane.*

2. All page citations given for Crane's war dispatches from Greece are taken from *Reports of War*, vol. 9 of *The University of Virginia Edition of the Works of Stephen Crane.*

3. All page citations given for Crane's war dispatches from Cuba and for "War Memories" are taken from *Tales of War*, vol. 6 of *The University of Virginia Edition of the Works of Stephen Crane.*

PRIMARY SOURCES

Crane, Stephen. 1970. *Tales of War*. Vol. 6 of *The University of Virginia Edition of the Works of Stephen Crane*. Charlottesville: University Press of Virginia.

———. 1971. *Reports of War*. Vol. 9 of *The University of Virginia Edition of the Works of Stephen Crane*. Charlottesville: University Press of Virginia.

———. 1973. *Tales, Sketches, and Reports*. Vol. 8 of *The University of Virginia Edition of the Works of Stephen Crane*. Charlottesville: University Press of Virginia.

Levenson, J. C., ed. 1984. *Stephen Crane: Prose and Poetry*. The Library of America. New York: Literary Classics of the U.S.

Stallman, R. W., and E. R. Hagemann, eds. 1964. *The War Dispatches of Stephen Crane*. New York: New York University Press.

———. 1966. *The New York City Sketches of Stephen Crane and Related Pieces*. New York: New York University Press.

SECONDARY SOURCES

Conrad, Peter. 1984. *The Art of the City: Views and Versions of New York*. New York: Oxford University Press.

Johnson, Willis Fletcher. 1926. "The Launching of Stephen Crane." *Literary Digest International Book Review* 4: 288–90.

Katz, Joseph, ed. 1970. *Stephen Crane in the West and Mexico*. Kent, Ohio: Kent State University Press.

Kwiat, Joseph J. 1980. "Stephen Crane, Literary-Reporter: Commonplace Experience and Artistic Transcendence." *Journal of Modern Literature* 8: 129–38.

LaFrance, Marston. 1971. *A Reading of Stephen Crane*. London: Oxford University Press.

Mencken, H. L. 1926. Introduction to *Major Conflicts*, vol. 10 of *The Work of Stephen Crane*. Ed. Wilson Follett. New York: Knopf.

Trachtenberg, Alan. 1974. "Experiments in Another Country: Stephen Crane's City Sketches." *Southern Review* 10: 265–85. Rpt. 1982 in *American Realism: New Essays*. Ed. Eric J. Sundquist. Baltimore: Johns Hopkins University Press.

Weinstein, Bernard. 1972. "Stephen Crane: Journalist." In *Stephen Crane in Transition: Centenary Essays*. Ed. Joseph Katz. DeKalb: Northern Illinois University Press.

JACOB A. RIIS

Howard Good

From out of the populous city men groan, and the soul of the wounded
crieth out.

—The Book of Job

By the time Jacob A. Riis published *How the Other Half Lives: Studies
Among the Tenements of New York* in 1890, the slum had been occasionally
investigated and continually reviled for close to fifty years.[1] But while Riis,
a long time police reporter, did not discover the slum, his book was easily
the most poplar and influential of the nineteenth century on the subject. Its
tremendous success frankly surprised him; he thought the title might have
had a lot to do with it (Riis 1901, 309). Actually, more important to the
book's popularity were the historical moment at which it appeared and the
penetrating and highly personal style in which it was written.

The slum, from its back alleys to its sweatshops, from its low saloons to
its great, weirdly picturesque mix of humanity, embodied in cruel and concentrated form the socioeconomic forces that were reshaping American life
in the late nineteenth century. Since the end of the Civil War, the tide of
population had been setting strongly toward the city, and by 1890 every
third American was a city dweller. Over the next ten years, the number of
cities with 4,000 or more inhabitants would grow from less than 9,000 to
almost 12,000, and the proportion of city dwellers would grow to about
two-fifths of the total population (Schlesinger 1933, 425, 435).

Tens of thousands were lured from the countryside to the city by the
seeming chance of better-paying jobs in shops, warehouses, railroad yards,
and gaunt, smoky factories. But this influx was exceeded by that of immigrants, first from Germany, England, and Ireland, then increasingly from
Southern and Eastern Europe. Four out of every five residents of New York

in 1890 were foreigners or of foreign parentage (Schlesinger 1933, 73). "The one thing you shall vainly ask for in the chief city of America," Riis observed, "is a distinctively American community. There is none; certainly not among the tenements" (1971, 1, 19).

And New York was splotched with tenements. Three-fourths of the city's population of 1.5 million lived in conditions of incredible squalor, packed into coal cellars and shanties and small, fetid, windowless rooms. Most tenements, Riis recognized, were not vicious, just poor and unfortunate (1971, 20, 133). They were the motley working class called forth by industrializing America and, quite simply, had no place else to live.

The native-born generation that came of age in the 1870s and 1880s still thought of America as a nation of farms and small towns, and they urgently needed someone to explain the grim urban-industrial landscape to them.

Little in their previous experience or their inherited frames of reference had prepared them to understand the world as they suddenly found it, bewildering in its rush and noise and menacing in its strangeness. They wanted to know, Who were these immigrants crowding into the cities? Why these dark, decrepit tenements? *How the Other Half Lives* undertook to answer their questions.

Riis often addressed his largely middle-class audience in the manner of a tour guide—a device, incidentally, earlier used by Charles Dickens, who took the readers of *American Notes* (1842) into the narrow, mazelike alleys and "leprous houses" of the New York slum know as the Five Points (1903, 76–77). "Be a little careful, please!" Riis warns, leading the way into a Cherry Street tenement. "The hall is dark and you might stumble over the children pitching pennies back there. Not that it would hurt them; kicks and cuffs are their daily diet." As the tour through the Lower East Side continues, he points out and interprets the sights: newsboys shooting craps in an alley; sweatshop slaves hunched over sewing machines, their faces and hands black with the color of the cloth on which they were working; tramps snoring in chorus in a seven-cent lodging house; the "Pig Market," where almost anything that could be hawked from a wagon—bandannas and tin cups, peaches and old coats—could be found, and at ridiculously low prices; the Short Tail Gang drinking beer under the docks, resting from its crimes; young women and mere girls toiling ten, twelve, sixteen hours a day as salesclerks and cashiers, some destined to be driven by their starvation wages to prostitution, others to suicide and an anonymous grave in Potter's Field (1971, 38, 72, 92, 100, 175, 183–89).

What made Riis's performance so effective was that he spoke with the authority of long experience. William Dean Howells might take an occasional "East-Side Ramble" or Stephen Crane conduct an infrequent "Experiment in Misery," but Riis was immersed in the slum.[2] For fourteen years now, he had explored its filthy courts and fever-stricken alleys as the police reporter of the New York *Tribune,* and he knew its residents and their miseries inside out. "The evils he exposed he discovered as a reporter," friend and former colleague Lincoln Steffens wrote in a profile of Riis; "as a reporter he wrung men's hearts with them" (1903, 419).

Even before his reporting days, Riis was intimately acquainted with tenement life. He had been one of about 125,000 Scandinavians to land in New York in the early 1870s. Although young, strong, and a trained carpenter, he could find no work in the city and soon took to the road, wandering down to Pennsylvania and up to Buffalo. He built huts for miners, hoed cucumbers, carted bricks, but mostly he went homeless and hungry. The road always seemed to lead him back to Mulberry Bend, which he later vengefully described as the "foul core of New York's slums." He passed many nights drowsing in doorways between the policeman's periodic "Move on!," punctuated by the prod of a club or the toe of a boot (1971, 49; 1901, chs. 2–4).

His three years of poverty and semi-starvation gave Riis a fierce sympathy for the poor and lost, while his decade and a half of police reporting gave him a seemingly inexhaustible supply of facts, anecdotes, and impressions with which to dramatically make the case for reform. A glance at the headlines in his scrapbook for the years 1883–87 reveals the range and obvious human-interest appeal of his *Tribune* stories: "Virus Farms," "Cute Tricks of Thieves," "Red Tape Extravagance," "Money Made at the Dumps," "Horses Stray Away" (Alland 1974, 25). Newspapers of the era prized "heart-writing," and Riis was an acknowledged master of it. Theodore Dreiser, who entered journalism about this time, recalled:

All specials were being written in imitation of the great novelists, particularly Charles Dickens, who was the ideal of all newspaper men and editors as well as magazine special writers (how often have I been told to imitate Charles Dickens in thought and manner!). The city editors wanted not so much bare facts as feature stories, color, romance. (1965, 59)

Riis, in fact, had learned English by reading Dickens as a boy in Denmark (Riis 1901, 4). In the process of puzzling out the words, he may have absorbed something of Dickens's literary style and humane spirit.

But whatever its source, Riis's sympathy ran extraordinarily deep, and it was perhaps never more poetically expressed than in the paragraph that concludes his chapter, "The Sweaters of Jewtown." The passage, simple yet strangely shimmery, suggests the stony vastness of the tenements and the vulnerability of the life struggling to maintain itself there. As always with Riis, his heart goes out most tenderly to the children of the slum, growing up amid dirt and degradation:

Evening has worn into night as we take up our homeward journey through the streets, now no longer silent. The thousands of lighted windows in the tenements glow like dull red eyes in a huge stone wall. From every door multitudes of tired men and women pour forth for a half-hour's rest in the open air before sleep closes eyes weary with incessant working. Crowds of half-naked children tumble in the street and on the sidewalk, or doze fretfully on the stone steps. As we stop in front of a tenement to watch one of these groups, a dirty baby in a single brief garment— yet a sweet, human little baby despite its dirt and tatters—tumbles off the lowest step, rolls over once, clutches my leg with unconscious grip, and goes to sleep on the flagstones, its curly head pillowed on my boot. (1971, 107)

Riis injected himself into many of the book's scenes and descriptions. He wrote in the first person of fire panics and murders and opium dens to emphasize that his was eyewitness testimony and thus deserved the reader's special attention and trust. But voice was not chiefly a trick of style; it was a moral quality. "The saddest of all things," he told Richard Watson Gilder, editor of *Century* magazine, "must be to go to one's grave with the feeling that in nothing one has been able to soothe or help the world's misery" (quoted in Lubove 1974, 64). Riis sought to help by arousing public indignation against the evils of the tenements. In hyperbolic prose, he brought the slum vividly to life for the Victorian gentlemen and ladies who lived uptown, insulated behind the dark, heavy furniture and easels, hand-painted rolling pins, china statuettes, and other bric-a-brac that cluttered their homes (Schlesinger 1933, 137). One can detect a deliberate attempt to shock the middle class into action in his account of a raid on a stale-beer dive, a basement saloon where unlicensed, doctored beer was served. He had accompanied the police as, in his phrase, "a kind of war correspondent."

"School is in," said the sergeant drily as we stumbled down the worn steps of the next cellar-way. A kick of his boot-heel sent the door flying into the room.
A room perhaps a dozen feet square, with walls and ceiling that might once have been clean—assuredly the floor had not in the memory of man, if indeed there was other floor than the hard-trodden mud—but were now covered with a brown crust that, touched with the end of a club, came off in shuddering showers of crawling bugs, revealing the blacker filth beneath. Grouped about a beer-keg that was propped on the wreck of a broken chair, a foul and ragged host of men and women, on boxes, benches, and stools. Tomato-cans filled at the kegs were passed from hand to hand. In the centre of the group a sallow, wrinkled hag, evidently the ruler of the feast, dealt out the hideous stuff. (1971, 61)

Someone had to tell of the misery and depravity in the depths of the urban-industrial order, of the "volcano under the city"; that someone, Riis said, was the reporter. "The power of fact is the mightiest lever of this or of any day," he declared, "and the reporter has his hand upon it" (1901, 99). Riis shared with many intellectuals and artists of the period what Phillip Rahv called an "intense predilection for the real" (1978, 11). This worship of the "tangible truths of actual life" was a reaction to both the stale gentility of Victorian culture and the new, complicated cityscape that seemed to cry out for investigation (Bremner 1956, 40). In *How the Other Half Lives*, Riis's faith in the efficacy of facts emerges in various ways, but most clearly in his mania for statistics. We learn that, by 1890, 37,000 of New York's 81,000 dwellings were tenements; that of the 508 abandoned babies received at the Infant's Hospital on Randall's Island in 1889, 333, or 65.5 percent, died; that the same year an average of 14,000 homeless men slept in flop-houses every night; and so on and so on (1971, 1, 72, 145). "Statistics are not my hobby," Riis once remarked. "I like to get their human story out of them" (1902, 81–82). Here they were often placed at the end of his vignettes of tenement life, like, or instead of, a string of exclamation points.

The urge to document urban conditions also lay behind Riis's foray into photography. In 1888 he had picked up an entire camera outfit for $25 and had started taking pictures of paupers, ashcans, shanties, scrubwomen, fire escapes, toughs, sweatshop workers—the thousand sordid images of which the slum was constituted (Alland 1974, 11). Unfortunately, when *How the Other Half Lives* was published, printers had yet to perfect the photoengraving process (Emery and Emery 1988, 224–46). Only seventeen halftones and nineteen drawings of Riis's photographs were included in the book, and none had the heartrending, revelatory power of the original pictures. The reviewer in the February 5, 1891 issue of the *Nation* complained, "The photographs are not very clear, and quite fail to suggest the squalor that they are intended to represent" (121). But this mattered far less than that Riis had explored new ways of seeing and telling. He had tried to use photography to supplement, or "thicken," his verbal description of the slum.[3] Lugging the cumbersome camera equipment of his day into alleys and tenements, he had hoped that his pictures at least, if not his words, would burn the plight of the poor into the public conscience.

"Ours is an age of facts," Riis said in *The Children of the Poor*, his 1892 sequel to *How the Other Half Lives*. "It wants facts, not theories" (iv). And yet he was no social scientist objectively observing the brutish life of the tenements. His writing combined the factuality of reportage with outbursts of sympathy, sorrow, anger, and disgust. Having seen dirty, ragged children go barefoot in the snow, sweatshop workers toil from dawn to midnight at their sewing machines, the dead wagon carrying the bodies of paupers to a trench in Potter's Field, he could write in no other way.

For example, he did not merely report the suffering the summer heat inflicted on the poor, but made it into a narrative. He selected and arranged the facts for maximum effect, just as he selected and arranged the slides that illustrated the lectures on the slum he delivered in churches and theaters around the city and later around the country.[4] His sentences were like a series of pictures projected by a magic lantern—flashes in the dark:

With the first hot nights in June police dispatches, that record the killing of men and women by rolling off roofs and window-sills while asleep, announce that the time of greatest suffering among the poor is at hand. It is in hot weather, when life indoors is well-nigh unbearable with cooking, sleeping, and working, all crowded into the small rooms together, that the tenement expands, reckless of all restraint. Then a strange and picturesque life moves upon the flat roofs. In the day and early evenings mothers air their babies there, the boys fly their kites from house-tops undismayed by police regulations, and the young men and girls court and pass the growler. In the stifling July nights, when the big barracks are like fiery furnaces, their very walls giving out absorbed heat, men and women lie in restless, sweltering rows, panting for air and sleep. Then every truck in the street, every crowded fire-escape, becomes a bedroom, infinitely preferable to any the house affords. A cooling shower on such a night is hailed as a heaven-sent blessing in a hundred thousand homes. (1971, 126–27)

As Riis went on to describe the terrible slaughter among the "army of little ones" during heat waves, his writing became even more emotive. He sentimentalized the "sleepless mothers [who] walk the streets in the gray of the early dawn, trying to stir a cooling breeze to fan the brow of a sick baby. There is no sadder sight," he said, "than this patient devotion striving against fearfully hopeless odds" (1971, 126–27). To the careful observations of the reporter and the fluid language of the poet, he joined a Christian sense of pity. He wrote, as it were, with a consecrated pen.

Whenever the fire bell rang in the press office opposite police headquarters in Mulberry Street, or there was a robbery or murder, Riis would offer a quick little prayer for strength and guidance. The idea of a police reporter praying to write a good murder story may seem ludicrous, but he believed that he was doing God's, as well as the *Tribune*'s, work. "The reporter who is behind the scenes," he explained in his autobiography, *The Making of an American*,

sees the tumult of passions, and not rarely a human heroism that redeems all the rest. It is his task to portray it that we can all see its meaning, or at all events catch the human drift of it, not merely the foulness and the reek of blood. If he can do that, he has performed a signal service, and his murder story may easily come to speak more eloquently to the minds of thousands than the sermon preached to a hundred in the church on Sunday. (1901, 199, 204)

Riis contended that his brother reporters did not understand this, or they "would waste no printer's ink idly" (1901, 365). *How the Other Half Lives* represented a sort of counter-journalism, a peeling back of the lies and distortions of the sensational press to reveal the real story hidden underneath. In a chapter titled "Waifs in the City's Slums," Riis noted:

Only the poor abandon their children. The stories of richly-dressed foundlings that are dished up in the newspapers at intervals are pure fiction. Not one instance of even a well-dressed infant having been picked up in the streets is on record. They come in rags, a newspaper often the only wrap, semi-occasionally one in a clean slip with some evidence of loving care; a little slip of paper pinned on, perhaps, with some message as this I once read, in a woman's trembling hand: "Take care of Johnny, for God's sake. I cannot." But even that is the rarest of all happenings. (1971, 145)

Although well researched and deeply felt, *How the Other Half Lives* was by no means a perfect book. Prominent among its flaws was Riis's xeno- phobia. He was suspicious of the ethnic groups that had most recently colonized the Lower East Side, doubtful that these illiterate, clannish peas- ants from Southern and Eastern Europe could ever be fully assimilated. His anxiety would cause him in later years to advocate immigration restrictions. Now it took the form of ugly racial stereotypes. Of Jews, for example, he said: "Money is their God. Life itself is of little value compared with even the leanest bank account" (1971, 76).

In a similar vein, Riis sometimes tried to wake up the middle class by appealing not to its pity, but to its instinct for self-preservation. Memories of the draft riots of July 1863, when the immigrant poor had streamed out of the tenements to murder, loot, and burn, were still fairly fresh, and Riis raised the spectre of a repeat of those bloody, turbulent days (Lubove 1974, 12). "The sea of a mighty population, held in galling fetters, heaves uneasily in the tenements," Riis warned. "Once already our city . . . has felt the swell of its restless flood. If it rises once more, no human power may avail to check it" (1971, 229).

This is not meant to imply that Riis's reputation was hollow or false, only that his writing was enmeshed in the conventions of his time and the contradictions of his personality. The same year *How the Other Half Lives* was published, he switched to the staff of Charles A. Dana's New York *Sun* and continued battling the slum as determinedly as ever. He forced the razing of Mulberry Bend, "the wickedest, as it was the foulest, spot in the city" (1902, 88). He drove bake shops, with their fatal fires, out of the tenement basements. He fought for, and got, stricter enforcement of child- labor laws, a truant school (boys who played hooky had been imprisoned with juvenile criminals), and parks for decayed neighborhoods. His influ- ence, spread through a steady procession of books, articles, and lectures, was simply tremendous. He did more than anyone else to prepare the way for the New York Tenement House Law of 1901, which Cordasco has called the "first major advance in the fight against the tenement slum" (1968, xxi).

Historians usually identify Riis as a precursor of the muckrakers of the Progressive Era or as a pioneer documentary photographer (Ware 1938, 15–28; Alland 1974, 225). But one can also accurately identify him as part of a long and valuable tradition of literary journalism. He is a link in a chain that stretches backward to Dickens's *American Notes* and forward through Crane's and Dreiser's sketches of New York low life and Jack

London's *The People of the Abyss* to George Orwell's *Down and out in Paris and London* and James Agee and Walker Evans's *Let Us Now Praise Famous Men*. All wanted to see for themselves how the other half lives, and all felt compelled on their return from the dark side to communicate what they saw. They were fiercely loyal to the ideal of the writer or photographer as witness. It is an ideal perhaps best summed up by the haunting refrain of the messengers in the Book of Job: "And I only am escaped alone to tell thee."

NOTES

1. A flood of cheap sensational subliterature, typified by such titles as *Mysteries and Miseries of New York* (1848), *New York: Its Upper Ten and Lower Million* (1854), and *Metropolitan Life Unveiled* (1882), poured from the presses in the second half of the nineteenth century. Allegedly factual exposés of crime and vice in the city, these works described in melodramatic style the gambling halls, brothels, and other temptations that brought country lads and maidens to ruin. Their authors appealed, as Bremner says, to "prurience behind a mask of outraged respectability" (1956, 68).

That there were respectable citizens who were genuinely outraged by the slum, and by the disease and immorality that seemed to characterize its inhabitants, is beyond question. The New York Association for Improving the Condition of the Poor (AICP), founded in 1843 by well-to-do merchants and businessmen, led the crusade for housing reform for two decades, partly out of sympathy for the teeming tenement population and partly, perhaps mostly, out of deep fear of it. The AICP believed that if the poor were more decently housed, they would be more decently behaved. Its annual report for 1853 indicated how very far there was still to go; "Crazy old buildings—crowded rear tenements in filthy yards—dark, damp basements—leaky garrets, ships, outhouses and stables converted into dwellings, though scarcely fit to shelter brutes—are the habitations of thousands of our fellow-beings in this wealthy Christian city" (Lubove 1974, 1, 4–7).

2. The remark about Howells and Crane echoes Bremner 1956, 55. Sims listed "immersion," which, in "its simplest form means time spent on the job," as one of the "essential features" of literary journalism (1984, 4, 8–12). Wolfe's term for this was "saturation reporting" (Wolfe 1973, 52).

3. The notion of "thick description" comes from anthropologist Clifford Geertz and refers to a "literary" method of interpreting other cultures. "As interworked systems of construable signs...," Geertz has written, "culture is not a power, something to which social events, behaviors, institutions, or processes can be causally attributed; it is a context, something within which they can be intelligibly—that is, thickly—described" (1973, 14).

4. See Sloan 1988, 36–37, for a description of a New York audience's startled reaction to Riis's stereopticon slides of the slum.

PRIMARY SOURCES

Riis, Jacob A. 1892. *The Children of the Poor*. New York: Macmillan.
———. 1898. *Out of Mulberry Street*. Rpt. 1906 as *The Children of the Tenements*.

New York: Macmillan. This is a selection of Riis's New York *Sun* stories and magazine articles. The *Sun* stories compare favorably with Stephen Crane's and Theodore Dreiser's New York vignettes. Among the best are "Death Comes to Cat Alley," "The Cat Took the Kosher Meat," "Nigger Martha's Wake," and "Abe's Game of Jacks."

———. 1901. *The Making of an American.* New York: Macmillan.

———. 1902. *The Battle with the Slum.* New York: Macmillan. Rpt. 1969. Montclair, N.J.: Patterson Smith.

———. 1971. *How the Other Half Lives: Studies Among the Tenements of New York.* New York: Dover. This edition contains one hundred photographs from the Riis Collection of the Museum of the City of New York and so comes closest to Riis's original conception of his master work.

SECONDARY SOURCES

Alland, Alexander. 1974. *Jacob A. Riis: Photographer and Citizen.* New York: Aperture.

Bremner, Robert H. 1956. *From the Depths: The Discovery of Poverty in the United States.* New York: New York University Press.

Cordasco, Francesco, ed. 1968. Introduction to *Jacob Riis Revisited.* Garden City, N.Y.: Doubleday.

Dickens, Charles. 1903. *American Notes and Pictures from Italy.* London: Macmillan.

Dreiser, Theodore. 1965. *A Book About Myself.* Greenwich, Conn.: Fawcett.

Emery, Michael, and Edwin Emery. 1988. *The Press and America.* 6th ed. Englewood Cliffs, N.J.: Prentice-Hall.

Geertz, Clifford. 1973. *The Interpretation of Cultures.* New York: Basic Books.

Lubove, Roy. 1962. *The Progressives and the Slum: Tenement House Reform in New York City, 1890–1917.* Pittsburgh: University of Pittsburgh Press. Rpt. 1974. Westport, Conn.: Greenwood Press.

Rahv, Phillip. 1978. "The Cult of Experience." In *Essays on Literature and Politics.* Ed. Arabel J. Porter and Andrew J. Dvosin. Boston: Houghton Mifflin.

Schlesinger, Arthur M. 1933. *The Rise of the City, 1878–1898.* New York: Macmillan.

Sims, Norman, ed. 1984. *The Literary Journalists.* New York: Ballantine.

Sloan, Kay. 1988. *The Loud Silents: Origins of the Social Problem Film.* Urbana: University of Illinois Press.

Steffens, Lincoln. 1903, Aug. "Jacob A. Riis: Reporter, Reformer, American Citizen." *McClures*: 419–25.

Ware, Louise. 1938. *Jacob A. Riis: Police Reporter, Reformer, Useful Citizen.* New York: Appleton-Century-Crofts.

Wolfe, Tom. 1973. *The New Journalism.* With an Anthology edited by Tom Wolfe and E. W. Johnson. New York: Harper and Row.

ABRAHAM CAHAN

Bruce J. Evensen

If a journalist "wants to influence real live people," Abraham Cahan told an interviewer in 1911, "he must first become a live man himself" (Poole, 474). For Cahan, who had developed by that time the reputation for being the most influential man on New York City's Lower East Side, becoming a "live man" meant immersion in the lives of the immigrant masses in their struggles to adapt themselves to America.[1] The adaptation that Cahan depicted in both the English-language and Yiddish press over the course of nearly seventy years made him a major mediator in American cultural history and an early advocate of a journalistic style that aimed to sensitize its audience to the experience of others by exploring the universalism of their humanity.[2]

Cahan's earliest writings about this immigrant community invests its members with "life-likeness" for the purpose of "not so much copying the outside nature but stimulating the sensation it evokes in us" (*Workman's Advocate*, 15 May 1889). During his first fifteen years in America, Cahan, a Jewish immigrant who had fled a czarist pogrom in his native Lithuania, wrote articles for both the Yiddish-language and the English press, while intensifying his campaign to organize Jewish workers for the Socialist Labor Party. His reporting at the *Arbeiter Zeitung* combined storytelling and social theory. In one issue he contrasts the wedding of a millionaire's daughter and the all-night dancing that follows it to the plight of newspaper peddlers, waiting at pickup points throughout the city for their early morning editions (6 Mar. 1890).

His writing for Charles Dana's *New York Sun*, however, was far less didactic. "Hebrews in Summer Hotels—How They Are Treated—A Strange but Strictly True Illustration" relies on a heavy dose of irony in showing how Jews use summer names to get hotel reservations (2 Sept. 1888). In articles for the *New York Press* and *New York Star*, Cahan strove for "artistic re-creation" of the life of the Lower East Side community. He consciously followed Dana's admonition that "a good newspaperman must know life." The basic course of a budding journalist was "life itself" (Stein et al. 1969, 357).

Life on the Lower East Side at the turn of the century found a Jewish community striving to adapt itself to the requirements of proletarian living at a time when they had been abruptly cut off from the cultural and religious institutions that had given their lives meaning and moral authority. "The shtetl was wretched enough," writes Irving Howe, a biographer of New York's Jewish ghetto, "but at least it was a thoroughly known place" (1976, 117). Cahan's work at the *New York Commercial Advertiser* between 1897 and 1902 reflected this struggle as part of the paper's larger effort to extend the sensibilities and enlarge the consciousness of its readers (Rischin 1985, xix). Lincoln Steffens, fresh from six years at the *New York Evening Post*, was determined to bring writers to the *Commercial Advertiser* whose curiosity would track social problems to their source (Winter and Hicks 1938, 130). In Cahan and Hutchins Hapgood he found journalists who shared his enthusiasm for culturally informed news. Together they helped develop a literary journalism that interpreted the turbulent spirit and rich complexity of New York's immigrant community to the paper's cosmopolitan readership.

Steffens, in his autobiography, credited Cahan with "bringing the spirit of the East side into our shop" and saw him at the center of the ongoing debate over how the paper could communicate journalistic observations through literary art (1931, 317). Steffens saw Cahan's *Yekl: A Tale of the New York Ghetto*, published in 1896 at the urging of William Dean Howells, as a pioneering work in fact-based fiction designed to get beneath the surface of things (Cady 1973, 256–57). Its portrayal of a cloak shop worker's bewildered attempt to become "an American feller, a Yankee," is told within the context of a ghetto Cahan had come to know intimately. Jake, the protagonist,

> had to pick and nudge his way through dense swarms of bedraggled half-naked humanity; past garbage barrels rearing their overflowing contents in sickening piles, and lining the streets in malicious suggestion of rows of trees; underneath tiers and tiers of fire escapes; barricaded and festooned with mattresses, pillows, and featherbeds not yet gathered in for the night. The pent-in sultry atmosphere was laden with nausea and pierced with a discordant and, as it were, plaintive buzz. (Cahan 1896, 27)

This plaintive buzz is brought to a sharp pitch within the pages of the *Commercial Advertiser*. At the Barge Office, where immigrants begin their lives in America, Cahan encounters a Hungarian-born flower maker, who supports her deaf-mute sister while saving to set up her intended in a business of his own (19 Jan. 1902). Then there is the story of Wilhemina Praast, detained at the Barge Office because she has neither money nor relatives to claim her. She is "in despair" because at twenty-eight she fears that she is too old to be wanted any longer (16 Feb. 1900). The uncertain future faced by immigrants is also reflected in Cahan's fiction of the period. "A fresh shipload of immigrants has arrived at the Barge Office," he wrote for *Cosmopolitan* in 1901. "It was made up of Slovaks, Magyars, Poles, Jews, some Syrians, some Armenians and a few lone representatives of other nationalities. The bay outside was overhung by a colorless, sullen sky. The 'detention pen' was filled with depressing twilight" (1901a).

The immigrant encounter with the shock of America is personified in Cahan's journalism through intimate portraits of the well-known souls of the city's Lower East Side. Perhaps none is more poignant than that of Rabbi Jacob Joseph, the leader of the Jewish community in Cahan's native Vilna, Russia, where he was revered as a Talmudic scholar. In 1887, Joseph answered a call to head eighteen of the largest orthodox synagogues of New York City. His first years were "happy ones" in which the immigrant community "clung to older forms of the faith." But as the people of the East Side "began to pick up American ideas," the celebrated exhorter of Old World ways "proved a disenchantment." When Cahan encounters Joseph in 1901 he finds a "hopeless invalid," helpless in a world he is unable to understand, pitied by a community he once led, his victimization "a symbol of the unspoken struggle between two worlds" and a reflection "of the sad history of the whole race" (*Commercial Advertiser*, 24 Jan. 1901).

Joseph's predicament is a metaphor not only for the struggle of the Jewish community but for Cahan's own difficulties in accommodating himself to a country he never imagined. "I do not know through what association of ideas the image came into my head," he writes, "but I remember distinctly that the word America would call to my mind a luxuriant many-colored meadow, with swarms of tall people hurrying hither and thither along narrow footpaths" (*Commercial Advertiser*, 6 Aug. 1898). His journalism is an exploration of these struggles and how he and the immigrant community attempted to adapt their ideals, sense of fraternity, and notions of moral order to a rapidly industrializing society.

Cahan records this adaptation in the many voices of the immigrant community. "Zu dir ist mein liebster Gang," Mrs. Gericke sings as she scrubs the staircase of her tenement house. "Mein liebster Gang, Mein liebster Gang!" (*Commercial Advertiser*, 14 Mar. 1899). "Look here, Sheeny, this is all you're going to get," Morris Sarner quotes his Gentile wife while explaining to a Harlem court judge why he wants a divorce from her. "Your honor, I am treated like a dog in my own house and fed like a pig." He pushes a package under Magistrate Brann's nostrils. "That looks like roast beef," the magistrate tells him. "Don't insult roast beef," Sarner says (*Commercial Advertiser*, 14 Mar. 1899).

Most of Cahan's encounters with the Lower East Side are not quite so comic. He defends the East Side housewife against the stereotypical portrayal of her as a nag and a gossip. "She lives," Cahan writes, "above the babble of a thousand voices, along with the fetid odors and heat glare from the street below." There she "wages perpetual warfare on the common enemy of all housekeepers, dirt." She is self-sacrificing. "For the sake of her children," Cahan reports, "she will go hungry if necessary." And her husband, "far from considering her an obstacle to his progress, regards her as a beacon light, leading him ever onward to a bank account and competency" (*Commercial Advertiser*, 29 June 1902).

Cahan's empathy for the plight of the immigrant family is expressed in the details of a writer intimately familiar with his subject. *Commercial Advertiser* readers learn of the crotchety butcher named Bauer, who opens a candy store off Avenue C with the $150 he gets for chopping off two of his fingers (8 July 1899). They learn of the fish peddler on Norfolk Street between Grand and Division who sells "fish, fish, living, floundering, jumping, dancing fish!" to housewives on Atonement Avenue (24 Sept. 1898). And they hear of the two-headed baby born in the basement of 58 Montgomery Street and the reassurance by the neighbor to a grieving father that the second mouth "will never be big enough to hold a cigarette" (18 Oct. 1899). And they listen in as the Social Science Club of 28 East 4th Street takes up the problem of the city's 1,500 pushcart operators, "hardly earning more than $5 a week," but forced to give fifty cents of it in bribes to police for being allowed to continue violating city ordinances (29 June 1898).

While Cahan was absorbed in the political life of the Jewish community, his writing about that community in the pages of the *Commercial Advertiser* is rarely didactic. His treatment of the cigar makers' strike of 1900 describes a dance by union members celebrating the sixteenth week of the work stoppage. "It's too hot to work for $5 a week," a striker tells Cahan. "This is the first vacation I ever got," another tells him (30 June 1900). In his autobiography, Cahan writes that "socialist and non-socialist schemes for ridding the world of its injustice" could best be communicated by seizing the human subject from within. This meant a commitment to what he saw as "realistic depiction" of working-class life. It emphasized those details of psychic reality that most acutely revealed the condition of the immigrant by causing the reader to recognize "the thrill" of finding himself within that portrait (Stein et al. 1969, 404–5). Cahan's fiction of the period has the same purpose. In "Tzinchadzi of the Catskills," David Tzinchadzi is the son of a Georgian nobleman, whose grandfather once led his tribe against the Russians. When Cahan encounters him in the Catskills, he is a melancholy man uncomfortably adjusted to living in America. He has made a small fortune selling real estate in New York City under the name of Jones. "America is a fine place," he tells Cahan, "but I have come to the conclusion that a man's heart cannot be happy unless it has somebody or something to yearn for."

Tzinchadzi appears to speak in behalf of Cahan, whose later journalism often reflected his own disappointment with life in America. "I have become oysgregreent—practical, as they say," he told readers of the *Jewish Daily Forward* in 1902. "I no longer gnash my teeth over the foolish world." But at the beginning of what would be a brilliant and highly profitable fifty-year career as editor of New York's most widely read Yiddish daily, Cahan admits to profound uncertainties over his role as mediator between the immigrant and American cultures. He questions his own "decency" and "self-respect." He has already seen his fire for social change, "my dear, my sacred idea," he calls it, overcome by the instincts of "a practical man" who "sleeps in peace and looks peacefully upon the world." Cahan laments that it has robbed him of "a single great faith" by which to live and left him with a "yearning for my yearnings of 20 years ago" (Sanders 1969, 168–70).

Cahan's intuitive penetration of immigrant feelings, along with his journalistic advocacy in behalf of social reform, transformed the *Forward* from a seldom-read offspring of the Socialist Labor Party into a powerful institution in Jewish immigrant life. Cahan produced not a party paper but a daily guidebook for Yiddish readers. His first edition of the *Forward* on March 16, 1902, set the tone under the lead editorial, "Send your children to college if you can, but don't let them become disloyal to their own parents and brothers." Cahan presents his point as if telling a parable. He opens his story by describing the way hundreds of Jewish boys start their days by walking to school up Second Avenue with books under their arms. Their faces "shine with a spiritual joy" at the prospect of learning, yet seem hardly aware of "the privation and spilt blood" Jewish families have endured to assure their children's education. Cahan relates the experience of a father who earns eight dollars a week and a mother who is ill refusing to allow their son to drop out of school and go to work. All the more reason, Cahan argues, "that college boys who betray their working class parents" by becoming "toadies to politicians" and "enemies of the people" are "traitors to their own people."

While Cahan's writing at the *Jewish Daily Forward* is characterized by strong appeal to sentiment and teaching by moral tales, it remains rooted in Cahan's certainty that "the most important question (about literature and journalism) always remains the same: does this feel like real life?" (21 Dec. 1903). The ambition for his writing was that it discover the universal through the particular. Good journalism was "novelistic," Cahan wrote in the *Forward*, as it "unfolded the thousands and thousands of life stories in tenement homes" to readers who saw themselves represented within those stories (21 Dec. 1903).

Cahan was assisted in constructing *emmeser romanen*, or true novels, by *Forward* readers, whose letters to Cahan, along with his replies, embody the fundamental struggle of accommodation and acculturation and its underlying irony—the sooner the Yiddish culture began to realize its goals of acceptance in America, the sooner it would destroy itself. To the "greenhorn" from Odessa who wrote that he could not forgive himself for abandoning Russia, where workers "are fighting for their lives," while he lived in America on five dollars a week, Cahan's advice was to stop feeling sorry for himself "and fight right here in America for a social order in which a man won't have to work like a mule for $5 a week" (30 Jan. 1903).

Cahan's ability to treat cultural nightmare through individual restlessness evoked a wave of response from his readers. Cahan counsels the tubercular who is afraid of suicide; the abandoned wife ready to give her children away "to someone who can give them bread"; the worker who scabs to buy his sick wife medicine; the thirteen-year-old raincoat maker who was docked two cents for arriving at a job ten minutes late; the barber who thinks of cutting his customers' throats; the cantor who wonders what will become of him since he no longer believes in God. Cahan's replies mix ideology and common sense, while attempting to be reasonable and reassuring.[3]

In the years leading up to World War I, Abraham Cahan's *Jewish Daily Forward* gave the immigrant community a window to the wider world while offering it a glimpse into its own soul. A circulation of 20,000 in 1900 topped 130,000 in 1918 and a quarter million by the middle of the next decade. The pass-along effect made the paper's penetration of the immigrant community far greater (Howe 1976, 539). Irving Howe points out that while the average immigrant home seldom had books, it was rarely without its *Daily Forward*. Not to take the paper when offered "was to confess you were a barbarian." To treat it with less than full respect was not without consequence. When one fish store owner wrapped carp in its pages, his store was boycotted until he stopped the practice and apologized.[4]

Cahan's identification with New York's Lower East Side raised his literary journalism to the art of community self-expression. Within hours of the Triangle Factory fire on March 25, 1911, the *Forward* put out a special edition decrying the loss of 146 ghetto residents. "The whole Jewish quarter is in mourning," Cahan wrote beneath the picture of Becky Kessler, a nineteen-year-old burned to death a week before her wedding. "Tears fall around this picture," Cahan wrote, while capturing the mood of the Jewish community. "There will be a funeral now instead of a wedding." Cahan's account of the tragedy and its aftermath is less an exercise in journalistic compassion than it is the outpouring of the collective sentiment of the Jewish community.

By the middle of the 1920s, the Yiddish community on New York's Lower East Side had passed its prime. The cultural shock and grave dispossession of one generation was giving way gradually to the limited successes of another, a generation that built on the sacrifices and profited from the mistakes of the ghetto's founding fathers to escape the ghetto altogether. Cahan chronicles the emergence of the "allrightnik" in a series of articles first written for *McClure's Magazine* and later expanded into the novel *The Rise of David Levinsky*.

The book is a diligent analysis of American social history posing as fiction, a delicately drawn rags-to-riches tale serving as a vehicle for social criticism. Levinsky's self-examination captures Cahan's own ambivalence over the Americanization of the shtetl community and Cahan's own role as mediator between cultures. Levinsky's rise from sewing machine operator to Garment District millionaire in the three decades leading up to World War I comes at the price of his own alienation. Levinsky echoes both Cahan and Tzinchadzi when he admits, "My sense of triumph is coupled with a brooding sense of emptiness and insignificance, of my lack of anything like a great, deep interest" (1969, 526). Levinsky's self-pity and loneliness speak to his alienation from an immigrant culture he has worked assiduously to escape and an American culture he has worked just as carefully to enter. Levinsky's success was at the expense of a way of life he labored unremittingly to put to death. Yet the life it left him he did not feel was altogether worth living.[5]

The settling of more than 1 million Jews on New York City's Lower East Side in the three decades leading to the outbreak of World War I was part of a larger historical phenomenon that saw more than 17 million immigrants settle in the United States, 1.5 million of them Jews.[6] What distinguished the Jewish settlement was the resolve to stay. Overall, one in five immigrants returned to the Old World, but only one in twenty-five Jews, and half of those returned not to the old country but to Palestine (Golden 1965, 5–7). The life that was scratched out by the pioneers who remained was summarized in the literary journalism of Abraham Cahan and aggressively promoted in his writing and his life as a social agitator. Cahan interpreted two distinct cultures to one another, cultures he was intimately connected to, yet eventually stood outside of. As socialist, journalist, and friend of the ghetto, he lived to see the material flourishing of a community he feared had lost a spiritual sense of how to live. Two generations after his passing, contemporary writers recognize in Cahan's cultural canvas chronicles of fitful adaptation, the modern paradox of people seeking community even at the loss of self.

NOTES

1. See Howe 1976, 524; Hapgood 1902, 183; Charles Regnikoff, ed., *Louis Marshall: Champion of Liberty* (Philadelphia: The Jewish Publication Society of America, 1957), 974–76; Yudel Mark, "Yiddish Literature," in *The Jews: Their History, Culture and Religion*, ed. Louis Finkelstein, vol. 2 (New York: Harper and

Row, 1949, 1960), 1216–19; Hillquit 1934, 15–40; Boris D. Bogen, *Born a Jew* (New York: Macmillan, 1930), 36–81; Learsi 1954, 157, 188–91; Rischin 1962, 78, 126–27, 158, 167; Sanders 1988, 165–66; and Sanders 1969, 6, 108, 217, 257, 416, 434–36, 452–53.

2. See Stein et al. 1969, 404–12. Also, *New York Commercial Advertiser*, 24 Feb. 1899. See also Howe 1970, 88–91; Sanders 1969, 105, 177; Joan Zlotnick, "Abraham Cahan, a Neglected Realist," *American Jewish Archives* 23 (April 1971): 33–46. For background, see chapter appearing in Melech Epstein's *Profiles of Eleven* (Detroit: Wayne State University Press, 1965), 76–109.

3. Isaac Metzker, ed., *A Bintel Brief* (New York: Ballantine, 1977), 118–19; Irving Howe and Kenneth Libo, *How We Lived: A Documentary History of Immigrant Life in America, 1880–1930* (New York: Richard Marek, 1979), 85–90; Howe 1976, 531–34. Also, *Congress Bi-Weekly*, 18 June 1971, 19.

4. Learsi 1954, 188–90; Howe 1976, 518–19, 528; Hillquit 1934, 15–23; Harold U. Ribalow, *Autobiographies of American Jews* (Philadelphia: Jewish Publication Society of America, 1965), 10–11, 90–91.

5. See John Higham's preface to *The Rise of David Levinsky* by Abraham Cahan. Also, Bernard G. Richards, introduction to *Yekl and the Imported Bridegroom and Other Stories of the New York Ghetto* by Abraham Cahan (New York: Dover, 1898, 1970); Chametzky 1977, 127–44; Daniel Walden, "Urbanism, Technology and the Ghetto in Novels by Abraham Cahan, Henry Roth and Saul Bellow," *American Jewish History* 23 (Mar. 1984): 296–300; Walter B. Rideout, "O Workers' Revolution . . . The True Messiah—The Jew as Author and Subject in the American Radical Novel," *American Jewish Archives* 11 (Oct. 1959): 161–62.

6. See Chametzky 1977, 3–5; Rischin 1962, preface; Howe 1976, 58–59; Sanders 1988, 151–52.

PRIMARY SOURCES

Cahan, Abraham. 1896. *Yekl: A Tale of the New York Ghetto*. New York: D. Appleton. Rpt. 1899.

———. 1901a, Mar. "Dumitru and Sigrid." *Cosmopolitan.*

———. 1901b, Aug. "Tzinchadzi of the Catskills." *Atlantic Monthly.*

———. 1926. *Bleter Fun Mein Lebe, Leaves from My Life*. New York: Forward Association.

———. 1969. *The Rise of David Levinsky*. Gloucester, Mass.: Peter Smith.

SECONDARY SOURCES

Cady, Edwin, ed. 1973. *William Dean Howells as Critic*. Boston: Routledge and Kegan Paul.

Chametzky, Jules. 1977. *From the Ghetto: The Fiction of Abraham Cahan*. Amherst: University of Massachusetts Press.

Golden, Harry. 1965. Annotation to *The Spirit of the Ghetto*, by Hutchins Hapgood. New York: Funk and Wagnalls.

Hapgood, Hutchins. 1902. *The Spirit of the Ghetto: Studies of the Jewish Quarter of New York*. New York: Funk and Wagnalls. Rpt. 1965.

Hillquit, Morris. 1934. *Loose Leaves from a Busy Life*. New York: Macmillan.

Howe, Irving. 1970, Mar. Review of *The Education of Abraham Cahan*, by Leon Stein, Abraham P. Conan, and Lynn Davison. *Commentary* 49: 88–91.

———. 1976. *World of Our Fathers*. New York: Harcourt Brace Jovanovich.

Learsi, Rufus. 1954. *The Jews in America: A History*. New York: World.

Poole, Ernest. 1911. "Abraham Cahan: Socialist—Journalist—Friend of the Ghetto." *Outlook* 99: 474.

Rischin, Moses. 1962. *The Promised City: New York Jews, 1870–1914*. Cambridge, Mass.: Harvard University Press.

———. 1985. *Grandma Never Lived in America: The New Journalism of Abraham Cahan*. Bloomington: Indiana University Press.

Sanders, Ronald. 1969. *The Downtown Jews: Portrait of an Immigrant Generation*. New York: Harper and Row.

———. 1988. *Shores of Refuge: A Hundred Years of Jewish Immigration*. New York: Henry Holt.

Steffens, Lincoln. 1931. *Autobiography of Lincoln Steffens*. New York: Harcourt, Brace.

Stein, Leon, Abraham P. Conan, and Lynn Davison. 1969. *The Education of Abraham Cahan*. Trans. from vols. 1 and 2 of *Yiddish Language Autobiographies*. Philadelphia: Jewish Publication Society of America.

Winter, Ella, and Granville Hicks, eds. 1938. Vol. 1 of *The Letters of Lincoln Steffens*. New York: Harcourt, Brace.

BIBLIOGRAPHIC NOTE

Moses Rischin's *Grandma Never Lived in America* (Bloomington: Indiana University, 1985) is a collection of Cahan's literary journalism during the five years he worked with Lincoln Steffens on the *New York Commercial Advertiser*. Rischin's introduction to that volume extends Rischin's analysis, which first appeared in the *American Jewish Quarterly* in September 1953, that Cahan's turn-of-the-century work with the English-language press reflected a "new journalism" that attempted to combine literary and journalistic techniques.

The most elaborate contextual works dealing with the development of Cahan's journalistic style at the *Jewish Daily Forward* are Irving Howe's *World of Our Fathers* (New York: Harcourt Brace Jovanovich, 1976) and Ronald Sanders's *The Downtown Jews: Portrait of an Immigrant Generation* (New York: Harper and Row, 1969).

Cahan's fact-based fiction has been the subject of growing analysis. Consider Jules Chametzky's *From the Ghetto: The Fiction of Abraham Cahan* (Amherst: University of Massachusetts Press, 1977), which is a summary of much of this literature. Also see Joan Zlotnick's article in the April 1971 issue of *American Jewish Archives* and Daniel Walden's analysis, which appears in the March 1984 edition of *American Jewish History*.

The two primary bibliographies of Cahan's work are found in Ephim Jeshurin's "A Cahan Bibliography," which the author printed himself in New York City in 1941. The Library of Congress has a photocopied edition of Jeshurin's bibliography since 1981. A second bibliography was compiled in 1970 by Sanford E. Marovitz and Lewis Fried, "Abraham Cahan, 1860–1951: An Annotated Bibliography," in

American Literary Realism, 1870–1910, vol. 3, 197–243. The publisher is the Department of English of the University of Texas at Arlington.

The last three volumes of Cahan's autobiography, describing his years as the editor of the *Jewish Daily Forward,* have yet to be translated into English. A biography of Cahan is being planned by Moses Rischin. It will complement two biographical chapters now available on the life of Cahan: Melech Epstein's *Profiles of Eleven* (Detroit: Wayne State University Press, 1965), 76–109, and Abraham Goldberg's *Pioneers and Builders: Biographical Studies and Essays* (New York: Abraham Goldberg Publications Committee, 1943), 284–330. Sanders's *The Downtown Jews,* despite its complete title, is essentially the story of New York's Jewish immigrant community told through the life of Cahan.

At this writing, the best way of studying the development of Cahan's literary journalism is to analyze the work itself in the Russian-, Yiddish-, and English-language presses in which it appeared.

LINCOLN STEFFENS

Peter Parisi

For all the connotations of superficiality and venality that sometimes attach to its name, American journalism is animated by an inspiring idealistic belief that everyday experience and the lives of ordinary people are "newsworthy," that journalism can present a feelingful account of the quality of daily life in a particular place at a particular time. When newspaper editors wax philosophic, they say that they want "the human stories," accounts of "the way we live now," a conception that would befit Balzac as readily as Abe Rosenthal. And whenever daily journalism attempts to register the quality of everyday experience, it necessarily becomes, in some measure, literary journalism.

But in what measure? In what literary mode? With what tone and what conception of human nature and society?

When Lincoln Steffens, as new city editor of the New York *Commercial Advertiser*, set out in 1897 to create a paper that would have "literary charm as well as information" (1938, 123) and "to beat the other papers ...in the way they presented the news" (1931, 317), he effected a subtle but significant shift in the literary quality of human-interest writing. A well-established tradition of journalistic feature writing had cohered around the Penny Press in the 1830s and thrived in his own day (and persists to ours). This tradition generally found the occasion for literary journalism in the "sentiment and humor of the daily life around us" (Mitchell 1924, 416–17), with the humor and the choice of story subjects usually governed by the famous adage that news is when "Man Bites Dog."[1] This tradition opened the way for the newspaper to register the texture of daily life, but it had fateful consequences for the expressive possibilities of literary journalism. For to write the news as a cavalcade of novelty, oddity, sensation, and sentiment is to write the "human story" as melodrama.[2] Steffens, in contrast, insisted that journalism could render tragic complexity and contradiction rather than melodramatic simplicity, that it could record beauty as well as novelty, and describe not just the odd but the "typical" and "characteristic."

Steffens thus formulated a critique of the routinization and flattening of the journalistic account of everyday life and sponsored journalistic writing of broader emotional and intellectual scope. To be sure, newswriting generally in the 1890s was more "literary" than it is today. The "inverted pyramid" structure had not yet transformed narrative into a hierarchy of fact. The spot news story was frequently told in chronological order with fully rendered character, setting, and dialogue. Although Steffens in his autobiography somewhat overstates the uniqueness of his editorial philosophy, he did acknowledge the literary power of the reporting of men like Julian Ralph and Richard Harding Davis: "The star men of the other papers ... likewise were laboring at the art of telling stories," he wrote (1931, 317). Steffens's achievement lies precisely in his insistence that an artistic approach to newswriting need not await the outbursts of genius. There have been "writer's papers" before and since, but no American newspaper has ever so thoroughly and self-consciously adopted an artistic attitude to the news as did the *Commercial Advertiser* under Steffens. Recognizing the journalistic solidity and ethical force of the artistic attitude, Steffens made literary journalism into editorial policy.

"The flash of a murder would come in," Steffens recalled in his autobiography, and, like any newspaper man, he would say, "There's a story in it." But his idea of the nature of the story, its telling, and its ideal reader response, all differed significantly from the typical human-interest approach. "Without any urge," Steffens said, he would instruct the reporter:

"Here, Cahan, is a report that a man has murdered his wife, a rather bloody, hacked-up crime. We don't care about that. But there's a story in it. That man loved that woman well enough to cut her all to pieces. If you can find out just what happened between that wedding and this murder, you will have a novel for yourself and a short story for me. Go on now, take your time, and get this tragedy, as a tragedy." (1931, 317)

Steffens's anecdote mounts an implicit critique of the conventional literature of journalism. The story is not the tale of the "bloody, hacked-up crime"—news as novelty and the unusual—but the "tragedy" of the transformation of love into murderous hatred. The subject, for a literary approach, was not the bare event but its suggestions about the deeper natures of people, society, "life." Steffens mocked the absurdity of the conservative *Evening Post*'s attempts chastely to report a "mere mean murder as news" when "there was no news in it, only life" (1931, 243).

"Our stated ideal for a murder story," Steffens wrote, "was that it should be so understood and told that the murderer would not be hanged, not by our readers." Steffens was not, let it be perfectly clear, campaigning against capital punishment. He was rather calling for newswriting that would elicit from the reader empathy and comprehension rather than shock and indignation. It was an extension of aesthetic distance to add to an ethical dimension of journalistic writing. Steffens saw that it was not in "sparkling," "saucy" prose that journalism gained true literary power, but in offering an account of the news that suggests its connections with larger patterns of individual and social life. The endeavor to portray the news event more fully linked the journalist and the artist. It was, Steffens insisted, "scientifically and artistically the true ideal for an artist and for a newspaper: to get the news so completely and to report it so humanly that the reader will see himself in the other fellow's place" (1931, 317).

In practice, the *Commercial Advertiser*'s literary journalism appeared in "timeless" portraits of city life more than in coverage of breaking news, and its best stories produced under this philosophy tended to appear on the first page of the paper's second section on Saturdays. (The *Commercial Advertiser* did not publish on Sunday.)

Getting the news completely, reporting it humanly, arousing empathy rather than awe, all meant enlarging the usual conventions of journalistic writing and thinking. Steffens said that he sought to hire "writers,... not newspaper men but writers." But he stressed the concreteness and openness of the writer's perception more than the fineness of his prose (1931, 314).[3]

He looked for reporters with "fresh staring eyes," adding, "When a reporter no longer saw red at a fire, when he was so used to police news that a murder was not a human tragedy but only a crime, he could not write police news for us" (1931, 314–15). The characteristic "try-out" at the *Commercial Advertiser*—"go and see and write the difference between Fifth Avenue and Broadway or Thirty-sixth and Thirty-seventh Streets" (1931, 311–12)—was an exercise in a kind of journalistic imagism, a test in rendering city life in its vivid, actual particularity, rather than bending it to fit a sentimental melodrama.

In the *Commercial Advertiser*, a story might be made of "What a Fire Escape Is Good For," with observations ranging from the aesthetics of the fire escape's lines and colors against the sky to description of how the Italian residents of a particular tenement use it as a balcony, garden, knife sharpener, and summer bedroom—everything but a fire escape (9 July 1898, 9). Here the journalist still observes noteworthy details of the public scene, but the "news" is the human creative faculty finding unpredictable and multiple uses for even utilitarian objects. Many *Commercial Advertiser* stories focused on popular creative activity itself, such as a piece on "Books Sailors Read" (*Ben Hur* and *Pilgrim's Progress* were favorites; 27 Nov. 1897, 4), and stories on "Songs Sold in the Streets" (5 Feb. 1898, 9) and

"Street Song Cynicism" (7 Jan. 1899, 9). These stories interpreted, some-what before their time, the ephemera of urban life as items of popular culture.

But more significant was the *Commercial Advertiser*'s ability to portray the creative dilemmas of the city's denizens, displaying in the process a remarkable ability to transform stereotypical journalistic categories. This pattern can be observed even in minor feature stories, such as "Sad Common Sense," a five-paragraph item that appeared at the bottom of the feature page one wintry Saturday:

She was a plain, practical sort of woman, who didn't take the little girl on her lap, but let her sway and stagger against other passengers as the car whizzed around curves. The little girl was rosy-cheeked; a blue woolen hood was drawn down over her ears and little fuzzy yellow ringlets curled around her face. Her coat was ob-viously an out-grown-elder-sister affair, and her hands were bare. At Fiftieth Street the woman spoke:

"Think it over, Bessie," she said. "You know how much you have. Take your choice! But let me know before we get out. I have no time to bother with you in the store. You can do as you like, and have the fur-lined gloves or the doll."

Bessie didn't look pleased at the prospect. She was standing near the door, where the wind blew in. At Twenty-seventh Street the woman spoke again.

"Have you decided?"

"Yes'm. The doll," faltered Bessie. Silence again until they neared Madison Square. The woman prepared to leave the car and handed several packages to the little girl. Flakes of snow blew in with the wind, and Bessie shivered as she went on the platform. They alighted and crossed the street. At the corner the little girl stammered: "I think I want the —the gloves, instead, please." And two tears for no reason whatsoever rolled down her cold cheeks. (12 Feb. 1898, 9)

The unknown reporter who observed and described this incident is, to be sure, in close contact with the personnel and machinery of melodrama. From Bessie's little blue hood and gold locks to the unloving mother who elicits the two tears that end the story, the outlines of a fairy tale hover in the background. But the writer makes no simple appeal to sentiment. The mother, for instance, is not a fairy-tale figure, mobilized essentially to arouse fear and pity. If she presses Bessie prematurely to choose between play and necessity, the portrayal of this "plain, practical woman" yet permits us to imagine that she has suffered something similar herself. As for Bessie, cer-tainly her "fuzzy yellow ringlets" and "faltering," "stammering" speech are aimed straight at our hearts. But she does not weep out of any simple, pathetic deprivation. She may, after all, "do as [she likes] and have the fur-lined gloves or the doll." By balancing the ironic observation that Bessie cries for "no reason whatsoever" against her tears, the climax of the story invites us not to weep, but to ask, "Why *is* Bessie crying?" Her tears mark the strain of accommodating mature choice in her young heart, the pain of passage from childlike desire to adult resignation. At the end of this Words-worthian rite of passage, Bessie knows all too well "how much [she has]."

This story contrasts vividly with the random actual incidents reported elsewhere in the New York press. Pulitzer's *World*, for instance, conspic-uously featured "Short Stories of City Life," and they are worthy pieces of local color journalism. But, as noted earlier, they turn upon oddity, novelty, or sentiment. For instance, one such *World* item, "Contrasts in a City Block," observes that "a strange human tide ebbs and flows... at the foot of East Twenty-sixth Street," where Bellevue Hospital and the city morgue stood hard by the New York Yacht Club. The sketch depends upon a stark, unelaborated contrast between rich and poor, secure and miserable, each stereotypically portrayed: "Weeping women on their way to the Morgue to claim their dead or in search of the missing are passed by charming belles and stately dames bound for a day's outing on the water" (15 Oct. 1899, 5).[4] Another of these "short stories," "A Bulldog His Missile," points an even more significant contrast with "Sad Common Sense." It describes a man ascending from a subterranean bar, who, as his arms reached street level, deftly snatched a bulldog that happened to pass by and hurled it back over his head, down upon the companions behind him. The conclusion of this Man-Hurls-Dog story, a classic *fait divers*, contrasts notably with the reflectiveness of the conclusion of "Sad Common Sense": "Why did he seize the dog? He says he doesn't know himself." And neither do we. The piece perfectly fits James Carey's observations about the potential resonance of the news as Man Bites Dog: "Unfortunately, no one knows what possessed the man who bit the dog; even psychiatrists are not likely to be much help. ... News of novel events must strain causality and credibility" (1986, 168). But in the same process, the journalistic story also loses the suggestiveness that surely characterizes any use of symbolism we would call "literary." Sensationalism shocks—and thereby silences—the mind. Literature elicits contemplation. And Bessie's story is literature in precisely this respect. Her tale illustrates how Steffens could, without absurdity or pretentiousness, link the idea of the tragic with journalistic writing. Slight as it may be, Bessie's story follows the tragic pattern in carrying her to what Frye calls "an epiphany of law, of that which is and must be" (1957, 208). Rather than evoking simple astonishment, her story calls forth the reflection and empathy Steffens believed could organize the composition of, and response to, journalistic writing.

The *Advertiser*'s imaginative sympathies for the denizens and scenes of the city also distinguished its writing from the more conservative papers, including the *Commercial Advertiser* before Steffens took over. For instance, in writing stories about the new immigrants, other reporters typically adopted the point of view of the Barge Office officials. A story about im-migrant arrivals in the pre-Steffens *Commercial Advertiser*, titled "Uncle Sam's Guards," enlivened its account with images of the commissioner of immigration and his deputies as "watchdogs," who "seem gifted with second sight" and "keep the unworthy from entering" (20 June 1896, 18). In the conservative *Evening Post*, the story "Held at the Barge-Office/Immigrants Before Boards of Inquiry" also adopted the watchful, suspicious perspective of the hearing officer, called "the Major" (14 Oct. 1899, 21). This tale paused over the impressive fact that the Major speaks twelve languages and his stenographer six. But Steffens, when he was with the *Evening Post*, and Cahan at the *Advertiser* centered their stories in the immigrants themselves. Steffens described the contradiction between an immigrant's statistical anonymity and his possibly contentious character in "Excise Candidate No. 15./A Man Who Does Not Think Much of His Examiners" (6 Apr. 1895, 5). In a similar vein, Cahan, sketching a group of immigrants, could suggest both the anonymity of the mass and its seething, vital variety:

A fresh shipload of immigrants had arrived at the Barge Office. There were Italians, Slovaks, Magyars, some Syrians and some Armenians in the consignment. As the detention pen was filling up, green, yellow and black asserted themselves as an extemporaneous tri-color in a mass of fluctuating hues and shapes. There was the usual rush and hubbub in the room. Everybody was on pins and needles to get out "into America." Everybody asked questions, pleaded, cried, cursed, or kissed the clerks' hands. (6 Sept. 1899)[5]

Here journalistic and literary ideals collide intriguingly: the literary pursuit of color and "rounded characters" brings into journalism a fuller account of the humanity of a people typically invisible in the official news narrative. The literary approach has ethical force. Steffens held, moreover, that "soft news" could yield solid journalism. Hapgood told of how he interviewed the new director of the city aquarium, Tammany-appointed and of course totally ignorant of piscine affairs: "When I asked Colonel Jones how he found out whether the water was right for the fish he said that when the fish died he knew it wasn't good for them." Steffens, Hutchins Hapgood recalled, put the story on the front page, and he could reasonably do so because the "colorful" quotation equally encompassed "a great political moment" (H. Hapgood 1939, 138–39).[6]

Technically, a more relaxed attitude toward quotation and attribution supported Steffens's literary approach. Stories might well be directly observed, as in "Sad Common Sense." But the newswriting conventions of the day also permitted long quotations from a single source, who, particularly in a human-interest story, was not necessarily specifically identified. As a consequence, the journalist, rather than "developing" a story from various bits of information and "quotes," often reported the source's telling of a story or of an observed incident. In a sense, the reporter reported stories already fully formed by their tellers. For instance, in "Pleas of an Old Tenant" (23 Sept. 1899, 9), an electrotyper (possibly for the *Advertiser*) who is looking for a place to live tells of his encounter with an old man who answers the door of a house to let. The old man tells the electrotyper that he will be evicted if anyone takes the rooms. He explains that he was born in the house and once occupied all of it, but he has lost ownership and now occupies but one top-floor room. Previously, the new owners somehow never got around to renting the house, but the latest one employs a rental agent who says that as soon as the top floor is rented, the man must leave. The *Advertiser* story contains long quotations from the old tenant, apparently reconstructed by the writer from the electrotyper's account. Of course, reporters in these cases were hardly giving up their literary control. They still accepted the story *as* a story, shaped structure, pace, and emphasis, decided when to set a scene, when to paraphrase, and when to use the source's narrative. A scrupulous editor of the present day might reject such stories as "hearsay," though these techniques are no more inherently unsound than is the frequently bemoaned, but still widespread, use of anonymous sources today. The long quotation and lack of attribution also had literary advantages, for the source/narrator could add valuable comment, and the lack of attribution projected characters and stories with a generality that enabled them more easily to represent a theme rather than a fragmented event.

In the end, perhaps, the paper was relatively unconcerned with facticity because its real subject was New York City itself. In his autobiography, Steffens said as much: "My inspiration was a love of New York, just as it was, and my ambition was to have it reported so that New Yorkers might see, not merely read of it, as it was; rich and poor, wicked and good, ugly but beautiful, growing, great" (1931, 311–12). The *Commercial Advertiser*'s openness to the life of the city led its literary *journalism* to function as vital and exact literary *sociology*. Many of the *Advertiser*'s human-interest stories may be read as parables of the humane consequences of urbanization, immigration, and commercialization. It is noteworthy, for instance, that Bessie's maturity is to be defined in a choice between commodities on sale in one of the great department stores. It seems significant too that her crisis takes shape in a remark of her mother's that springs equally from the woman's character and from the jostle and hurry of urban life: "Take your choice! But let me know before we get out. I have no time to bother with you in the store."

Similarly, it is the city's sprawling, disjointed growth that set in motion the stories of the forlorn tenant discussed above. In another story, a poor but well-bred lady wrests considerate service from a rude department store clerk through unremitting, genuine politeness—a little drama of gentility confronting commercialism (11 Feb. 1899, 9). Yet another story describes a sporting mare crossing the Grand Circle who was so spooked by motor traffic that she just sat down, quivering in the traces. The motorists and trolleymen stopped their vehicles and waited patiently, neither laughing nor mocking, as the steed regained her composure and her owner led her off (31 Dec. 1899, 9). Reported because it was interesting in itself, the anecdote today tellingly indexes the transition into the motor age.

For all its merits, Steffens's literary journalism was not without its limitations. A genteel propriety often seemed to hem in the writing of the *Commercial Advertiser*. This is perhaps not surprising considering the paper's wealthy, conservative readership. Michael D. Marcaccio says that Hutchins Hapgood's portraits of bums and con-men ignored the brutality of their lives (1977, 72). And in this connection, it is worth noting that it is hard to imagine, say, Stephen Crane's dark, naturalistic New York City sketches appearing in the pages of the *Commercial Advertiser*. Less just is Hapgood's judgment that Steffens was "An Interesting Failure" who simply tired of his literary experiment (1970, 107–12). The characterization seems more to reflect Hapgood's own profound disillusionment with journalism, evident in his grim, brilliant analysis of the toll upon the creative spirit exacted by a life devoted to pursuing news novelties (95–106). It was, arguably, precisely in his work with Steffens at the *Commercial Advertiser* that Hapgood came to understand the distinction he so preceptively draws between journalism that believes that "the interesting exists only in the unusual" and journalism that focuses instead on "the inexpressible significance of the usual" (97). No better description of Steffens's own achievement can be found.

Certainly, too, the general intellectual and aesthetic climate of the Progressive Era supported Steffens's journalistic orientation. The active debate between realism and romance in itself suggested the possibility of making art from the mundane materials of journalism. Steffens described his inspiration as literary, but his aesthetic *responsiveness* implied powerful journalistic *responsibility*. As he posited the resonance of literature in the city's daily life, Steffens told journalism's "human story" so as to return to public life a richly complex, yet realistic, image of its own possibilities and dimensions.

NOTES

A grant from the Capital College Research Fund of Penn State–Harrisburg supported the research for this essay.

1. The maxim is John Bogart's, city editor of the New York *Sun* under Charles A. Dana. When a cub reporter demanded a definition of news, Bogart replied, "When a dog bites a man, that is not news; but if a man bites a dog, that's news." See, for instance, Frank Luther Mott, *American Journalism, A History: 1690–1960* (New York: Macmillan, 1962), 376.

2. This quality has often been noted in journalistic interpretation of experience. See, for instance, Michael Schudson, "Why News Is the Way It Is," *Raritan* (Winter 1983), 119, 122–23. Ironically, journalism's notorious penchant for instantly dub-

bing any and every disaster a "tragedy" is precisely a sign of its impulse toward melodrama.

3. Chief among the *Commercial Advertiser* writers was Abraham Cahan, whose advocacy of socialism and Russian realism inspired Steffens's journalistic ideas. Cahan specialized in coverage of the Jewish ghetto for the *Commercial Advertiser*; he produced the ghetto novel *Yekl* before joining the paper, and later became editor of the *Jewish Daily Forward*. Cahan's writing for the *Advertiser* is collected in *Grandma Never Lived in America*, ed. Moses Rischin. See also Rischin's "Abraham Cahan and the New York *Commercial Advertiser*," *Publications of the American Jewish Historical Society* 43 (Sept. 1953): 10–36.

Other writers included Hutchins Hapgood, who at the *Commercial Advertiser* specialized in Bowery and ghetto characters, and later wrote *Types from City Streets*, which reflected upon the journalism of the 1890s and the *Commercial Advertiser* under Steffens (Rischin 1967 includes some of his writing for the *Commercial Advertiser*); Carl Hovey, whose *Commercial Advertiser* stories Steffens commended for revealing political realities through effective human-interest description, and who became editor of *Metropolitan* magazine; and Norman Hapgood, the paper's drama critic and Hutchins's brother, who carried on a democratic theory of journalism at *Collier's Weekly* (see Marcaccio 1977, 51 and passim, on both brothers). See also Steffens's description of the paper's writers in his *Autobiography* (1931), 315–16.

4. Other urban short stories on this day possessed about as much literary suggestiveness as the contemporary "people" item. They included "Admiral Dewey's Favorite Flower" and "Mrs. Frank Leslie's Pet Is Dying," which reported the moribund state of "the most petted and pampered dog in New York." Longer *World* features depended heavily on sex and sentiment, e.g., "Lured Her Lover to Die with Her"; "Murder of a Farmer and His Adopted Son"; "How Police Cared for the Multitude"; "Ends Her Life for Lack of Love" (1 Oct. 1899, 3).

5. Reprinted in *Grandma Never Lived in America*, 123. Rischin remarks aptly that Abraham Cahan's portraits of Jews in the *Commercial Advertiser* brilliantly evaded stereotype: "Here were objects neither of commiseration nor outrage, neither financial titans nor merchant princes, neither a mystical people nor a tenement proletariat, neither comics nor grotesques" (1967, xxi).

6. For another anecdote of "feature" coverage effectively conveying the "news," see Steffens's *Autobiography*, 322.

PRIMARY SOURCES

Steffens, Joseph Lincoln. 1931. *The Autobiography of Lincoln Steffens*. New York: Harcourt, Brace.

———. 1938. *The Letters of Lincoln Steffens*. Ed. Ella Winter and Granville Hicks. New York: Harcourt, Brace.

———. 1962. *The World of Lincoln Steffens*. Ed. Ella Winter and Herbert Shapiro. New York: Hill and Wang.

SECONDARY SOURCES

Cahan, Abraham. 1985. *Grandma Never Lived in America*. Ed. Moses Rischin. Bloomington: Indiana University Press.

Carey, James W. 1986. "The Dark Continent of American Journalism." In *Reading the News*. Ed. Robert Karl Manoff and Michael Schudson. New York: Pantheon Books.

Connery, Thomas B. 1986, Spring. "Hutchins Hapgood and the Search for a 'New Form of Literature.' " *Journalism History*: 2–9.

Dunn, Robert. 1956. *World Alive: A Personal Story*. New York: Crown.

Fine, David M. 1973. "Abraham Cahan, Stephen Crane, and the Romantic Tenement Tale of the Nineties." *American Studies* 14: 95–107.

Frye, Northrop. 1957. *Anatomy of Criticism*. Princeton, N.J.: Princeton University Press.

Hapgood, Hutchins. 1902. *The Spirit of the Ghetto: Studies of the Jewish Quarter in New York*. Rpt. 1967. Cambridge, Mass.: Belknap Press of Harvard University Press.

———. 1939. *A Victorian in the Modern World*. New York: Harcourt, Brace.

———. 1970. "An Interesting Failure." In *Types from City Streets*. New York: Garrett Press.

Hapgood, Norman. 1930. *The Changing Years: Reminiscences of Norman Hapgood*. New York: Farrar and Rinehart.

Higham, John. 1965. "The Reorientation of American Culture in the 1890s." In *The Origins of Modern Consciousness*. Detroit: Wayne State University Press.

Horton, Russell M. 1974. *Lincoln Steffens*. New York: Twayne.

Kaplan, Justin. 1974. *Lincoln Steffens: A Biography*. New York: Simon and Schuster.

Marcaccio, Michael D. 1977. *The Hapgoods: Three Earnest Brothers*. Charlottesville: University Press of Virginia.

Mitchell, Edward P. 1924. *Memoirs of an Editor*. New York: Scribner's.

Palermo, Patrick F. 1978. *Lincoln Steffens*. Boston: Twayne.

Rischin, Moses. 1902. Introduction to *The Spirit of the Ghetto: Studies of the Jewish Quarter in New York*, by Hutchins Hapgood. Rpt. 1967. Cambridge, Mass.: Belknap Press of Harvard University Press.

———. 1953, Sept. "Abraham Cahan and the New York *Commercial Advertiser*." *Publications of the American Jewish Historical Society* 43: 10–36.

———. 1985. Introduction to *Grandma Never Lived in America*, by Abraham Cahan. Bloomington: Indiana University Press.

Schudson, Michael. 1988. "What Is a Reporter? The Private Face of Public Journalism." In *Media, Myths, and Narratives: Television and the Press*. Newbury Park, Calif.: Sage Press.

Stinson, Robert, 1979. *Lincoln Steffens*. New York: F. Ungar.

George Ade

John J. Pauly

The writings of George Ade have received much critical scrutiny, yet very little of that criticism takes seriously Ade's achievements as a journalist. For most critics journalism was a youthful way station at which young Ade paused to quench his thirst for experience, a whistle stop on the road to becoming the celebrated author of *Fables in Slang* and a successful Broadway playwright. Without diminishing at all the achievement of Ade's later work, today's reader might, in fact, prefer to remember Ade for his journalism. For six years Ade explored nearly every literary possibility that a newspaper column could offer. If critics have forgotten that impressive body of work, it may be that they have taken their cue from Ade himself. Though he died in 1944 at age seventy-eight, Ade abandoned daily journalism at age thirty-four. His new career as an acclaimed literary celebrity removed him, physically and psychologically, from Chicago and, over time, erased the memory of his early journalism.

Ade owed his success to a fortuitous combination of talent, ambition, and historical happenstance. Born in Kentland, Indiana, he acquired his love for literature and theater while attending Purdue University. After graduation he spent a year in Lafayette, Indiana, writing news and advertising copy. He came to Chicago in 1890 at the urging of a former Purdue classmate, the illustrator John McCutcheon, who told him of an opening at the *Morning News*. Ade started as a writer of daily weather stories. Within two years he had become a star reporter, covering major events such as the Democratic and Republican conventions of 1892, the Homestead Steel strike, and the Sullivan-Corbett fight. In those years Chicago earned its modern reputation as a great newspaper town, and the *Morning News* was an especially good place for an ambitious young writer. Soon to be renamed the *Record*, it was the morning daily of Victor Lawson and Melville Stone, who also owned the popular afternoon *Daily News*. With writers such as

Ade, Eugene Field, Ray Stannard Baker, Edward Price Bell, and Trumbull White on staff, the *Record* was arguably one of the most literate American newspapers of its generation.

Ade had arrived in Chicago at a particularly robust moment in that city's history. Chicago had spent the past fifty years making itself the center of America's agricultural and industrial economy and transportation network. It now imagined itself challenging the financial and cultural preeminence of New York. Those predictions of greatness were seemingly confirmed when, in 1891, Congress chose Chicago for the site of a world's fair celebrating the 400th anniversary of Columbus's voyage to the New World. That World's Columbian Exposition provided both Ade and McCutcheon with their greatest opportunity. From May till October 1893 the two contributed a daily column called "All Roads Lead to the Fair"—Ade writing vignettes of the fair and its people, McCutcheon rendering its scenes in pen and ink. The popularity of this series led Charles Dennis, the *Record*'s managing editor, to encourage Ade to write similar stories about Chicago itself. On November 17, 1893, the first of the "Stories of the Streets and of the Town" appeared, with illustrations by McCutcheon.

The sheer number of "Stories" that Ade wrote would astonish a modern reporter. Unlike today's columnists, who often hire earnest young assistants to do the research, Ade did his own footwork. During January 1894, the first full month of their publication, Ade wrote twelve "Stories." He wrote 15 in February, then 27 in March, 26 in April, and so on through the year— almost 300 stories in just the first full year. Day after day he turned out stories of 1,000 and 1,500 words each, skipping Sundays only because the *Record* did not publish a Sunday edition. Month after month, for the next six years, Ade maintained that pace, producing over 1,800 in all. Twice during those years Ade took time off to visit Europe. Even then, however, he sent home regular reports about his adventures. The popularity of Ade's column encouraged the *Record* to publish eight paperback collections of the "Stories" as part of a quarterly series that included the *Daily News* almanac. But even those collections, which included from forty to eighty stories each, reprinted less than a third of the work that had originally appeared in the *Record*. Subsequent anthologies have winnowed an even smaller number of stories from those original collections.

The George Ade of the "Stories" does not entirely resemble the genial cracker barrel humorist who won renown before World War I, received polite esteem in the 1920s, and went virtually unread by the 1930s. Many critics have written off Ade's time in Chicago to youthful exuberance and have stressed the enduring small-town values of his rural upbringing, a life to which he later returned. Ade's stories do occasionally betray the fastidious tone that became more insistent and priggish in later life. But for the most part Ade's journalism echoes the sounds of the city, revealing a young man utterly fascinated with the sheer vitality and absurdity of city life. He often stood back and listened to the hubbub without passing judgment on it.

Ade frequently explored the paths of city life by trailing workers through their jobs. In particular he was drawn to occupations in which workers had to deal with "the public." He wrote stories about railroad advertising agents, hat restorers, train conductors and porters, postmasters, coachmen, private detectives, assessors, policemen, and coroners, among others. Such stories often describe the day-to-day life of an occupation, linking together anecdotes the workers told Ade. But Ade often drew a larger meaning from those simple tales. He often used workers' stories to comment upon public manners. Ade responded to the strange and unpredictable behavior of the public by letting workers themselves tell how "You meet all kinds in this line of work."

Ade also paid close attention to the settings in which his characters worked. He tirelessly catalogued all the nooks and crannies of the city. The dime museum, police court, tugboats, farmers market, and trolley car were all on his beat. Ade was there at the grand opera observing the behavior of the crowd, as well as at the vaudeville theater. For one story he described the city's small shops, many of which were only four to eight feet wide, tucked between large, new buildings. He explored the Chinese laundries and the stands of sidewalk merchants as well as the grand institutions, such as the Art Institute. In a city as sprawling and lively as Chicago, a story waited around every corner.

A recurring but relatively unnoticed theme in Ade's journalism is the uncertainty of city people's knowledge of one another. Writing in an age when large numbers of people were being recruited as audiences for newspapers, magazines, theater, and novels, Ade regularly commented on the differences between popular culture representations of urban life and occupations and the actual experiences of workers themselves. For instance, in "About Arrests and Those Arrested," he asks policemen to contrast stage versions of an arrest with actual arrests that they had made (9 Mar. 1894). In "The Story-Book Detective and the Detective," Ade compares the dull routine of private detectives to the romantic adventure of dime novel accounts of the Pinkertons (5 Mar. 1894). In "Sidewalk Merchants and Their Wares," he notes that the flower girl "is a thing of beauty on the stage, where she wears bangs and a pink dress and does a neat song and dance." By contrast, the flower girl of Clark Street "is a frowsy young creature . . . saucy, forward, and with a frightful knowledge of the things which children should not know" (13 Sept. 1894).

Time and again, across a variety of genres, Ade noted the ambiguity of urban identity. Sometimes he dramatized the uncertainty of social relations in order to convey a sense of the city's anonymity and loneliness; at other times he strove for comic effect. Ade often paid meticulous attention to styles of dress. His story "Some of the Unfailing Signs" offers tongue-in-cheek advice about how to identify different social classes and occupations—the alderman, the telegraph operator, the young businessman from the board of trade, the undercover policeman, the lawyer (5 Oct. 1894).

When a story features a surprise ending, in the style of O. Henry, the surprise often hangs upon the reader's mistaken impression of a character. In "The Mystery of the Back Roomer," for example, a mysterious young man leaves his boarding house late each night and returns every morning. Eventually his perplexed fellow boarders confront him and learn his secret: he is a chiropodist in a Turkish bath (28 Feb. 1894). One of Ade's most famous stories, "Mr. Benson's Experience with a Maniac," tells of a medical student who, when given the opportunity to visit a hospital for the insane, finds himself confronted, pursued, and cornered by a huge inmate. Finally the inmate reaches out, touches the terrified Benson, and says, "You're it! Now see if you can catch me" (28 Nov. 1894).

Ade enjoyed but never ridiculed these confusions of identity. In one of his funniest stories, "Trying to Identify Two Men," Ade shows photographs of two men to Chicago police detectives and asks if they have ever seen either one. Several detectives do not recognize the men at all. But others comment on how dangerous the two look, and still others remember having arrested the men or seeing them at the station house or in court. Some of the detectives wonder whether the two photos are of the same man, one picture older than the other, or one taken with and one without a disguise. At the end Ade reveals the identities of the men. The first is William Dean Howells, the eminent novelist and literary critic, the second, Archibald Forbes, a famous war correspondent. Ade notes only that "Mr. Howells was in Chicago several weeks during the Exposition, but as far as can be learned his conduct was exemplary" (24 Feb. 1894).

Ade found other examples of ambiguous social identity in the plentiful con games of 1890s Chicago. One item in a potpourri titled "Some Incidents Peculiar to a Big Town" tells of an apparently poor man who enters a prosperous business, claiming to have found an elaborately decorated horseshoe on the sidewalk out in front. The poor man says that he assumed that the businessman owned the horseshoe and would hate to lose it. The businessman, impressed by the man's earnestness and honesty, buys the horseshoe, only later to discover that the "poor" man uses this scam to sell off the inventory from a friend's now-defunct blacksmith shop (1 Mar. 1894). A story published about a week later, " 'The Gold Eye-Glasses' and Other Stories," discusses a similar scam, in which "gold-frame" eyeglasses are sold to a well-dressed pedestrian, who later discovers that the glasses are made of brass (10 Mar. 1894).

Among the con games Ade most carefully documented were those of politics. Ade described in meticulous detail the inequities of the tax assessment system, the cynical conversion of a crooked alderman facing reelection, and the techniques commonly used to rig ballot boxes and recruit ghost voters. Ade never relished the telling of such tales as a Damon Runyon, Jimmy Breslin, or Mike Royko later would, but neither did he rail against such practices with the evangelical fervor of a muckraker like William Stead. For the most part Ade related these stories of corruption with an air of bemused detachment and gentle cynicism.

Ade reserved his greatest respect for citizens who reject pretense in order to live responsible, ordinary lives. He believed in the value of being middling—not necessarily middle-class, for many of his characters are hard-working, simple, respectable working-class clerks and laborers. The decent, ordinary citizen, for Ade, was someone who neither steals from others nor lords it over them. He was as skeptical of the artifice of upper-class society as of the political demagoguery and connivery of the lower classes. One of Ade's most praised stories, "Effie Whittlesley," takes up precisely this theme. Edward Wallace's wife hires Effie as the new family servant, only to find that her husband and Effie grew up in the same small town. Without self-consciousness Effie and Ed address each other by first name. As in many of Ade's stories, the wife is the one who puts on airs, who strives to maintain the "proper" class distinctions of servant and employer (13 Mar. 1896).

This praise for simple folk often appears in Ade's stories as a commentary on the manners of young people. Though himself a young man, Ade often preferred the style and manners of older people, who remembered the days before "society" overtook Chicago. Critics have often interpreted this preference as evidence of Ade's unshakable small-town values. But his "Stories" do not trade freely in nostalgia, as so much of his later work does. Ade praises city dwellers' worthy and humane impulses wherever he finds them. If young people appear to disadvantage, it is because they are so often taken in, Ade thinks, by fashion, fads, and pretension.

In one of the anecdotes in " 'The Gold Eye-Glasses' and Other Stories," for instance, some young passengers on a suburban train mock a woman who is knitting on her ride home. "If she would only eat caramels, or read a yellow book, or play whist, it would be a proper form, but knitting was old-fashioned." Ade clearly sides with the older people on the train, who nod approvingly at the woman's quiet industry (10 Mar. 1894). In "Her Visit to Chicago," a woman from a small town in Ohio visits her son and daughter-in-law. At first the young wife tries to use her social connections to impress the mother-in-law. But soon the older woman objects that "I didn't come to Chicago to get my name into the newspapers." The two spend the rest of the visit enjoying simpler pleasures—visiting the panoramas, Auditorium tower, and stockyards and going to theaters, where the mother can "sit down with the rest of the people and laugh" (13 Mar. 1894).

From the very first story Ade remained a democratic moralist and gentle critic of urban manners. But he did not, by implication, merely glorify the

small town. He wished only that the city could retain the easygoing camaraderie of country life. In his story "The Advantage of Being 'Middle-
Class,'" Ade explicitly argues for the superiority of simple, democratic
manners. The middle class, Ade writes, refers to "all those persons who are
respectably in the background, who work either with hand or brain, who
are neither poverty-stricken nor offensively rich, and who are not held down
by the arbitrary laws governing that mysterious part of the community
known as society." To illustrate the advantages of being middle-class, he
describes a dreamy, warm evening in June. Middle-class families relax on
their front stoops, in casual dress, eating and smoking. Young working-
class couples walk arm in arm in the moonlight or go out onto a double-
decked steamer on the Chicago River to dance. Meanwhile upper-class
families stay boarded up in their houses, out of a sense of propriety, one
family even refusing to come out to listen to an organ grinder who is playing
on the sidewalk in front of their house. Ade imagines that ordinary Chi-
cagoans "must feel sorry for the millionaire, who cannot go to a public
park in the evening to stroll or sit for the reason that so many other persons
go there" (14 June 1894).

Throughout the 1890s, Ade experimented freely with a variety of literary
forms. Often his columns string together six or more short anecdotes, sometimes, but not always, connected by a common theme. Many of his stories
employ the indirect leads and extended quotations commonly found in the
modern feature story. Others resort to fables and parables, question-and-
answer interviews, mock dramas, and short stories. From day to day Ade
experimented with all those genres. For example, though critics have often
treated the fables in slang as an invention dating to 1897, one can find
intimations of that style in much earlier work. One of Ade's very first stories,
"A Young Man in Upper Life," offers a sad parable about a young writer
of promotional brochures who watches himself rise, then fall behind, in the
race for success (20 Nov. 1893). In "The Advertising Agent and Others,"
Ade ends his final anecdote with an explicit moral, much in the style of the
later fables (17 Feb. 1894).

The single technique Ade came to rely on most heavily, however, was
dialogue. His "Stories" are filled with wonderful skeins of speech and snip-
pets of conversation. (In this sense the later fables were unrepresentative,
for many of them were written entirely in Ade's own voice, with little or
no dialogue.) Like today's feature writers, Ade sometimes allowed subjects
to tell their own stories at length, though one always senses that he has
reworked the conversation in order to heighten its drama, as any storyteller
would. Dialogue helps Ade establish the social class and personal style of
his characters, but his purpose is to do much more than represent the
idiosyncrasies of word choice and diction. Time and again Ade is drawn to
the occasions and places where strangers and acquaintances talk to each
other. The boarding house, for instance, frequently appears in the "Stories"

as a stage for comical encounters. Even stories without dialogue are often told as something Ade overheard, or something someone told him, or something that "they say." By comparison, contemporary journalism works with a corrupt and truncated understanding of conversation, cutting the talk of citizens into sound bites or papering it over with the holy writ of official sources. For Ade, conversation was the life of the city, and journalism his mode of understanding that life.

Ade never introduces himself as a character in his "Stories," but he frequently appears in a variety of guises. In his question-and-answer stories Ade is the unidentified questioner. In other third-person narratives, the reader senses that the "young man" or "stranger" spoken of is probably Ade himself. The story "A Run to a Fire," for instance, describes the experience of two young men walking home from the theater who stop to watch firemen douse a blaze. It seems likely that the two men were Ade and McCutcheon, fast friends and theater-lovers. "The Former Kathryn" is an extended monologue by a gossipy department store clerk, elicited by a customer's question about what happened to the girl who used to work at the counter (9 June 1898). In this, as in so many other stories, Ade is probably working with an incident he experienced or witnessed.

Ade typically did not luxuriate in extended description. But the following passage from "The Advantage of Being 'Middle-Class' " shows that he was capable of such work:

Dearborn Avenue leads to the lights and shadows and cool depths of Lincoln Park. First there is a broad, smooth roadway, which shows boldly in the electric glare, and then there is a deeply shaded drive between solid walls of trees. It widens and brings into dim outline a dark statue with a massive pedestal. Each wheelman coursing the drive is marked by a speck of lantern, and the illusion is that of racing fireflies. No carriages disturb the night with a clatter of hoofs. Under the trees, right and left, the shade is so deep that sometimes voices may be heard where no one can be seen. Only a few feet away a flood of light shows every blade of grass and every pebble. All roads into the park lead to some circling pathway which is laced with the black shadows of trembling leaves, while misshapen blotches of the blending light fall on the figures and the benches. (14 June 1894)

More typically, Ade kept his descriptions brief and simple, presuming that the reader already knows something of the places and people he is discussing. Ade worked like a draftsman rather than a colorist. His short, deft strokes suggest the contours of a setting and set the stage for his characters' encounters.

Ade's preference for character over plot or color enriched his journalism but ultimately condemned him to a lower status as a writer. Ade himself understood what was expected of a serious writer in that age, and in his later "Stories" one occasionally hears him straining to sound more literary and serious. As Ade moved into national syndication and away from Chicago, his work changed. He had always excelled at evoking the small scenes of city life. His was not the intellectual vision of a nineteenth-century novelist, conjuring up the grand dramas of modern society. The pleasure of Ade's text lay in the ephemeral yet familiar quality of his observations. But critics and publishers wanted whole fables and stories, and Ade obliged. In the hierarchy of literary prestige, short stories served as practice for a long, serious novel—a novel that Ade never wrote.

The economic limits of journalism also drove Ade to abandon the "Stories." According to Ade's biographer, Fred Kelly, after nearly ten years as a newspaper reporter Ade was making only $65 a week, which was considered a top salary at the *Record*. When Ade first syndicated his "Fables in Slang," he sold them to two papers for $30 a week each. In a few months he was making $200 a week and in a few years $500 to $1,000 a week (1977, 15–52). But Ade's success changed his art. Critics have often attributed Ade's declining popularity to his audience's changing tastes: after World War I, they say, readers lost interest in Ade's style of nostalgic humor. But that exaggerated style of nostalgia was itself the motif that Ade invented to market himself to a wider audience. As his work moved into national syndication, it necessarily abandoned its local references. Without actual reporting to reinvest it with new life, Ade's nostalgic idiom eventually wore thin.

The literary marketplace offered few other options to someone of Ade's talent and temperament. Daily journalism was exhausting and unrewarding, especially for an aging writer. Ade was making five to ten times as much money writing one or two fables a week as he did writing six "Stories." Nor did Ade possess the reformer's zeal that would inspire him to write muckraking tracts or pursue in-depth sociological investigations. Ade started out to market his work, but found that all he had left to market was his own literary persona. Along the way he and his critics buried a substantial body of literary journalism. But it is still there, a treasure waiting to be unearthed.

PRIMARY SOURCES

Ade, George. 1903. *In Babel: Stories of Chicago.* New York: McClure, Phillips.
———. 1947. *The Permanent Ade.* Ed. Fred C. Kelly. Indianapolis: Bobbs-Merrill.
———. 1961. *The America of George Ade.* Ed. Jean Shepherd. New York: G. P. Putnam's Sons.
———. 1963a. *Artie and Pink Marsh.* Chicago: University of Chicago Press.
———. 1963b. *Chicago Stories.* Ed. Franklin J. Meine. Chicago: Regnery.

SECONDARY SOURCES

Ashforth, Albert. 1987, Autumn. "Hoosier Humorist, Three Letters." *American Scholar* 56: 565–73.

Kelly, Fred C., ed. 1977. *George Ade, Warmhearted Satirist*. Westport, Conn.: Greenwood Press.

Matson, Lowell. 1961, Autumn. "Ade—Who Needed None." *Literary Review* 5: 99–114.

Meine, Franklin J. 1963. Introduction to *Chicago Stories*, by George Ade. Ed. Franklin J. Meine. Chicago: Regnery.

Pekar, Harvey. 1981, Fall. "George Ade: Forgotten Master of American Literature." *Gamut* 4: 59–72.

Hutchins Hapgood

Thomas B. Connery

In a state of "feverish excitement" over New York City, Hutchins Hapgood resigned his teaching position at Harvard in 1897 and joined the staff of the New York *Commercial Advertiser* as a reporter. Five years earlier he had graduated from Harvard at the head of his class, and, not wishing to return to his home in Illinois, he had first traveled and studied in Europe and then obtained a master's degree from Harvard before he started teaching.

Hapgood's brother, Norman, was already working for the *Advertiser*, and Hutchins was convinced that the newspaper under Lincoln Steffens was conducive to his own temperament and talents and that he would fit well with other staffers who believed in "Steffens's idea of literary journalism" (Hapgood 1939, 140). Hapgood did some rather standard reporting for Steffens, but mostly he wrote articles "something like the feuilleton—a short article which is a mixture of news and personal reaction put together in a loose literary form" (Hapgood 1939, 138).

Thus, from the beginning of his journalistic career, Hapgood experimented with a form of literary journalism. His ideas for depicting reality by mixing literary technique with standard reporting methods would later blossom into a theory of literary journalism, making Hapgood somewhat of a pioneer and visionary. Although Hapgood did not employ as many literary devices as other literary journalists, his writing can be treated as literary journalism because of the philosophy and ideas that informed and shaped it.

Hapgood's later efforts at book-length literary journalism were more daring and interesting theoretically, but his work at the *Advertiser* was more accomplished and, perhaps, more significant. It was at the *Advertiser* that Hapgood and other reporters were encouraged to look beyond the typical news account, even being asked to write "an impressionistic description"

of two streets (Hapgood 1939, 138). Hapgood later explained what Steffens's approach meant to him:

For I could see, and was permitted to express, the beauty of the commonplace and
the everyday. The news instinct had not at that time made the slightest impression
on me. I was pure and was not looking for the exceptional. I despised the exceptional
with a simple and profound contempt. It was more important to describe the quality
of Eighth avenue than to secure a Rapid Transit "beat." And an interview with
some commonplace person who was enjoying life was more important than an
interview with a big dignitary who was too busy to enjoy life. (1913, 6)

Many of Hapgood's attempts to depict the common and ordinary, and
therefore much of his literary journalism at this period, consisted of writing
about New York's East Side and particularly the Jewish ghetto. When Hapgood turned his focus elsewhere, it usually was to record a personal vignette
or something that caught his eye in a shop or on a New York City street.
For instance, in "Two Men—Four Years" he relates a reunion of two
twenty-nine-year-olds who had been close companions in Europe four years
earlier. The piece presents the reunion as an actual experience, although the
two men are not identified by name. The first paragraph explains how the
two men got together, and the remainder of the article consists of the
conversation between the two over how they have changed in four years,
and how in that time they have become less willing to seek excitement and
novelty, how they now find a certain amount of enjoyment in monotony
and routine. That is the extent of the article; there is no connection or peg
to current events or traditional news. Instead, by allowing readers to eaves-
drop on a conversation that takes place on a river bank on a summer
afternoon, the article serves up a melancholy acknowledgment of aging and
change.
   Hapgood would later write, "What we call important news is, as a rule,
singularly unimportant to humanity, and that which is most important to
humanity is not news" ("The Real News"). His account of two men talking
wistfully about their lives is Hapgood's attempt to report on an aspect of
life common to all humankind as he perceived it. Like much of literary
journalism, this article deals with typical human behavior and cultural attitudes rather than with the facts of an extraordinary action, and bears a
striking resemblance in approach and content to New Yorker "Talk of the
Town" pieces.
   Perhaps Hapgood's most important reporting, and his most important
literary journalism, is his depiction of the lives of the East Side Jews. To
capture this important, emerging subculture, Hapgood immersed himself in
the community. He learned Yiddish and was guided through the ghetto by
Abraham Cahan, who also worked for the Advertiser and who was a fiction
writer and editor of the Jewish Daily Forward.

Hapgood's articles on the ghetto, collected and published in 1902 and reprinted twice since then, lack imaginative power and vividness, but nevertheless contain subtle themes and conceptualizations missing from most reports on the Jewish ghetto found in the mainstream press. As Irving Howe notes, Hapgood "brushed past the trivialities of journalistic 'local color,' " thereby conveying experience and meaning in an immigrant world of vitality and richness rather than one of stereotypes and superficialities" (1967, 7). Moses Rischin describes Hapgood's articles as "a major cultural breakthrough" because "in an era when immigrant stereotypes were rife, Hapgood's Russian Jews did not fit into established literary categories" (see Hapgood 1967, xxi).

Hapgood takes the reader into the ghetto streets with the peddlers and merchants, into the homes of sweatshop workers and Talmudic scholars, the cafes of artists, intellectuals, and socialists, the synagogues of the rabbis. He relies heavily on extensive quotations and portions of conversations to define tone, character, and theme, but stops short of the extensive scene-setting and storytelling common to literary journalism.

Too often, his Jewish ghetto articles carry the pacing and tone of an ethnographic report. But when Hapgood wrote about an individual, such as a poet, writer, or ticket-taker, he made greater use of descriptive writing that produced stronger visual images. Such articles are more likely to capture a piece of time and to depict the human condition in the manner of literary journalism rather than as a sociological study might.

For instance, "A Lone Russian Genius" begins broadly and generally, as most of his articles do. But this is the story of a bitter, unhappy man, and Hapgood establishes a contrast between the man, an "aloof" inventor, and the warm, convivial cafe where he sits. Here are the first two paragraphs:

In the Russian-Jewish tea and coffee cafes of the east side gather an earnest crowd of men, who discuss with passion all the great, unsolvable questions of humanity. Literary men, poets, actors, business men, most of whom were driven from Russia, delight in expressing at these the ideas for which they were persecuted abroad. Enthusiasm for progress and love of ideas is the characteristic tone of these gatherings and an entire lack of practical sense.

Very striking, therefore, was the attitude of a Russian-Jewish inventor, who took his lunch the other day at one of the most literary of these cafes. Near him were a trio of enthusiasts, gesticulating over their tea, but he sat aloof, alone. He listened with a cold, superior smile. He neither smoked nor drank, but sat with his thin, shrewd face, chillily thinking.

Hapgood tells us that the man is considered a genius who invented a means of extending the life of electric lamps. Instead of reaping the fame and fortune that should have come from his idea, he was cheated by "unscrupulous lawyers."

Then Hapgood becomes a part of the scene as an American who sometimes visits the cafe. The American sits and carries on a conversation with the inventor, who speaks critically of writers and artists of the Russian-Jewish community, smiling "sarcastically" one time and "coldly" another, or sneering and responding "dispassionately." When the American praises a novelist, a journalist, and Russian actors, the inventor tells him that he is "deceived by the surface," and when the American challenges the inventor, calling him a pessimist, the inventor replies that he sees "things just as they are." In the end, enough ambiguity remains to suggest that the inventor's posture may be the correct one.

The article on the inventor was only one full column in length, running down the right side of the newspaper. Hapgood's purpose was to take the reader into the cafe to meet a man in the same manner as if the reader were visiting the cafe. The piece does not have sufficient depth for thematic development. But it does create an impression of a type and successfully captures the state of mind of an immigrant whose enthusiasm for life and whose dreams have been shattered. A picture of the inventor emerges, one character from the larger subculture of the Jewish ghetto.

Hapgood next immersed himself in a broader, ill-defined subculture, that of Bowery low-life. But the Bowery's array of bums, thieves, and street people became philosophers and natural artists in articles written by Hapgood for the *Commercial Advertiser* and the *Morning Telegraph* and collected in *Types from City Streets*.

The control he had maintained in his Jewish ghetto writing disappears in the Bowery pieces as Hapgood sentimentalizes and romanticizes his bums, generally ignoring the cruelty of their poverty, because for Hapgood their very poverty made them noble and more "real," urban examples of Rousseau's natural man. Chapter and article titles reveal Hapgood's bent: "The Bowery's Sentiment," "The Town's Philosophers," "His Sensitive Soul," "Anything for a Good Fellow," and "Virtue on 'De Lane.' "

In many of the *Types* articles, Hapgood merely allows the subjects to speak, providing direction for their thoughts and attempting to give his speakers a greater depth and seriousness than is evident. In "Jacky Doodles in His Cups," however, he takes readers into a Bowery bar to hear an exchange between Jacky Doodles and Chuck Connors, known as the "mayor of Chinatown." The exchange is over a down-and-out woman called Tough Louise, but Hapgood's story is designed to show readers kindness and compassion in the Bowery.

After setting the scene in the bar and outlining the characters, Hapgood has Connor chastise Jacky in typical Bowery language. But suddenly, Connors, whose "heart is tender," stopped "his flow of invective" because he saw that Jacky was weeping. Everyone in this tough, dirty dive stops to look at Jacky. They are all puzzled, but not Connors, who, Hapgood writes, "understood as he always does." Connors then goes to Jacky, slaps him on the back, and says: "Cheer up, Jacky, if you feel that way, my boy, you're all right. Wait and see de play out. Take her home, my boy, and do better de next time."

Instead of ending the story there, Hapgood awkwardly intrudes on the narrative with a clumsy personal reflection: "As I went home that night I reflected deeply on the relation between 'booze' and virtue." The reader must contend not only with Hapgood's silly attempt to idealize alcohol, but also with Hapgood's sudden presence in the story. Such intrusions are common in the *Types* articles.

In the Jewish ghetto articles, Hapgood's own literary deficiencies, such as his inability to present more creatively what he observed and learned in the ghetto, stop his work from being particularly strong literary journalism. In the *Types* articles, however, his vision, his interpretations of what he sees and learns, weakens the articles as much as his lack of literary ability. He was so determined to impose his own romantic sensibility on his low-life characters that he neglected their true humanity and their genuine predicament. This is particularly evident in the book's final chapter, "The Town's Philosophers."

The "philosophers" are boxers whom Hapgood categorizes according to a specific outlook on life: "Jim Jeffries, Cynic," "John L. Sullivan, Fatalist," "Kid McCoy, Optimist," and "Tom Sharkey, Mere Man." The piece on Sullivan begins pretentiously:

John L. Sullivan was in a philosophical mood. He was between theatrical engagements, and was using his leisure time in thought, deep thought about the universe. He sat in a comfortable chair and looked pensively out of the window of his room at the Hotel York into the cold day. He nursed his mild attack of the gout by resting his foot nonchalantly upon a friendly stool.

"Glad to see you," he said. "I just feel like talking today. I have been thinking, and whenever I think I like to talk." (1970, 337)

Sullivan then tells Hapgood just what he wants to hear: "I'm a philosopher, and I like to think a lot. I believe in fatalism." It's almost as if Sullivan is responding to a prod from Hapgood, who might have asked, "Do you think of yourself as a philosopher? Are you a fatalist, Mr. Sullivan?" Neither irony nor satire seemed to have been a part of Hapgood's literary or intellectual makeup.

Each of the articles on the fighters suffers from the same forced attempt to make the men fit Hapgood's preconceived interpretation. The article on McCoy begins, " 'Kid McCoy' sat quietly and pensively in his gymnasium on Forty-second Street and told about his philosophy of life" (342). Sharkey, the "Mere Man," was a bit more difficult when "he was visited by one who desired to discover what Tom's philosophy of life might be," because "he does not use his brain too much," and "his ideas are in the nature of protoplasmic tendencies" (346).

Hapgood, however, was able to elicit some marvelous quotations from these boxers. For example, Sullivan is comical, yet perfectly Boston and Irish, when he says in deepest seriousness, "I suppose I'm a philosopher because I came from Boston—the Hub of the universe, you know; I learned to play baseball there, and to think" (340). Or when he says: "I don't think there's any harm in a few drinks. After a man's work is over for the day, it's a good thing to take a few drinks, say ten or twelve. It helps a man's fatalism a lot, I find, and I have seen a whole lot of the world" (340–41).

These fighter articles contain a thread of character that could lead to fuller, more satisfying portraits, but the form of the articles allows only for a jumbled sense of these men that borders on caricature. In the preface to *Types*, Hapgood says that the sketches are intended to "throw light upon the charm of what from one point of view is the 'ordinary' person—careless, human, open, democratic" (10). But the light is too dim. He does nothing to unify the quotes that come tumbling out of these fighters. His light is false and prevents us from seeing the essence of the fighters and their true humanity.

Although Hapgood used largely the same approach in the Jewish ghetto articles as in the boxer pieces, in the ghetto writing he provided a context; he established a larger cultural perspective within which his subjects were able to come alive in a specific setting where they confronted specific issues and specific problems. In the Jewish articles, Hapgood did not stamp the word "philosophy" over each piece, begging the question. Consequently, in the Jewish articles Hapgood's judgments and interpretations are more subtle, less awkward, and more convincing than in the fighter articles.

It is not clear whether Hapgood's strict adherence to a very unadorned and unimaginative use of the interview technique was due to his lack of literary talent or to his sincere commitment to the interview as a basis of a distinct literary form. Such a form, Hapgood maintained in an article in 1905 in *Bookman*, would be more artistically and realistically valid than either the fiction or the journalism written at the turn of the century.

In that article, "A New Form of Literature," Hapgood argues that the interview could provide the "force and vitality" that were missing from contemporary writing, that it could be "carried into literature" by being developed into "autobiography of an unconventional kind" (424). He asked why talented writers did not

go directly to the lives of the people? Why not interview men and women, get their points of view, discover their stories and then tell them in print? Instead of artificially constructing a plot, why not look for a real tale? Instead of imagining a character, why not go forth and discover one? And when an expressive personality is discovered, why should not the writer find plenty of use for his sympathy and imagination in understanding and re-constructing this expressive personality? (424)

Ultimately, Hapgood hoped that by using his approach, "a section of life would thus be portrayed and a human story told at the same time" (424).

Of course, Hapgood had already experimented with his ideas in the Jewish ghetto articles and the *Types* articles. But a significant step toward a longer attempt at Hapgood's interview-biography approach occurred in *The Autobiography of a Thief*, the story of Jim Caulfield, a professional thief and pickpocket, as told to Hapgood. Hapgood simply spent some time sitting in bars, recording Caulfield's life, and then wrote an introduction and conclusion, otherwise never appearing in the book as either observer or narrator.

Hapgood played a more important role in the narration of *The Spirit of Labor*, published in 1903, four years after *Thief*. For *Labor*, Hapgood spent a considerable amount of time observing Anton Johannsen, a Chicago woodworker and labor union member. He rented a room in a boarding house near Johannsen's home so that he could be near the man. He "became almost a member of his family, and came to occupy an acknowledged place in the circle of his radical friends" (19). To avoid getting an inarticulate worker, Hapgood carefully selected Johannsen and chose him only after closely following the Chicago labor movement, attending meetings and frequenting labor saloon hangouts. He came upon Johannsen in a bar where the worker was "gesticulating, making impressive statements about organized society" (13). When Johannsen proved less impressive in interview situations, Hapgood collected his information by watching him in more spontaneous instances.

The book is not entirely in Johannsen's own words. Rather, it is a retelling in a conventional, straightforward style that contains quotes and pieces of conversations throughout, and only rarely description. Some of the chapters are similar to those of *The Spirit of the Ghetto* in that Hapgood recreates a scene in an apartment or bar by reproducing discussion or dialogue. For instance, a chapter that deals with the ethics of using violence in the labor struggle begins this way: "Anton and I and Schmidtty—a woodworker with a ready fist and an honest soul—were sitting in a down-town cafe, drinking beer and talking philosophy and other things" (375). Then most of what follows is the actual dialogue. In such instances, the reader gets a strong sense of personality, a feel for people who live in a particular manner, but little else. It fails to capture that "Spirit of Labor" that motivated Hapgood to do this project. Rather, the book looks at one individual who happens to be part of the labor movement, an individual who is a nuisance to both management and union leaders, a man who shuns traditional morality. But Hapgood never sufficiently explores why Johannsen takes his stands and behaves as he does.

Hapgood again tried his method in 1909 with *An Anarchist Woman*, the story of a maid who tries to escape to better things while experimenting with life. Hapgood described the book as an attempt "to show the moral and social disintegration of some victims of the industrial system" (1939,

192). But despite the extremely strong character of Marie, the book suffers from the same limitations as *The Spirit of Labor*: insufficient atmosphere, lack of a larger significance, insufficient development of unifying themes, and an overdependence upon the commentary and words of the principal subject, without any elaboration or imaginative shaping of those words and commentary by Hapgood.

Michael Marcaccio correctly identified Hapgood's major deficiency when he said that Hapgood "was more interested in personality than in complex background . . . more interested in personality than in literary craftsmanship . . . too tied to seeing one individual as a type, to escape confinement in his literary method" (1977, 145–46). Hapgood believed so strongly in the nobility of his subjects and thought so little of the importance of imagination that he was blind to the inadequacy of reliance on the subject's words alone. Therefore, his attempt to go beyond the facts led him to a method just as confining and limited as sticking to the facts. The problem was not so much in his thinking as in its narrow execution, and because of that his practice never matched the promise of his theory.

In the end, his literary journalism or his in-depth "human documents," as he called them, seem as similar to the "documentary nonfiction" described by William Stott in *Documentary Expression and Thirties America* as they do to more recent literary journalism. Nevertheless, Hapgood clearly recognized the need for a type of writing that captured real life, that dealt with actual people and events but had a literary touch in the presentation, and he perceptively developed an early theory of what we now call literary journalism. Even if his own writing lacked polish and imagination, his thought foreshadowed a movement and is an important part of literary journalism's history and tradition.

PRIMARY SOURCES

Hapgood, Hutchins. 1897. "The Reporter and Literature." *Bookman* 5: 119–21.

———. 1898, July 16. "Two Men—Four Years." *Commercial Advertiser*.

———. 1900, Mar. 10. "A Lone Russian Genius." *Commercial Advertiser*. In *Spirit of the Ghetto* the article is called "A Cynical Inventor" and is part of the last chapter, "Odd Characters."

———. 1903. *The Autobiography of a Thief*. New York: Fox, Duffield.

———. 1905. "A New Form of Literature." *Bookman* 21: 424–27.

———. 1907. *The Spirit of Labor*. New York: Duffield.

———. 1909. *An Anarchist Woman*. New York: Duffield.

———. [1912 or 1913]. "The Real News." *New York Globe*. Undated in the Hapgood Papers at Yale. I was unable to locate it in the *Globe*, but it was probably printed in 1912 or 1913.

———. 1913, Feb. 21. "The Bath." *New York Globe*. This column is one of a number of newspaper clippings in the Hutchins and Neith Boyce Hapgood Papers in the Beinecke Rare Book and Manuscript Library, Yale University,

New Haven, Connecticut. Unfortunately, most of the clippings, including this one, are not dated.

———. 1939. *A Victorian in the Modern World.* New York: Harcourt, Brace.

———. 1967. *The Spirit of the Ghetto: Studies of the Jewish Quarter in New York.* Cambridge, Mass.: Belknap Press of Harvard University Press. Orig. pub. by Funk and Wagnalls in 1902, with a second printing in 1909. The Belknap Press edition is simply a reprint of the 1902 edition, but with an introduction by Moses Rischin. Funk and Wagnalls also came out with a new edition, with a preface and notes by Harry Golden, in 1965.

———. 1970. *Types from City Streets.* New York: Garrett Press. Orig. pub. 1910.

SECONDARY SOURCES

Connery, Thomas B. 1986, Spring. "Hutchins Hapgood and the Search for a 'New Form of Literature.' " *Journalism History* 13: 2–9.

Howe, Irving. 1967, Mar. 19. "The Subculture of Yiddishkeit." *New York Times Book Review.*

Luhan, Mabel Dodge. 1936. *Intimate Memories.* Vol. 3 of *Movers and Shakers.* New York: Harcourt, Brace.

Marcaccio, Michael D. 1977. *The Hapgoods.* Charlottesville: University Press of Virginia.

William Hard

Ronald S. Marmarelli

They spent the afternoon outlining what they wanted to say in the full page of newspaper copy the two of them were putting together for the campaign. They shared the hope that it would persuade readers in Tennessee to push for passage of laws to protect property rights of married women. But they differed on how the text should be written.

Later on that Friday in December 1912, in a letter from Nashville, William Hard reported that he had suggested to Ida Clyde Clarke that they use stories about people—perhaps about women in situations that result from present laws—and she had seen the merit of his approach to writing "entertaining articles on unentertaining but important subjects." That kind of writing takes effort, Hard observed in his letter, but "the entertainment is always there if the writer is willing to work" (William Hard Papers).

As he sat in his room at the Hermitage Hotel writing the letter to his wife, Ann, Hard might have paused to consider that his accomplishments in a half-dozen years as a magazine journalist provided ample evidence of what he referred to in the letter as "the possibilities of the anecdote method."[1] As a newspaper interviewer in Houston, Texas, had written earlier that year, Hard's magazine work had taken him around the nation in search of his stories, "prying into shady corners of character and disposition and between time writing stuff that has made the country sit up and take notice" ("Hard's Mission" 1912, 3).

If it had been suggested to Hard that the "stuff" of which the country had taken notice might be viewed years later as warranting attention as part of a tradition of *literary* journalism, he probably would not have objected. He knew that "literary skill," "artistic coloring," and "emotion" were essential for a writer who wished to be read. People need more than facts, he wrote. "For mental health they need the pleasures of art, and one of the domains of art is [literary] style" (1901a, 16). He also knew that literary skill was useful to the writer who wished to sell his work, for "the man who writes real stories is the man most indispensable to magazines" (Hard Papers, letter to Ann Hard, 9 Dec. 1906). In his successful endeavors in the magazine marketplace of the Progressive Era, Hard consistently turned out appealing articles that stand out as some of the most interesting of a career that continued until 1960.

In that period from 1901 through 1920, Hard, while making a living as a journalist, put his skill to work in service to Progressivism and wrote about many of the issues on its eclectic, kaleidoscopic agenda. The range of his work reflected the broad scope of Progressive journalism, which included "muckraking" and other "new forms of journalism" that were part of a "wide-ranging literature on public affairs" Progressives used in their efforts to effect reform (Welter 1962, 254).[2] The magazine *Everybody's* made up an important element of that literature, and Hard did some of his most creative Progressive journalism for that publication.[3]

Trying to be helpful as well as interesting, Hard promoted causes and ideas, or at least promoted awareness of current issues, through his "anecdote method," entertaining writing that was factual in content and literary in quality. In "picturesque" stories showing "human beings in action," Hard used a variety of techniques, not just anecdotes, in a variety of inventive ways in the effort to produce entertaining articles on important subjects (Hard Papers, letter to Ann Hard, 15 Dec. 1906).

That could be seen in editorials he wrote for the *Chicago Tribune*, where he worked from July 1901 to April 1905, "writing my daily snatches of contemporary history with enormous amazements of discovery" (1920a, 169). Robert W. Patterson, *Tribune* editor, had hired Hard because he read some of Hard's early articles for the *Neighbor*, the monthly publication of the Northwestern University Settlement House, where Hard got his start in reform journalism in April 1901. Among the various pieces he wrote for the *Neighbor* for more than two years was a series of nine "Scenes" done between August 1901 and December 1902 that consisted of narrative essays full of detail and colorful writing. They also contained a good bit of what has been called "tour-guide reporting" (Francke 1985, 80), with Hard taking the reader to various sites on the Northwest Side of Chicago. In "Mass at St. Stanislaus'" Hard led the way to the church by way of the Milwaukee Avenue streetcar:

The rails will be wobbly and the car itself will seem to be blind drunk and appear likely to leave the track at any moment and go off and lie down in the gutter, but at Noble Street you may alight and you will find yourself in the heart of a transplanted Cracow or Warsaw. (1901b, 7)

Soon after he embarked on his career in magazine writing in 1906, Hard wrote for the *World To-Day* a number of "Silhouettes" similar in style and

content to the earlier "Scenes." In one of them, " 'John Knezoshamlutosko——,' " which is given as John's real name—at least, "as much of it
as I could catch"—Hard contrasted John, who worked six months a year
in Kansas City and spent the other six months in Chicago not working,
with Sanders, a native New Englander and foreman of a factory. Sanders
tried without success to cajole John into going to work for him in his factory.
The piece closed with John contemplating his environment:

And John looked out at the belching smokestacks of the mills, at the deep mud of
the street, at the innumerable wires on the telegraph poles, at the countless tracks
of the switching yard, at the freight trains, at the decaying plank sidewalks, at the
row of saloons on the other side of the street, at the pale-pink spot in the sky where
the sun was tapping for admittance on the farther side of the smoke-wall of the air,
and John was happy. His round innocent face was burnished with contentment. He
was in the midst of his annual six months' vacation. (1907a, 820)

From the middle of 1907 through the end of 1910, Hard wrote several
major pieces—an article for *Munsey's* and one article and two series for
Everybody's—that represented perhaps his greatest achievements in literary
journalism.

In "Where Poison Haunts Man's Daily Work," one of a few articles he
wrote for *Munsey's*, he created scenes of encounters with human embodi-
ments of the conditions caused by exposure to deadly substances used in
making some products. He noted that while going home from work in a
streetcar you might observe that

the man across the aisle of your car smiles over a joke on the back page of his
newspaper. As his mirth broadens you notice that along his gums, looking like some
hideous band of metal placed there by the dentist, there runs a distinct line of deep
blue. That line is lead. That man works in lead—and lead works in him.

The street-car passes a factory. Out of its heat and roar come four or five dripping
men. You notice that the perspiration on their bare arms shows greenish; and their
hair, sprouting green from its roots, gives each man's head the appearance of a
grotesque vegetable. That factory turns out a certain kind of brass.

The lead man across the aisle drops a button. His neighbor stoops to pick it up.
As his fingers gather around the button they suddenly quiver and stop. Their master
urges them on. They refuse to obey him. They will not come together. Their master—
their former master—grins. When he first saw danger he saw it with terror. Now
that he sees it every day, terror is distilled to ironic humor.

Turning towards the lead man, the humorist with the rebellious fingers conducts
a little physical experiment. He tries to place the tip of his little finger on the tip of
his thumb. When he has done his best, an amusing gap of half an inch remains.
The lead man displays the blue line of his gums in an appreciative smile. He recognizes
that gap. He knows the handiwork of dinitrobenzin. He is familiar with the consequences of helping to make certain explosives. (1907b, 717)

Here and there in the article, in a manner akin to chanting, Hard recounted the various names ("hatter's shakes, diver's paralysis, shoemaker's chest, miller's itch") by which "modern medicine tries to catch up with modern industry, the doctor endeavors to keep pace with the inventor" (1970b, 717–18). " '*Sunt lacrimae rerum,*' " Hard concluded, quoting from classical literature. " 'There are tears in things.' That is the epitaph of the man who encounters poison in his ordinary, daily work" (1907b, 721).

Throughout the Progressive Era, Hard continued writing about conditions of work and life in the modern industrial city. For *Everybody's*, for which he started working in 1907 after serving briefly as Chicago editor of *Ridgway's*, a short-lived weekly started in 1906 by the company, he wrote " 'De Kid Wot Works at Night,' " which has probably been his most widely known work.[4] The story was told largely through the experiences of one newsboy, in an article notable for Hard's carefully shaped narrative.

Hard opened "De Kid" with a lengthy, elaborate description of Chicago at dusk, each paragraph consisting of periodic sentences with parallel syntax and adverbial phrases to create a sweeping prose poem of Chicago being transformed from day to night. The passage was fashioned into a series of three long paragraphs followed by three short ones, all beginning with "when" phrases, leading up to "between five and six o'clock in the afternoon." Next came three paragraphs ("Then it is") that introduced the main characters, "the night newsboy and the night messenger boy," who "turn another page once more to the thronging, picturesque, incoherent characters of the night life of a big American city" (1908a, 26).

The article began with the approach of night.

When the shades of night look as if they were about to fall; when the atmosphere of Chicago begins to change from the dull gray of unaided local nature to the brilliant white of artificial illumination;…when the sound of the time-clock being gladly and brutally punched is heard through every door and window—
When all these things are happening, and, besides—

The next two paragraphs added more detail of activity—"fat men" beating "lean and energetic and profane men" to aisle streetcar seats, department store clerks throwing "the night-covers over bargain ormolu clocks just as you pant up to the counter," a suburban man buying a steak at a meat market "in order to have the laugh on the high-priced suburban butcher," railway station clocks and the sights and sounds of the comings and goings in the street (1908a, 25–26).

Hard presented the newsboy starting his work as he

approaches his favorite corner, grins at the man who owns the corner news stand, receives "ten *Choinals*, ten *Murrikins*, ten *Snoozes*, and five *Posts*"; goes away twenty feet, turns around, watches the corner-man to see if he has marked the papers down in his note-book, hopes that he hasn't marked them down, thinks that perhaps he has forgotten just how many there were, wonders if he couldn't persuade him that he didn't give him any *Murrikins*, calculates the amount of his profit if he should be able to sell the *Murrikins* without having to pay the corner-man for them, turns to the street, dodges a frenzied automobile, worms his way into a hand-packed street-car (which is the only receptacle never convicted by the city government of containing short measure), disappears at the car-door, comes to the surface in the middle of the aisle, and hands a *News* to a regular customer. (1908a, 26–27)

Taking up the social questions of what the youth who is employed in the nighttime "street trades" does and sees, and how it affects him, Hard summarized the reasons why newsboys should be regulated by law, particularly adverse effects on their health, noting that the newsboy had been given the status of "merchant" who, thus, "occupies the same legal position as Marshall Field & Co." "Therefore he does not fall within the scope of the child-labor law. Therefore no rascally paternalistic factory inspector may vex him in his pursuit of an independent commercial career (1908a, 28)."

After a summary of the evolving composition of the newsboy population, Hard told the story primarily through the career and experiences of an Italian newsboy who later moved up to the more prestigious job of messenger boy. "The best specimen of the finished type of newsboy, within my knowledge, is an Italian boy named 'Jelly.' His father's surname is Cella, but his own name has been 'Jelly' ever since he can remember" (1908a, 32).

The article ended with a scene that began outside a downtown hotel, where the messenger boys were playing "craps."

Two hours and a half pass playing craps. The honesty of the engineering construction of the dice is several times impugned. And, apparently, not without reason. The boy who is winning at any given time is the boy who is playing with his own dice. (1908a, 37)

A man carrying a satchel staggers into the scene. Hard describes him as "a very old man, about thirty-six years of age," whose "eyes stagger almost as much as his legs." His satchel contains a device that would make him rich, the man tells the boys. They "solemnly" kick the satchel until it is battered, cracked open, and "revealed as being empty." The boys then gaily kick the satchel even more. The scene continues:

The man staggers into the street. A policeman turns the corner.

"Time to go swimmin'," yells the leader....

The light of dawn is chilling and freezing the warm nocturnal radiance of the arc-lamp. The policeman's face is gray and sick. To the man who has worked all night it seems unreasonable, impossible, like a nightmare, that within another hour or two thousands of people should be resuming their frantic, insane, energetic labor in the office buildings about him....

The policeman looks down the street, eastward, after them. A gleam of sunlight strikes the metal on his helmet. The night is over. (1908a, 37)

Hard's major work for *Everybody's* between 1907 and 1911 consisted of two long series of articles on issues related to modern womanhood. The articles in "The Woman's Invasion" series (six parts) contain lengthy passages of narrative and description that are rich in detail and figurative language.[5] For the second series, "The Women of To-Morrow" (five parts), Hard made even more striking use of narrative structure, characterization, description, and dialogue and interior monologue.[6]

His skill in creating scenic passages rich in figurative language was shown in several of the articles in the two series. The first article in the first series, "Fall River, an Outpost on the Edge of the Future," describes the coming of a new working day at Fall River, Massachusetts. There, Hard presents "a transformation scene of a most thrilling sort, with a hillside for a stage, with the lamps of docking boats for footlights, and with a black sky for a proscenium arch." He describes the activity that begins about 5 A.M. and continues until

the moment has come . . . for light, for power, for work, for the down-to-a-second and down-to-a-cent precalculated frenzy of modern manufacturing. At six-thirty precisely, not a second sooner, not a second later, there is a blinding blaze of light from every window in the mill; there is a belching clamor of machinery through the open door.

Then the door swings shut and absolute silence is restored to the street. So is absolute loneliness. (1908b, 582)

In Part III of the same series, Hard described another scene of Chicago streets, in a manner similar to " 'De Kid,' " although briefer. "Through the orchestral roar that is Chicago, through the bellows and brasses that is The Loop," he wrote, giving an impression of the activity that continued until 8:30 in the morning, when "25,000 women are at work" (1908b, 73).

The opening of the final installment, "The Working Home," consisted of an extended narrative about Bessie Smith, a widow and mother forced to work outside the home after her husband's death. It begins: "Bessie Smith got through work at five. A block down the street, in her favorite department store, she bought, in little, very thick paper pails (like the pails they use for oysters) a mutton stew, a rice pudding, and two codfish balls" (1909c, 521). Bessie then went to a day nursery to get her son, Harry, who was almost three years old.

That evening, in her flat (just around the corner from the mottled-brick building), the little boy struggled, between mouthfuls of zwiebach drenched in milk, to find words for the happenings of the day. His mother sat at her table beside him, piecing together the fragments of his gossip, inciting him to the construction of new baby-phrases, and forgetting (almost till they were spoiled) the mutton stew and the rice pudding warming for her supper in the oven of the gas range. (1908c, 521)

Mrs. Smith postponed putting her son to bed so that she could spend more time with him. She ran out of reasons for putting it off, then chastised herself for keeping him awake. But, she thought, "if tomorrow were only Sunday! She could make him talk all day then!"

But to-morrow she will get up at half past six, and after the two codfish balls (warmed in the oven) and a cup of coffee have made her breakfast, and a bowl of glutena and cream has made Harry's, she will reach the day nursery by half past seven and hand Harry back to the blue-and-white-stripe-clad nurse. And then, at eight sharp, she will punch the time-clock in a big down-town store. (1908c, 521)

The final three articles in "The Women of To-Morrow" series illustrated three phases of modern womanhood—economic independence, empty leisure, and social services and citizenship—in ways that made them exceptional examples of Hard's skill. They included inventive characterization to depict women representing those three phases.

In "Love Deferred," Part III of "Women of To-Morrow," Hard noted that his central figures are "compositely imagined," and he contrasted them with some cases that "are individually (though typically) existent in real life in one of the large American cities" (1910a, 489). That was followed by several brief case studies in which the people were identified by initials only, as in "R—— J——" (1910a, 489–90).[7]

The central figures in "Love Deferred" were John and Mary. The article told of their sensible decision that Mary continue to work for two years after they got married, two years "in which she had helped John to start a home" (1910a, 494). The story of their "progressive" lifestyle was told with long passages of dialogue and interior monologue ("Mary felt she would wait for John even if, instead of going away on a career, he were going away on a comet" [486]), interwoven with statements from experts and with statistics. Hard also admitted his artifice in telling of John's profession: "We will pretend that John was a doctor. No, that's too professional. He was a civil engineer" (1910a, 486).

Part IV of "Women of To-Morrow," titled "The Wasters," presented a contrasting case study of an apparently invented character, Marie, a woman of the leisure class, whose father and husband "had removed from her life all need, and finally all desire, to make efforts and to accomplish results through struggle in defiance of difficulty and at the cost of pain" (1910b, 767). Hard showed the reader "the social ceremony" that occurred when Marie got a headache.

The decorations, which were very elaborate, comprised, besides the usual tasteful arrangement of thermometers, eau-de-Karlsbad, smelling salts, bottles, cracked ice, and chocolate creams, a perfect shower of tourmaline roses, the odor of which, alone among all the vegetable odors in the world, had been found after long experimentation to be soothing to Marie on such occasions. It was not thought that

Marie could vanquish a headache except after a plucky fight of at least one day's duration. (1910b, 767)

Later Hard conceded that the leisure class made a significant "contribution" to society.

Marie and her friends greatly increased the number and prosperity of tailors and milliners and candy-dippers and perfume manufacturers and manicurists and hairdressers and plumed-bird hunters and florists and cab-drivers and Irish lace-makers and Chinese silk-worm tenders and violet-and-orris sachet-powder makers and matinee heroes and French nuns who embroider underwear and fur-traders, and pearl-divers and other deserving persons, not forgetting the multitudes of Turks who must make nougat or perish. (1910b, 770)

In "Mothers of the World," Part V of the series, Hard pushed closer to simply fictionalizing as he presented a scene showing his dialogue with a symbolic character representing the maternal and social spirit of womanhood.[8] The voice told the writer that "the greatest reserve fund of energy in any American city is the leisure and semi-leisure of certain classes of its women" (1911, 100) and suggested that this energy be used to make the city more livable. Most of the article consisted of descriptions of the work of various women's groups rendering service to the city of Chicago, but it was artfully framed at beginning and end with the dialogue on the roof of a Chicago building. It begins:

Leaning over a tiled parapet, we looked down at the streak of street so far below. Motor-cars, crawling—crawling, glossy-backed beetles . . .
"But look at that!" she said.

The voice directed his attention variously around the landscape visible from the rooftop until "she waved her hand and blotted out the city from before me" (1911, 98–99).

Hard then saw a scene of a primitive camp where, the voice told him, she was housekeeper. She restored the city to his sight and told him that he was "the real housekeeper" there. She asked why he didn't ask her to help, noting the reserve fund of energy that women represented. The writer responded:

"But they can give their leisure to 'good works' now if they want to," I answered.
"Yes," she said, "but if they do that, they'll want to go farther. Look!"
And this is what she showed me—what she told me. (1911, 100)

Six pages of text with photographs presented instances of the social and civic service work of the Chicago Woman's Club and associated organizations, from kindergartens to the juvenile court.

In the closing section of the article Hard returned again to the roof and his companion. "We crossed the roof's tarred gravel once more, and once more leaned over the tiled parapet and looked abroad at the city" (1911, 108). The voice then told in a monologue spread over a page and a half the implications of what she had shown. Suffrage is just an extension of housekeeping of the world, she noted. At the end, the writer asked:

"But who?" I said, "who are you?"
"I," she said, "I am the spirit that made woman love her child, and that shall yet make her love her kind." (1911, 108)

In 1917, Hard became a regular contributor to the *New Republic*. Since 1915 he also had been featured correspondent for *Metropolitan*. " 'I See by the Newspapers'—But Do You?" and "The Toy Tyrants," both written in 1920, when Hard's work dealt almost exclusively with postwar labor issues and repression of civil liberties, were notable for their tone of irony and creative use of dialogue. "Tyrants" consisted entirely of a dialogue between the writer and his wife in which the record of the Red Scare was recounted.

A number of articles from Hard's weekly work for the *New Republic*, both during the war and in the postwar period, exhibited his skill in the use of first-person narrative and description in political commentary. Two of his most notable pieces were "Cannon: The Proving" and "In Judge Anderson's Courtroom." His talents were valued at the *New Republic*. Willard Straight, who supported the journal with his money and advice, wrote Herbert Croly, *New Republic* editor, in 1918 that although some tightening of the belt was necessary, Croly should retain Hard. His lighter tone was needed in order for the magazine to reach a wider audience because, Straight wrote, most of the writers were "too high-brow."[9]

Hard's work offers the student of literary journalism several notable examples of the genre prior to the emergence of the New Journalism of the 1960s and 1970s. As a Progressive Era interpreter, Hard sought to make important subjects attractive and compelling for readers, whether members of the general audience of magazines such as *Everybody's* and *Munsey's* or the activist and intellectual audiences of the *Neighbor* and the *New Republic*. As a journalist, he sought to inform and entertain. His work was factual because it was based on extensive reporting, and it was entertaining because of his artistry, which developed, *Everybody's* noted, out of "imagination based on facts rather than on rainbows" (Dec. 1913, 866).

NOTES

1. Hard also wrote, "With the exception of Steffens and myself, I don't believe that there is anybody who understands the possibilities of the anecdote method and he won't use it any more, since he got so interested in what he thinks."

2. That there was a vital interrelationship between journalism and Progressivism in those years generally has been acknowledged by scholars, although most have limited their attention to muckraking. The development of a broader conceptualization of Progressive journalism remains a task needing attention.

3. He also contributed to the reform work of the *Delineator*, a companion to *Everybody's* in the Butterick Company. Hard directed the magazine's campaign on behalf of women's legal rights, of which his collaboration with Mrs. Clarke in Nashville was a part.

4. The article was included in *The Muckrakers: The Era in Journalism That Moved America to Reform—The Most Significant Magazine Articles of 1902–1912*, ed. Arthur and Lila Weinberg (New York: Simon, 1961), 369–84; and in *Popular Writing in America: The Interaction of Style and Audience*, ed. Donald McQuade and Robert Atwan (New York: Oxford University Press, 1974), 228–37 (but excerpted in their 4th ed., 279–85); and also excerpted in *Years of Conscience: The Muckrakers*, ed. Harvey Swados (Cleveland: World, 1962), 160–61. McQuade and Atwan noted its kinship with works of New Journalism (212).

5. The announcement of the "Woman's Invasion" series in the May 1907 "With *Everybody's* Publishers" stated that the articles would be "real, human documents—not mere masses of economic facts, but the embodiment of actual experiences and fraught with conviction and character" (720). Hard used material from his own research and material gathered first-hand by Rheta Childe Dorr, who had initially proposed and been given the assignment. Dorr was identified as Hard's collaborator on the series and was credited in an editor's note with having done the early research. She was not happy with the way the series came out. See Dorr 1924, 160–64, 193–99, 201.

6. The articles were reprinted, without revision, in book form. Reviewers generally commended Hard's style, although one noted that "the somewhat sensational style will tend to prejudice the educated reader" (see the review in *Booklist* 8 [1912]: 330).

7. In another piece for *Everybody's*, "Spiking Down an Empire," Hard crafted a narrative populated by a number of characters named "the Engineer," "the Investor," "the Sub-Contractor," and "the Stranger," among others.

8. Hard's device was similar to one Tom Wolfe used in his early versions of the material that became, in different form, *The Right Stuff*. Originally, Wolfe's story of the experiences of test pilots and astronauts was told in the voice of a sort of composite astronaut; the articles' text represented the monologue in which the voice told "Tom" the story. One writer termed this device "collective unspoken" (Weber 1975, 49).

9. Straight to Herbert Croly (20 Feb. 1918). Willard Straight Papers (Cornell University Library, Ithaca, N.Y.). Other commentators on Hard's *New Republic* work have noted his vividness and "spare and racy style" (*Ministers of Reform: The Progressives' Achievement in American Civilization, 1889–1920*, ed. Groff Conklin [New York: Dodge, 1936], 556) and his "brilliant reporting" (Frank Luther Mott, *Sketches of Twenty-one Magazines 1905–1930*, vol. 5 of *A History of American Magazines* [Cambridge, Mass.: Harvard University Press, 1968], 211).

PRIMARY SOURCES

Hard, William. 1901a, Dec. 22. " 'Eloquence' and 'Facts.' " Editorial. *Chicago Tribune*.

———. 1901b, Aug. "Scenes on the Northwest Side: I. Mass at St. Stanislaus'." *Neighbor*: 7–8.

———. 1904, May 22. "The Submarine Mine." Editorial, *Chicago Tribune*: 16.

———. 1907a. "Silhouettes of Life: 'John Knezoshamlutosko—.' " *World To-Day* 13: 818–20.

———. 1907b. "Where Poison Haunts Man's Daily Work." *Munsey's* 38: 717–21.

———. 1908a. " 'De Kid Wot Works at Night.' " *Everybody's* 18: 25–37.

———. 1908b. "The Woman's Invasion: I. Fall River, an Outpost on the Edge of the Future." *Everybody's* 19: 579–91.

———. 1909a. "Spiking Down an Empire: Canada's New Farthest-North Trans-continental Railway." *Everybody's* 21: 633–45.

———. 1909b. "The Woman's Invasion: III." *Everybody's* 20: 73–85.

———. 1909c. "The Woman's Invasion: VI. The Working Home." *Everybody's* 20: 521–32.

———. 1910a. "The Women of To-Morrow: III. Love Deferred." *Everybody's* 23: 486–96.

———. 1910b. "The Women of To-Morrow: IV. The Wasters." *Everybody's* 23: 767–77.

———. 1911. "The Women of To-Morrow: V. Mothers of the World." *Everybody's* 24: 98–108.

———. 1918. "Cannon: The Proving." *New Republic* 15: 136–38.

———. 1919. "In Judge Anderson's Courtroom." *New Republic* 20: 373–77.

———. 1920a. "Farmer-Labor: The Background." *New Republic* 24: 168–70.

———. 1920b, Feb. " 'I See by the Newspapers'—But Do You?" *Metropolitan*: 25–27 + .

———. 1920c, Apr. "The Toy Tyrants." *Metropolitan*: 16–17 + . William Hard Papers. Archives of Contemporary History. American Heritage Center, University of Wyoming, Laramie, Wy.

SECONDARY SOURCES

Dorr, Rheta Childe. 1924. *A Woman of Fifty*. 2nd ed. New York: Funk.

Francke, Warren. 1985, Winter. "Sensationalism and the Development of Nineteenth-Century Reporting: The Broom Sweeps Sensory Details." *Journalism History* 12: 80–85.

French, George. 1912. " '*Everybody's*' Business." *Twentieth Century* 6: 241–49.

Greene, Theodore P. 1970. *America's Heroes: The Changing Models of Success in American Magazines*. New York: Oxford University Press.

"Hard's Mission in Houston to Help Texas Wives Reform Laws." 1912, July 27. *Houston Chronicle*: 3.

Kittle, William. 1909. "The Making of Public Opinion." *Arena* 41: 433–50.

Marmarelli, Ron. 1986. "William Hard as Progressive Journalist." *American Journalism* 3: 142–53.

Review of *The Women of Tomorrow* by William Hard. 1912. *Booklist* 8: 330.

"Straight Talk with *Everybody's* Publishers." 1913. *Everybody's* 29: 865–66.

Weber, Ronald. 1975, Summer. "Moon Talk." *Journal of Popular Culture* 9: 142–52.

Welter, Rush. 1962. *Popular Education and Democratic Thought in America*. New York: Columbia University Press.

Wilson, Christopher P. 1983. "The Rhetoric of Consumption: Mass-Market Magazines and the Demise of the Gentle Reader, 1880–1920." In *The Culture of Consumption: Critical Essays in American History, 1880–1980*. Ed. Richard Wightman Fox and T. J. Jackson Lears. New York: Pantheon.

———. 1985. *The Labor of Words: Literary Professionalism in the Progressive Era*. Athens: University of Georgia Press.

"With *Everybody's* Publishers." 1907. *Everybody's* 16: 719–20.

———. 1908. *Everybody's* 18: 863–64.

———. 1910. *Everybody's* 23: 575–76.

———. 1912. *Everybody's* 26: 863–64.

THEODORE DREISER

Marilyn Ann Moss

Theodore Dreiser's journalistic writing was a configuration of factual data that ultimately coalesced into a personal mythos—a tale of how a young journalist might invent himself as a spokesman for American lives at the turn of the century. Within this mythology of selfhood, people, places, and events in the American landscape became the raw material by which Dreiser unwittingly used journalism to romance himself toward a literary career. For when he came to write his first novel, *Sister Carrie*, in 1900, Dreiser invented his fictional characters in the image of those American masses who populated his newspaper columns and magazine pieces. Both literature and journalism—interchangeable as they were, simultaneous as they were— became an imaginative marketplace from which Dreiser selected the details of his own mythology as a writer. In Dreiser's view, American cities had stories to tell of themselves, and he made it his responsibility—in fact his career as a journalist—to become a representative storyteller of his generation. To tell a story, however, meant that journalism and literature enlist to exhibit the public persona of Dreiser himself.

Storytelling became this journalist's first experience with writing for the public. During his first years working for newspapers such as the Chicago *Globe*, Dreiser learned quickly and exceedingly well the nature of writing what were termed "features," human interest stories that moved in the rhythms of literature as well as journalism. These were stories that reflected the reverence of the times for sensationalism and which were characterized by either "lengthy colorful meandering pieces that vividly evoked the look and sound of a particular chapter of city life," or that presented "a human interest tale that would capture the reader's imagination" (Fishkin 1985, 95). As Dreiser, in his autobiography, *Newspaper Days*, would later account for these stories, Chicago journalism in the 1890s "was still in that discursive stage which loved long-winded yarns upon almost any topic. Nearly all news stories were padded to make more of them than they deserved, especially as to color and romance" (1974, 65).[1]

Thus Dreiser's early experiences may be viewed as working in journalism and imaginative fiction simultaneously. His very first feature story, a piece on Chicago slum life, exhibited as much of his literary skills as it did of the factual world around him.

Saloon lights and smells and lamps gleaming smokily from behind broken lattices and from below wooden sidewalk levels gave it a shameless and dangerous color. Accordions, harmonicas, jew's-harps, clattering tin-pan pianos and stringy violins were forever going; paintless rotting shacks always resounded with a noisy blasphemous life between twelve and four; oaths, foul phrases, a Hogarthian shamelessness and reconciliation to filth everywhere. (66)

Dreiser's view of slum life was appropriately bleak, and even more decidedly fatalistic, much like the account of New York's Bowery that would find its way into his earliest work of novelistic invention. Within the fatality of slum life, however, lurked the characteristic Dreiserian sensuality and eroticism that came to mark all of his fiction: the forces of life in all parts of the city that fought a battle against that which would serve to repress it. As narrator of this "tale," Dreiser was powerfully attracted to a life that he *conceived* of as "shameless" and "dangerous" no less than "foul" and "forbidden." He was just as concerned with the color and the sound of the life as he was with the facts that may have initially presented themselves to him. The literary imagination that fed this piece envisioned tin-pan pianos as "clattering" and violins as "stringy." More attractive still were the "foul phrases" that bespoke "a noisy blasphemous life" and that led to an eroticized blend of "dangerous color" and a "reconciliation to filth everywhere." Even in this first journalistic piece, Dreiser was well on his way to viewing American city life as the stuff of a grand American drama.

The close relationship between social fact and literary fancy exhibited in his earliest newspaper pieces became the wellspring of Dreiser's invention of himself as a prophetic "seer" into American culture. As he wrote in *Sister Carrie*, culture itself could easily be defined by those erotic and "dangerous" forces that drew people to American cities. Thus Dreiser set for himself the task, as a journalist, of understanding those forces which controlled the lives of ordinary men and women yet which these men and women could not themselves perceive. In order to procure this role of seer for himself, however, Dreiser had first to invent himself as a persona in his journalistic pieces. And it was in his early days with newspapers and magazines that fact flirted with literary convention as a means for this young writer to convey the drama he sensed in city life. Moreover, he wanted to write of what he saw as no other journalist could. Upon this foundation Dreiser conveyed his unique moral vision of the world in which he lived.

Writing feature stories gave Dreiser the first taste of his imaginative powers; yet he also learned early on the benefits of out-and-out lying in print. It could become the quickest means of pleasing an editor and the best means of being handed another assignment. At the St. Louis *Globe-Democrat* in 1892, for example, Dreiser began a five-month tenure as probably the sole contributor to a column called "Heard in the Corridors," supposedly a series of interviews with notable if not simply colorful hotel guests in the city of St. Louis. In truth, however, the column emerged as a string of fabrications from Dreiser's own imagination. Anxious to further his career and excited at the prospect of shaping his own creative powers, Dreiser literally invented himself as interviewer *and* "hotel guest." In his mind these short "features" were little other than extended, if not romanticized, human interest stories. As he would later recall the experience:

I discovered that it gave free rein to my wildest imaginings which was exactly what I wanted. I could write any sort of story I pleased, romantic, realistic or lunatic, and credit it to some imaginary guest at one of the hotels, and if it was not too improbable it was passed without comment. . . . I went forth to get names of personages stopping at the hotels. . . . I returned and racked my brain, decided I could manufacture names as well as stories, and forthwith scribbled six marvels attaching such names as came into my mind. (134)

Although Dreiser soon resigned from the *Globe-Democrat* after having been found out for writing fictitious theater reviews, he had honed his art as a clearly literary journalist and had prepared for himself the persona that would soon earmark his career as a magazine writer. At this new post he would be able to sustain himself financially for the rest of his career as a novelist.

In 1895 Dreiser became editor and principal contributor to *Ev'ry Month*, a magazine founded by his brother, the popular songwriter Paul Dresser, and the music publishing firm of Howley, Haviland and Co., as a means of promoting the firm's songs. The magazine's chief readership was women, and its pages consisted not only of Dreiser's editorials and departments but also of household and decorative features. Within the pages of *Ev'ry Month*, nonetheless, Dreiser established himself as a kind of social philosopher, a purveyor of American "truth-telling" that extended far beyond the concerns of domestic households. One major contribution to his reputation as a social commentator was his column, "Reflections," a journalistic feat of iconoclastic dimensions. Penning himself as "The Prophet," Dreiser meant to have his readers believe the column to be the work of more than one writer. In this role, he ventured into avenues of American thought and American city life, now perceiving himself to be an allegorical construction of both artist and public spokesman, seer and, in his own terms, "Genius." This would make for journalism in purely literary terms.

Within the margins of his "Reflections" column, Dreiser discovered not only his literary voice but also the allegorical persona and thematic center of an oeuvre of Dreiserian novels to come. As Donald Pizer has noted, the column revealed a journalist who was, if anything, the subject of his own mythology.

The allegory centers on the character and experience of the Genius. . . . The circumstances of modern life bring him to the City . . . but the Genius soon discovers that the city contains not only the glorious spectacle which is life at its most compelling but also the struggle for existence which is inseparable from all life. . . . He realizes that though the individual is insignificant in the overwhelming fury of the battle of life, the laws of life are themselves beneficent for the mass of men and for the progress of the race. And the Genius senses that the artist's response to this insight contains three fused emotions: awe toward the vast, impersonal forces of life; compassion for the victims of these forces, and wonder at the "color" or aesthetic appeal of the variation and conflict caused by these forces. (Pizer 1977, 20)[2]

Dreiser located a drama being played out in the modern American city between the forces of good and evil that men and women did not understand to the extent that the Genius perceived it. Thus it was his responsibility to enlighten these men and women as to the nature of their modern condition: to the struggles between the strong and the weak, and between individuals and the masses. He sought, therefore, to expose the hard facts beneath these struggles. For Dreiser this agenda was felt to be a moral responsibility. That is, he desired sincerely to lift the curtains of romantic fallacy from behind which, he felt, Americans viewed their own lives. Within this moral drama Dreiser's archenemy was the force of conventional codes which, he felt, distorted the vitality of human beings and imprisoned them in a passive acceptance of their impoverished lives. Dreiser would likewise write novels about such men and women, and in his journalistic pieces he developed the crucial terms of his dramatic and literary sensibility. It was indeed an allegory conceived in literary dress wherein Dreiser was both narrator and fictional subject. He regarded himself as an impassioned voice who would, unwittingly, exalt the very color and flavor of the city's impersonal forces that he aimed to expose.

Thus, in the *Ev'ry Month* columns the informed and wholly compassionate "Prophet" contemplated and commented upon ordinary city scenes that became at once the fabric of an enormous moral and philosophical yarn. Yet his eye was always toward the real men and women who played out their lives in Dreiser's city. Stating his editorial policy, he wrote:

No cynicism will you find in this steady contemplation of the trend of events; no assertion that the world or the Union is treading irretrievably toward ruin; on the contrary, a firm and undisturbed faith in nature, and in men true to nature, despite the decay of a few of the species, or schools, or tribes, of which there are so many. (104)

Dreiser was irremediably drawn to those American "tribes" whose lives would fill his columns, individuals with real experiences and real emotional data who became subsumed into a large canvas of American cityscapes. Because, ultimately, Dreiser was fascinated more by forces than he was by individuals. Moreover, he was fascinated by the extent to which he might participate in and comment upon the American scene passing before him: a scene he estimated to be a collision between men and women who profited in society and those who merely endured. Contemplating the heroic terms within which he might participate in the scene, he held fast to his conception of Dreiser the seer. In an early *Ev'ry Month* column, he wrote that "he is a wise man who . . . can logically distinguish the good from the evil—and a true savior is he who can marshal the nobler sentiments of the people and array them for successful combat" (105). He was, of course, speaking of himself.

In this way Dreiser conceived of journalism within literary configurations, and factual data became allied with imaginative narratives and an authorial voice that competed with objective fact for a privileged place in the text. He was never so much a recorder of human events as he was an interpreter of culture, and he interpreted his culture as a great tale of human lives as they were controlled by the flux of social forces. Moreover, Dreiser found fascinating the mood of the sensational, and he tended to view the men and women he wrote of as case histories in a contemporary drama of heroic proportions.

Thus, in one particular "Reflections" column for 1896, Dreiser was irresistibly attracted to what he termed an ordinary "New York Tragedy." While he eventually offered the facts of this tragedy, he was more immediately drawn to the opportunity to comment on its spectacle.

In this world of struggle and discontent nothing so tends to alleviate one's disgust with one's own condition as the honest contemplation of the conditions of others. It is not by reading that this can be done, for reading begets a false sentiment, nor by retiring within one's self, as it were, and there brooding; but by going out among the people and into the places where misery gathers. (81)

In calling for public contemplation of "the conditions of others," Dreiser wished to amplify ordinary events until they indeed became a social spectacle by which others might measure their lives. In his literary sensibility he was fascinated by the romance of struggle, the spectacular if not awesome contest between good and evil. And, as "A New York Tragedy" demonstrated, he looked at the social world around him within these terms so as to become an exemplary social philosopher for the masses. That is, he intended to notice what other journalists hadn't the "talent" to notice about their own society.

It is curious that more misery does not show itself upon the pages of daily newspapers, when one realizes that no day is without its shadow somewhere. It is curious and yet explainable because it requires talent to perceive true suffering and talent, also, to write of and describe it, and when the newspaper world is sifted so very much talent is not discoverable after all. (81)

For Dreiser in this piece, "when a fitful tale show itself," most reporters "either have not the heart to appreciate" this tale, or "lack the ability to describe," or are "lazy or indifferent, or hardened by long labor in the same field" (81). Having reached this opinion, it was Dreiser's self-appointed role as editor of *Ev'ry Month* to locate a "tragic" or "fitful" tale that he believed was a seer's gift, the business of the "Prophet."

This "Prophet," like other human beings, lived in an imperfect and, what is more, an *indifferent* world. And the fact of such indifference became the prototypical Dreiserian subtext throughout the journalistic pieces. As "A New York Tragedy" demonstrated, then, Dreiser's mission was to locate the large picture embedded within the everyday occurrence.

One such story appeared during the past month in one of our New York papers, and it concerned a woman who was very poor, whose husband was a wandering vagabond, and whose dwelling-place was a cell of a room, bare, unodorous, and dark. This creature was sick and weak, and while she was physically unfit to support herself she had a child to care for and that was enough to fire her strength, though it could not increase nor preserve it. (82)

Dreiser weaved the facts of this woman's life into a compelling narrative whose subject matter was the business of a literary landscape, a picture of city life as much the way Dreiser experienced it as did the woman herself. She became, then, nothing less than the heroine in a great tragedy; moreover, she was invested with the writer's sympathies to the extent that a novelist would invent a literary character from the experiences of his own psychology. For Dreiser, this heroine, upon her death, became a victim of a world indifferent to the mere fact that she lived. "All day the body...lay there on its mattress in the heat" as "grimy, half naked children...came and played about the doorway, not thinking of the pitiful thing within." While those "who had known her stopped in to look at the body," there was "no one to feel deep sorrow for the dead" (82).

The landscape of this tragedy was as factual as a woman's death yet as grand as the paradox of "grimy" children who came to play about the body of a dead woman while people who knew her expressed their "sympathy" and "sadness" in "crude fashion." Furthermore, for Dreiser the fact of a woman's death in the slums of New York was a paradox in light of the wealthy who buried their dead in fashionable and public ceremony. Yet American cities were felt by Dreiser to be places of contradiction, and the desire to relay this feature of modern American life lay at the core of Dreiser's desire to be a journalist. He wrote of people as if they were metaphors for the embattled condition of human nature itself. As he wrote in a piece called "The Right to Kill" in 1918, "it is time that we cleared away all the cobwebs of altruism and all fine-spun religious notions, sweet as they may be, and faced the facts, disturbing as they may be, but healthy; that life is a chaffering bickering game" (229).

For Dreiser, the journalist had a responsibility to look at real events and human beings with an eye toward their representative place in a modern world whose elements were the conditions of flux. Further, he had little interest in reporting facts only to let the story end there. If people lived within the conditions of fluctuating forces, then indeed these people, as they were revealed in print, had to be viewed in a way that exhibited their representativeness, their symbolic nature, in their social communities. Human beings were embroiled in a vortex of shifting values and tragic circumstances. There could be no means of understanding the actualities of life at the turn of the century in America other than by attending to the complex dramas that lay embedded within the fact of a woman's death in the slums or a man's standing in line in the Bowery seeking a bed for the night. For Dreiser, journalism was also a literary endeavor. And as the "Prophet," he used his imaginative powers to ensure not only that stories were written but also that he be understood as the representative storyteller in print. Dreiser's journalistic writings, thus, were a collision of fact-finding and a powerful desire to locate a literary persona. The two served each other equally well.

NOTES

1. All page citations given for Dreiser's early work (on the Chicago *Globe* and the St. Louis *Globe-Democrat*) are taken from *Newspaper Days* (originally published as *A Book About Myself*) by Theodore Dreiser.

2. All page citations given for Dreiser's "Reflections" columns from *Ev'ry Month* magazine are taken from *Theodore Dreiser: A Selection of Uncollected Prose*, ed. Donald Pizer.

PRIMARY SOURCES

Dreiser, Theodore. 1974. *Newspaper Days*. New York: Beekman.

———. 1985. *Selected Magazine Articles of Theodore Dreiser: Life and Art in the American 1890s*. Ed. Yoshinobu Hakutani. Toronto: Associated University Presses.

———. 1988a. *Journalism/Theodore Dreiser*. Ed. T. D. Nostwich. University of Pennsylvania Dreiser Editions. Philadelphia: University of Pennsylvania Press.

———. 1988b. *Theodore Dreiser's "Heard in the Corridors," Articles and Related Writing*. Ed. T. D. Nostwich. Ames: Iowa State University Press.

SECONDARY SOURCES

Fishkin, Shelley Fisher. 1985. *From Fact to Fiction: Journalism and Imaginative Writing in America*. New York: Johns Hopkins University Press.

Lingeman, Richard. 1986. *Theodore Dreiser: At the Gates of the City 1871–1907*. New York: G. P. Putnam's Sons.

Moers, Ellen. 1969. *Two Dreisers*. New York: Viking Press.

Pizer, Donald, ed. 1977. *Theodore Dreiser: A Selection of Uncollected Prose*. Detroit: Wayne State University Press.

Swanberg, W. A. 1965. *Dreiser*. New York: Charles Scribner's Sons.

JOHN REED

Robert E. Humphrey

When John Reed graduated from Harvard College in 1910, he harbored few definite plans beyond finding an opportunity to write poetry and fiction. After a walking tour of Europe, he rented third-floor rooms on Washington Square in Greenwich Village, an old section of New York City that was becoming the bohemian capital of America. He met other youthful insurgents who, rejecting the restraints of respectability, sought to create a haven of freedom, creativity, and adventure. Rebels against conventional society and its values, Villagers celebrated sexual freedom, avant-garde art, social justice, and political radicalism (Humphrey 1978).

Immersion of the swirling currents of Village life pulled Reed away from propriety and pushed him toward radicalism. He had enjoyed a privileged background: middle-class upbringing in Portland, Oregon, a preparatory education at Morristown Academy in New Jersey, and Harvard. But Reed and other rebels of his generation sensed that reality existed beyond the sheltered confines of middle-class culture, hence the urge to reside in the Village close to the poor and disreputable. Not academically oriented, Reed felt that experience provided the best education, and in the city he "saw that reality transcended all the fine poetic inventions of [academic] fastidiousness and medievalism" (Reed 1936, 334).

In the Village Lincoln Steffens, the "muckraking" journalist already famous for exposés of political corruption, became his mentor. Steffens brought to American journalism two beliefs that influenced Reed: development of an individual literary style when writing news stories and an admiration for social outcasts. Steffens also provided practical help, securing Reed a position as assistant editor for *American Magazine*.

In early 1913, Reed also became editor and contributor to *The Masses*, a lively new Village monthly filled with poetry, fiction, cartoons, illustrations, editorials, and news features written from a leftist perspective. For

Reed and other Villagers *The Masses* provided an outlet for works too radical for commercial publication. He wanted to write something that would "stir" the "emotions" of all men (1921, 209). Lacking any newspaper experience, Reed approached journalism as a writer eager to immerse himself in events and to recount his understanding of truth through description, character, dialogue, and personal observations. He was attracted to violent episodes that exemplified the struggle of ordinary men and women for freedom and justice.

Reed was first exposed to industrial strife during the Paterson, New Jersey, silk workers' strike in the spring of 1913. When Big Bill Haywood, leader of the militant Industrial Workers of the World, told Villagers that strikers were incarcerated simply for manning picket lines, Reed decided to visit Paterson and see for himself. He was promptly jailed for four days in Passaic County.

Reed wrote two accounts of his experiences in Paterson. The piece for *Metropolitan* magazine, "Sheriff Radcliff's Hotel," detailing fetid, filthy cells endured by "petty criminals" and "bums with the animal need for warmth and shelter," exposed a submerged existence that "respectable people" with the "churches, city halls, theaters, and automobiles" never encountered (1913b, 14). In portraying poor, luckless creatures ensnared in a heartless criminal system, he attempted to shame and move middle-class readers.

The second version in *The Masses*, "War in Paterson," a political narrative with himself in the action, centered on the strikers' struggle against the mill owners and the police. Reed openly identified with the underdog workers. There existed, he declared, a "war in Paterson" pitting poor immigrant workers against the police, the courts, the churches and the newspapers; in short, the "machinery" of society was mobilized against oppressed immigrants. Taking issue with other newspaper reports, he held the "Mill Owners" and "their servants, the police," responsible "for the violence" (1913a, 17).

Reed did not explicate the issues; he neither explained precipitating causes of the strike nor disclosed what the workers hoped to achieve. Instead he focused on what he witnessed: the setting, the combatants, and the suffering endured by the valiant immigrants. He skillfully recreated a dramatic incident of confrontation. "Six men," he wrote,

had taken shelter from the rain under the canopy of a saloon. "Come on! Get out of that!" yelled the . . . policemen advancing. The men quietly obeyed. "Get off this street! Go on home, now! Don't be standing here." They gave way before him in silence, drifting back again when he turned away. Other policemen materialized, hustling, cursing, brutal, ineffectual. No one answered back. Nervous, bleary-eyed, unshaven, these officers were worn out with nine weeks incessant strike duty. . . .

A little further along the street we saw a young woman with an umbrella, who had been picketing, suddenly confronted by a big policeman.

"What the hell are you doing here?" he roared. "God damn you, you go home!" and he jammed his club against her mouth.

"I no go home!" she shrilled passionately, with blazing eyes. "You big stiff!" (1913a, 17)

By recreating scenes and dialogue, Reed brought authenticity and immediacy to his reporting. He wanted to show how ordinary people faced adversity and participated in historical events. And yet, while he individualized the participants, either by quoting their remarks or describing their actions, he utilized them to illustrate the vicissitudes of larger events.

It was impossible for Reed to remain detached and ignore the disadvantaged and their cause. In this instance, he immediately took issue with two "cops," who "leaped up the steps, seized my arm, and violently jerked me to the sidewalk!" Arrested and placed in the overcrowded county jail, he was befriended by immigrant strikers. Little wonder he contrasted the "intelligent, cruel, merciless face of the police magistrate" with the brave Italians, Lithuanians, Poles, and Jews, who, though having endured "grinding routine in the sunless mills" and the "hopeless brutality" of the police, "glowed with hope and understanding." Reed admired Bill Haywood, whose "massive, rugged" face "radiated strength," but the real heroes were the immigrant workers, "gentle, alert, brave men ennobled by something greater than themselves." Having endured "twelve solid years of disappointments and incalculable suffering," they "must not," he avowed, "lose again" (1913a, 17).

Reed's partisan account, which disputed mainstream, antilabor newspaper coverage of the strike, was not simply propaganda. Although he perceived a binary world divided into the powerful few and the unempowered many, capitalists and proletariat, he was a humanist, not a political ideologue. His encounter with the strike in Paterson confirmed for him the stories he wished to cover firsthand, namely, violent struggles of the poor against political injustice. He found another opportunity for such reporting when the editor of *Metropolitan* magazine asked him to cover the Mexican civil war.

In February 1913, General Victoriano Huerta seized power from Francisco Madero, a moderate liberal, and used the Federalist army to establish a military regime. Almost immediately popular movements arose to defeat Huerta and restore constitutional government; the northern leaders were Venustiano Carranza, the elderly governor of Coahuila, and Pancho Villa, a former bandit. Carranza, a conservative landowner, was primarily interested in political reforms, while Villa wished to break up large haciendas and redistribute land to peasants and Indians who had been reduced to peonage.

American political leaders were concerned about the Mexican civil war because of its proximity to the southern border and because American capitalists, including newspaper magnate William Randolph Hearst, had substantial investments in Mexican land, mining, and railroads. Some Americans even urged the government to send troops into Mexico to protect these U.S. interests.

Reed was captivated by the daring exploits of Pancho Villa, who won brilliant victories at Juarez and Chihuahua City. In early December 1913, he crossed the border and for four months lived with various elements of the rebel Constitutional army, sending back written accounts of his adventures. Later these pieces were published as *Insurgent Mexico* (1914), a book that brought him considerable praise. Three years afterwards he recalled happily riding, "sleeping on the ground with the hombres, dancing and carousing in looted haciendas all night after an all-day ride." Being with them "intimately in play" and in battle "was perhaps the most satisfying period of my life" (1936, 336). A need to demonstrate his masculinity to himself and to others prompted Reed to plunge into dangerous situations where humble men and women endured hardship and death for noble causes. Rebelliousness inclined Reed to sympathize with the poor, those without middle-class comforts and inhibitions who suffered real deprivations. Consequently he wrote about those at the bottom of the social order. This radical posture placed him outside traditional journalism and elite sources of information.

Reed's ability to befriend the Mexican peons and rebel soldiers made his coverage unique. He interviewed and traveled with Pancho Villa, the "Mexican Robin Hood," an unpretentious but decisive leader who seemingly lacked political ambitions. Reed described gleefully how Villa accepted a medal presented to him by the artillery corps "for personal heroism on the field."

Villa put out both hands eagerly, like a child for a new toy. He could hardly wait to open the box and see what was inside.... Villa looked at the medal, scratching his head, and, in a reverent silence, said clearly: "This is a hell of a little thing to give a man for all that heroism you are talking about!" (1914a, 115–16)

Since Reed had only a fragmentary understanding of Spanish, he could not have reproduced Villa's comments (or any dialogue) with stenographic accuracy. Not bound by the traditional strictures of news reporting, he portrayed scenes, characters, dialogue, and incidents that conveyed his sense of truth.

Reed ignored the overall picture: the strategy of war, politics between rebel factions, U.S.-Mexican relations, or the problems besetting Mexico. Instead he focused on participants at a very personal level, building sympathy for the Mexican rebels. In so doing, of course, he invested his impressions with political implications; he hoped to persuade American readers and Wilson administration officials that Villa was far superior to Carranza.

He admitted that Villa executed captured Federal army officers, but pointed out that the rebel general freed "common soldiers" because "most were conscripts" who "thought they were fighting for their country." Reed emphasized Villa's human qualities, a desire for justice, a willingness to bear discomfort, and an easy relationship with his men:

Often I have seen him slouched in his cot in the little red caboose in which he always traveled, cracking jokes familiarly with twenty ragged privates sprawled on the floor, chairs and tables. When the army was entraining or detraining, Villa personally would be on hand in a dirty old suit, without a collar, kicking mules in the stomach and pushing horses in and out of the stock-cars. Getting thirsty all of a sudden, he would grab some soldier's canteen and drain it, in spite of the indignant protests of its owner, and then tell him to go over to the river and say that Pancho Villa said that he should fill it there. (1914a, 144–45)

Contrastingly, Reed told his readers that Carranza, who had "contributed nothing but congratulations" to the revolt, was surrounded by secretaries, officials, and cabinet members who kept probing correspondents at bay. Only after promising not to ask any questions was he finally ushered into Carranza's darkened room:

It was so dark within that at first we could see nothing. Over the two windows blinds were drawn. On one side was a bed, still unmade, and on the other a small table covered with papers, upon which stood a tray containing the remains of breakfast. A tin bucket full of ice with two or three bottles of wine stood in a corner. As our eyes became accustomed to the light, we saw the gigantic, khaki-clad figure of Don Venustiano Carranza sitting in a big chair. There was something strange in the way he sat there, with his hands on the arms of the chair, as if he had been placed in it and told not to move. He did not seem to be thinking, nor to have been working,—you couldn't imagine him at that table. You got the impression of a vast, inert body—a statue. (1914a, 144–45)

In juxtaposing these portraits, he intimated their contrasting capacity for leadership. For Reed personal qualities, not political policies, offered the surest indication of commitment and ability.

It was the radical point of view, namely, a sympathy for lowly Mexicans and an antipathy for Americans, that distinguished Reed from the typical correspondent. Whereas the "incredibly poor [but] lavishly hospitable" peons suffered and died for a better world, the American mercenaries enlisted merely for "excitement" and "loot." Reed hated these "hard, cold misfits" who "despised the cause for which they were fighting" while "sneering" at the "gaiety of the irresponsible Mexicans" (1914a, 160). The Americans contemptuously referred to Mexican women as "whores"; Reed found relaxed sexual encounters refreshingly liberating. His open acceptance of Mexican values and customs made him an exceptional journalist.

Reed did not pen a propagandistic celebration of Mexican peasants and the rebel cause, for he showed that selfish and materialistic as well as idealistic motives induced Mexicans to join the fight. Using dialogue of the participants, he humanized his story while building credibility. He recounted that one little, bald-headed soldier, a former school teacher, said that he did not expect to gain anything from the struggle: "No, it is not the trooper, the starved, unfed, common soldiers who profit from the Revolucion. Officers, yes—some—for they get fat on the blood of the Patria. But we—no." When Reed asked him why he was fighting, the soldier explained, "I have two little sons. And they will get their land." But fourteen-year-old Gil Tomas said laughingly: "I'm fighting so I can get a thirty-thirty rifle from some dead Federal, and a good horse that belonged to a millionaire."

Another peon confessed, "I fight because it is not so hard as to work [sic]." An apothecary, who had been elevated to a major and "doctor" in the rebel army, told Reed: "This Revolucion. Do not mistake [sic]. It is a fight of the poor against the rich. I was very poor before the Revolucion and now I am very rich." Reed's honesty in reporting these self-seeking motives did not deflate his own idealism about ordinary Mexicans. On the trail one night he encountered two impoverished peasants whose goats had been taken by soldiers, and yet they remained optimistic about the future. These "two human beings" were "symbolic of Mexico—courteous, loving, patient, poor, so long slaves, so full of dreams, so soon to be free" (1914a, 25, 37, 78–79, 170).

Reed became involved in two deadly battles. The first occurred at La Cadena, where Federalist cavalry overran Reed and a band of rebels. He barely escaped with his life. In telling the story he skillfully recreated the enormity of war:

A little running horse appeared on the rise, headed our way, the rider outlined in a radiant dust. He was going at furious speed, dipping and rising over the rolling land.... And as he spurred wildly up the little hill where we stood, we saw a horror. A fan-shaped cascade of blood poured from the front of him. The lower part of his mouth was quite shot away by a soft-nosed bullet. He reined up beside the colonel, and tried earnestly, terribly, to tell him something; but nothing intelligible issued from the ruin. Tears poured down the poor fellow's cheeks. He gave a hoarse cry, and, driving his spurs deep in his horse, fled up the Santo Domingo road. (1914a, 83)

Unlike correspondents who typically concerned themselves with military tactics, movement of regiments, and exploits of individual heroes, Reed conveyed an intimate sense of what battle conditions were like for ordinary peons, and he did so with the sensitivity and style of a writer. In the battle for Gomez Palacio, he was so close to the front lines that he was able to describe the scene and interview soldiers during the battle.

Up the track in the hot morning light straggled a river of wounded men, shattered, bleeding, bound up in rotting and bloody bandages, inconceivably weary. They passed us, and one even fell and lay motionless nearby in the dust—and we didn't care. . . . A little company of horsemen jogged out of the thicket and drew up on the track, looking toward town. One man got down from his saddle and squatted beside us.

"It was terrible," he said suddenly. "Carramba! We went in there last night on foot. They were inside the water-tank, with holes cut in the iron for rifles. We had to walk up and poke our guns through the holes and we killed them all—a death trap! . . . And then this morning thousands came—thousands came—reinforcements from Torreon—and their artillery—and they drove us back again. They walked up to the water-tank and poked their rifles through the holes and killed all of us—the sons of the devils!" (1914a, 214)

Having experienced the excitement of war and struggle, Reed could never again really adjust to conventional existence. After Mexico Reed became more critical of America and government policies. Adopting a socialist perspective, he rejected support for the Allied cause when war broke out in Europe in 1914. He viewed the war as simply a fight for commercial gain; none of the European powers, he thought, had right on its side. Unlike the Mexican war, Europeans were not fighting for idealistic goals, and that explained why there was "no enthusiasm" among ordinary citizens (1914b, 17).

Arriving in Paris soon after the outbreak of hostilities, Reed was dismayed to see Frenchmen being transported to "military centers," which crushed "all their impulses and ideas, and turned them into infinitesimal parts of an obedient machine to hurl against the youth of Germany, who had been treated the same way" (1914c, 14). When he traveled by train to Berlin and then to the German lines in France, he observed the same obedience to "that superior intelligence, the Government." Not bothering to interview high government and military officials, he wanted to know what ordinary soldiers faced. Contrary to the bloodthirsty images painted by Allied propaganda, he found German soldiers to be "big, jovial, childlike people" who took pride in the "gallant pageantry" of "royalties, uniforms, [and] decorations" (1915a, 13). But splendor vanished at the front. Trudging through trenches near Ypres, he discovered that men lived like moles in muck-filled dugouts. In describing horrible conditions at the front and in recreating conversations with German soldiers, he humanized the enemy. Using a visit to a field hospital where a general was handing out Iron Crosses to three wounded soldiers, Reed showed the tragic losses for those on the other side:

The next man was still too weak to speak.

"Shot through both lungs," went on the general, "while bringing food from the camp-kitchen to the men in the trenches." He laid the cross on the bedclothes.

The third man's skin looked like ivory, so tightly was it drawn over his wasted face. I noticed his great eyes fixed steadily on the general as he spoke—he had had one leg carried away by a shell and the other wounded. Gangrene had set in and both legs had been amputated at the thigh. He was a famous long-distance runner. The general dangled the Iron Cross before him, and he slowly reached out his hand for it and held it for a moment in front of his eyes, twisting it this way and that. Then, without a word, he deliberately held it out at arm's length and dropped it on the floor. (1915b, 8)

Reed used this poignant scene (real or fictive) to demonstrate the utter tragedy for men fighting in a meaningless war and to prove that some Germans also lacked fervor for this war.

When the French government banned Reed from the Western front, *Metropolitan* editor Carl Hovey suggested that he and illustrator Boardman Robinson cover the Eastern front. From April to October 1915, Reed traveled throughout Eastern Europe, reporting on those who endured filth, disease, stench, and unspeakable atrocities. He documented the mass killing of Serbian men, women, and children without fully understanding that nationalism had generated such barbarism. Otherwise he found little of interest to report because idealism was missing. So he became a wandering traveler, observing individuals and nationalities.

What struck him most vividly were the appalling conditions, both physical and psychological, endured by Jews trapped in Russia. He was both repelled by their habits and sensitive to their plight. In crowded, narrow, filthy streets full of "evil-smelling rubbish" and "clouds of bloated flies," he saw "cringing men with their 'sacred fringes' showing under their long coats," boys with "unhealthy faces," girls "prematurely aged with bitter work and eternal humiliation, grown women wrinkled and bent, in wigs and slovenly mother hubbards" (1916a, 170).

Reed used a discussion with an infantry officer to reveal the brutal, irrational logic of Russian anti-Semitism. The colonel told him, "You Americans do not understand what we have to endure from these people. The Jews are all traitors to Russia." Reed admitted that he was puzzled because the Jews in Austria and Germany were "entirely loyal." " 'That is different,' replied the colonel firmly. 'In Germany and Austria the Jews have civil rights; therefore naturally they are patriotic. In Russia, however, the Jews had no civil rights. So they betray us. So we kill them' " (1916a, 235).

By the time Reed returned to America in late 1915, his interest in the war had flagged. Since the European conflict lacked moral purpose, the idealist could only wait until the killing stopped. He argued in *The Masses*, the only journal in which he could express himself freely, that the country was "being scared into an 'heroic mood' by Wall Street," which wanted "a great army and navy to protect its foreign investments." Patriotic crusades, he maintained, were a hoax perpetrated by "imperialist bankers" and "predatory plutocrats" in order to launch the United States on a "gigantic adventure in World Imperialism" (1916b, 7). Even before an American declaration of war against the Central Powers, he accurately prophesied "an ugly mob-madness, crucifying the truth tellers, choking the artists, sidetracking reforms, revolution and the working of social forces" (1917a, 11).

After President Wilson asked for and received an American declaration of war in 1917, Reed renounced his previous support of the president. His sense of alienation deepened as America became convulsed by a patriotic frenzy. To recharge himself morally and artistically, he decided to go to Russia. He already perceived that the Council of Soviets, "the real revolutionary head of the new Russia," was growing "stronger hourly as the power of the awakened proletariat" broke through "the veneer of capitalism smeared thinly over the face of things." Brimming with optimism, he envisaged "a new human society on earth" (1917b, 35). Reed and his wife, Louise Bryant, arrived in Petrograd in September 1917. He wrote to Boardman Robinson: "We are in the middle of things, and believe me, it's thrilling. There is so much dramatic to write that I don't know where to begin. For color and terror and grandeur this makes Mexico look pale" (1917c). His luck in being present as the Bolshevik coup unfolded made Russia a stimulating assignment, for Reed wanted both to experience and to write about revolution. He called his reports, published in 1919, *Ten Days That Shook the World*, a title that proclaimed his sense of the revolt's earthshaking significance.

Because Reed sailed into the eye of the political storm, his writing became less personal. As he followed the machinations for power, he worked like a traditional journalist, attending meetings, copying down speeches, proclamations, and documents (though he spoke and understood very little Russian), and interviewing high-level leaders and a few citizens. He tried frantically, amid disorder and confusion, to record what he considered the most significant event since the French Revolution. He successfully caught the chaos and passion generated by the quest for power in Russia.

Reed's dream of a popular revolt and the creation of a utopian society were finally being realized, or so he imagined. Overwhelmed by the ferment and promise of the Bolshevik Revolution, Reed became a Communist without fully understanding the party's ideological and organizational principles. To him the Bolsheviks were patriots, like the Mexican rebels, ready to distribute land and ensure freedom for the Russian people. Subsequently, he dismissed all criticism of the Bolsheviks and ignored the authoritarian nature of the new government. Reed became an apologist of the regime and a political activist, thereby ending his career as a literary journalist.

Reed's itch to pursue, experience, and communicate violent political struggles made him an important witness to history. Because he eschewed techniques and perspectives of conventional journalism, Reed could offer a picture of history's underside. Unfortunately, neither his political stance nor his literary approach was adopted by American journalism.

PRIMARY SOURCES

Reed, John. 1913a, June. "War in Paterson." *The Masses.*

———. 1913b, Sept. "Sheriff Radcliff's Hotel." *Metropolitan.*

———. 1914a. *Insurgent Mexico.* New York: D. Appleton.

———. 1914b, Sept. "The Traders War." *The Masses.*

———. 1914c, Dec. "With the Allies." *Metropolitan.*

———. 1915a, Mar. "German France." *Metropolitan.*

———. 1915b, Apr. "In the German Trenches." *Metropolitan.*

———. 1916a. *The War in Eastern Europe.* New York: Scribner's.

———. 1916b, July. "At the Throat of the Republic." *The Masses.*

———. 1917a, Apr. "Whose War?" *The Masses.*

———. 1917b, July. "The Russian Peace." *The Masses.*

———. 1917c, Sept. 17. Reed to Boardman Robinson. Reed MSS., Houghton Library, Harvard University.

———. 1919. *Ten Days That Shook the World.* New York: Boni and Liveright.

———. 1921, Jan. Letter to Harriet Monroe. *Poetry*: 209.

———. 1936, Apr. 29. "Almost Thirty." *New Republic.*

SECONDARY SOURCE

Humphrey, Robert E. 1978. *Children of Fantasy: The First Rebels of Greenwich Village.* New York: John Wiley.

RING LARDNER

Donald R. Hettinga

If Ring Lardner were to hear Tom Wolfe's claim of his discovery in the 1960s of a new literary journalism, he might be tempted to reuse his famous line, "Shut up, he explained." He might, that is, if he were alive in 1973 to read Wolfe's claim (Wolfe 1973, 9). The fact that he was not would make such a retort all the more valid, for despite Wolfe's claims to the contrary, in the teens and twenties of this century, Lardner was writing a kind of literary journalism that looks suspiciously like New Journalism. In his journalistic pieces on sports and culture in America, Lardner employed the same strategies that he employed in his fiction, strategies Wolfe identifies as characteristic of the New Journalists: heavy reliance on authentic dialogue, use of reflector narrators, presentation of culturally symbolic details.

To be fair to Wolfe, I should note that he anticipates the question of whether the New Journalism is really new and recognizes that "the person who usually asks if the New Journalism is really new," as the contributors to this volume of essays do, "often supplies names of writers who he believes did it all years ago, decades ago, even centuries ago" (42). Wolfe's rejoinder to such querists is to assert that "upon inspection one finds that these writers usually fall into one of four categories: (1) those who were not writing nonfiction at all—as in the case of Defoe, and Addison and Steele in the 'Sir Roger de Coverley Papers'; (2) traditional essayists, doing very little reporting and using few if any of the techniques of the New Journalism—such as Murray Kempton, I. F. Stone, and James Baldwin, in the often cited case of *The Fire Next Time*; (3) autobiographers; (4) Literary Gentlemen with a Seat in the Grandstand" (42). Though elsewhere in his piece he mentions Lardner, Wolfe must have forgotten him here, for upon inspection of his work in magazines and newspapers, one finds that Lardner is writing nonfiction, that he is not a traditional essayist, that he is not simply an autobiographer, and, most certainly, that he is not a literary gentleman with a seat in the grandstand.

My point is not so much to quibble with Wolfe as it is to turn to him for his useful catalogue of the narrative strategies of the New Journalists and to use that catalogue to open up the journalism of a man who in the mid-1920s was one of the best-known writers in the United States but who now is relatively unknown. Although Lardner has perhaps been overlooked because he gets reductively categorized as a humorist or as a sports writer, he bears our attention because as a journalist he does what Norman Sims suggests that the best literary journalists do: "Reporting on the lives of people at work, in love, going about the normal rounds of life, they confirm that the crucial moments of everyday life contain great drama and substance" (1984, 3). Lardner's ability to use the kind of literary techniques that Wolfe terms New Journalistic earned him high praise from his own generation. T. S. Matthews, for example, is typical if a bit extravagant in grouping Lardner with Chekhov and Shakespeare, "for Lardner, like Shakespeare and Chekhov, has owed his literary existence (and has repaid it by writing for them) to the common people of his day, the people who have been talking prose all their lives, and will never know it" (Elder 1956, 315).

Most noticeable to his contemporaries was Lardner's ability to record the dialects of ordinary Americans. In fact, H. L. Mencken, writing in *The American Language*, regularly refers to Lardner as a kind of standard source of common American speech. According to Mencken, "in his grotesque but searching tales of baseball-players, pugilists, movie queens, song writers and other such dismal persons," Lardner "set down common American with the utmost precision (1936, 424). He notes, moreover, that one attempt by a grammarian to provide a comprehensive grammar of the United States drew not on a field study of speakers of American English, but upon materials found "in the pages of that incomparable reporter, Ring Lardner" (333).

Lardner uses dialogue as the literary journalists of the sixties and seventies do—to show readers scenes that they would otherwise be unable to see. In "Some Champions," for example, by having us follow as he stumbles into a hotel room, he allows us to overhear some off-the-field conversation of major baseball figures talking about that year's World Series and about baseball in general:

"We were wondering," explained Bill, "what Honus, here, would have done to that ball they played with today."

"He couldn't have hit it much farther than he hit the old one," I said, waving myself to a seat on the floor.

"You're right, boy," said the big Dutchman approvingly.

"Where do you get that 'boy'?" said Dan. "This guy was in the Central League with me in 1906, scoring an error against the third baseman if I hit the right-field fence on the fly."

"In South Bend?" said Chick. "I pitched an exhibition game there in 1906. They didn't have fences."

"Not after you got through pitching," said Dan. (1976, 14)

The point Lardner is making here is the same one that he made elsewhere more sarcastically:

The master minds that controls baseball says to themselfs that if it is home runs that the public wants to see, why leave us give them home runs, so they fixed up a ball that if you don't miss it entirely it will clear the fence, and the result is that ball players which use to specialize in hump back liners to the pitcher is now amongst our leading sluggers. (Elder 1956, 170)

These conversational exchanges, however, presented as they are without narrative editorializing, work more effectively than the direct satirical statement that tells readers what to think. The dialogue characterizes these ball players, showing us their wit and spirit of camaraderie, even while it critiques changes in the game, like the new, more dynamic baseball.

In his "Wake" column in the *Chicago Tribune*, Lardner regularly used dialogue to report on life in the bleachers, covering an aspect of the game that did not otherwise get reported. Here, for example, he incorporates dialogue into his piece on the Cubs and the Phillies to satirize the fans. He opens the article by stating that he "had long wondered what manner of manager and man this Evers was" and that he "learned in the sixth, after Bob Emslie had canned the Trojan for kicking at a decision at second base." Lardner then airs the fans' interpretation of these events:

"That's right, Bob. Send the crab to the clubhouse. It'll strengthen the team."

"Robber! Robber! If you can't beat us fair, you'll do it by puttin' our best man out of the game."

"Best man, eh? If he's the best man, it's a heluva team."

"It'd been a heluva team if he wasn't manager. You'll notice he's got 'em up there fightin'."

"Yes, and when there's a chance to win he breaks up the team by gettin' put out."

"Accordin' to your dope, the team's better when he's out. You got your wires crossed."

"Oh, go on and get your hat cleaned." (Elder 1956, 99–100)

After this dialogue, Lardner does not need to offer further comment on the behavior of the manager or the correctness of the umpire's call; the churlish conversation of the fans has shown his point of view.

But of even greater note than his use of dialogue is Lardner's strategy of employing personas to reflect the minds of characters on which he was

reporting. In this he was behaving as chameleon-like as Wolfe, who acknowledges that "sometimes I used point-of-view in the Jamesian sense in
which fiction writers understand it, entering directly into the mind of a
character, experiencing the world through his central nervous system
throughout a given scene" (Wolfe 1973, 19). While at least one critic sees
the dialect of Lardner's personas as a definable idiom (Webb 1960, 482),
it is not quite that, for he writes under the guise of several different identities,
and the idiolect of each speaker is distinct. Though each shares the distinction of being a shade or two off from standard English, the athlete speaks
differently from the average American, the average American speaks differently from the working woman.

Lardner became famous for the "busher" language he developed fully in
the *Saturday Evening Post* pieces that later became *You Know Me Al* (1916),
but a prototype of that idiolect appeared earlier when he adopted the persona
of an "unassisted athlete" to report a baseball game in his column in the
Chicago Tribune. The slang-speaking athlete drops a few final consonants
in his self-righteousness, but otherwise he avoids the malapropisms that
other of Lardner's personas would fall into:

We ought to of trimmed 'em. When Egan, the big shot, said I was out at second he
musta been full o' hops, the big boob. I like t' known where he was at las' night,
the big bum. Some o' them umps oughta be on the chain gang, the big boobs. . . .
    Wisht Mac had let me wallop when I had the big Indian three and nothin' that
time. 'Member? Merkle was on third base. I looked 'round and Mac gives me the
sign to take one. That's rotten baseball. I think. I took one that I could hit out o'
the park. Then the big Indian hooks one on me and I missed. Then I'm lookin' for
another hook and he comes with a fast one. And the Catfish calls me out. If I'd
known he was goin' to call it on me, I'd a hit that one out o' the park. The big
rum. (Elder 1956, 98)

The repetition of the name-calling quickly establishes the character of this
ball player as the type "who hates umpires, blames everyone else for his
mistakes, and maintains a constant bad humor" (Elder, 99). The persona's
self-righteousness and bad humor undercut his own credibility, and the
readers are left with Lardner's report that the umpires and managers performed well but that the players left something to be desired.

Lardner speaks in a slightly different voice when writing as what several
critics term "the wise boob," an average American " 'bright guy, usually
in the know or thinking that he is,' holder of 'a good opinion of himself'
and quite willing to let others share it" (Patrick 1963, 28). If he lacks the
self-righteousness of the athlete, this character does not lack in confidence,
particularly confidence in his own wit and perceptions. Lardner combines
this naive confidence with malapropisms and grammatical errors to render
the persona's assertions ironic. For example, readers can immediately see
the difference between Lardner and the persona when in a piece on education

in *Some Champions* he asserts that "from 12 to 17 or 18 ain't no time to waste on books," and that he knew because he "was one these smart Alex that graduates from high school at 16" (1976, 4). This speaker is in the know about schools, and he successfully directs his wit at the foibles of the systems, as when he wryly quips that he does not know how it is these days, "but in those times practically all the teachers in high schools was members of the fair sex. Some of them was charter members" (6). While readers are still chuckling, Lardner turns the wit to satire, for this persona's academic prowess is due to the deafness and incompetence of these "charter members." The persona's language undercuts his pride in subverting the system.

These various voices, these idiolects, allow Lardner to do what Wolfe proudly notes he was accused of doing as he reported on the manners and morals—"entering people's minds," using interior monologue. Lardner, like Wolfe, apparently "figured that was one more doorbell a reporter had to push" (Wolfe and Johnson 1973, 21). One of the more interesting doorbells that Lardner pushes is that of Clara Meyers, a working woman who, as she reveals her "innermost thoughts," reveals a lot about a new American woman who was to inhabit the twenties:

I believe that's [her conversational ability] what gives me the advantage over other girls because some girls seems to think that because they're pretty they don't have to say nothing but I don't rest on my looks but it's the combination of my looks and the things that I say that gives me the advantage and Joe Klein that's the staff lyric writer down to the office says they ain't nothing freshs him up so after he's wrote a song and is all fagged out mently as looking at me and listening to me talk. (Elder 1956, 152)

Here again, the voice undercuts the content; in this syntax, Clara's very claims of depth characterizes her as shallow.

Lardner reportedly once denied being a satirist by saying, "I just listen" (Webb 1960, 482). The cadences of his personas testify to the accuracy of his ear; in part, these voices are recording what Wolfe terms "status details," the behaviors "through which people express their position in the world" (Wolfe 1973, 32). But Lardner also had an eye for the potential of symbolic possessions, that dimension of status details in which Wolfe has a particular interest. His "average American" persona, for example, conveys a conventional middle-class perspective on the notion of purchasing a fur coat for his spouse:

In the first place I am not a sucker enough to invest hundreds and hundreds of dollars in a garment which the chances are that the Mrs. will not wear it more than a couple of times all winter as the way it looks we are libel to have the most openest winter in history. (Elder 1956, 173)

Implicit in this rationalization is both the spouse's desire for an upper-class status symbol and the speaker's penuriousness. But Lardner's eye encompasses the nouveau riche as well as the average American. In a profile in the *New Yorker* he captures the type:

Mrs. Kaufman is the perfect hostess. If a guest expresses a taste for Kirman rugs, the next time he enters her apartment he will trip over one of them. If he raves about Gobelin tapestries, Mrs. Kaufman will have some hung in a conspicuous spot on the occasion of his second visit. If he is crazy about Rembrandts, the walls will be reeking with them when he comes again. This, I should say, is the ne plus ultra of hospitality, and not so expensive as one might suppose, since very few people visit the place twice. (1928, 16)

Because of his eye for the status implications of material objects, Lardner can equate the specific styles of rugs and tapestries with the works of a master, thus indicting his nouveau riche subject for her insecure conspicuous consumption.

Here, as throughout his journalism, Lardner employs literary strategies to report critically on culture and manners. In the jargon of literary criticism, we could note that "Lardner, through his own texts, instructs the reader in the shortcomings of his culture's behavioral and conception codes" (Gilead 1985, 332). In the plainer language of H. L. Mencken, we could note that Lardner "delighted in his creatures as comedians . . . but was filled with a vast contempt for them as men. One could almost discern a moral purpose in him" (1926, 255). Without the dialogue, without the personas, without the status details, that moral purpose would not have been nearly as clear, the prose would not have been nearly as effective. We could note that for all its literary attributes, Lardner's journalism still is not New Journalism, but if we did, we should be ready to hear, "Shut up, he explained."

PRIMARY SOURCES

Lardner, Ring. 1928, July 7. "Dante and ———." *New Yorker* 4: 16–17.
———. 1976. *Some Champions: Sketches and Fiction.* Ed. Matthew J. Bruccoli and Richard Lyman. New York: Scribner.

SECONDARY SOURCES

Elder, Donald. 1956. *Ring Lardner: A Biography.* Garden City, N.Y.: Doubleday.
Gilead, Sarah. 1985. "Lardner's Discourses of Power." *Studies in Short Fiction* 22: 331–37.
Mencken, H. L. 1926, June. "A Humorist Shows His Teeth." *American Mercury*: 254–55.
———. 1936. *The American Language.* 4th ed. New York: Knopf.
Patrick, Walton R. 1963. *Ring Lardner.* New York: Twayne.
Sims, Norman, ed. 1984. *The Literary Journalists.* New York: Ballantine.

Webb, Howard, Jr. 1960. "The Development of a Style: The Lardner Idiom." *American Quarterly* 12: 482–92.
Wolfe, Tom. 1973. *The New Journalism*. With an Anthology edited by Tom Wolfe and E. W. Johnson. New York: Harper and Row.

DAMON RUNYON

John J. Pauly

Today the continuing achievements of the *New Yorker* and the triumphs of the New Journalism symbolize the modern tradition of literary journalism. Magazine writers predominate in that tradition, for they have proved more willing than newspaper writers to cross the fact-fiction border—to employ literary technique in the service of journalism, and reporting in the service of literature. Newspapers did not always shun or ignore literary journalism, however. The career of Damon Runyon reminds us that not so long ago journalists consciously employed literary techniques in their news work. Runyon remained—by preference—a newspaper man till his death, despite his profitable forays into magazine fiction and screenwriting. He was perhaps the best-known and most widely read news columnist and reporter in America from the 1920s to the 1940s. From first to last he found the newspaper a congenial home for his work.

Runyon has become so identified with Broadway that one easily forgets that he was born in Manhattan, Kansas, and grew up in Colorado. The son of an itinerant printer, Runyon entered newspaper life by age twelve, became a full-fledged alcoholic by fifteen, fought in the Spanish-American War, rode the rails after his discharge, then returned to Colorado and gained notice as a reporter for the *Rocky Mountain News*. Financial and literary ambition drove him to New York City in 1911 and shortly thereafter convinced him to abstain from alcohol for the rest of his life. Through all the long nights at Lindy's, Runyon would chain smoke, drink cup after cup of coffee, and listen to the talk.

Runyon never made it past the sixth grade, but he was an enthusiastic autodidact throughout his life. In a column entitled "The Discriminating Thief," Runyon attributed his success to his willingness to steal material from history's best writers: "I steal from everybody and as bold as brass." He offered a long catalogue of his "intellectual larceny":

Sometimes I wonder if youse appreciate me. I steal from Plato, Socrates, Woodrow Wilson, Shakespeare, Montaigne, Mr. Dooley, Euripides, Nat Fleischer's All-Time Ring Record, Lincoln's speeches, Ingersoll's lectures, LaGuardia's readings of the comic strips, Caesar (Irving and Arthur and Julius), Butler (Nick, Sam, Ben and Bill), Dickens, Cato, Thoreau, Emerson and Whitman.

I steal from Dante, Goethe, Aesop, Confucius, Karl Marx, Yussel Stalin, Conrad, James G. Blaine, Demosthenes, Sheridan (Dick and Phil), Disraeli, Nick the Greek, Joe Louis, Bob Fitzsimmons, Hans Christian Anderson, Grimm, L. B. Mayer, Henry Mencken, Good Time Charley, George Jean Nathan, George Washington, Grover Cleveland, Clay, Calhoun, Talleyrand, Thomas Paine and Jim Farley (1946, 45–46)

That passage, like so many in Runyon's work, subtly blends self-effacement with braggadocio. But even if one discounts his claims, there is reason to suspect that Runyon was smarter than he let on. He certainly possessed the general knowledge that newspaper journalists readily acquire. He had traveled widely—in the Army, on the rails, for assignments—and he remained till the end an inveterate conversationalist. (After he lost his larynx to cancer, Runyon simply passed handwritten notes to his companions.) Yet there was something more. Those who knew him have testified to the range of his knowledge. The sportswriter Jimmy Cannon wrote that "one of the odd things about Damon was that he was a very cultured man" (quoted in Introduction to Runyon 1986, 23). Biographer Edwin P. Hoyt said that Runyon often surprised his Hollywood friends with his knowledge of European culture. "Damon went to Romanoff's nearly every night, where he and the Prince astounded some of the Hollywoodians from the Ozarks by discussing Kafka, Spengler, Hermann Hesse, and the art museums of Europe" (1964, 280).

Although Runyon came to be known as America's greatest sportswriter, he also covered some of the biggest news stories of his era. He wrote about "Blackjack" Pershing's expedition to Mexico in search of Pancho Villa; the First Army campaigns during World War I; the Black Sox scandal; the Johnson-Willard, Dempsey-Willard, and Tunney-Dempsey fights; the Hall-Mills murder, Al Capone tax evasion, and Lindbergh baby kidnapping trials; the 1933 Senate investigation of the House of Morgan; and the four inaugurals of Franklin Delano Roosevelt. Though hospitalized in the final stages of his cancer, Runyon insisted upon traveling to Washington to cover FDR's funeral.

Runyon often used feature writing techniques even when covering regular news stories. When the Senate investigation of J. Pierpont Morgan opened, he began with a bit of verse:

Morgan, the mighty, is on the spot!
We wait, anxiously, for the earth to rock.
Nothing happens, except a slight tremor of excitement, as the world gets up on tiptoe to look and listen.

It turns out to be an income tax inquiry, something like Al Capone's or any of the other boys.

Morgan, the mighty, one of the richest men on the face of the globe, pays no income tax in 1931 or 1932. He does not remember about 1930.

His twenty partners in the J. Pierpont Morgan firm, many of them supposed to be very wealthy, pay an aggregated income tax of $48,000 in 1930, and none whatever in 1931 or 1932. That's all of them, understand. Losses, you know, losses, losses, losses. (1947, 252)

Some reporters still write in such a fashion, though rarely in a straight news story. Compared to the clotted prose found in today's newspaper, Runyon's writing was remarkably clear, concise, and witty.

Runyon also found opportunities for literary journalism in his columns, which appeared under titles such as "The Mornin's Mornin'," "This Sporting Life," "Says Damon Runyon," "The Brighter Side," and "My Old Home Town." Runyon was only one of an impressive stable of column writers employed by New York newspapers in the 1920s and 1930s. His contemporaries included Don Marquis, Heywood Broun, Walter Lippmann, O. O. McIntyre, Arthur Brisbane, Mark Hellinger, Franklin P. Adams, Westbrook Pegler, and Runyon's good friend Walter Winchell. Each newspaper heavily advertised its best columnists in order to attract readers in the competitive New York market. William Randolph Hearst further promoted Runyon's column as part of his national syndication service.

Through his syndicated columns, and later his magazine stories, Runyon made Broadway a national state of mind. Indeed, one biographer has aptly called Runyon and Winchell "the men who invented Broadway." That street would provide Runyon with events and characters for his journalism and fiction alike. For example, the fictional story "A Piece of Pie" recounts an epic eating contest much like the ones in which Runyon himself had taken part (1989, 203–18). In a 1920 story from the Yankees' training camp, "Ruth and Irwin Cobb Top-Heavy Choices in Feed Stakes," Runyon told of just such a contest pitting sportswriters against ballplayers (*New York American*, 5 Mar. 1920). The story "The Brain Goes Home" offers a fictionalized account of an actual event—the murder of gambler Arnold Rothstein—that Runyon had covered as a reporter (1989, 85–96).

Runyon's characters step off the street and into news or fiction, as the occasion demands. As critics have noted, Runyon's fictional characters often had real-life equivalents: Waldo Winchester was inspired by Walter Winchell, Miss Missouri Martin by Tex Guinan, "The Brain" by Arnold Rothstein, Regret by Abba Dabba Berman, "Bookie Bob" by Billy Warren, Angie the Ox by Ciro Terranova, and so forth (1986, 18–19). In a more general way Runyon's work chronicled the habitués of the new nightclubs and restaurants. Runyon's obituary of the waiter Harry Tibbetts describes the regulars at Jack Dunstan's all-night restaurant and might also serve as a catalogue of the characters in his own stories: "Actors and actresses, rich brokers, polo players, song writers, newspaperman, authors, artists, pamphleteers, poets, prize fighters, ball players, promoters, 'grifters,' hotel keepers, jockeys, billiard players, horse owners, chorus girls, gunmen, gamblers" (quoted in Mosedale 1981, 131).

Runyon would have remained an ordinary writer had he merely borrowed characters and plots from New York nightlife. But along Broadway he glimpsed something more: a dark vision of public hypocrisy. Jean Wagner has argued that Runyon's stories systematically transvalue American morals by discovering humane sentiments and honor among the low and reprehensible, and cruelty and corruption among the well-born and upright (Wagner 1965, 52–53). Though at times Wagner may overstate his case, he at least acknowledges the seriousness of Runyon's purpose and method. A writer in the 1920s might have chosen any number of events, from World War I to the 1919 World Series to the Teapot Dome scandal, to symbolize the disenchantment of that era. Runyon, the former alcoholic, chose Prohibition. As others have observed, speakeasies blurred the boundaries of proper behavior, because all the patrons of speakeasies were law-breakers regardless of their social standing. And it was Prohibition that encouraged the modern forms of organized crime and made gangsters a new corporate plutocracy, at once celebrated and excoriated.

Runyon's work as a reporter undoubtedly fed his cynicism. Larzer Ziff has identified a similar mood in the reporters of the 1890s. Those reporters developed twin defenses of cynicism and sentimentality, Ziff argues, because they could not fully report upon the corruption and inequity that they witnessed each day. "[Cynicism] kept [the reporter] from allowing his sentimentality to make him vulnerable; [sentimentality] kept him from allowing his cynicism to cut him off from the human interest that was his stock in trade."[1] Although Runyon erected those same defenses, the 1920s presented new problems for reporters. The simultaneous expansion of newspapers, movies, radio, and magazines as consumer media encouraged new types of media events, directed by a steadily enlarging army of public relations consultants. The trade show, Congressional investigation, Broadway opening, Hollywood premiere, championship prize fight, World Series, murder trial, and gangster funeral now fell on the reporter's beat.

Runyon covered all such events with a cynical wink. He developed literary techniques that deflated the presumptions of the powerful and righteous and afforded him ironic distance from the proceedings. Sometimes Runyon expressed his cynicism by parodying the publicist and his clichés. In a 1916 feature story about the annual New York automobile show, Runyon described the show's publicist as the "publicity accelerator of the show," a man who "flutters excitedly from twig to twig, chirping a gruesome song" (New York American, 1 Jan. 1916). In a column titled "About Bosh," Runyon responded to drama critic George Jean Nathan's claim that more "bosh" was written about actors than about any other subject. Runyon replied that the clichés employed by boxing promoters and sportswriters surely rivaled those applied to actors:

Q. Have you ever read, Mr. Nathan, of the Prize Fighter who

(a) Is a gentlemanly Little Fellow that you might take for a young broker rather than a Prize Fighter, out of the ring, barring his Tin Ear?

(b) Bought his Maw a home with his Very First Earnings?

(c) Always keeps himself in the Best of Condition?

(d) Never tasted Licker?

(e) Never smoked or chawed? (*New York American*, 5 Mar. 1920)

That passage suggests how fully Runyon understood the role clichés played in the work of a reporter. Runyon deliberately mimics the style of George Ade's *Fables in Slang*, capitalizing the clichés, just as Ade had, in order to register his own distance from the pseudo-events he was asked to cover.

Runyon's much-remarked use of a first-person narrator in his fiction grew directly from his earlier experiments as a newspaper columnist. He essentially translated the personal voice of the columnist into a point of view for his fiction. Runyon's narrator in the Broadway stories obeys the conventions of news reporting, writing only about what he has observed or what someone else has told him. When action occurs out of his view, Runyon's narrator simply presents a whole segment of the story as "told to me by ———." That technique, of course, basically imitates the journalist's habit of quoting sources.

First-person point of view also offered another advantage to Runyon: it let him capitalize on his fame as a syndicated columnist. Runyon's narrative voice in the short stories blurs the distinction between Runyon the columnist and Runyon the fiction writer. Much of the audience, after all, had read his columns on Broadway nightlife for years before his short stories began appearing in *Collier's* and *Cosmopolitan* around 1930.[2] Though we cannot entirely equate Runyon with the narrator in the Broadway stories, many in the audience probably connected the two. And those who knew Runyon personally noticed similarities between the narrator and the writer.

Besides borrowing characters and events for his Broadway stories, Runyon adapted a style of expression that he had been developing for years in his journalism. That style came to be known as "Runyonese," and the characters who spoke that way as "Runyonesque." As John Rees has argued, Runyon's style did not entirely originate in New York City. Forms of it appear in the stories of western writers such as Bret Harte and Alfred Henry Lewis, particularly the latter's 1912 collection *The Apaches of New York* (1968, 77). Rees concludes that Runyon is the last of a dying breed of "local colorists" in American fiction—a description meant to denigrate rather than flatter Runyon's abilities. More severe critics have argued that Runyon's style amounted to little more than a heavy reliance on slang in order to simulate a streetwise realism. The most literal-minded have insisted that Broadway people did not really talk in Runyonese. Such criticisms serve mostly to keep Runyon in his place and to deny that his immense popularity necessarily signaled literary worth.

What such criticism generally misses is how fully Runyon's journalistic experience shaped his fiction. Runyon's slang was no mere coloration added to enliven an otherwise formulaic plot, but simply one element in a detailed re-creation of a whole way of life. David Maurer, a longtime student of subcultural argot, has written that while doing his own research he often saw Runyon checking his manuscripts with underworld characters (Wagner 1965, 86). Critics who treat the Broadway stories as a form of slang forget that, however striking individual terms may have seemed to the audience, they always constituted a relatively small part of a Runyon story. Runyon, in fact, gave the general interest magazines just what they wanted: stories that simulated the feel of Broadway through highly stylized speech, but never engaged in graphic violence or overly arcane forms of underworld jargon. Runyon satisfied readers' expectations by playing himself in his stories and by borrowing characters, places, and events from the headlines. Runyon also did his homework. Wagner has noted that he filled the Broadway stories with technical details about crime that only an insider could know (for instance, how to tie up and bag a kidnap victim so that when the victim awakens he will instinctively move in such a way that he strangles himself) (Wagner 1965, 51–52).

The convergence of publishers' demands, audience expectations, and Runyon's journalistic habits is also apparent in his use of "historic present tense." Runyon's Broadway characters incessantly employ present tense verbs, even when describing past events. A typical example of this technique can be found in the story "Tobias the Terrible": " 'Why,' Joey Uptown says, 'I never hear of a greater outrage in my life, although,' he says, 'I can see there is some puppy in you at that, when you do not return this Trivett's punch' " (1989, 49). Somehow such passages give the impression of a less-educated speaker trying to speak in an amusingly formal way (perhaps as he might respond to a reporter's questions). The technique, while generally entertaining, does not always work, especially for female characters. In the same story, Tobias's sweetheart Deborah sounds awkward when she speaks in present tense:

"Toby, darling," she says, "it is nobody but Deborah who loves you dearly, and who always knows you will turn out to be the greatest gunman of them all. Look at me, Toby," she says, "and tell me you love me, too. We never realize what a hero you are until we get the New York papers in Erasmus last night, and I hurry to you as quickly as possible."

Present tense works in Runyon's stories as a style of men's talk, such as one might hear in a speakeasy or locker room. Although that style made women's speech sound merely awkward (he did not care much for women's company, anyway), it improved the efficiency of his art. Like other journalistic techniques, present tense enhanced speedy, simple writing.

In his columns Runyon had often created fictitious narrators who anticipate his Broadway characters. A 1916 column purported to give the text of a speech by Kid Botts, "Brooklyn's Rugged Lightweight, World's Challenger at 140 Pounds," on "How to Have Muskels Like Mine," delivered at a smoker of the "Boys' Gawanus Athletic Union." Botts explains, "I got them by exercise, which is very healthy, and would do people good if they done them right along." One would only need to change *got* to *done* to *do*, to hear a voice very like those in the Broadway stories. Or consider the political observations of one "Amos Mugg," who occasionally filled in for Damon Runyon: "One thing about William Jennings Bryan, he will never pull any such boner as this Charles E. Hughes pulls on election night when he goes off to the hay thinking he is elected President, because any time William Jennings Bryan goes to the hay on election night he knows dam well he is not elected, which is where the old experience comes in" (*New York American*, 2 Mar. 1920). Long before Runyon turned his attention from sports to Broadway in the mid-1920s, he was developing the styles of speech and characterization that later made him famous as a short story writer.

Critics who dismiss Runyon's stories as sentimental miss their dark side. One can certainly find maudlin moments in Runyon's stories. When he strives too hard for effect, Runyon sometimes falls short. His much-admired report on FDR's funeral, for example, contains some moving description but also more than its share of mawkish dialogue. Running all through Runyon's work, however, is an unredeemed if unspoken strain of violence, corruption, and suspicion. By the late 1920s there is not much left to block his slide into cynicism, and nothing or no one escapes his sarcasm. In the story " 'Daddy' and 'Peaches,' " an account of Edward W. "Daddy" Browning's attempt to get a court decree of separation from Frances Heenan "Peaches" Browning, his child bride, Runyon refers to Browning as "that gallus old codger" and notes that "when it comes to the dolls, old Daddy Browning seems to be of the genus sap" (1947, 97). He describes "Peaches" as a "buxom matron of sixteen summers and 160 pounds" (117).

Nor does Runyon spare the audience. He notes that nearly a hundred reporters had attended the trial, and that "the populace expects to hear more or less 'dirt.' It would be a terrible blow to the nation if this should turn out to be a dull narration of conjugal incompatibility without any paprika in it" (97). On the second day of the case Runyon wrote, "I regret to report that the opening scene of the great moral opus, entitled 'The Saps of 1927,' and featuring the inimitable Daddy and Peaches Browning, fell a little flat today" (101). He describes the courtroom as "jammed with men and women and young girls, with their ears distended, and a street packed with people almost rioting in their desire to get a peep at the principals in a duel of defamation" (107).

After the case had ended, another New York newspaper published an editorial condemning the sensational publicity given the case. Runyon responded:

It is a good editorial, at that, well written, and timely, and it appears on a page hard by one carrying advertisements of some highly moral and uplifting plays now running on Broadway, and dealing with such interesting topics as miscegenation, male and female perversion, divorce, seduction, Negro honky-tonks, night life dead-falls, larceny, assault and battery, bootlegging, burglary, forgery, murder, and perhaps some lesser peccadilloes of this great human race. (134–35)

Beyond mocking the editorial's self-righteous tone, Runyon was revealing a deeper purpose in his coverage. He observed that the real problem was not the newspapers but New York law, which forbade desertion or incompatibility as grounds for separation, and thus forced couples to justify their separation in an open court hearing. Read in this context, Runyon's stories about "Daddy" and "Peaches" constituted a thoroughgoing satire—of separation hearings as media events, or reporters as panderers, of the government as moral hypocrite, of the audience as a prurient mob.

It is a truism of journalism history that the Civil War ended the Age of the Editor and began the Age of the Reporter. What we sometimes forget is that the late nineteenth century drove newspapers in two somewhat opposite directions. One path led journalism toward the ethereal goal of objectivity and reduced reporting to a bureaucratic function within the new system of economic and political administration. The other path led into the streets and plunged the reporter into the myriad forms of city life. The contemporary newspaper plods along that first wide, flat, and dusty path. The beauty of Damon Runyon's work is that it leads us back to the second path. And along the way we begin to understand what journalism has lost in its rush for certainty.

NOTES

1. Larzer Ziff, *The American 1890s* (New York: Viking, 1966), 152.
2. Publishers reportedly found that an issue containing a Runyon story could increase sales by up to 60,000 copies (Weiner 1948, 170).

PRIMARY SOURCES

Runyon, Damon. 1946. *Short Takes*. New York: McGraw-Hill.
———. 1947. *Trials and Other Tribulations*. Philadelphia: J. B. Lippincott.

————. 1954. *Runyon from First to Last*. London: Constable.

————. 1986. *Romance in the Roaring Forties and Other Stories*. New York: Beech Tree Books.

————. 1989. *Dream Street*. London: Folio Society.

SECONDARY SOURCES

D'Itri, Patrice Ward. 1982. *Damon Runyon*. Boston: Twayne.

Hoyt, Edwin P. 1964. *A Gentleman of Broadway*. Boston: Little, Brown.

Mosedale, John. 1981. *The Men Who Invented Broadway*. New York: Richard Marek.

Rees, John O. 1968. "The Last Local Colorist: Damon Runyon." *Kansas Magazine*: 73–81.

Wagner, Jean. 1965. *Runyonese*. Paris: Stechert-Hafner.

Weiner, Ed. 1948. *The Damon Runyon Story*. New York: Longmans, Green.

DOROTHY DAY

Nancy Roberts

Many know Dorothy Day (1897–1980) as the co-founder of the lay Catholic Worker movement, with its scores of soup kitchens and shelters for the homeless. But Day was also a writer. Essayist, novelist, nonfiction book author, she was, most of all, an advocacy journalist. For nearly fifty years (1933–1980) Day edited the *Catholic Worker* in New York City, hewing it to her movement's vision of social justice and peace.

Before her conversion to Roman Catholicism in 1927, Day served her apprenticeship as a secular radical journalist at the socialist *Call*, Max Eastman's *Masses*, and the *Liberator*. To Day, as to so many of her contemporaries, including Meridel LeSueur, Mary Heaton Vorse, and Agnes Smedley, journalism represented one of the few socially acceptable ways for women in radical movements to function as activists. Day viewed journalism as a catalyst for social change, believing that the journalist could employ the printed word "to move the heart, stir the will to action, to arouse pity, compassion, to awaken the conscience" (Day 1948, 145). And she never forgot the lesson she learned at *The Masses*. In a day when many of her Wobbly, socialist, and communist journalist colleagues wrote rather utilitarian prose, fearing that too much color and style might undercut the seriousness of their messages, Day and the staff of *The Masses* knew that writers who wished to win radical ideas a hearing must present them as compellingly as possible. Neither style *nor* substance could be neglected.

Day sensed that the most interesting way to get across her ideas about peace, poverty, and social justice was to use the fiction writer's techniques. Fiction was not unfamiliar to her. She had written one novel, *The Eleventh Virgin*, before making a final commitment to social activism and advocacy journalism. Her earliest journalistic work shows mastery of a variety of fiction techniques, including description and scene-setting, the juxtaposition of contrasting images, and characterization, to a degree not usually found in journalism. Consider "A Coney Island Picture," a piece the twenty-year-old Day wrote for the *Liberator* in April 1918. In just a few words, she set the scene: "Last night it stormed. The ocean spit far up on the beach huge cakes of ice, bits of driftwood glazed over with foamy crystals." The sea has also cast ashore the body of a destitute girl, whom Day characterized briefly but movingly. She noted the eighteen cents that had been found in the girl's pocket, "tied up in the corner of her handkerchief," as well as "the blister on her frozen heel as though she had walked—as we all have walked, to deaden the misery or to get warm." Her stockings had "many neat darns," and her "thin cotton crepe underwear" was "yellow because it had been washed and washed in the bathroom of a rooming house, and hung over the heater to dry. Poor little chemise" (1918, 46).

In "South Street," an article she wrote for *The Masses* about the same time, she deftly evoked the simultaneous beauty and squalor of the harbor:

South Street, where the truckmen and deckmen sit around on loads of boxes and wait for a boat to come in, where men idle in the September sunlight and dream and yawn and smoke, where the horses clatter along the cobbles dragging huge heavy trucks with a noise resembling a mob of people aroused after long repression, and where the kids sit on the edge of the dock and look with wishful eyes at the water below that swirls with refuse and driftwood. (1917, 26)

Day further contrasted "a wave of soft silence, golden in the September sunlight with its autumny smell" with the "heavy foul odor from God knows what storehouse, and from the river that gulps and gulps at the docks all day long" (1917, 26).

Many years later, she would reflect: "An ordinary journalistic device is to paint a picture with contrasts. It is an emotional way of making a point" (1948, 145). Much of her writing, including the innumerable columns, essays, reviews, and muckraking articles she wrote for *Catholic Worker* and her several books based on her Catholic Worker life, was just that: expressions of her convictions made memorable and moving not by simple statistics or other "objective"-seeming data, but by the "feel of the facts." A particularly effective example is her 1936 series of articles about Arkansas sharecroppers, which was published in both *America* and the *Catholic Worker*. Here, her writing communicates an almost visceral feeling of what it means to be poor, cold, and hungry:

It was seventeen above zero when we started out this morning with a carload of flour, meal, lard, sugar, coffee and soup....

It wasn't until late in the afternoon that we reached the worst place of all, just outside Parkin, Arkansas. There drawn up along the road was a tent colony, which housed 108 people, four infants among them, and God knows how many children.

The little girls giggled and laughed with their arms around each other while we talked to this evicted crowd of sharecroppers. Only one of them had on a sweater,

and the heels and toes of all of them were coming out of their shoes. Their giggles started them coughing and woke up one of the babies who cried fretfully, weakly.
. . .

The little tent where we stood on the frozen earth was filled with fourteen children and there were thirteen more in the camp. Here too were four infants, wrapped in scanty cotton blankets. . . .

While surveys are being made and written the Southern Tenant Farmers' Union carries on . . . organizing the sharecroppers. . . . They have had a hard struggle in the past and the future looks dark. But combined with faith and charity they have hope, and the terror that walks by day and by night in Arkansas does not daunt them. (1936, 516–17)

A gifted storyteller, Day often used dramatization to communicate the mysteries of her religion. For instance, she began her December 1934 *Catholic Worker* piece with a description of her seven-year-old daughter, Tamar Teresa, at play with her friend Freddy. The children were drawing pictures of the Nativity. Day recounted the pair's conversation as they told the Christmas story to each other: " 'And the cow breathed on the little baby Jesus and kept it warm,' Teresa says delightedly. "Cows are very warm animals, I know. . . . I'm sure the baby Jesus didn't mind being in a stable at all. Probably there were chickens, too. And maybe the shepherds brought their littlest lambs to show them to him' " (1934, 4).

Then, Day's narrative described how she told the children:

"Christ came to live with the poor and the homeless and dispossessed of this world, . . . and he loved them so much that he showed himself to the workers—the poor shepherds—first of all. It wasn't until afterward that he received the Kings of this earth. So let us keep poor—as poor as possible—"

"In a stable with cows and chickens," Teresa finished joyfully. "And then it will be easier for me to have God in my heart." (1934, 4)

Day often noted that "it is people who incarnate ideas, who make ideas come alive."[1] Not surprisingly, she was particularly effective in evoking the realities of poverty through her characterization of individuals, ordinary men and women whose lives she presented in a vividly detailed, sympathetic, yet unsentimental way. Referring to the poor by their first names helped break down the barriers between her audience and them, as did her unfailing eye for the telling detail. For instance, she recounted the life of John Ryder, an alcoholic farm worker:

All of you ride the Pennsylvania or the Lehigh pass by those pig farms set in the swamps, ugly as sin, evil-smelling holes, where thousands of pigs are raised and fattened on garbage from New York hotels. . . . John Ryder worked in this setting, cleaning out pig sties, caring for the hogs. . . . On pay days he would come over to New York and too often spend his holidays on the Bowery. He told us the pay was good and the meals too, but it was another case of needing heroic virtue to live under such surroundings. Too often the men sought surcease and rest and dreams in drink. . . . But it is difficult to clamber out of the trough of the destitute. . . .

John, like the prodigal son, came home to us after feeding off the husks of the swine. And he could not be feasted because he was dying. Instead, he had that real feast, the bread of the strong [the Eucharist], and he died and was laid out in the chapel at Maryfarm, and each night before his burial we said the office of the dead as though he were one of the mightiest of the sons of God. (1946, 6)

Because Day lived for nearly fifty years in voluntary poverty at the Catholic Worker house in New York in close communion with the destitute, the homeless, and the terminally ill, her prose had an uncommon integrity—and power. "There was," as Robert Ellsberg has observed, "absolutely no distinction between what she believed, what she wrote and the manner in which she lived" (Day 1983, xv). Day's articles in the *Catholic Worker* frequently began as conventional journalistic reportage, complete with factually verifiable names, dates, and events. Then her passion for peace and social justice, the integrity of her life, and her ever-present skills as a raconteur coalesced into a powerful narrative. Day's writing moved gracefully from the everyday to the ultimate, as in her piece "A Baby Is Born" in the January 1941 *Catholic Worker*. Poverty, homelessness, and peace are weighty issues, but how effortlessly Day dealt with one after the other in this piece ostensibly about the experience of an unwed mother giving birth:

Every night before we went to bed we asked the young mother, "How do you feel?" and asked each other . . . "Is there taxi money?" in case it would be too late to call an ambulance.

And then, one morning at five I heard rapid footsteps in the room above, the voice of the ambulance intern in the hall, "I'll be waiting downstairs," and I realized the great moment had arrived. It was still dark out, but it was indubitably morning. Lights were on in the kitchens of surrounding tenements. Fish-peddlers, taxi drivers, truckmen, longshoremen, were up and on their way to work. The business of life was beginning. And I thought, "How cheerful to begin to have a baby at this time of the morning!" Not at 2 A.M., for instance, a dreary time, of low vitality, when people sink beneath their woes and courage flags.

Five o'clock is a cheerful hour. Down in our little back yard . . . down in that cavernous pit with tenements looming five and seven stories up around, we could hear them dragging out the ash cans, bringing in the coffee cans for the line. . . .

Out in front the line was forming already and two or three fires in the gutters brought out in sharp relief the haggard faces of the men, the tragedy of their rags. The bright flames, the blue-black sky, the grey buildings all about, everything sharp and clear, and this morning a white ambulance drawn up in front of the door.

This is not the story of the tragedy of the mother. . . . But . . . it was a miserable shame that the departure of the young woman for her ordeal should be witnessed by a long, silent, waiting line of men. They surveyed her, a slight figure, bundled on that cruelly cold morning (and pain and fear make the blood run cold), come running down from the dark, silent house to get into the ambulance.

Not one man, not a dear husband, not a protector on whom she could lean for comfort and strength. There was no Joseph on this winter morning. But here were hundreds of men, silent, waiting, and wondering perhaps as they watched the ambulance, whether it was life or death that had called it out. (1941, 1, 7)

Day did not stop here, but moved on to other themes of consequence. She linked the lonely terror of the woman giving birth alone to that of the soldier, "with his guts spilled out on the battlefield, lying for hours impaled upon barbed wire." But while the mother was rewarded for her suffering with the gift of her child, the soldier's agony was only relieved by death. Day contrasted the joy that accompanies birth with the suffering that much of the rest of life brings, from war to homelessness. She did not end this complex piece on a cheerful note as she gazed at the "rosy and calm and satisfied" infant. Without embracing hopelessness, she contemplated how little the newborn knows of what the world holds, of "what horrors beset us on every side."

Like much of Day's writing, "A Baby Is Born" is an intense, moving exploration of the realm of the poor and the forgotten. As this piece shows, Day's ability to tell a story through characterization, description, scene-setting, and ironic juxtaposition meant writing that approached literature in its power to evoke the "feelings behind the facts." Again and again, Day transports the reader far beyond conventional journalistic reportage.

Day's masterful report of the atomic bombing of Japan begins simply enough: "Mr. Truman was jubilant. He went from table to table on the cruiser which was bringing him home from the Big Three conference, telling the great news, 'jubilant,' the newspaper said. *Jubilate Deo*. We have killed 318,000 Japanese."

Nearly half a century later, we realize that no conventional reporting could have even begun to deal with the dreadful implications of Hiroshima. Day sensed this, and she abandoned conventional reporting in "We Go on Record," her September 1945 commentary, with the sentence, "We have killed 318,000 Japanese." She continued:

That is, we hope we have killed them, the Associated Press, page one, column one, of the Herald Tribune says. The effect is hoped for, not known. It is hoped they are vaporized, our Japanese brothers, scattered, men, women and babies, to the four winds, over the seven seas. Perhaps we will breathe their dust into our nostrils, feel them in the fog of New York on our faces, feel rain on the hills of Eason [a Catholic Worker farm in Pennsylvania]. (1945, 1)

The juxtapositions in this piece are powerful indeed—as they are in Day's 1953 *Catholic Worker* piece about the execution of Julius and Ethel Rosenberg for atomic spying. Where was Day that summer evening when the Rosenbergs went to their fate? She was out in the country at a Catholic Worker farm, she told her readers, where "the air was fragrant with the smell of honeysuckle" and where, "out under the hedge...the black cat played with a grass snake, and the newly cut grass was fragrant in the evening air." Just before the Rosenbergs were electrocuted, Day wrote, she was busy bathing her grandchild. "My heart was heavy, as I soaped Nickie's dirty little legs, knowing that Ethel Rosenberg must have been thinking with all the yearning of her heart, of her own soon-to-be-orphaned children." Without exonerating the Rosenbergs, Day observed that if the couple had indeed been spies for Russia, then "they were doing what we also do in other countries." In their way, Day observed, the Rosenbergs had been "serving a philosophy, a religion."

And religion was not without its distortions, she added,

when Christian prelates sprinkle holy water on scrap metal, to be used for obliteration bombing, and name bombers for the Holy Innocents, for Our Lady of Mercy; [and] bless a man about to press a button which releases death on fifty thousand human beings, including babies, children, the sick, the aged, the innocent as well as the guilty.

Therefore, she concluded, "Let us have no part with the vindictive State and let us pray for Ethel and Julius Rosenberg" (1953, 2, 6). Once again, Day moved effortlessly from the everyday to the eternal.

Dorothy Day is usually thought of as an apostle of the homeless. But she should also be remembered as a gifted storyteller who communicated the realities of poor people's lives in a thoughtful and compelling way. In doing this, she also reflected upon the madness of modern society's materialism and warmongering, linking the issues of peace and social justice. The result is a large body of writing that transcends conventional journalism in both the gravity of its themes, which more commonly are literature's province, and in its degree of insight into human beings, who are vividly and compassionately evoked.

NOTE

1. Dorothy Day, quoted by Ade Bethune, personal interview, Newport, R.I., Apr. 26, 1983.

PRIMARY SOURCES

Day, Dorothy. 1917, Nov.–Dec. "South Street." *The Masses.*
———. 1918, Apr. "A Coney Island Picture." *Liberator.*
———. 1924. *The Eleventh Virgin.* New York: A. and C. Boni.
———. 1934, Dec. "Christmas." *Catholic Worker.*
———. 1936, Mar. 7. "Sharecroppers." *America.*
———. 1938. *From Union Square to Rome.* Silver Springs, Md.: Preservation of the Faith Press.

———. 1939. *House of Hospitality*. New York: Sheed and Ward.

———. 1941, Jan. "A Baby Is Born." *Catholic Worker*.

———. 1945, Sept. "We Go on Record." *Catholic Worker*.

———. 1946, Nov. "For These Dear Dead." *Catholic Worker*.

———. 1948. *On Pilgrimage*. New York: Catholic Worker Books.

———. 1952. *The Long Loneliness: The Autobiography of Dorothy Day*. New York: Harper and Row.

———. 1953, July–Aug. "Meditations on the Death of the Rosenbergs." *Catholic Worker*.

———. 1960. *Therese*. Notre Dame, Ind.: Fides.

———. 1963. *Loaves and Fishes*. New York: Harper and Row.

———. 1970. *Meditations*. Ed. Stanley Vishnewski. New York: Newman Press.

———. 1972. *On Pilgrimage: The Sixties*. New York: Curtis Books.

———. 1983. *By Little and by Little: The Selected Writings of Dorothy Day*. Ed. Robert Ellsberg. New York: Alfred A. Knopf.

SECONDARY SOURCES

Coy, Patrick, ed. 1988. *"A Revolution of the Heart": Essays on the Catholic Worker Movement*. Philadelphia: Temple University Press.

Klejment, Anne, and Alice Klejment. 1986. *Dorothy Day and "The Catholic Worker": A Bibliography and Index*. New York: Garland.

Miller, William L. 1973. *A Harsh and Dreadful Love: Dorothy Day and the Catholic Worker Movement*. New York: Liveright.

———. 1982. *Dorothy Day: A Biography*. San Francisco: Harper and Row.

Piehl, Mel. 1982. *Breaking Bread: The Catholic Worker and the Origin of Catholic Radicalism in America*. Philadelphia: Temple University Press.

Roberts, Nancy L. 1984. *Dorothy Day and the "Catholic Worker."* Albany: State University of New York Press.

ERNEST HEMINGWAY

Paul Ashdown

Returning from an East African safari during the winter of 1933, Ernest Hemingway sat against a stone wall and watched grebes swimming in the Sea of Galilee. Capturing those moments of repose by the fisherman's sea in a postscript to *Green Hills of Africa*, Hemingway gives an important clue to a truth he expresses in much of his work. The Galilee fishermen Jesus selected as his first disciples knew the proper use of time. Whether mending nets on the shore or casting them into the sea, fishermen live by patient and careful observation of nature and attention to detail. A fisherman must not be rushed and must believe the bounty will be provided.

Hemingway's famous fishermen, Nick Adams in "Big Two-Hearted River" and Santiago (named for the Apostle James, a Galilee fisherman) in *The Old Man and the Sea*, know how to wait and, by waiting, learn something about the sanctification of time. Hemingway shows this deference to time early and often in his literary journalism. For example, in his dispatch "Fishing the Rhone Canal," which appeared in the *Toronto Daily Star* in 1922, Hemingway recalls catching a trout in the Swiss canal by carefully timing his cast in the afternoon shadows. He wraps the trout in a copy of the *Daily Mail*, which is filled with the ephemeral news of the day, none of which is as satisfying or timeless as the trout. By fishing slowly down the edge of the stream, he knows he sooner or later will catch a trout again. Walking near the stream on the road to Aigle, he thinks of French, Hunnish, and Roman armies passing along the road long before, wondering if they took time to fish in the same stream. Arriving at the train station near Aigle, he eats and drinks joyfully in a beautiful cafe, knowing that he has a long wait for the next train, and secretly wishing it will never come (1967a, 33–35).

The little grebes Hemingway watches on the Sea of Galilee live by fishing too. They are not mentioned in the Bible, he decides, because "those people were not naturalists." Biblical writers were not naturalists but had eyes sufficiently keen to identify twenty-seven species of birds. All creatures of the earth live in harmony with time, and, Hemingway seems to suggest, humankind prospers only to the extent that it shares in that harmony. Writers, especially, must make accommodation so that they see the world properly. Hemingway said in the Foreword to *Green Hills of Africa* that he tried to write it as "an absolutely true book to see whether the shape of a country and the pattern of a month's action can, if truly presented, compete with a work of the imagination." He wanted "to try to write something about the country and the animals and what it's like to someone who knows nothing about it" (1967b, 194). In order to do this, he enriches characters and dialogue with the techniques of the novel and uses dramatic time to advance the action. Rhetoric intrudes, occasionally, but is often masked as parody. Hemingway invents a campfire literary discussion ostensibly to show up "the lice who crawl on literature," at the same time effectively commenting on the book he is writing (1967b, 109).

The naturalist, Hemingway insists, must avoid rhetoric. He praises Melville for telling "how things, actual things, can be" but then condemns those who pay closer attention to Melville's rhetoric, "which is not important. They put a mystery in which is not there" (1967b, 20). True mysticism, he says in *Death in the Afternoon*, should never be

confused with incompetence in writing which seeks to mystify where there is no mystery but is really only the necessity to fake to cover lack of knowledge or the inability to state clearly. Mysticism implies a mystery and there are many mysteries; but incompetence is not one of them; nor is overwritten journalism made literature by the injection of a false epic quality. (1932, 54)

Hemingway says that he cannot read other naturalists like Thoreau unless they are being extremely accurate and not literary (1967b, 21). To get the kind of accuracy Hemingway wants takes time, and *Green Hills of Africa* is saturated with references to doing things slowly, carefully, and properly. Traveling through Masai country, which he thinks is the loveliest part of Africa, he objects to being forced to hunt rapidly. He dreams about coming back to "hunt that country slowly, living there and hunting out each day ... and get[ting] to know it as I knew the country around the lake where we were brought up." He would "lie in the fallen leaves and watch the kudu feed" or "watch them on the hillside and see them long enough so they belonged to me forever" (282).

Difficulties arise on the safari when the hunters are rushed: "I thought he'd do well off by himself with no one to hurry him or rattle him ... I rattle him trying to get him to speed up" (63). "Something is always tricking him, the need to do things other than in regular order, or by an inexact command in which details are not specified, or to have to do it in front of

people, or to be hurried" (131–32). Everything on the hunt and, by extension, in life in general, reminds us that time is terribly short, that we are
always being caught by time, tripped up by time, forced by time to do things
for which we are not ready.

Hemingway calls this "that most exciting perversion of life: the necessity
of accomplishing something in less time than should truly be allowed for
its doing" (12). The country is also a captive of time. Marveling at elephant
tracks "sunk a foot deep in the loam of the forest floor," Hemingway reflects
that mammoths traveled through the hills in southern Illinois "a long time
ago" and made the same tracks, but now the biggest game in America is
gone (249–50). America had been a good country, but now it is too late.
"A continent ages quickly once we come. . . . Let the others come to America
who did not know that they had come too late. Our people had seen it at
its best and fought for it when it was worth fighting for. Now I would go
somewhere else" (284–85).

He expresses something of the same sentiment in an *Esquire* magazine
article he wrote at about the same time he was writing the Africa book.
Recalling a visit to his hometown of Oak Park, Illinois, five years earlier,
Hemingway laments that "the house where I was born was gone and they
had cut down the oak trees. . . . So I was glad I went away from there as
soon as I did. Because when you like to shoot and fish you have to move
often and always further out and it doesn't make any difference what they
do when you are gone" (1967a, 188).

Now, casting time as a central enemy to one's work, one's spirit, one's
enjoyment of life, is an understandable prejudice for a journalist. As a
newspaper reporter, Hemingway "told what happened and, with one trick
and another, you communicated the emotion aided by the element of timeliness which gives a certain emotion to any account of something that has
happened that day" (1932, 2). The apparent urgency of the information
swindles the reader into imagining it, but a month later the time element is
gone and the account is forgotten. "But if you make it up instead of describe
it you can make it round and whole and solid and give it life" (1967a, 215–
16). Then and only then is it worth remembering. Moreover, the constraints
of time virtually ensure that a reporter might be able to learn what happened
but seldom why it happened (Hotchner 1959, 10).

Hemingway's use of journalism as source material for his fiction and his
achievements and limitations as both a novelist and a journalist have been
thoroughly analyzed.[1] Some of the stories he wrote as a teenager for the
Kansas City Star in 1917 and 1918 before he went to Europe with the Red
Cross have been collected by Bruccoli in *Ernest Hemingway, Cub Reporter*.
Although largely routine and unremarkable, these stories show a writer
cautiously attempting to break out of the boundaries of conventional
straight news reporting. Hemingway was always more comfortable with the
literary feature approach to news writing. He developed this approach from

1920 to 1923 as a reporter and foreign correspondent with the *Toronto Daily Star* and the *Toronto Star Weekly*, and then continued it through most of his life by contract work for leading magazines, newspapers, and the North American Newspaper Alliance (NANA). Anthony Burgess argues that the Hemingway of the Toronto papers "was a man who saw things sharply and sharply delivered what he saw, keeping himself discreetly in the background. When it was necessary for him to come forward and make a judgment, it was usually done with a flash of individuality wholly charming" (1978, 61).

Hemingway could always build a simple story around the purely sensual pleasures of life, usually by placing himself in the center of the story, and it is these shared celebrations of commonplace joys that many people remember most readily from his writing. The hard, cynical edge of his reporting was always ready to surrender to beauty. An early story, "Christmas on the Roof of the World," cabled to the *Toronto Star Weekly* in 1923, captured both the exhilaration of celebrating the Christmas season on a Swiss mountain and the poignancy of being homesick in Paris. The young Hemingway, his wife, and youthful companions rush into their clothes and tear down an icy road "in the glory of the blue-white glistening alpine morning." From the top of a mountain they "could look over the whole world, white, glistening in the powder snow, and ranges of mountains stretching off in every direction." After a seven-mile rush down the slope "in the dusk, past chalets that were a burst of lights and Christmas merriment in the dark," the skiers race into the black woods past chalets, "their windows alight with the candles from the Christmas trees," overshooting their own chalet, and then hiking back up the hill toward lights "very cheerful against the dark pines of the hill, and inside was a big Christmas tree and a real Christmas turkey dinner."

The narrative concludes with a scene that could come from Puccini's *La Bohème*:

Paris with the snow falling. Paris with the big charcoal braziers outside the cafes, glowing red.... Snow is never more beautiful than in the city. It is wonderful in Paris to stand on a bridge across the Seine looking up through the softly curtaining snow past the grey bulk of the Louvre, up the river spanned by many bridges and bordered by the grey houses of old Paris to where Notre Dame squats in the dusk. It is very beautiful in Paris and very lonely at Christmas time.

Two lovers visiting the city walk up the Rue Bonaparte longing for their own homes (in a purely invented conversation, unless the lovers are the Hemingways themselves, or Hemingway had an extraordinary capacity for eavesdropping) and worrying about their future. After eating an unsatisfactory Christmas dinner in a little restaurant, they return to the street, where "snow was still falling. And they walked out into the streets of old

Paris that had known the prowling of wolves and the hunting of men and the tall old houses that had looked down on it all and were stark and unmoved by Christmas." The lovers are too homesick to enjoy themselves. The perfect Hemingway ending: a lesson learned in the losing of something, a clean, well-lighted place cast against a gathering darkness, reverberations of eternity, and the slow, steady lapping of time in its fullness against a remembered shore (1967a, 124–31).

Hemingway distinguished between "writing against deadlines, writing to make stuff timely rather than permanent" and writing he produced on his own schedule. He told a bibliographer, "No one has the right to dig this stuff up and use it against the stuff you have written to write the best you can" (Cohn 1931, 112). Although Hemingway's journalism as a body of work has been placed "among the best newspaper and magazine reporting available in our troubled times," his Spanish Civil War reporting has been called everything from "meager, rambling and self-centered" to "abysmally bad."[2] Burgess argues that Hemingway's war correspondence is still very readable only because he treated it as a minor form of fiction-writing. He contends that Hemingway's journalistic patrons in effect subsidized his research for fictional books and had to "make do with second-best Hemingway" (1978, 79).

Robert O. Stephens takes a more balanced approach to Hemingway's journalism by placing it in the context of his entire nonfictional output. This "public voice"—including journalism, essays, prefaces, program notes on painting and sculpture exhibitions, self-edited interviews, scripts, works of literary journalism such as *Death in the Afternoon* and *Green Hills of Africa*—"constitutes an intermediate voice between the private and the masked voices" (1968, x). This gives a better sense of what Hemingway was doing as a man of letters and offers the nonfictional work as a parallel art to the fiction rather than a sort of subordinate dream landscape from which to mine the fictional archetypes.

As part of his "public voice," then, Hemingway's journalism might be seen as a rough draft for the "private voice" of fiction, or it might stand on its own merits. Stephens demonstrates how Hemingway practically transcribed portions of his journalism into fiction. The second draft—the fictional form—pushed beyond the boundaries of time not only in its more leisurely creation but also in expanding the interior life of the characters and the narrator's response to them. He evidently was not chary about fictionalizing portions of his journalism. His gift for inventing dialogue results in characters who could have stepped out of the pages of *The Sun Also Rises*. Did these people really say these things *just this way*? But, on the other hand, we may be willing to accept that what the stories lack in journalistic accuracy they gain in dramatic unity.

For example, a NANA dispatch, "A New Kind of War," cabled from Madrid in 1937 during the Spanish Civil War, begins with a grainy film noir quality, suggesting Raymond Chandler and Humphrey Bogart. Hemingway lies in bed in a dark room, listening through an open window to the rattle of gunfire and thinking, "It is a great thing to be in bed with your feet stretched out gradually warming the cold foot of the bed and not out there in University City or Carabanchel. A man is singing hardvoiced in the street below."

In the morning he is awakened by an exploding shell and looks out to see a man sprinting across the pavement. Downstairs in the lobby, he sees a woman, blood spurting from her abdomen, being carried into the hotel. Vapor rises from a broken gas main in the sidewalk, "looking like a heat mirage in the cold morning air."

One man has been killed by the explosion, but the "dead man wasn't you," so Hemingway goes to breakfast, passing a woman scrubbing blood off a marble floor. Conversations about the incident heighten the sense of fatalism. The awareness of the closeness and randomness of death becomes palpable. The correspondent finds that he can obtain a bigger room on the side of the hotel near the explosion and closer to the shelling for less than a dollar. Why not? "It wasn't me anymore."

Stopping at a hospital behind the front lines, Hemingway is told that a severely injured American named Jay Raven wants to see him. Raven tells Hemingway that he was blinded by a grenade after he helped rally retreating Republican soldiers and defeat some Fascist troops. But Hemingway does not believe the story because it was "the sort of way everyone would like to have been wounded." During World War I he had known that "men often lied about the manner of their wounding."

Nevertheless, he plays along with Raven, who "did not sound like the wreckage of a soldier somehow." A doctor tells Hemingway that Raven will recover but will be permanently maimed. Later Hemingway meets Raven's wounded commanding officer and learns that Raven's story is quite true. And as Hemingway already suspects, Raven is not really a soldier, but a social worker with no military training. "This is a strange new kind of war where you learn just as much as you are able to believe," he concludes. We are left with the sense that in this war and probably in the coming war we must not only believe that we will go on living, but we must have faith in order to believe anything at all. In this new kind of war, the possibility of bravery may be the only thing worth believing in (1967a, 272–64).

With only some minor adjustments, the dispatch could have been and perhaps should have been published as a short story. But there is a double meaning for the reader, who, having every reason to believe that the dispatch is largely fiction, may fall into the same trap as Hemingway in the story. This brilliant technique—hardly second-rate Hemingway—creates a truly literary piece of journalism. The objection should be raised that the reader is entitled to know what is fact and what is invention. Burgess charges that Hemingway's fiction-writer's talent "impelled him to invent, organize reality into aesthetic patterns, cultivate the 'impressionism' which Ford Madox Ford encouraged writers to carry over from fiction to real life. Truth, according to Ford, was not facts but vision—a view which justified suppression and distortion of facts, what ordinary people call lying" (Burgess 1978, 79). But the literary journalist could respond that you take your knavery one way or another—either the trick of timeliness or the artifice of literary invention.

Especially in his war dispatches, as in his war fiction, Hemingway insists that the reader accept the hard reality of existence and not mix it up with rhetoric or propaganda. His writing is often a response to what passes as timely news in the press, and, as Stephens points out, "he wrote with a sound and sometimes cynical knowledge of the predilections of newspaper and magazine readers who were his major public" (1968, 324). In a graphic piece of commentary about the Italian invasion of Ethiopia, "Wings Always over Africa: An Ornithological Letter," published in *Esquire* in 1936, he begins by citing a press dispatch that reported the passage through the Suez Canal of almost 10,000 Italian casualties. He points out that the dispatch did not say that the soldiers were being sent to hospital concentration camps on an Italian island so that they would not depress the Italian enthusiasm for the war. He says that it is easy to be patriotic when you fail to know what really happens in a war. While the Italian planes are swooping down on the lightly armed Ethiopians, terrible carrion birds are swooping down on wounded Italian soldiers and eating them alive. Describing this ghastly process in some detail, he points out the need for the Fascists to conceal this aspect of war from the troops. He reflects on the consequences of World War I for the common people of Italy and denounces those who profited from the conflict. In this senseless war against Ethiopians, it is the poorest Italians who will suffer again. "Mussolini's sons are in the air where there are no enemy planes to shoot them down," he says. But poor men's sons are the foot soldiers, who will hear "the whish of wings when the birds come down," and will die never knowing their real enemy (1967a, 229–35).

This is effective literary journalism, building on the faulty and probably hasty press dispatch that fails to tell the whole story, and then exploiting the analogy of the predatory birds and the Italian planes. Beginning as a commentary on the limitations of timely journalism, it continues in essay or editorial form to explicate the history, causes, and consequences of what Hemingway later called the "bullying, murderous, slovenly crime of war" (1948, x). Ultimately, Hemingway found that as a literary journalist he could not win either way. He had written of the Castilian sense of death in *Death in the Afternoon*:

They think a great deal about death and when they have a religion they have one which believes that life is much shorter than death. Having this feeling they take an intelligent interest in death and when they can see it being given, avoided, refused and accepted in the afternoon for a nominal price of admission they pay their money and go to the bull ring. (1932, 266)

When he returned to the subject in his last journalistic writing, published as "The Dangerous Summer" in *Life* magazine shortly before he died, he was criticized for writing journalism and not literature (L. Hemingway 1980, 280). But whatever labels could be attached to his writing, Hemingway's suicide in 1961 left a void in American letters that has never been filled. As Norman Mailer puts it: "Hemingway had given the power to believe you could still shout down the corridor of the hospital, live next to the breath of the beast, accept your portion of dread each day. Now the greatest living romantic is dead. Dread was loose" (1970, 14).

NOTES

1. See, for example, Fenton 1954; Kobler 1984; Fishkin 1985.
2. See Hemingway 1967a, xiv; Shaber 1980, 421; Knightley 1975, 213.

PRIMARY SOURCES

Hemingway, Ernest. 1932. *Death in the Afternoon.* New York: Charles Scribner's Sons.
———. 1948. *A Farewell to Arms.* New York: Charles Scribner's Sons.
———. 1967a. *By-Line: Ernest Hemingway.* Ed. William White. New York: Charles Scribner's Sons.
———. 1967b. *Green Hills of Africa.* New York: Collier Books.
———. 1970. *Ernest Hemingway, Cub Reporter.* Ed. Matthew J. Bruccoli. Pittsburgh: University of Pittsburgh Press.

SECONDARY SOURCES

Burgess, Anthony. 1978. *Ernest Hemingway and His World.* New York: Charles Scribner's Sons.
Cohn, Louis Henry. 1931. *A Bibliography of Ernest Hemingway.* New York: Random House.
Fenton, Charles A. 1954. *The Apprenticeship of Ernest Hemingway.* New York: Viking.
Fishkin, Shelley Fisher. 1985. *From Fact to Fiction.* New York: Johns Hopkins University Press.
Hemingway, Leicester. 1980. *My Brother, Ernest Hemingway.* Miami Beach: Winchester House.
Hotchner, A. E. 1959, Oct. 18. "Ernest Hemingway Talks to American Youth." *This Week.*
Knightley, Philip. 1975. *The First Casualty: From Crimea to Viet Nam: the War*

Correspondent as Hero, Propagandist, and Myth-Maker. New York: Harcourt Brace Jovanovich.

Kobler, J. F. 1984. *Ernest Hemingway: Journalist and Artist*. Ann Arbor: University of Michigan Research Press.

Mailer, Norman. 1970. *Of a Fire on the Moon*. Boston: Little, Brown.

Shaber, Sarah. 1980, Autumn. "Hemingway's Literary Journalism: The Spanish Civil War Dispatches." *Journalism Quarterly*.

Stephens, Robert O. 1968. *Hemingway's Nonfiction: The Public Voice*. Chapel Hill: University of North Carolina Press.

JAMES AGEE

Paul Ashdown

Anyone attempting to read James Agee's *Let Us Now Praise Famous Men* should first read John Keats's poem "On Sitting Down to Read King Lear Once Again." Keats feared the consuming fire of Shakespeare's great tragedy, that "fierce dispute / Betwixt damnation and impassion'd clay," as the reader of *Let Us Now Praise Famous Men* should fear James Agee (*Norton Anthology* 1986, 2: 803–4).

The great claims made for *Let Us Now Praise Famous Men* (one British reviewer called the book "perhaps the greatest work of reportage of this century") rest upon its power to force a reader to confront the sort of dark torments Keats found in *King Lear* (McDonald 1978, 147). Something primeval, something supernal, lurks in the darkling fields of Agee's Alabama and Keats's ancient oak forests and clouds of Albion. These are lands where poetry is heard in the call of a fox, where fathers are blind, where sons and kings must go mad to feel what wretches feel, and where the claims of one group of human beings upon another are pressed with benumbing ferocity.

Even before his twenty-first birthday, Agee had plans to combine "huge geometric plots such as *Lear*" with the spare beauty of Chekhov (Agee 1978, 47). Agee began writing his *Lear* six years later, after he found his Chekhov in the photographer Walker Evans. Together they found their heath in Alabama, a plain where "poor naked wretches" endured the pitiless storms of the Great Depression. Agee took poor Lear's epiphany on the heath as the first theme of the sonata form he said that he had deployed in the service of his accusatory document; the second theme, words that he said he quoted, "to mislead those who will be misled by them" (Agee and Evans 1941, xix), was the rallying cry of the *Communist Manifesto*. The result was, as William Stott describes it, "a book of doom and desperate resignation" (1973, 313).

Of course, it is homage to Agee that readers may discern in his book parallels with great works of art. Some have found in *Let Us Now Praise Famous Men* a thing so grand that it falls closer to works by Blake or to Melville's *Moby Dick* than to a form of documentary journalism. Others have noted that Agee was too much moved by Joyce for signs of Bloom and Dedalus to be absent from his work. Agee has sometimes been compared to Orwell, Whitman, and Proust, and an American president said that Agee reminded him of Van Gogh. He has been called "a sovereign prince of the English language" and an American writer of prose passages rivaled only by Hemingway and Thoreau. The book has been called "the great prose lyric of American literature."

The structure and meaning of such a book, accordingly, has been much debated. Musical and religious forms have been observed, philosophies and aesthetics have been delineated, extolled, and, not infrequently, debunked. For the work has always had its critics, some of whom have seen its posturings as an inchoate form of dementia. Damning Agee with faint praise, some critics have seen *Let Us Now Praise Famous Men* as cultic, its author as, at best, a minor literary figure whose genuine talents were dissipated by journalism, Hollywood, and besotting sins of the flesh that took him to an early grave. Others have viewed Agee as a photogenic bohemian more to be placed in the company of Jack Kerouac and James Dean than of Shakespeare, Melville, Blake, and Joyce. Can literary journalism begin to embrace such a figure?[1]

Although Agee's career included almost two decades of popular magazine writing and the publication of two novels, a volume of poetry, occasional short stories, and memorable screenplays ("The African Queen," "The Bride Comes to Yellow Sky," and "Abraham Lincoln: The Early Years"), we must attend to *Let Us Now Praise Famous Men* as an icon of literary journalism.[2] For it is that major work, begun in 1936 as an assignment for *Fortune* magazine, that calls to account the very reductivist substance of journalistic modernism: a scientific obsession with facts and documentation in pursuit of objective reality. This faith in documentation had become acute in the 1930s, especially in Britain. In his history of that decade, Malcolm Muggeridge recalls that a new breed of writers tried "to portray life as it is without attempting to reveal its imagined significance" (1967, 278). To the contrary, Agee concludes in *Let Us Now Praise Famous Men*, the "very blood and semen of journalism.... is a broad and successful form of lying" (Agee and Evans 1941, 235). His answer was, in Stott's assessment, "a form we might call antidocumentary or metaphysical documentary or neo-Christian documentary, a form of repeated prefaces and incidental notes to a book that cannot be written" (1973, 310).

This kind of literary reportage attempts to see real people as something more than sociological units of analysis or informational commodities to be brokered in the offices of New York magazine publishers. But Agee's methods, taken at face value, have disturbed many readers. Agee's doubts and dualisms sometimes undermine the enormous edifice of detail he erects almost as a parody of documentary realism. Is the purpose objective subjectivity or subjective objectivity? Or something else?

Tom Wolfe, master craftsman of a later form of literary journalism which some believe originated with Agee, wondered why Agee couldn't just abandon his own point of view and let his subjects speak for themselves. Agee, he believed, was just too diffident to interview anyone other than himself (Wolfe 1973, 44). Priscilla Robertson, a rival documentary writer who was Agee's contemporary, questioned Agee's bleak conclusions and charged that *Let Us Now Praise Famous Men* was "not much more to be trusted as a source book for life in the '30s than *King Lear* for early Britain" (Stott 1973, 311–12). And that is precisely the point. "Thus *Macbeth* would be documentary," Muggeridge quipped, "if the number of Thanes on Macbeth's and on Malcolm's side were accurately given, and the political forces brought into play by Macbeth's attempt to found a dynasty, subjected to a careful analysis" (1967, 278).

Neither Shakespeare nor Agee was terribly interested in writing objectivist social history. Both sought something rather more universal. *King Lear*, a play that clearly shows the difference between an imaginative and scientistic view of life, is the perfect vehicle for Agee.[3] He tells us what he is about by quoting Shakespeare's Lear and then using as his first documentary source a third grade geography textbook belonging to the ten-year-old daughter of a cotton tenant farmer. In a section on food, shelter, and clothing, the textbook asks the child to consider what every person needs. "Let us imagine that we are far out in the fields. The air is bitter cold and the wind is blowing. Snow is falling, and by and by it will turn into sleet and rain. We are almost naked. We have had nothing to eat and are suffering from hunger as well as cold" (Agee and Evans 1941, xx).

King Lear asks us to imagine the same conditions, and Agee reminds us that the child's needs are no less than those of the mad king and his ragtag retinue on the heath. To press his point he begins the second, longer section of his work with a poem dedicated to Walker Evans. The poem alerts the reader that the authors are spies "moving delicately among the enemy," or, as Lear would have it, God's spies, angels that "take's upon the mystery of things" (1941, 5).

Agee's poem intrudes into the fourth act of the play and brings Edgar, disguised as Lear's philosopher, the mad Tom of Bedlam, and his blind father Gloucester to Dover. Agee casts himself in the role of Edgar, a younger son seemingly mad in his rantings while growing in moral awareness. He describes what he sees in photographic detail for his blind father, a surrogate for the moral blindness of the reader of *Let Us Now Praise Famous Men*. After his "part wakened" father believes that he has jumped from the cliff, Agee's Edgar withdraws, for now, undisclosed. Complete revelation and subsequent action are deferred.

At the end of *King Lear*, Edgar proclaims that the time is long overdue for all to say what we feel and not what we ought to say. For this is a play about prophetic language and a way of seeing. Shakespeare's Edgar trusts in a coming divine justice, foreshadowing, perhaps, the coming Christian era. Afflictions in the here and now are to be borne with compassionate patience. Agee takes up prophetic language of the play to warn later in *Let Us Now Praise Famous Men* that although "rescuing feet" are surely on their way, for now there can be no more immediate end for the problems in Alabama than there could be for Lear and the poor naked wretches of Celtic Britain (1941, 392). He, too, counsels patience and resignation. The poem concludes: "Not yet that naked hour when armed, / Disguise flung flat, squarely we challenge the fiend. / Still, comrade, the running of beasts and the ruining heaven / Still captive the old wild king." The fiend in this context is Tom of Bedlam, Edgar's now-exorcised shadow self. Although Edgar has shed his disguise, Agee is not yet ready to do so, for his guilt-ridden presentiments are still to be cleansed by his literary act of atonement.

One instrument for that atonement is the raging storm in which he finds himself near the end of the book, corresponding with Tom of Bedlam's meeting with Lear during the terrible storm on the heath. The heath in Shakespeare's time was the unfenced countryside where lunatics and brigands roamed beyond the reach of law or social restraint. Conan Doyle later used the wild countryside of Dartmoor as the setting for *The Hound of the Baskervilles*. There the escaped convict Selden and even Sherlock Holmes sought shelter in Neolithic huts on Grimspound Bog. The Elizabethans and the Victorians had the same feelings toward the heath that many Americans still have today toward the rural Deep South. Despite his East Tennessee heritage, Agee comes to "deepest Alabamian rurality" little better prepared to meet the people of the heath on their own terms than are his readers. But as he huddles with a sharecropper family in their tenebrous "holy house," a meager cabin affording little protection from the deteriorating moral order symbolized by the wind and thunder, he bonds with them through small acts of love and shared humanity. The fiend will only be challenged in this world by those in communion with the company of "famous men" praised by Jesus Ben-Sirach in the Apocrypha. Like Lear on the heath, Agee learns in Alabama that it is the naked who are truly clothed and the poor who shall inherit the kingdom (1941, 393–407).

Agee has been faulted for sentimentalizing the poor and seeing only goodness in them (Stott 1973, 305–6). His notebooks show that he was even more nostalgic than he revealed in the book. He has been accused of appearing to be more concerned with God's creatures than God is. Writers continue to hunt down the Alabama sharecroppers Agee and Evans seemed to deify, as if to try to show them less than ennobled by the hardships their families endured. Some, indisputably, are angry, resentful, and embarrassed about the book, which Agee could have foreseen. Ironies, such as the fact that a photograph of Annie Mae Gudger, "the Mona Lisa of the Depression," sells for $4,000, or that the sharecropping system virtually ended within several decades of the book's publication, have been used to undercut its moral and prophetic power.[4] Yet the literary journalist assumes risks that the unbridled imaginative writer does not. No journalists sought interviews with Shakespeare's Edgar or walked the heath to photograph beggars newly released from the mental hospitals in Albany's Britain.

Agee somehow found a way to return to the payroll of those employers he counted among his "most dangerous enemies" when denouncing the assignment that ultimately led to the publication of the book in 1941. But after *Let Us Now Praise Famous Men*, Agee's inward journey, as journalist, was largely complete. He had begun as a poet, had attempted conventional magazine journalism, and had detonated the form in *Let Us Now Praise Famous Men*. Next he would work backward through memory, producing two autobiographical novels. The twenty-seven-year-old James Agee of the Alabama book becomes the twelve-year-old Richard of *The Morning Watch* and finally the six-year-old Rufus Follet of *A Death in the Family*. Taken as a single autobiographical work and read in chronological order, the parts illuminate the whole and help us understand Agee's intense spiritual struggle.

While working out the struggle in the novels and with *Let Us Now Praise Famous Men* behind him, Agee continued to work as a literary journalist through the 1940s, but with a greater sense of control. This he exhibited most effectively in the film criticism which W. H. Auden in 1944 called "the most remarkable regular event in American journalism today. What he says is of such profound interest... that his articles belong in that very select class... of newspaper work which has permanent literary value." Although these reviews continue to tell us a good deal about Agee, they tell us a great deal more about America in the 1940s.

As a social and cultural critic, he had a genius for pithy assessment and sagacious judgment of a changing order. His shorter essays, reviews, and reports for *Time* relieved him of some of the burden he previously had imposed on himself to wring all he could out of a longer assignment. Yet he still raised the prophetic voice he had used in the early *Fortune* articles to warn of fascism and to predict the social changes that would be brought about by the automobile and the growing network of roads and highways in the United States. Toward the end of World War II he turned his attention to what the war had wrought for American society. He feared that the individual would be tested in the collectivist postwar environment. He doubted that Americans were ready to accept the responsibilities the war had imposed upon them, and he feared that they would be seduced by the promise of affluence and corrupted by power. He sensed that the family would be under attack and that generational conflicts would worsen as Americans who had never left home before were intoxicated with a new sense of possibility. He worried about a landscape cluttered with tawdry

motels and fouled with industrial pollution. Most of all he feared the growing power of science as demonstrated by the atomic bomb. In his most
powerful *Time* essay, a teleological lamentation about the destruction of
Hiroshima and Nagasaki, he argued that splitting the atom divided both
the physical and the spiritual order. By playing God and using the awful
power of the atomic bomb on fellow creatures, he believed that mankind
had opened a "bottomless wound in the living conscience of the race." From
now on, reason and spirit would meet "on final ground."

Although Agee remained a journalist for several more years before turning
his attention to screenplays and fiction, nothing he subsequently wrote better
expressed his spiritual vision than this *Time* essay. What he wrote was
grafted to him from early childhood as a religious sense of the universe,
which he made clear in *A Death in the Family* and *The Morning Watch*.
Schooled by the monks of the Order of the Holy Cross at St. Andrew's
School in Tennessee, he lived the Anglican sense of the Incarnation derived
from the Greek Fathers, a world both of outward and spiritual natures. In
this world sacraments defined reality and material objects were consecrated
by scriptural allusion.[5]

When he was a student at Exeter and Harvard, he was a frequent visitor
at St. Francis' House, the monastery chapel and guest house of the Cowley
Fathers in Cambridge, Massachusetts (Agee 1978, 39–40). These austere
Anglo-Catholic monks, members of the Society of St. John the Evangelist
founded in England by Richard Meux Benson in 1866, lived a simple life
at once both cloistered and involved with the social concerns of the world.
Benson and others of the Oxford Movement, paralleling the Danish philosopher Kierkegaard in some respects, found ways to distance themselves
from Christendom while moving closer to Christ.[6]

Despite his respect for the monks and his love for his old St. Andrew's
teacher, Father Flye, Agee lost no love on the clergy in general, preferring
a form of Christian anarchy or Christian existentialism to the formal beliefs
and practices of the Church.[7] His exposure to both the Cowley Fathers and
the Holy Cross monks shaped the unusual liturgical and literary style of his
writing and intensified his suspicion of all forms of power. "Official acceptance is the one unmistakable symptom that salvation is beaten again," he
wrote in *Let Us Now Praise Famous Men*, sounding much like Benson or
Kierkegaard (Agee and Evans 1941, 15).

With the prophecies of the Cistercian monk Joachim of Fiore and the
spiritual zeal of the Franciscans, poverty had been raised to cosmic significance in Western philosophy during the Middle Ages. Having been brought
up in the romantic tradition of Anglo-Catholicism, Agee, when he came
upon the tenant farmers in Alabama, could only envision writing about
them as "an independent inquiry into certain normal predicaments of human
divinity" (1941, xiv). As a literary journalist, therefore, Agee was always
writing on a cosmic stage. Even when he could not find in his personal life

the source of the power that drove his literary imagination, he never lost the inspiration in his work. Agee's Christianity, Walker Evans wrote, "was a punctured and residual remnant, but it was still a naked, root emotion" (1941, xii).

NOTES

1. For example, see Stott, 308; Fitzgerald, 27; W.J.T. Mitchell, "The Ethics of Form in the Photographic Essay," *Afterimage* (Jan. 1989): 13; Robert Phelps's appreciation in *Letters of James Agee to Father Flye*, 1; Alfred T. Barson, *A Way of Seeing* (Amherst: University of Massachusetts Press, 1972), 45. Also see the memoirs by Matthews and Macdonald in *Remembering James Agee*, edited, with an introduction, by David Madden. Madden and other scholars contrasted Agee with many writers and artists during the "The Agee Legacy," a conference at the University of Tennessee held Mar. 27–Apr. 1, 1989.

2. While *Let Us Now Praise Famous Men* is a masterpiece of literary journalism, some of Agee's magazine journalism can be treated as literary journalism as well. See Ashdown 1985.

3. My reading of *King Lear* owes a great deal to essays by A. C. Bradley and Harry Levin in *The Tragedy of King Lear*, ed. Russell Fraser (New York: New American Library, 1963); Michael Ignatieff, *The Needs of Strangers* (New York: Viking, 1985); Lionel Trilling, *The Experience of Literature* (New York: Doubleday, 1967); Northrop Frye, *Northrop Frye on Shakespeare* (New Haven: Yale University Press, 1986); and Ernest Ferlita, *The Theatre of Pilgrimage* (New York: Sheed and Ward, 1971). *King Lear* also enters into Agee's *A Death in the Family*, 163.

4. For example, see Howell Raines, "Let Us Now Revisit Famous Folk," *New York Times Magazine*, May 25, 1980; Stott, 313; Dale Maharidge and Michael Williamson, *And Their Children After Them* (New York: Pantheon, 1989).

5. See *James Agee: Selected Journalism*, edited, with an introduction, by Paul Ashdown (Knoxville: University of Tennessee Press, 1985); Peter Ellertsen, "James Agee, the Bomb and Oliver the Cat," *The Christian Century*, July 31–Aug. 7, 1985, 709–11; Adam Dunbar McCoy, *Holy Cross: A Century of Anglican Monasticism* (Wilton, Conn.: Morehouse-Barlow, 1987).

6. See *Benson of Cowley*, ed. Martin L. Smith (Oxford: Oxford University Press, 1980).

7. For example, see *Agee on Film*, 246; Agee's characterization of Father Jackson in *A Death in the Family*; "Religion and the Intellectuals," *Partisan Review* 17 (Feb. 1950): 106–13; Victor A. Kramer, "James Agee," in *Literature of Tennessee*, ed. Ray Willbanks (Macon, Ga.: Mercer University Press, 1984), 133–47; Father Flye discusses Agee's religious beliefs in *Remembering James Agee*, 14–22.

PRIMARY SOURCES

Agee, James. 1957. *A Death in the Family*. New York: McDowell, Obolensky.

———. 1964. *Agee on Film: Reviews and Comments*. Boston: Beacon Press.

———. 1978. *Letters of James Agee to Father Flye*. 2nd ed. Dunwoody, Ga.: Norman S. Berg.

Agee, James, and Walker Evans. 1941. *Let Us Now Praise Famous Men*. Boston: Houghton Mifflin.

Ashdown, Paul, ed. 1985. *James Agee: Selected Journalism*. Knoxville: University of Tennessee Press.

Fitzgerald, Robert, ed. 1962. *The Collected Short Prose of James Agee*. Boston: Houghton Mifflin.

SECONDARY SOURCES

Auden, W. H. 1964. "A Letter to the Editors of *The Nation*." In *Agee on Film*. Boston: Beacon Press.

Matthews, T. S., and Dwight Macdonald. 1974. In *Remembering James Agee*. Ed. David Madden. Baton Rouge: Louisiana State University Press.

McDonald, Donald. 1978. "Is Objectivity Possible?" In *Enduring Issues in Mass Communication*. Ed. Everette E. Dennis, Arnold H. Ismach, and Donald M. Gillmor. St. Paul: West.

Muggeridge, Malcolm. 1967. *The Thirties*. London: Collins, 1967.

The Norton Anthology of English Literature. 1986. 5th ed. New York: W. W. Norton. 2: 803–4.

Stott, William. 1973. *Documentary Expression and Thirties America*. New York: Oxford University Press.

Wolfe, Tom. 1973. *The New Journalism*. With an Anthology edited by Tom Wolfe and E. W. Johnson. New York: Harper and Row.

JOSEPH MITCHELL

Norman Sims

One of the true symbolists among the literary journalists, Joseph Mitchell created cultural portraits of the Fulton Fish Market in New York City, the Bowery, and several communities in New Jersey and Staten Island. Mitchell's profiles looked deeply into the psychological core of his subjects, achieving the kind of knowledge we normally find only in clinical texts or fiction. Occasionally, he created a symbolic foundation for his nonfiction that can be considered as a fusion of realist and modernist styles.

In 1938, Mitchell came to the *New Yorker* after several years of writing feature stories for the New York newspapers. He arrived at about the same time as a number of newspaper writers who invigorated the magazine's reportage. Mitchell had become friends with A. J. Liebling at the *World-Telegram*. They were joined at the *New Yorker* by such writers as John McNulty, Joel Sayre, St. Clair McKelway, Philip Hamburger, John Bainbridge, Lillian Ross, John Hersey, Berton Roueche, and Meyer Berger. By 1965, Mitchell had written dozens of articles, many of which were collected in five books, then he suddenly fell silent and, although he continued to work at his office, had published nothing else by 1990.

Old Mr. Flood (1948) contained his profile of a 93-year-old retired house-wrecking contractor who ate a seafood diet and maintained that he would live to be 115. "Mr. Flood is not one man," Mitchell explained. "Combined in him are aspects of several old men who work or hang out in Fulton Fish Market, or who did in the past. I wanted these stories to be truthful rather than factual, but they are solidly based on facts" (Mitchell 1948, vii). Among the characters who made Mr. Flood was Joe Mitchell, who preferred a seafoodetarian diet himself.

One of his most important books, *The Bottom of the Harbor* (1960), collected six nonfiction articles that demonstrated his maturing craft. In the same year he published a lasting profile of "The Mohawks in High Steel," about a group of Indians with no fear of heights who worked on the New York skyscrapers. His last book, *Joe Gould's Secret* (1965), contained two profiles of a Greenwich Village character who provided Mitchell with an avenue of self-expression rarely found in nonfiction. Off and on since 1965, Mitchell has been writing another book with new autobiographical and journalistic contributions.

Part of Mitchell's inspiration for *The Bottom of the Harbor* came from Herman Melville's *Moby Dick*. He hoped to write in a way that captured something of the spirit of the community surrounding the Fulton Fish Market in southern Manhattan, in the same way Melville wrote about whaling. Two of his articles were not focused on his beloved fish market, but rather on the small town of Edgewater, New Jersey, just across the Hudson from the Upper West Side of Manhattan, and on a black neighborhood called Sandy Ground on Staten Island.

The imagery in "The Rivermen," his article on Edgewater, reflects Mitchell's peculiar attraction to graveyard humor. One of the most powerful images emerged as he was talking with an old woman who was setting out some bulbs at the family gravesite in the Edgewater cemetery. They fell into a discussion of the roses that grew freely in the cemetery, roses originally brought to the New World 200 years earlier in Dutch times. "I know why they do so well in here," the woman said. "They've got good strong roots that go right down into the graves" (1961, 190). Like the roses, the rivermen of Edgewater had their roots in some traditional occupations of the past. They lived by working on tugboats and excursion boats on the Hudson River, by fishing for the shad that still made their annual run up the Hudson from the ocean, and before that by cutting paving blocks for New York City from a local quarry. All their skills as fishermen and rivermen were endangered, as were the shad themselves, by changes in the city and pollution in the river. Yet they endured. Mitchell caught their spirit in his article, preserving a way of life that stood as a background to the rivermen. Despite all the changes engulfing them, the rivermen had an attitude toward life and death that was unchanging. The image of the enduring roses symbolized that attitude.

Mitchell wrote so often about disappointed old men and women for whom nothing had turned out the way they thought it would that he got a reputation for what he calls graveyard humor. Another term might be graveyard irony, because he meant a perspective on life, often acquired by the elderly, that revolves around comparing life's troubles to the grave. One day Harold Ross, founder of the *New Yorker,* stepped into Mitchell's office to discuss one of his articles. "You know," Ross said, "you're a pretty gloomy guy." After a moment, Ross added, "Of course, I'm no God-damned little ray of sunshine myself" (personal interview, 1988). Actually it was the strength in the "graveyard humor" perspective that Mitchell wrote about, not its morbid qualities.

"Mr. Hunter's Grave," another of the articles in *The Bottom of the Harbor*, profiled an elderly black bricklayer who lived in a traditionally black community on Staten Island. In typical fashion, Mitchell set out to find a free-growing patch of wild flowers in New York City and ended up in a graveyard tangled with weeds, vines, and symbols. The profile became a family portrait, centered on the family cemetery plot and the gravesite Mr. Hunter had reserved, and beyond that a cultural portrait of the entire community.

His profile of Mr. Hunter reached into the man's psychological core in a way rarely achieved in journalism.

You're trying to report, at the beginning without knowing it, the unconscious as well as the consciousness of a man or woman. My whole idea of reporting—particularly reporting on conversation—is to talk to a man or a woman long enough under different circumstances, like old Mr. Hunter down on Staten Island, until, in effect, they reveal their inner selves. Once I had what I considered the revealing remark, I could use that to encourage them to talk more about that aspect of their lives. They were able to talk, like Mr. Hunter could talk about his first wife's death, about his son's death, about his stepfather whom he hated and who I guess hated him. That way I could go far deeper into the man's life than I could any other way. (Personal interview, 1988)

No casual reporting technique can achieve what Mitchell was looking for. He spent day after day listening to Mr. Hunter and taking notes, gradually gaining his trust and learning about his life. "One thing you have to do, if you're going to write this sort of thing," Mitchell explained, "is realize that people have buried their pain and have transformed experience enough to allow them to endure it and bear it. If you stay with them long enough, you let them reveal the past to themselves, thereby revealing it to you" (personal interview, 1988).

Mitchell describes his approach to writing as a portrayal of a person against his cultural background. Representing the person against that background "gives the story meaning and significance, rather than plot." He compares this to what T. S. Eliot called the objective correlative. "It's where you write about one thing and you're actually writing about another. Or where you make one thing represent another" (personal interview, 1988). Several of Mitchell's works contained that sort of symbolic representation, everything being implied by the context and the setting rather than stated outright. "In recent years," Mitchell once said, "I have written mostly about what I guess could be called the unusual in the usual, such as a description of the bottom of New York Harbor, in which, without seeming to do so, I tried to make the reader conscious of parallels between the litter and the marine life down there—the old wrecks and the eels and the polluted oyster-beds—and the beauty and the ugliness stored up in his own mind" (*North Carolina Authors* 1952, 83).

The symbolic element in *The Bottom of the Harbor* was recognized by literary critic Stanley Edgar Hyman when he analyzed the imagery of the several articles contained in the book:

Dusty hotel rooms shut up for decades and now reluctantly explored are infantile experience; the wrecks on the bottom of the harbor, teeming with marine life, are festering failures and guilts; the rats that come boldly out of their holes in the dark before dawn are Id wishes; Mr. Poole's dream of the draining of New York harbor by earthquake is a paradigm of psychoanalysis; Mr. Hunter's grave is at once tomb and womb and marriage bed. (1978, 83)

Mitchell was born on July 27, 1908, near Fairmont, North Carolina. His father raised cotton and tobacco, and bought cotton on the local market and also speculated in futures on the New York Cotton Exchange. His family had lived and farmed in the area since before the Revolutionary War. After attending the University of North Carolina, but not graduating, Mitchell moved to New York City. He had realized, standing on the local cotton-trading platform with his father, that arithmetic was a foreign language. He could not pass the math classes at college. Cotton-trading was a risky and cut-throat business where an instantaneous grasp of mathematics was required. Instead of going into his father's business, Mitchell left for Greenwich Village, although he retained a love for his birthplace. Since 1976, when his father died, Mitchell has helped his two brothers and three sisters with the management of his father's farms, dividing his time between New York and North Carolina. Many of his interests in New York—his love of cemeteries and wildflowers, for instance—had their origins in his North Carolina childhood. "I always felt like an exile," Mitchell said (personal interview, 1989b), and that feeling drew him to one of the most unusual characters he ever wrote about, Joe Gould.

In 1942, Mitchell published a profile of Joe Gould in the *New Yorker*. Gould was a disheveled bohemian who cadged drinks by entertaining barroom customers. He would demonstrate, for example, how he could carry on conversations with sea gulls. This Bowery eccentric had graduated from Harvard and was the son of a New England doctor, and his ancestors had been in America since 1635. Like Mitchell, he was an exile from the world of his father.

Gould's lifetime project was the Oral History of Our Time. He collected scraps of conversation, biographies of bums, harangues from speakers in Union Square, dirty stories, graffiti, gossip, and arguments about free love, birth control, psychoanalysis, and art. He eavesdropped, and scribbled in nickel composition books. Over the years, as several writers had reported in different publications, the Oral History had grown to millions of words. The idea fascinated Mitchell, whose own work resonated with Gould's idea. Critic Noel Perrin noted of *The Bottom of the Harbor* that each story is told "so much in the words of its characters that it feels like a kind of apotheosis of oral history" (1988, 21).

"I could see the whole thing in my mind," Gould told Mitchell about the Oral History:

Long-winded conversations and short and snappy conversations, brilliant conversations and foolish conversations, curses, catch phrases, coarse remarks, snatches of quarrels, the mutterings of drunks and crazy people, the entreaties of beggars and bums, the propositions of prostitutes, the spiels of pitchmen and peddlers, the sermons of street preachers, shouts in the night, wild rumors, cries from the heart. (Mitchell 1965, 68)

Mitchell, who chronicled ordinary lives in New York City modeled after Stendhal's treatment of the French bourgeoisie, recognized that this down-and-out genius Gould was on to something.

One thing troubled Mitchell about the 1942 profile. He had never actually seen the huge stack of composition books. After Gould died, Mitchell went in search of the man's life work. His digging revealed a few notebooks filled with repetitive and obsessive memories of Gould's father, centered on a psychologically damaging remark about his son's chances in life. Soon Mitchell discovered Joe Gould's secret: the Oral History did not exist.

After *Joe Gould's Secret* was published in 1965, Mitchell fell strangely silent. Not another word had been published by 1990, although Mitchell was said to be constantly working on a major nonfiction book. Almost everyone familiar with Mitchell's work has realized that all of his work since 1965 might be nothing more than an Oral History. Literary critic Stanley Edgar Hyman wrote of *Joe Gould's Secret*:

We realize that Gould has been Mitchell all along, a misfit in a community of traditional occupations, statuses, and roles, come to New York to express his special identity; finally we realize that the body of Mitchell's work is precisely that Oral History of Our Time that Gould himself could not write. (1978, 85)

Mitchell does not entirely deny it. "We were in the same boat," he said of Gould. "We both came from small towns and didn't fit in, and both had an idea. He had the same feeling about people on the park bench talking. I was talking about myself here. He was talking about himself and I was talking about himself and I was talking about myself" (personal interview, 1989a). Yet everything about Gould was factual, he said. It was all documented.

Joe Gould's Secret was about Mitchell in the same way that *Ulysses* is about James Joyce. Many writers who deal in extended narrative nonfiction discover that they can write only when they have a personal connection with their material. In Mitchell's case, his interests merged with Gould's so thoroughly that the two are sometimes inseparable. Other writers have explored the same ground. A. J. Liebling, writing about Colonel John R. Stingo, "The Honest Rainmaker," shaped a portrait that was a composite of two real men, himself and another. James Agee's personal involvement made *Let Us Now Praise Famous Men* a memorable classic, as did George Orwell's in *Homage to Catalonia* and *Down and out in Paris and London*. Mitchell's presence in *Joe Gould's Secret* is more hidden—it may have been unconscious at the time he wrote it—yet his personality merged into Gould's.

Interpretation of nonfiction works such as Mitchell's has suffered because of a necessary realist strategy. Literary journalists bring us reports from the world, reports that represent reality in everyday terms. Edgewater, the Fulton Fish Market, and Mr. Hunter's family on Staten Island all existed. Mitchell's articles about them captured some portion of their realities. Accepting the literary strategy, we readily assume that, because something really happened or really existed, any symbolism contained in the story must be either accidental or unintentional. Yet the creative forces that motivate writers like Joe Mitchell or A. J. Liebling to create an extended work of narrative nonfiction are not terribly different from the juices that feed the labors of novelists. In writing about Joe Gould and Old Mr. Flood, Mitchell found a means of self-expression. He became a part of the narrative without interjecting himself into it. His work remained formally realist—meaning that it dealt with realities outside of the author's point of view. Yet at the same time it was modernist, in the sense that the reality had been filtered through the author's own system of values and perspectives. The roses in the Edgewater cemetery, Mr. Hunter's family story, and Joe Gould's personality can be actual and symbolic. Mitchell spent so much time with Joe Gould, for example, that he could choose from a panoply of conversations. He could describe the "true Gould," as he put it, and talk about Joe Mitchell at the same time (personal interview, 1989b).

Writing about Coleridge's "The Ancient Mariner," Kenneth Burke once said, "The main ideal of criticism, as I conceive it, is to use all that is there to use." If we are to understand the "symbolic enactment going on in the poem," Burke wrote, "we must study the interrelationships disclosable by a study of Coleridge's mind itself" (1973, 23). Critics of nonfiction tend to neglect the personal relationships the author has with his material. In Joseph Mitchell's case, the full meaning of his writing, and the symbolism of the imagery, can only be achieved if one is willing to accept a symbolic element in nonfiction and to respect nonfiction as a form of personal expression. There have been a few masters of symbolism in nonfiction during the twentieth century, and Mitchell is one of them. If his work since 1965 turns out to be an autobiography, we may yet learn more about the full meaning of his nonfiction.

PRIMARY SOURCES

Mitchell, Joseph. 1938. *My Ears Are Bent*. New York: Sheridan House.

———. 1943. *McSorley's Wonderful Saloon*. New York: Duell, Sloan and Pearce.

———. 1948. *Old Mr. Flood*. New York: Duell, Sloan and Pearce.

———. 1960. *The Bottom of the Harbor*. Boston: Little, Brown; London: Chatto and Windus, 1961.

———. 1965. *Joe Gould's Secret*. New York: Viking Press.

———. 1988, Oct. 14. Personal interview.

———. 1989a, Mar. 23. Personal interview.

———. 1989b, Aug. 14. Personal interview.

Mitchell, Joseph, and Edmund Wilson. 1960. *Apologies to the Iroquois with a Study of the Mohawks in High Steel*. New York: Farrar, Straus.

SECONDARY SOURCES

Burke, Kenneth. 1973. *The Philosophy of Literary Forms*. Berkeley: University of California Press.

Cowley, Malcolm. 1943, July 26. "The Grammar of Facts." *New Republic*: 113; Rpt. in *The Flower and the Leaf*. New York: Viking Press, 1985.

Hyman, Stanley Edgar. 1978. "The Art of Joseph Mitchell." In *The Critic's Credentials*. New York: Atheneum.

North Carolina Authors. 1952. Chapel Hill: University of North Carolina Library.

Perrin, Noel. 1983, Spring. "Paragon of Reporters: Joseph Mitchell." *Sewanee Review* 91, no. 2: 182.

———. 1988. "A Kind of Writing for Which No Name Exists." In *A Reader's Delight*. Hanover, N.H.: University Press of New England.

Sims, Norman. 1990. "Joseph Mitchell and *The New Yorker* Nonfiction Writers." In *Literary Journalism in the Twentieth Century*. Ed. Sims. New York: Oxford University Press.

JOHN HERSEY

Dan R. Jones

As the author of more than a dozen novels, John Hersey has firmly established himself as a writer of fiction. Yet it is his reputation as a journalist, earned as a correspondent for *Time* and *Life* during World War II, that may ultimately define his career. Tom Wolfe, in his landmark 1973 essay "The New Journalism," declares that Hersey's wartime reportage comprises the direct ancestry of contemporary literary journalism. While claiming to be uncomfortable with the progeny with which he has been credited, Hersey is nonetheless responsible for a number of important technical and stylistic achievements in the development of literary journalism. In particular, *Hiroshima*, Hersey's account of the first wartime use of the atomic bomb, must be considered one of the central works of the genre.

Born in 1914 in Tientsin, China, to American missionary parents, Hersey began his journalistic career in 1937 as a correspondent for *Time*, the magazine he considered "the liveliest enterprise of its type" (Sanders 1967, 21). Hersey quickly mastered *Time's* anonymous writing style and employed it effectively on a series of overseas assignments. His first, to report on the Sino-Japanese War from the magazine's Chunking bureau, led to the writing of *Men on Bataan* in 1942, an account of the fighting in the Philippines. The book, written from the New York bureau using letters, interview materials, and *Time* files, won Hersey critical praise, even though his depictions of the valor of American fighting men are so thoroughly mired in the morale-building effort that they fail to comprise innovative or even very convincing journalism.

Into the Valley, an account of a Marine detachment dug in during a particularly perilous battle at Guadalcanal, followed in 1943. Though not entirely free of the patriotic excesses that marred *Men on Bataan*, *Into the Valley* benefits from Hersey's participation in the events he depicts, and in that respect presages some of the techniques he used to advantage in *Hi-*

roshima two years later. *A Bell for Adano*, for which Hersey won the 1945 Pulitzer Prize in fiction, was published in 1944. The book is loosely based on a *Life* article he wrote about a day in the life of the American military governor of Licata, Sicily. The novel recounts the efforts of Major Joppolo, an American military government commander of a small Sicilian village, to find a bell for the village belltower to replace the one stolen by the Fascists and thus restore the villagers' sense of community. As in Hersey's previous efforts, the book is tinged with nationalist pride, as is evident in the following characterization of Joppolo and his mission:

Until there is a seeming stability in Europe, our armies and our after-armies will have to stay in Europe. Each American who stays may very well be extremely dependent on a Joppolo, not only for language, but for wisdom and justice and the other things we think we have to offer to Europeans. (2)

David Sanders, author of the first book-length study on Hersey, has characterized Hersey's wartime writing as the work of "a man who had to write too much too soon" (1967, 38). Of course, the same could be said of any number of correspondents assigned to cover World War II, for whom the demands of wartime reporting, political as well as journalistic, dictated the production of supportive, morally unambiguous chronicles of the war effort—a kind of journalism that contains what Dwight MacDonald has called the "built in reaction." In MacDonald's words, such writing "includes the spectator's reactions in the work itself instead of forcing him to make his own responses" (1960, 228). In short, Hersey's journalism of this period was intended to augment, rather than interpret, the images and understandings of the war his readers had gathered from a variety of popular sources. Had he not encountered a subject worthy of challenging and expanding his abilities, both as a journalist and a literary stylist, he likely would be remembered primarily as one of a host of correspondents who translated their experiences and perceptions into popular, yet transitory, accounts of the war.

He found that subject in the first wartime use of the atomic bomb. *Hiroshima*, published in 1946, remains Hersey's best example of literary journalism. Much of the success of *Hiroshima* has to do with its subject. Unlike the war in general, the use of an atomic bomb to obliterate a city was an event unparalleled in human history, one for which no adequate model of understanding existed. This reality produced a sense of awe in his readers which Hersey could tap, but it also meant that he could not depend on the "built in reaction" to help tell his tale. If the story were to be told in a credible fashion, it demanded that Hersey not only gather and document information, but also provide forms for understanding what has been called history's least imaginable event.

Hersey employs a number of techniques to achieve this end. The basic narrative structure of the book is chronological: the account opens a few hours before the bombing and closes almost exactly one year later. The chronological scheme provides a simple, easily imagined frame for guiding the reader's perception of the event. As circumstances become unimaginable, storytelling becomes more conventional, as we rely increasingly on our most basic perceptual strategies. Ultimately, the most simple form of storytelling is to convert the event into a series of episodes, related by time.

Hersey achieves a sense of authenticity by adopting an almost clinical tone in his prose. Missing from *Hiroshima* are the moral pronouncements of *Into the Valley* and *A Bell for Adano*; in their place are spare and meticulously documented details gleaned from close observation and careful research. The exact location of the center of the blast, for example, is identified as "a spot a hundred and fifty yards south of the torii and a few yards southeast of the pile of ruins that had once been the Shima Hospital" (96). Although this datum is of little interpretive value, it demonstrates to the reader that much about the bombing can indeed be ascertained and communicated in familiar terms; precise description becomes an instrument of comprehensibility.

The book chronicles the fortunes of six survivors for a year following the blast. The six—a German Jesuit priest, two doctors, a Japanese Methodist minister, an office girl, and a tailor's war widow—are decidedly unrepresentative of the general population of Hiroshima. For example, Hiroshima, with its population of 250,000, had only 150 doctors; 2 of these appear in *Hiroshima*. Likewise, even though Christians numbered less that 1 percent of predominantly Buddhist and Shintoist wartime Japan, two of Hersey's subjects are Christian clergymen. Yet the very qualities that make Hersey's survivors atypical of Japanese culture make them recognizable and even sympathetic to American readers. Hersey's choice of subjects is thus consistent with the book's basic agenda: to provide a frame for comprehending the incomprehensible reality of the atomic bomb blast. Because Hersey's nonfiction novel is populated with figures who, though Japanese, nonetheless conform to American social types, the characters become guides to understanding the event.

The survivors' attempts to understand the function and effects of the bomb, and their uncertain progress toward that end, trace an important narrative movement in the book in which readers participate. Rumors abound, such as the theory that the destruction was the result of gasoline or magnesium dust sprinkled over the city and then ignited; an exact understanding is never achieved. Technical explanations were of course available to Hersey, yet they do not appear in the book. Rather, he allows the bomb to remain ultimately inexplicable, partly to authenticate the survivors' own understandings, and partly so as not to violate the sense of awe that his readers are likely to attach to the bomb. His journalistic technique in this regard is thus not to tell all that is known about the bomb, but rather to report on the reality of the bomb in ways that are consistent both with his subjects' perceptions and with the prior understandings of the readers to whom the account is offered.

In addition to locating terms that would adequately symbolize the atomic bomb, Hersey was faced with the task of translating Japanese culture into a vocabulary that would be accessible to Western sensibilities. He does this by choosing as settings for the book institutions that would be common to both Japanese and American cultures: churches, banks, a police station, a lower-middle-class home, hospitals, and doctors' offices. When he can, Hersey describes Japanese life by using terms familiar to Americans; Hiroshima's outlying residential districts, for example, are referred to as "suburbs" (8). When no adequate terms exist for describing a uniquely Japanese custom or institution, it is labeled an oddity and explained, often in detail. Dr. Fujii's single-doctor hospital, for example, is described as "a peculiarly Japanese institution" (13); a detailed explanation of Japanese customs for ministering to the sick follows. The city of Hiroshima thereby assumes a quality of everyday life that readers can associate with their own lives. Hersey's journalistic agenda is thus not only to report the facts of the event, but to accommodate the needs of his American readers by providing a perceptual frame within which the event assumes significance.

In 1985, Hersey published a fifth chapter to *Hiroshima* in which he documents the fates of the six survivors. Two—Dr. Fujii and Father Kleinsorge—have died, while the others have encountered various fortunes and misfortunes. Dr. Sasaki, the idealistic young surgeon who worked tirelessly in the days following the initial blast to care for the wounded and dying, has become wealthy, while Mr. Tanimoto, the equally selfless Methodist minister, has met with only mixed success and much disappointment in his efforts to teach the world about the horrors of the atomic bomb. The updated accounts bring the reader no closer to a comprehensive moral understanding of the bomb, and Hersey skillfully resists the temptation to use the new stories to bring narrative closure to the original text. To do so would violate his original journalistic agenda: to translate the reality of the bomb into terms that are salient to Western habits of mind, while declining to either justify or condemn its use. The true achievement of *Hiroshima*, then, and that which sets it apart from Hersey's earlier journalism, is that its journalistic credibility is not flawed by the injection of moralistic sentiment.

Here to Stay, first published in 1963, was Hersey's next venture into literary journalism. The book is a collection of nine tales of survival—from war, natural disasters, concentration camps, and other extreme situations. The complete text of *Hiroshima* is included as the last piece. The stories are gleaned from a variety of sources. Some are previously unreported products of Hersey's World War II experiences, such as "Joe Is Home Now" and "A Short Talk with Erlanger," both of which address the problems of returning war veterans. Other stories in the collection appear to have been sought out precisely because they typify for Hersey the theme of survival. An example is the first story in the collection, "Over the Mad River," which chronicles the experiences of an elderly survivor of the floodwaters spawned by Hurricane Diane in Connecticut in 1955.

Hersey opens his preface to the 1988 edition of *Here to Stay* with the following statement: "The great themes are love and death; their synthesis is the will to live" (vii). The statement provides not only a unifying theme for the stories in the collection, but may also offer some insight into Hersey's motivations as a writer of nonfiction. Also in the preface he writes:

I could wish that a great secret could have been embedded in these tales, so that a reader could unriddle it between the lines—a clear answer of some kind to the most mysterious of all questions, the existential question: What is it that, by a narrow margin, keeps humankind going, in the face of its crimes, its follies, its greed, its passions, its sorrows, its panics, its hatreds, its hideous drives to pollute and waste and dominate and kill? (vii)

The stories, of course, provide no final answers, yet it is significant that Hersey chooses to explore these basic issues through the telling of nonfiction "tales." While claiming to remain faithful to the factual demands of journalism, Hersey imbues his tales with a parable-like quality that is quite consistent with the thematic character of fiction.

The Algiers Motel Incident, an account of the murders of three young black men during the Detroit riots of 1967, represents Hersey's only other significant attempt at extended literary journalism. Published in 1968, the book consists of carefully transcribed interviews with witnesses to the shooting, family members of the dead, the police and legal authorities involved in the shooting, and a host of secondary figures. There are also court transcripts, media accounts, and other official records, all linked by Hersey's own narrative. While presenting a tremendous amount of data about the shootings, the book suffers from a number of flaws, not the least of which is Hersey's intervention into the narrative. Unlike *Hiroshima,* in which the author remains invisible, and *Here to Stay,* in which he appears only in the preface and introductions to individual stories, Hersey enters directly into the telling of *The Algiers Motel Incident.* However, his purpose in doing so is cloudy. Early in the text he explains that, while he has always "stayed out of my journalism" as a matter of principle, "this account is too urgent, too complex, too dangerous to too many people to be told in a way that might leave doubts strewn along its path" (24). Presumably, Hersey is freeing himself to make judgments on the facts he presents, but this rationale does not satisfy, nor does it justify Hersey's failure to recognize the moral complexity of the tale he is telling. His blame for the police involved in the shooting is unequivocal; their victims were guilty, he says, of no more than "being, after all and all, black young men and part of the black rage of the time" (195)—despite the fact, as *Atlantic* reviewer Edward Weeks observed, that most had police records and all "had a cynical contempt for the legal process" (1968, 92).

Such behavior hardly warrants murder, of course, and Hersey's moral judgments may have been correct, if only in a legal sense. Yet the book was published long before the legal issues in the case were settled, and in any event, credible literary journalism must do more than use reporting as an instrument for the placing of blame. Essentially, Hersey was unable to accomplish in *The Algiers Motel Incident* what he could do in both *Hiroshima* and *Here to Stay*: the conversion of a set of factual incidents into true-life parables of survival and endurance. Hersey attempts to construct a parable of race relations and the effects of prejudice in America out of the incidents described in *The Algiers Motel Incident,* but the victims are not sufficiently ennobling, nor are the perpetrators sufficiently malicious, to reduce the tale to these terms. Ironically, it may be Hersey's integrity as a journalist that prevents *The Algiers Motel Incident* from being a more compelling story. Hersey was driven to uncover every scrap of available data in his quest for the truth behind the murders at the Algiers Motel, yet the circumstances and issues of the case he revealed turned out to be too complex to fit the parable-like narrative he seems to have envisioned for the book.

Hersey is not a greatly self-reflective writer, although he has occasionally commented on his role as a literary journalist. In an article entitled "The Novel of Contemporary History," which appeared in the November 1949 issue of the *Atlantic,* he defends the use of literature as a "clarifying agent" (80) for the chronicling of world events, and says that fiction may be a more effective instrument for the conception of history than is historical writing itself. Further, Hersey codifies the qualities that the writer of historical novels should possess, including a need for understanding, a desire for communication, "anger," and a "will for world citizenship" (84). The essay reveals more about Hersey's attitude toward the handling of fact than he perhaps intends; it is his self-conscious attempt to demonstrate anger, for example, that makes *The Algiers Motel Incident* an ultimately unsatisfactory account of a historically significant event.

Hersey's headnotes to the individual stories in *Here to Stay* offer additional insights into his practices and beliefs as a nonfiction writer. For example, he includes in almost every headnote a statement of how the information for the particular piece was gathered, as if to prove its authenticity. At the beginning of "Flight," a story about a family of Hungarian refugees following the 1956 suppression, he includes the following statement:

I became acquainted with the Fekete family in Austria, at a teeming refugee camp, a few days after the family's eruption from its homeland, and it was there that the gaunt paterfamilias told me most of this story; I lived parts of its last chapters with him. (1963, 33)

Similar statements of Hersey's fact-gathering technique appear in the head-notes to most of the stories, perhaps to assure the reader that the fictional quality of the "tales" presented in the book should not be considered in-consistent with the journalistic integrity of the facts contained therein.

In the headnote to the section "Strength from Without," Hersey offers a further defense of his literary handling of factual material, in this case, his creation of composite characters and situations in the stories "Joe Is Home Now" and "A Short Talk with Erlanger." "Something needs to be said about the reportorial technique used in this story and the one that follows," Hersey writes, adding that his technique in these two stories is different from that used in the "orthodox journalistic tales that constitute the rest of the book" (1963, 107). His explanation is as follows:

These two accounts...are dovetailings, in each case, of the actual experiences of a number of men...The story of [Joe's] struggles is not "fictionalized," because noth-ing was invented; it is a report. Joe does and says things that were actually said and done by various men with whom I talked; I simply arranged the materials. (107–8)

Again, Hersey hopes to demonstrate that the literary quality of his writing does not detract from its journalistic authenticity, yet the technique he is defending—the blending of composite characters and situations into a single narrative line—is not a conservative one. In general, Hersey's approach to the construction of journalistic narrative is much more traditional than the approach he employs in these two stories.

This traditional approach is well articulated in a 1980 essay entitled "The Legend on the License," in which he declares that "journalism is on a sickbed and is in a very bad way" (1). The article launches a belated attack on Truman Capote's *In Cold Blood* and presents as well stinging rebukes of Tom Wolfe, for bending the rules of journalistic objectivity in *The Right Stuff,* and of Norman Mailer, for tampering with documentary evidence in *The Executioner's Song.* Hersey closes with what he considers a simple dictum: "The writer of fiction must invent. The journalist must not invent" (25). Such an edict has the ring of common sense about it, but does not go far toward clarifying the relationship between factual content and fictional technique which even Hersey displays in his best literary journalism.

While Hersey has not ventured into extended literary journalism since the publication of *The Algiers Motel Incident,* his latest novel, *Blues,* is nonetheless a curious blend of fact and fiction that presents a wealth of data, lore, and insights gleaned from Hersey's twenty years of fishing for bluefish along the coast of Massachusetts. Set as a series of dialogues between a seasoned fisherman and a novice identified only as "stranger," the book is a vehicle for Hersey to explore his own fascination with the sea by tracing the dramatic revelations that are opened to the stranger as he learns to fish. While *Blues* can hardly be considered literary journalism in the sense that *Hiroshima* is, it is nonetheless an appealing concatenation of scientific data, folklore, and wisdom set in a literary frame.

As Hersey nears the end of his writing career, it appears that his most substantial accomplishment is still one of his earliest. *Hiroshima* represents Hersey's most successful blending of literary technique with journalistic content, largely because it is one of his least self-conscious works. Hersey's characteristic shortcoming as a literary journalist has been his desire to employ journalistic findings in the service of preconceived moral intentions. His early World War II journalism clearly displays this flaw, as does *The Algiers Motel Incident*. *Hiroshima* escapes this defect, largely because the simple moral judgments that might have typified the event were not available. Consequently, the novel provides an honest and compelling account of a morally ambiguous event in a journalistically credible fashion, as well as in aesthetically and dramatically effective terms. Perhaps unwittingly, Hersey has provided in *Hiroshima* one of the seminal examples of contemporary literary journalism.

PRIMARY SOURCES

Hersey, John. 1942. *Men on Bataan*. New York: Alfred A. Knopf.
———. 1943. *Into the Valley*. New York: Alfred A. Knopf.
———. 1944. *A Bell for Adano*. New York: Alfred A. Knopf.
———. 1946. *Hiroshima*. New York: Alfred A. Knopf. Reissued with new material, Knopf, 1985.
———. 1949. "The Novel of Contemporary History." *Atlantic* 184: 80–84.
———. 1963. *Here to Stay*. New York: Alfred A. Knopf. Reissued with new preface, New York: Paragon House, 1988.
———. 1968. *The Algiers Motel Incident*. New York: Alfred A. Knopf.
———. 1980, Autumn. "The Legend on the License." *Yale Review*: 1–25.
———. 1987. *Blues*. New York: Alfred A. Knopf.

SECONDARY SOURCES

Huse, Nancy Lyman. 1978. *James Agee and John Hersey: A Reference Guide*. Boston: G. K. Hall.
———. 1983. *The Survival Tales of John Hersey*. Troy, N.Y.: Whitston.
MacDonald, Dwight. 1960, Spring. "Masscult and Midcult." *Partisan Review* 27: 203–33.
Sanders, David. 1967. *John Hersey*. New York: Twayne.
———. 1968. "John Hersey: War Correspondent into Novelist." In *New Voices in*

American Studies. Ed. Ray Browne, Donald M. Winkleman, and Allen Hayman. West Lafayette, Ind.: Purdue University Press.

Weeks, Edward. 1968, July. Review of *The Algiers Motel Incident,* by John Hersey. *Atlantic*: 92–93.

JOHN STEINBECK

Giles Fowler

In 1958, long after the war he had "attended" as a correspondent for the *New York Herald Tribune,* John Steinbeck looked back with some pensiveness at the old newspaper dispatches finally being issued in book form. "Reading them over after all these years," he wrote in his introduction, "I realized not only how much I have forgotten but that they are period pieces, the attitudes archaic, the impulses romantic, and, in the light of everything that has happened since, perhaps the whole body of work untrue and warped and one-sided" (1958, xi). It was almost an apology, as though the author were predicting, and hoping to neutralize, unfriendly reactions to the book, *Once There Was a War.*

In fact, Steinbeck's deprecating words were in some ways justified. More than a few pieces in the collection do seem dated and corny, "warped and one-sided"—which is not surprising, given their age, as well as the haste, the stress, and especially the constraints of censorship under which they were written.

At the same time, many of the stories to this day have an unexpected vibrancy. At their best, they survive as vivid evocations of a chaotic, lethal, sometimes heroic era, and of some of the people—mostly unnamed and quick-sketched—who passed through it.

In all, Steinbeck filed sixty-six articles of around 1,000 words each, date-lined from June 20 to December 13, 1943 (the last dozen or so apparently written from notes following his return to the States in October). Steinbeck's intent from the first was to focus on the human side of war and leave the straight news to other correspondents. Almost exclusively, his subjects were ordinary servicemen and civilians, bit players in a drama far too huge for them to grasp. Thus, while Steinbeck's reportage covers a broad expanse of the war zone, from England to North Africa to the bloody beaches of Italy, his stories explore much smaller worlds of the immediate and personal:

crewmen of a PT boat staring at a body bobbing in the sea (1958, 164); two neighbors in Dover examining a rosebush damaged by last night's air raid (49); a wounded GI who worries that his wife "wouldn't like a cripple" (101).

Steinbeck also gives us glimpses into the small world of his own terror. His numbed, almost dreamlike third-person account of battle, after he had come under heavy fire on the beachhead at Salerno, is one of many moments in *Once There Was a War* that far transcend ordinary journalism (157–60).

The collection is journalism, of course, right down to its lapses into banality and the "raggedness" (Steinbeck's own term) of much of the writing. But it also approaches literature in at least three ways. First, it relies heavily on forms and devices borrowed from the fiction writer's craft: the short story structure, impressionistic imagery, characterization, and extensive use of dialogue. Second, it is interwoven with themes associated with Steinbeck's literary works. Finally, the best articles capture and interpret with an artist's sensibilities the experience of actually being there on the staging grounds and killing grounds of a great war.

Even when his prose is hurried, Steinbeck can give these experiences the stark immediacy of stop-action frames in a living newsreel. Often this effect has as much to do with the author's rhythms as with his images, as in this scene from the battle for Salerno:

He might have seen the splash of dirt and dust that is a shell burst, and a small Italian girl in the street with her stomach blown out, and he might have seen an American soldier standing over her twitching body, crying . . . He would have smelled the sharp cordite in the air and the hot reek of blood if the going has been rough. The burning odor of dust will be in his nose and the stench of men and animals killed yesterday and the day before. (158)

This may not represent Steinbeck at his very best, but neither can it be casually dismissed. *Once There Was a War* contains numerous passages of similar power, and for these alone the book merits serious attention.

Nevertheless, the collection often has been treated as little more than a footnote in critical analyses of Steinbeck's work. Although some of the initial reviews were favorable, others in such periodicals as *Saturday Review,* the *New York Times,* and the *New Yorker* were cool or damning. (Notably, by the late fifties Steinbeck had fallen out of favor with many critics, who felt that his talent was in decline.) Scholarly opinion has been equally mixed.

At least a few who have reexamined the work some years after its release have suggested that *Once There Was a War* deserves far more respect than it has usually received. One such scholar, Sanford E. Marovitz, in a 1974 article in the *Steinbeck Quarterly,* compares the collection favorably with Bill Mauldin's *Up Front* and Ernie Pyle's *Brave Men,* and concludes that

Once There Was a War revealed the author as "a distinguished literary journalist" (1974b, 98). And Lester Jay Marks, writing in *Thematic Design in the Novels of John Steinbeck,* asserts that in "tone, characterization, and theme, these pieces bear the weight of comparison with Steinbeck's fiction" (1969, 90).

The stories were written only four years after the publication of Steinbeck's masterpiece, *The Grapes of Wrath,* and two years after the major nonfiction work *Sea of Cortez* (in collaboration with Edward F. Ricketts). The author at age forty-one was still at or near the height of his creative vigor, although in the previous year he had published two works of scant value, the novel *The Moon Is Down* and the quasi-journalistic *Bombs Away: The Story of a Bomber Team.*

The latter, done as a wartime propaganda piece, has its effective moments but hardly deserves serious study. However, an earlier Steinbeck foray into journalism, a series of newspaper pieces about California's migrant farm workers, is worth more than passing note.

Written in 1936 for the *San Francisco News,* the seven articles plus an added epilogue appeared two years later in pamphlet form under the title *Their Blood Is Strong.* (In 1963 the full text was republished by Warren French in his book, *A Companion to "The Grapes of Wrath."*) Though openly didactic, the work is a well-reported, tersely written record of the appalling conditions under which the harvesters lived and of the social and economic forces that led to their plight. More important, as French observes, readers of the tract will recognize "many details which Steinbeck subsequently put to artistic use" in *The Grapes of Wrath,* though of course the novel "is art rather than propaganda" (1963, 52–53).

As Steinbeck gathered material for *Their Blood Is Strong* and *The Grapes of Wrath,* part of his secret, it seems, was the use of total-immersion reporting in which he spent days and weeks with the migrants, at times sharing the harshness of their lives. Although Steinbeck gives little hint of his later reporting techniques for *Once There Was a War,* it seems fair to assume that again he sought to blend with his subjects in order to win their trust and tap their feelings. At the same time, however, there is much reason to doubt F. W. Watt's assertion in *Steinbeck* that a characteristic of the author's wartime reporting was "his resolute refusal to go beyond his personal knowledge—he wrote only what he saw, and 'faked' nothing" (1962, 77).

Steinbeck certainly "faked" the narrative point of view in many of his dispatches, as he admits in his introduction to *Once There Was a War.* One of his "coy little tricks with copy," he writes, was to put descriptions of scenes "in the mouth of someone else," perhaps because he felt that they would be "more believable" that way (1958, xvi).

There are other reasons to question whether Steinbeck always adhered to the letter of the facts. Some stretches of narrative and dialogue have a slicked-up, processed feel. A few pieces, such as a stock, predictable ghost story told by an American sergeant (68–71), come off as barrack-room whoppers. And the journalistically fastidious will be put off by the author's occasional habit of entering characters' minds.

Misgivings of another kind arise from our knowledge that the stories were subjected to heavy military censorship and even heavier self-censorship. In his introduction, Steinbeck describes at length the absurd rules imposed by the military command, then writes: "In the pieces in this book everything set down happened. It is in the things not mentioned that the untruth lies" (xiii).

Plainly Steinbeck understood that all journalism is a compromise between the whole truth and the reporter's limitations. He ends his introduction with a remark that might describe many a journalistic record: "[The stories] are as real as the wicked witch and the good fairy, as true and tested as any other myth" (xxi). This statement may also indicate that the author wished the book to be taken more as literature than as journalism in the strictest sense.

Marks and Marovitz have suggested that the articles together have a kind of structural unity not unlike that of Steinbeck's episodic novels, *The Pastures of Heaven, Cannery Row,* and *Tortilla Flat.* Although this seems somewhat exaggerated (too many of the stories simply do not fit in, in terms of subject matter, style, or tone), it is true that many of the dispatches are loosely linked by setting, by character, and especially by theme.

Throughout the stories we encounter familiar Steinbeck motifs: man's instinctive will to survive (as an individual as well as a faceless component of the mass); the theme of "group man" engaged in coordinated effort to serve a common cause; the workings of the dark, irrational unconscious in shaping human behavior.

As in *The Grapes of Wrath,* Steinbeck the war correspondent concerns himself largely with the struggle of plain people to endure and adapt to a world of much inhumanity and danger. These soldiers and civilians are swept up in a vast effort that both subordinates and puts terrible demands upon the self. At such times, individuality may be the loser, as in this grotesquely memorable scene aboard a troop ship:

The men wear their helmets, which make them all look alike, make them look like long rows of mushrooms. Their rifles are leaning against their knees. They have no identity, no personality. The men are units in an army. The numbers chalked on their helmets are almost like the license numbers on robots. (1958, 3)

But within the herd existence and depersonalizing violence of war, we keep finding characters who refuse to relinquish their grip on personal identity. Their reactions to war vary throughout the book, and some are amusingly or eerily idiosyncratic. As Peter Lisca notes in *John Steinbeck: Nature and Myth,* the war dispatches contain repeated evidence of Steinbeck's interest in Jungian psychology—the ways people revert to "unconscious or dreamlike or atavistic behavior" under terrible stress or exhaustion (1978, 224).

In two of the stories, for instance, Steinbeck writes of the almost consuming power of superstition over fighting men's lives. At a bomber base in England, a tail gunner misplaces his St. Christopher medal and the whole crew scrambles in search of it while an uneasiness "creeps all through the room" (1958, 30). Among soldiers at the front, many wear steel-bound Testaments in their breast pockets to deflect bullets, one man carries a locket his dead wife wore as a child, and a sergeant holds an Indianhead penny against the stock of his rifle as he fires (195–96).

It was Steinbeck's conviction (reinforced by his contemplations of sea life during the marine biological expedition described in *Sea of Cortez*) that the survival of any species, man included, hinges on its ability to adapt—to accept and live according to what "is."

The ultimate symbol of adaptation is a character called Big Train Mulligan, a private assigned to a motor pool in London. An uncannily resourceful fellow, wise to the stratagems of borrowing money, mooching food, romancing English girls, and playing on the vanities of officers, Big Train has made such a cozy life for himself that his war is more of an extended holiday (1958, 84–87, 102, 105). In some ways, as Marks observes (p. 89), he is like other happy-go-lucky nonconformists who show up in Steinbeck's novels *Cannery Row* and *Tortilla Flat*.

Yet the treatment of Mulligan illustrates a frequent shortcoming of *Once There Was a War*: a failure to give characters full-blown lives of their own. Somehow, Big Train appears to be less a quirky, independent human being than a figure manipulated to represent an idea. He is described but not *revealed,* and, worse, he is predictable.

Even characters' dialogue in certain passages has a tooled, reconstructed quality, leaving the nagging suspicion that the original reality has been so overworked for effect that what now lies on the page is less than real.

This same sense of calculated manipulation dulls the impact of one of the more consciously literary segments of the book, the six pieces that wind up the collection (1958, 212–33). Set out as a kind of serialized short story, they describe the capture of an Italian island by a force of American paratroopers. The moment Steinbeck describes these GIs with their uniformly pale eyes, their "almost shy good manners," and their lethal readiness to become "very rough if anybody shoots at them," one almost expects John Wayne to step forward as their commanding officer. And other stereotypes are on the way: the Italian soldiers jabbering absurdly as they surrender without a fight; the crisp German officer who is bamboozled into thinking that his own superior force is badly outnumbered. Steinbeck not only enters the German's mind briefly, but also chronicles every thought of the lone U.S. lieutenant who is the story's hero.

Granting that the events must have happened, did they happen as Steinbeck wrote them? Did the characters really look, behave, and think these ways, and did the real-life events fall into so neat a narrative structure, right down to the closing punchline? Some readers will be justified in doubting whether Steinbeck was even there during the taking of that island.

The majority of the stories are untainted by this aura of artificiality, however. Even when Steinbeck obviously puts description "in the mouth of someone else," he is able more often than not to convey the feel of first-hand experience. Here, for instance, is an excerpt from a unnamed soldier's supposed description of the Salerno landing:

We were out there all packed in an LCI and then all hell broke loose. The sky was full of it and the star shells lighted it up and the tracers crisscrossed and the noise—we saw the assault go in, and then one of them hit a surf mine and went up, and in the light you could see them go flying about...

It didn't seem like men getting killed, more like a picture, like a moving picture. We were pretty crowded up in there, though, and then all of a sudden it came to me that this wasn't a moving picture. (155)

The words are hardly literary, but the keenness and tautness of the telling are. Whether or not the voice is really John Steinbeck's and the GI a convenient fiction, the story fails not at all in capturing the terror of that beachhead.

In tone, *Once There Was a War* varies according to content. At his worst, Steinbeck attempts a roguish cuteness, as in the particularly silly piece about an "elf" who supplies the war correspondents with hard-to-find whisky (190–94). Much of the best writing, on the other hand, is marked by a cool precision and leanness that serve the author especially well in some of the action scenes. His account of a PT boat's attack on a German ammunition ship is reminiscent of passages from Hemingway:

[The captain] issued his orders and took the wheel himself. Then he swung the boat and called softly, "Fire!" There was a sharp explosive whisk of sound and a splash, and the torpedo was away. He swung again and fired another. And his mouth moved as though he were counting. (208)

Still other dispatches bear some kinship to the famous interchapters in *The Grapes of Wrath*, in which descriptive vignettes are used to dramatize general conditions in Depression America. Steinbeck writes, for instance, about a huge "bone yard" for wrecked tanks, not unlike an American auto junkyard. What makes the piece is its use of poignant details: "In this tank which has been hit there is a splash of blood against the steel side of the turret. And in this burned-out tank a large piece of singed cloth and a charred and curled shoe" (138).

Here is evidence, surely, of the true reporter's eye for those telling bits of reality that lend scale and texture to the larger picture. Such an eye belongs also, of course, to the true literary writer, which is one reason we are not surprised when journalist and novelist merge in a single person.

Inarguably, the best of Steinbeck's work lies in the best of his fiction. There is nothing in the wartime dispatches to match the eloquence and power of *The Grapes of Wrath* or the raffish comedy of *Tortilla Flat*.

Nevertheless, *Once There Was a War* may stand as the best journalistic writing Steinbeck ever produced; certainly he rarely, if ever, equaled it in succeeding years. *A Russian Journal* (1948), describing a journey to the Soviet Union with photographer Robert Capa, has been justly criticized for superficiality. *Travels with Charley: In Search of America* (1962), Steinbeck's account of a tour to rediscover his native land, enjoyed popular success but now seems thin and simplistic. *America and Americans* (1968), a bleak discourse on the state of the nation's moral health, does little more than rework the author's familiar concerns about a softening America. And most of the dozens of magazine and newspaper pieces produced in the period demonstrate, as Marovitz writes, that "the vital force of Steinbeck's creative imagination markedly deteriorated during the late 1940s" (1974b, 96).

It was still a creatively vital John Steinbeck, however, who in 1943 telephoned his war stories home to the *Herald Tribune*. He was even tempted to turn out a book about his war experiences, but he resisted the impulse at the time, believing, as he explains in his introduction, "that unless the stories had validity twenty years in the future they should stay on the yellowing pages of dead newspaper files" (xi).

Steinbeck needn't have worried. In a broad sense, his war stories surely have much the same validity today as they had in 1943. While written and flawed as journalism, they sometimes meet the test of art.

PRIMARY SOURCES

Steinbeck, John. 1938. *Their Blood Is Strong*. San Francisco: Simon J. Lubin Society of California. Rpt. 1963. In *A Companion to "The Grapes of Wrath."* Ed. Warren French. New York: Viking Press.

———. 1942. *Bombs Away: The Story of a Bomber Team*. New York: Viking Press.

———. 1948. *A Russian Journal*. New York: Viking Press.

———. 1958. *Once There Was a War*. New York: Viking Press.

———. 1962. *Travels with Charley: In Search of America*. New York: Viking Press.

———. 1966. *America and Americans*. New York: Viking Press.

SECONDARY SOURCES

French, Warren, ed. 1963. *A Companion to "The Grapes of Wrath."* New York: Viking Press.

Howarth, William. 1990. "The Mother of Literature: Journalism and *The Grapes*

of *Wrath*." In *Literary Journalism in the Twentieth Century*. Ed. Norman
Sims. New York: Oxford University Press, 53–81.

Lisca, Peter. 1978. *John Steinbeck: Nature and Myth*. New York: Thomas Y.
Crowell.

Marks, Lester J. 1969. *Thematic Design in the Novels of John Steinbeck*. The Hague:
Mouton.

Marovitz, Sanford E. 1974a, Spring. "The Expository Prose of John Steinbeck, Pt.
I." *Steinbeck Quarterly*: 41–52.

———. 1974b, Summer-Fall. "The Expository Prose of John Steinbeck, Pt. II."
Steinbeck Quarterly: 88–102.

Watt, F. W. 1962. *Steinbeck*. Edinburgh and London: Oliver and Boyd.

LILLIAN ROSS

Arthur W. Roberts

Just how far a writer of nonfiction should go in the use of literary techniques has been debated for a long time. Early in the movement known as the new journalism, such taboos as the use of the pronoun "I" and the re-creation of extensive dialogue were abrogated when the writers began entering scenes as direct participants. As more liberties were taken, these same writers separated into two camps: those favoring the more liberal use of fictional techniques and those favoring the more journalistic. Writers like Gay Talese, Tom Wolfe, and Norman Mailer have insisted that their reporting is accurate even when they have entered the heads of people to reveal their thoughts. These writers have "maintained that the portrayal of interior mind states, while a dramatic device drawn from fiction, could be harmonized with the factual basis of journalism since the material was derived from reporting. The writer simply interviewed the subject about thoughts and emotions as well as everything else," subsequently incorporating these revelations into a dramatic narrative. Wolfe believed, after all, that as long as he did not make up anything, his readers ought to "allow me a certain leeway *if* it leads towards a better grasp of what actually took place" (Weber 1980, 29).

Clearly in the conservative camp of the new journalism, however, is Lillian Ross, one of the earliest practitioners of the art. From the beginning of her career, Ross has used dramatic scenes filled with dialogue in her literary reporting; but in response to claims that she helped pioneer literary journalism, Ross, a staff member of the *New Yorker* since 1949, pooh-poohed the idea, maintaining that "fictional 'devices' have been used in reporting for centuries—this is not a recent 'invention' " (1983, 9). Nevertheless, after World War II when American magazines had shifted their emphasis from fiction to nonfiction, she became, along with others such as John Hersey and Joseph Mitchell, an early contributor to the movement away from the purely objective reporting that had characterized most journalistic practice till then.

Written in a style simple and direct, Ross's works range from short—2,000-word—portraits of such celebrities as Ed Koch, Edward Albee, and Yehudi Menuhin to longer works such as *Picture,* the in-depth study of the making of MGM's *The Red Badge of Courage.* In these she makes use of a number of fictional devices, proving her own words: "Careful observation, significant details, characterization, insight into a character or a situation—all these can be as much as part of good factual writing as they are fiction . . . in reporting there can be not only characterization and character development but also a 'story'—even a plot" (1983, 9–10). But Ross, throughout her work, is careful to limit her use of fictional devices to protect the credibility of her reporting. She is more an observer than a participant. On the scene, often as a first-person narrator, as in *Picture,* she is at most a very minor character referring to herself only to establish a rationale for the reader's view of the scene. For example, in the opening paragraph of *Picture* she tells us that director John Huston was in New York in connection with the making of *The Red Badge of Courage* and "on the occasion of his visit, I decided to follow the history of that particular movie from beginning to end, in order to learn whatever I might learn about the American motion picture industry" (1964, 223–24).

This said, Ross records her first scene. We listen as Huston and his assistant Arthur Fellows greet her at the door to Houston's hotel suite, but then she recedes as Huston and Fellows do the talking. Ross nods in assent and accepts a drink, but her participation is ancillary. Our focus is on Huston; we are hardly aware of her presence as she softly surfaces only now and then.

Often, as in "The Yellow Bus," one of her *New Yorker* pieces, she makes no mention of herself at all but simply reports what occurs as an invisible observer would describe the scene. The effect, in both works, is to place the reader dramatically close to the action, practically on stage.

Such a point of view is consistent with her perception of her role as narrator, while she observes and reports without direct comment. In 1983 she formally separated herself from a number of writers of the new journalism. Discussing the difference between fictional and factual writing, she wrote:

The two kinds of writing differ in important ways, however . . . The reporter keeps his opinions, his sentiments, his prejudices to himself. And something . . . peculiar to fiction is the author's freedom to say what people think and feel. Contrary to what some writers believe today, what is inside another person's head is "unreportable." The closest a person can come is to tell what a person says he thinks or feels or thought or felt. (1983, 10)

With the candid high school seniors in "The Yellow Bus," Ross has no particular need to examine the private thoughts of the characters. They say what they feel. But the literary portrait of such a sophisticated personality as the late John Huston presented unusual challenges.

MGM's making of *The Red Badge of Courage* was a high-risk venture. With behavior in battle as its subject and men as its characters, it lacked a strong story line and had no traditional love interest, elements considered necessary for success at the box office. Huston, as a principal advocate in MGM's decision to make the movie, was under considerable pressure. We see him as he works and relaxes in a wide variety of situations, but always, as in life, from the outside. Huston's frustration, anger, gentleness, and relief each come into play; but Huston carefully controls his swings of mood, making their detection by his colleagues difficult. Without the convenience of interior mindviewing, the writer, who must rely upon less direct methods, faces a challenge. Here is how Ross suggests Huston's slight irritation as he directs John Dierkes in a scene with Audie Murphy, the protagonist:

Huston elbowed Dierkes aside and put Murphy's hand on his own arm. "When you say 'No, no, no leave me be,' start to go down and make him let go of you," he told Dierkes. He stumbled and fell forward, loosening Murphy's grip. "All right, try it again—by yourselves this time."

Huston lit a brown cigarette as the actors moved back up the path to do the scene again. Inhaling deeply, as though in anger, he said that [Royal] Dano was wonderful. "That boy is an actor," he said. "He's a great actor. I don't have to tell him a goddamn thing. The only other actor I've known who had that was Dad [Walter Huston]. But Dierkes will be wonderful in the picture. That face! Even when an actor is limited in his acting experience, you can cover for him. You can get him to do things that don't require acting." He threw his cigarette down and ground it out. "You make him let go of you as you start to go down," he said to Dierkes in a soft voice.

Dierkes looked puzzled. "Don't I pull my arm away from him?"

"Do whatever you want to do with your goddamn arm," said the director. "The point is you make him let go of you by falling."

Dierkes looked more puzzled. "I see, John," he said.

"Once more," Huston said crisply. (1964, 277)

Later, since Ross will not presume to divine Huston's thoughts, we must infer the director's state of mind. Dierkes, seeking some recognition from the director, comes upon Huston as he talks with a cameraman.

Huston returned the greeting exuberantly but mechanically. Then, as though something had just occurred to him, he stepped down from the dolly and motioned Dierkes to come closer with one of his conspiratorial gestures. The two men squatted on the ground. "I just want to tell you how glad I am to have you in this picture," Huston said, with slow, dramatic emphasis. "I just know you'll be good, John."

The orange stubble of beard appeared to redden as Dierkes said, "Thanks." Then he added, "I sure wish the picture was shot."

"It'll be over before you know it," said Huston. "It always is. Too soon." (1964, 297)

Here we see the director dealing with pressures on location:

He slumped down in his seat, arranging his long legs in a comfortable position. Reinhardt [the producer] stepped on the gas. "Don't rush," Huston said, looking out at passing fields of haystacks. "We're in no hurry, Gottfried. I like to see this kind of country. I just love to see this." (1964, 305)

Rarely does one of Ross's characters reveal his or her state of mind. In *Picture,* this is about as close as Ross comes to commentary: "It bothered him, [Huston] said, that there was no big scene at the finish. He felt that something was missing" (1964, 307).

However confining her point of view, we can see the fidelity with which she holds to her role as reporter when we read her own words on its limitations: "What is said must be said in the presence of the reporter. It cannot be 'reconstructed' from what the reporter *thinks* may have been said or from what someone else thinks he *remembers* having been said" (1983, 4). Thus, Ross excludes fabrication and most commentary, but in so doing she requires a perceptive audience whom she challenges to be sensitive to very slight changes in nuance. Those who ignore such refinements can misread the work.

Perhaps this explains what John Hollowell called "Lillian Ross's infamous sketch of Hemingway" (1977, 41). The "infamous sketch" was her "Portrait of Hemingway," originally published as a profile for the *New Yorker* in 1950, which Ross later referred to as "a sympathetic piece." She wrote of her surprise when readers' reactions were sharply divided. Her comments indicated, in effect, that a number of readers had misread her tone. While Hemingway fans had been pleased with her article, a number of Hemingway haters also reacted favorably, convinced that Ross shared their negative attitude toward Hemingway. In fact, many wrote her letters. However, Hemingway himself reacted positively. As Ross related: "When he heard about all this he wrote to reassure me. On June 16, 1950, he wrote that I shouldn't worry about the piece and that it was just that people got things all mixed up." Having found it complimentary, he remained on good terms with the writer. Later Ross wrote:

If some of the people who misunderstood the Profile [of Hemingway] were to read it now, they...would see that although I did not reveal my viewpoint directly, implicit in my choice and arrangement of detail and in the total atmosphere created, was my feeling of affection and admiration. I liked Hemingway exactly as he was. (1961, 14)

Ross's above-mentioned "choice and arrangement of detail" is an integral unit of her style. Like the caricaturist who draws a likeness in a few lines, Ross often captures the essentials of a person early in a work with a deft phrase or two. Those who have seen and heard John Huston in a television interview may recognize the aptness of her initial description of him in *Picture*: "He had a theatrical way of inflecting his voice that can give a commonplace query a rich and melodramatic intensity ... Huston is a lean, rangy man, two inches over six feet tall, with long arms and long hands, long legs and long feet" (1964, 224–25). Ross also carefully selects details for use as "status" symbols, described by Tom Wolfe as details or patterns of behavior and possessions through which people experience their position in the world (Wolfe 1973, 31–35). Louis B. Mayer's office, described in *Picture* as cream-colored from desk to walls, represents Mayer's simple and sentimental character. Huston's ever-present "brown cigarette" helps to humanize a figure regarded with awe by many of his contemporaries. Ironically, the emphysema that plagued Huston's last days casts a sad hue over this detail.

Thus, she chooses and arranges details as commentary. In "Terrific," as the Junior League volunteers eagerly make ready for their annual charity ball for the poor, they find that the piano is out of tune. Nothing disparaging about the Junior League is said in "Terrific," but this detail, mentioned several times, suggests that the world of the affluent and well-meaning women of the Junior League is out of tune with the poor. This idea becomes clearer as Ross again and again adds and arranges details of their over-abundant enthusiasm and superlative reactions.

Mrs. Adams dashed into the main ballroom for a quick look at the decor. She waved gaily to Coleman, who struck up "Stranger in Paradise." Then she turned around and around, looking at the room. "Goodness, isn't it the prettiest decoration ever?" she said as a few guests strolled in.

"Heavenly," one of them said.

"Terrific," said another. (1964, 138)

Gradually the title "Terrific" takes on a wry irony as the reader senses the contrast between the activities of the Junior Leaguers and those people, like Dorothy Day and other activists, who at that time were in the nearby Bowery washing and feeding the destitute.

Another group subject is the "Bean Blossom Township High School seniors" in "The Yellow Bus." Ross uses details to establish a character trait of the whole group. As the seniors set out for their first meal in the big city they walk, "for some reason, in Indian file." Then we find them again playing follow-the-leader when, inside the cafeteria, they are led by "Mike Richardson, a husky, red-haired boy with large swollen-looking hands and sunburned forearms." Mike "took a plate of fish and then filled the rest of his tray with baked beans, a roll, iced tea, and strawberry shortcake"; the others "quickly and shakily filled their trays with fish, baked beans, a roll, iced tea, and strawberry shortcake" (1964, 14–15).

Thus we see the teenagers as unsophisticated travelers sharing an inability to cope with the unknown. By the end of the tale other details, along with the dialogue, will help us see them as rather naive but pragmatic Midwesterners whose values remain much the same as their parents', in spite of their senior trip to New York. All but perhaps two will live their lives with the comfortable assurance that they are at one with their forbears.

Ross has written about a variety of subjects—often a person: Hemingway, Adlai Stevenson, Picasso. Other times she has chosen a group, such as the Junior League in "Terrific," an institution, such as the American motion picture industry in *Picture* or the American diamond industry in "The Big Stone." Her method is to explore her subject through major scenes with trenchant dialogue, recording relevant images while viewing characters from without. What the close reader can expect by the end of a Ross piece is a sense of understanding achieved through careful attention to the dialogue, the detail, and the overriding tone.

Just where in the annals of literary journalism does her work belong? Some observers might classify Ross as a cautious or a conservative new journalist; for while she has freely used fiction techniques in her work, she has eschewed such new journalism conventions as interior monologue and created dialogue. As the title *Reporting* suggests, she places a great value on fidelity to traditional reportorial conventions and practices. Hers is a body of work, characterized by restraint, which readers will find tightly controlled as it challenges their perceptions. So perhaps Lillian Ross may be most accurately characterized as a traditional literary journalist. Historically, journalism has tended to focus upon work that departs from tradition. Yet amid all the hubbub over the new journalism, the work of Lillian Ross deserves to be savored.

PRIMARY SOURCES

Ross, Lillian. 1961. *A Portrait of Hemingway*. New York: Simon and Schuster.
———. 1964. *Reporting*. New York: Simon and Schuster. This volume contains Ross's series of articles called *Picture*, published in the *New Yorker* in 1952. A paperback edition of *Picture* was published in 1984 by Limelight Editions of New York.
———. 1983. *Takes: Stories from the Talk of the Town*. New York: Congdon and Weed.

SECONDARY SOURCES

Hollowell, John, 1977. *Fact and Fiction: The New Journalism and the Nonfiction Novel.* Chapel Hill: University of North Carolina Press.

Weber, Ronald. 1980. *The Literature of Fact.* Athens: Ohio University Press.

Wolfe, Tom, 1973. *The New Journalism.* With an Anthology edited by Tom Wolfe and E. W. Johnson. New York: Harper and Row.

TRUMAN CAPOTE

Gary L. Whitby

Truman Capote is regarded by many as the founding figure in the 1960s movement loosely referred to as the "New Journalism," which sought to apply fiction-writing techniques to news reportage. His book *In Cold Blood* (1965), the powerful documentary of the 1959 murder of a Kansas farm family and its aftermath, was the first so-called news novel. Long before this, however, Capote (born Truman Streckfus Persons in New Orleans, September 30, 1924; he later took the name Capote from his mother's second husband) was well acquainted with some of the best that literary journalism had to offer, having gone to work for the *New Yorker* as a copy boy when he was only eighteen.

In his work before *In Cold Blood,* Capote displayed a clear interest in fact-related fiction. His three most significant fictional pieces—*Other Voices, Other Rooms*; *The Grass Harp*; *Breakfast at Tiffany's*—are, according to literary critic Kenneth T. Reed, "veiled, loosely autobiographic tales that reflect to some limited extent the author's personal history" (1981, 123). What would become in Capote's further work a characteristic, enduring tendency to use fictional techniques in reportage can be traced from his early local color writings, through his interviews and profiles, to the significant amount of research and interviewing that went into the writing of *In Cold Blood.*

LOCAL COLOR

Between 1946 and 1950, the *New Yorker* published nine of Capote's travel pieces. These were later collected in a book titled *Local Color,* published by Random House in 1950. The pieces, in the order of their placement in the book, are about New Orleans, New York, Brooklyn, Hollywood, Haiti, Europe (France, Italy, London), Ischia (an island near Capri), Tangier, and a train ride through Spain. In these stories Capote evinces the literary/ journalistic style for which he would later become famous, especially the particularly of his eye and ear, recording a disparity of images and sounds and showing his ability not only to put down human utterance with a convincing realism but to do so along a tight story line, one containing completely convincing characterizations of real people and including his own impressions of—and reactions to—them.

Local Color contains numerous examples of Capote's ability to depict character. In "New Orleans," there is "Mr. Buddy," the one-man band (banjo, drum, harmonica) who fancies himself a great womanizer: "Been all over, been in and out, all around; sixty-five, and any woman takes up with me ain't got no use for nobody else; yessir, had myself a lota wives and a lota kids, but christamighty if I know what came of any of 'em— and don't give a hoot in hell" (Capote 1950, 9). In "New York," there is the "Black Wido," Joe Vitale (Wido*w*" is the *male* spelling, he tells a young-ster), an Italian radio-repair man who fancies himself a great swimmer and who puts a sign on his storefront ("Watch this window for news of the Black Wido") announcing an upcoming swimming feat which results in his being rescued by life-savers and "forced upon the beach like a half-dead shark" (17). In "Brooklyn," there is "Miss Q. who complains that her whole neighborhood is being turned by 'Africans'...into a black nightmare; first Jews, now this; robbers and thieves, all of them—makes my blood run cold" (26). Here also there are "radio [volume] battles" which lead one Brooklyn landlord to make plans to murder the culprits (30). In "Haiti," there is the "tall, slant-eyed, ragged girl" who is kept tied to a tree because she is too vicious to be let loose (46). In "To Europe," there is "Lucia," the sixteen-year-old ragged beggar girl who "would sit herself down, drain a whole bottle of Strega, smoke all the cigarettes she could lay hold of, then fall into an exhausted sleep" (58).

Here, too, one finds Capote's ability to turn poetic figures of speech that commit a scene to memory, a trait that would serve him well throughout his career and give readers the impression that they were reading fiction when what they were reading was really heightened fact. "To Europe," for example, opens in "storm-green air" (55). The lakes are like "green wine in the chalice of volcanoes, the Mediterranean flickering at the bottoms of cliffs" (60). In "Ischia," the yacht *Princepessa* "spank[s] across the bay like a sassy dolphin," and the islands are "like ships at permanent anchor" (64). The grape fields outside the town contain bees that are "like a blizzard and lizards burn greenly on the budding leaves" (69). In "Tangier," a mischie-vous youth has a tongue that is "like a ladle stirring in a cauldron of scandal" (76). In "A Ride Through Spain," the seats of the train "sagged like the jowls of a bulldog" (85), and "the southern sky was as white and burning as a desert; there was one cloud, and it drifted like a traveling oasis" (86).

Although Capote once claimed that poetry was "not his field," he clearly possessed the transformational powers of the poet. In addition, *Local Color* reveals a writer with a fine eye for detail, a command of vocabulary without being heavy, a remarkable ear for dialogue, and (what would later serve him so well in interviewing the killers for *In Cold Blood*) a remarkable memory.

INTERVIEWING AND PROFILING

The *New Yorker* sent Capote in the winter of 1955–56 to cover the Everyman Opera's presentation of Gershwin's *Porgy and Bess* to audiences in the Soviet Union. The cast was black (something the Russians were not prepared for); the first stop was Leningrad. This was to be an iron-curtain raising event, and Capote was to go along and write a journalistic account of it. The result was *The Muses Are Heard,* which, rather than being a purely chronological account, was, in Capote's mind, a comic novel: "I wanted it to be very Russian, not in the sense of being reminiscent of Russian writing, but rather of some Czarist *objet,* a Fabergé contrivance, one of his music boxes, say, that trembled with some glittering, precise, mischievous melody" (Clarke 1988, 291).

The piece does indeed glitter, with everything from Soviet paranoia to American concupiscence. There are unforgettable images and scenes throughout: a fat man being beaten in an alley, apparently by government officials (Capote 1956, 422);[1] the critical reaction of a Russian audience to the "decadent" sensuality of Gershwin's work (448); a one-eyed Russian beer-drinker who can make beer run from his empty socket (428). However, what glitters most, perhaps, is Capote's remarkable memory for dialogue and scene. The former is rendered so convincingly as to make the reader believe that the author used a tape recorder. He did not.

Instead, Capote perfected interviewing, if it can be simply called such in his work, to a fine mnemonic art, aiming it at such unsuspecting targets as Marlon Brando during the making of James Michener's novel *Sayonara* into a motion picture in 1957. Encouraged by the journalistic success of *The Muses Are Heard,* Capote persuaded the *New Yorker* to send him to Kyoto, Japan, filming site of the movie. What Capote had in mind was another comic novel similar to *The Muses Are Heard.* What he produced, instead, was a long, revealing interview/profile of Brando, whom he obviously disliked.

This piece, published by the *New Yorker* later in 1957, is a devastating deadpan satire of Brando, in which the actor's own glowing statements about himself are used against him. Brando, for example, had referred to himself in context with his friends and hangers-on as "the duke in his domain," and it was this which Capote picked up and used as a title. Perhaps not suspecting that Capote could remember what amounted to an almost seven-hour monologue by the actor, Brando poured his heart out to Capote, who had begun the interview by seeming to pour his own out to Brando. This, however, was a subtle interview technique used by Capote to get the interviewee to talk: "The secret to the art of interviewing," wrote Capote, "—and it is an art—is to let the other person think he's interviewing you. You tell him about yourself, and slowly you spin your web so that he tells you everything" (Clarke 1988, 302). This technique worked like a charm on Brando, who later wrote of the interview: "The little bastard spent half the night telling me all his problems. I figured the least I could do was tell him a few of mine" (Clarke 1988, 302).

Capote eviscerated Brando as a pretentiously inflated prima donna who went to bed with men he didn't care about, as an unfeeling son who had deserted his mother, and as a renowned actor who regarded acting with contempt. The piece was a journalist tour de force that resulted in an inflamed Brando railing, "I'll kill him [Capote]" (Clarke 1988, 303). Capote used heavy description to set the scene, a flashback to when he had first met Brando ten years earlier, and filled the piece with literary figures of speech: Brando was a "salamander" who slithered into his roles (Capote 1987, 522). When the actor spoke, it sometimes seemed as if he "were slowly turning over a coin to study the side that seemed to be shinier" (532). Describing to Capote his realization that he was famous, Brando said that he had awakened one day to find himself "sitting on a pile of candy" (533). Capote picked this up and used it as a barbed literary motif, speaking of Brando's "precandy days" (533) and closing the piece with a late-night, sixty-foot-high billboard vision of Brando in "a squatting position, a serene smile on a face that glistened in the rain and the light of a street lamp. A deity, yes; but more than that, really, just a young man sitting on a pile of candy" (544).

If "The Duke in His Domain" was vintage Capotean satire, it was also an instance of the author's continuing concern with psychology. Upon arriving at Brando's suite, Capote found the actor reading Freud, and throughout the interview the two men exchanged self-analyses. Capote claimed that Brando had an inferiority complex that made him avoid powerful people and beautiful women, preferring to "pick on," according to Capote's interview of the actor's grandmother, "the cross-eyed girls" (533). And Brando is rendered as the "emotional contemporary, a co-conspirator," of children (539). Only the comedian Wally Cox thinks of him as a "a creative philosopher, a very deep thinker" (541).

Capote's ability to put together an interview with a natural story line, one that (as evinced in the Brando interview) includes a psychological examination of his characters, is what makes his work so readable and what gives it the feel of fiction. As he once told an interviewer: "My work must be held together by a narrative line. Even the Brando piece was narrative" (Nance 1970, 142). Other such narrative interviews, coming well after the acclaim of *In Cold Blood* in the mid-1960s, were "Then It All Came Down" (1979), an interview with convicted murderer Bobby Beausoleil; and *Handcarved Coffins* (1979), a first-person news novella about a serial killer in "a western state" otherwise unidentified.

Beausoleil had murdered a man in a way not dissimilar to the way the actress Sharon Tate and friends had been butchered by the Charles Manson "family." Capote interviewed the killer in the San Quentin penitentiary, attempting to get Beausoleil to admit that the Sharon Tate murders had been an attempt to free him by trying to persuade police that the real murderer was still at large. Here was vintage Capote, structuring the interview by way of pointed questions, the answers to which themselves provide a narrative line. And here too, as in "The Duke in His Domain," Beausoleil was stabbed with his own words, revealing his psychologically deranged belief that murder was all right "if that's how it came down" because— and this becomes a motif in the piece—"everything that happens is good" (Capote 1987, 461).

Handcarved Coffins tells the story of state bureau investigator Jake Pepper's five-year search, with Capote's occasional assistance, for the killer of eight residents of an unnamed midwestern town (Capote apparently planned to publish parts of the story while the investigation was still in progress). The killer sends his victims a small, packaged handcarved coffin with their photographs inside before killing them, days or months later, in a variety of bizarre and grisly ways: by putting amphetamine-injected rattlesnakes in their cars, by trapping them in a basement and incinerating them, by cutting one's head off with a fine, razor-sharp wire strung between a tree and a telephone pole, and by poisoning one's ulcer medication with liquid nicotine.

Although the case is never solved, Pepper is convinced that a local rancher, Robert Quinn, whose "private river" has recently been partly diverted to meet the water needs of neighboring ranchers, is the guilty party, the eight victims having been part of local board of nine appointed by the municipal government, in time of drought, to make the decision whether or not to divert. The committee's decision had gone against Quinn, who strongly opposed changing the river's course. Quinn is a World War II marine who has killed more than his share of Japanese, as well as two gambling debt collectors from Las Vegas who had earlier appeared at his ranch. During the five-year investigation, Officer Pepper falls in love with the local first-grade school teacher, Addie Mason, who is on Quinn's murder list and who is drowned, shortly before her planned marriage to Pepper, in the river near Quinn's land.

The story, as human-interest journalism, was itself larger than life. Quinn owned more than 3,000 acres of land and was so politically well connected that Pepper could not obtain a warrant to search his property. Pepper's love for Ms. Mason, who had never been married, came after he had been widowed and left with four grown sons. And the townspeople, after the rumor was out that the investigator suspected Quinn, flocked to the rancher's support so that Pepper feared that even if he did find evidence against the rancher the townspeople would lynch him instead of the murderer.

In contrast to his aesthetic distance as third-person narrator in *In Cold Blood*, Capote involves himself as a character in *Handcarved Coffins*. He is fascinated with the violence and at several points tries to explain the psychology of it. His reactions are like those of a first-person narrator in a novel:

> Outside, crusts of snow laced the ground; spring was a long way off—a hard wind whipping the window announced that winter was still with us. But the sound of the wind was only a murmur in my head underneath the racket of rattling rattlesnakes, hissing tongues. I saw the car dark under a hot sun, the swirling serpents, the human heads growing green, expanding with poison. I listened to the wind, letting it wipe the scene away. (Capote 1987, 465)

One also sees in *Handcarved Coffins* Capote's powers of language and characterization at play. The vast prairie wind, itself almost a character in the story, is personified: "the only sound in the room was the meowing wind clawing at the window" (473). The first-grade teacher whom Pepper loves is dwelt on thus: "The sway of her hips, the loose movements of her fruity breasts, her contralto voice, the fragility of her hand-gestures: all ultra seductive, ultra feminine without being effeminate" (475).

On the other hand, the face of the murderer's wife, a Mexican American, is "like a fist" (491). Quinn himself, viewed at the end of the story's five-year time span, is almost mythologized as a malign river god:

> I [Capote] thought of the young bulls I had seen parading in the golden pastures; Quinn, glistening in his rubber suit, reminded me of them—vital, powerful, dangerous. Except for his whiter hair, he hadn't aged an iota; indeed, he seemed years younger, a man of fifty in perfect health. (513)

Quinn's characterization is partly accomplished by way of a Capote flashback in which the author remembers the murderer's alter ego, one Reverend Billy Joe Snow, who violently baptized the author when he was a five-year-old in Alabama. Like the fundamentalist evangelist Snow, Quinn has a "messiah complex," apparently feeling it his duty to protect "my river," as he refers to it, from other human beings. Once, he tells Capote, Blue River was so pristine as to produce a six-pound rainbow trout on a fisherman's first cast. Now that a part of it has been diverted, the river's potency has been weakened, and the fishing is not so good.

The river, like the wind, indeed becomes something of a character in *Handcarved Coffins* and is made to merge with the human characterizations as well. It is involved in the motivation of the murders. It is used to depict and heighten the characterization of Quinn. One of its waterfalls is the scene of Addie Mason's death. And, as a contextual link between Quinn and the murders, it whispers to the author: "Always I could hear the river, a slow soft churning roar; then, at a curve in the path, I saw it; and saw Quinn, too" (513). Presided over by the river god Quinn, the river is the last image of the novella, and Capote here depicts Quinn almost as a demented transformation of the Reverend Snow. Speaking of the death of Addie Mason, Pepper's drowned fiancée, Quinn closes the piece: " 'The way I look at it is: it was the hand of God.' He raised his own hand, and the river, viewed between his spread fingers, seemed to weave between them like a dark ribbon. 'God's work. His will' " (514).

IN COLD BLOOD

Handcarved Coffins, begun in 1975 and published in 1979, shows Capote at the peak of his creative journalistic powers. *In Cold Blood,* published in 1965, had won him both large financial reward and critical acclaim. However, the fact that the "Santa Claus killer" case (so-called because of the "gift" of the handcarved coffin to the victims before their deaths) was never solved prevented its receiving the full news-as-sociology/psychology treatment given to the murderers in *In Cold Blood.* Another difference between the two works is point of view: *In Cold Blood* was written in the third person, *Handcarved Coffins* in the first. The fact that some few critics thought *In Cold Blood* not so expressive as it might have been (Reed 1981, 118) may have prompted Capote to write *Handcarved Coffins* in the first person, allowing the author to characterize himself and thus inject his own emotions and perceptions into the story.

In any case, Capote made it a point to keep himself out of *In Cold Blood.* Some months after the publication of the book in 1965, he remarked to George Plimpton in an interview: "For the nonfiction novel to be entirely successful, the author should not appear in the work. Once the narrator does appear, he has to appear throughout, all the way down the line, and the I-I-I intrudes when it really shouldn't" (Plimpton 1966, 38).

In Cold Blood traced the shotgun murders of a wealthy Holcomb, Kansas, farm family, the Clutters, in November 1959. The two murderers, Perry Smith and Dick Hickock, were parolees from the Kansas state penitentiary. They were apprehended in late December 1959, brought to Kansas for trial, found guilty, and sentenced to death by hanging. After numerous appeals, they were executed in April 1965. Capote, who had first seen news of the crime in the *New York Times* shortly after it occurred, immediately decided to go, with his friend the novelist Harper Lee, to Holcomb. There followed approximately five years of intense investigative interviewing and research by Capote, resulting in his compiling more than 4,000 pages of typed notes (Clarke 1988, 331).

Capote's excellent memory served him well in the writing of *In Cold*

Blood. He quickly gained the confidence and liking of Smith and Hickock—
so much so that before their execution they willed him their belongings—
and was able to interview them almost daily at the Kansas state penitentiary.
Although the interviews are submerged in the book, they clearly have gone
into the making of Smith and Hickock's characterizations.

In *Local Color* Capote had occasionally shown a fascination with violence. In "Then It All Came Down" and *Handcarved Coffins,* he would
show a fascination with both violence and the psychological motivation
behind it. In the Smith-Hickock crime, he had the perfect combination:
grisly violence and emotionally afflicted criminals. Convinced that he should
keep himself out of the story as a character, his task was to use the real
characters he had and to tell the story qua story, in much the way a reporter
might tell it if he or she could have *all* the relevant facts, including early
influences on Smith and Hickock that might have contributed to their
actions.

Capote had used the flashback technique in earlier work, including "The
Duke in His Domain." Now he used it as a means of letting the reader in
on events in the childhood of the criminals that might have led to their
crime. Smith had been mistreated by his parents, although Hickok was
"devoted" to his. Smith, however, was much the more likeable of the two
men. These differences Capote built on, establishing Smith as a sympathetic
character driven by childhood events beyond his control, and portraying
Hickok as a cheap crook who enjoyed running over dogs on the highway
but who was really a "blowhard." Such positive/negative techniques are
familiar to the news writer and to the cinema writer as well; broad stereotypes are necessary and common to both areas. To give these depth,
Capote used autobiographical statements from Smith and Hickok, as well
as detailed psychiatric reports on them following their incarceration.

The setting itself is made to support the vacant extremes of characterization and incident. Nature seems uncaring. The streets of Holcomb turn
in the seasons from the "thickest dust" to the "direst mud" (Capote 1965,
3). The day of the murder is "bright-skied, glittery as mica" (77). Suggesting
the lonely, predatory nature of the two criminals, one chapter begins:
"Mountains. Hawks wheeling in a white sky" (110). The trip to intercept
Smith and return him to Kansas takes Kansas Bureau of Investigation agent
Alvin Dewey across an Arizona landscape "of hawks and rattlesnakes and
towering red rocks" (232). Another chapter begins with two stray cats,
suspiciously suggestive of reductions of the two killers, looking for dead
birds in the grills of automobiles (246).

What is going on here and throughout *In Cold Blood* is that Capote,
forced to follow the natural plot of the story he has chosen from the newspaper (and thereby having been prevented from "creating" incident and
scene), is deepening the context and texture of the story by focusing on
seemingly irrelevant details which, when added up, scenically undergird the

story with the resonance of a concrete particularity. These details are precisely what a strict news report of the incident would omit and what, conversely, a novelist would have to create.

Nonetheless, Capote remains "objective" about his material.[2] He does not wish to pass judgment on either Smith or Hickock because (1) he believes them to have been pushed by circumstances beyond their control to do what they did; and (2), like a good 1960s reporter, he does not wish to commandeer the reader's reaction. Capote really thought of Smith and Hickock as pawns of fate in the committing of the crime, which, at one point in the book, he referred to as "a psychological accident, virtually an impersonal act; the victims might just as well have been killed by lightning. Except for one thing: they had experienced prolonged terror, they had suffered" (245).

Finally, *In Cold Blood* is written in eighty-five short reportlike chapters and placed within the context of four large sections: "The Last to See Them Alive," "Persons Unknown," "Answer," and "The Corner." In other words, the book is handled as if it were a breaking news story, some of the chapters appearing almost as features or sidebars. The temporality of the major sections is crossed, and the reader has the feeling that he or she is reading simultaneous accounts of the crime in several different newspapers or magazines. The style is much more like journalism than anything else Capote had written before or would write later. Gone are the poetic turns of phrase found in *Local Color*. Gone are the satirical jabs of *The Muses Are Heard* and "The Duke in His Domain." And vanished below the surface are the hundreds of interviews Capote conducted before sitting down to write. What remains is a surface of pure story, *real* story, a highly informed and volatile residue of the actual event.

It is worth noting that one Capote critic, Philip K. Tomkins, has argued that certain "facts" in *In Cold Blood* have been fictionalized. Although Tomkins argues convincingly, even he admits that the questionable passages are a problem in the short run and that the issue will be forgotten over time.

Future literary historians and scholars will undoubtedly place Capote's discrepancies of fact as well as his pretensions and rationalizations in perspective, and they will join with the present and future public in enjoying the work for its own sake. "Time," as Auden wrote, "... worships language and forgives Everyone by whom it lives." (1966, 125)

Capote's contributions to literary journalism, then, are significant ones. Although Theodore Dreiser in *An American Tragedy* had much earlier written a novel based on a murder in New York, Dreiser did not put nearly as much research into his work as did Capote. It was this huge amount of data that imparted a good deal of the authority one feels in the story of Perry Smith and Dick Hickock. Capote's local color stories, or what might be called his "travel sketches," contain imagery and characterizations unsurpassed in that genre. Capote developed the interview itself into something of an art form, later employing it as a method of objectivity in *In Cold Blood*, and later still, after the doctrine of objectivity had come under fire, as a means of involving himself as first-person narrator in *Handcarved Coffins*.

NOTES

1. Citations from *The Muses Are Heard*, "The Duke in His Domain," "Then It All Came Down," and *Handcarved Coffins* are from *A Capote Reader* (New York: Random House, 1987).

2. One should keep in mind that the heavy critique mounted against objectivity in the 1970s was not present when Capote wrote *In Cold Blood*. By the time he wrote *Handcarved Coffins* in 1979, however, he was no doubt aware of it.

PRIMARY SOURCES

Capote, Truman. 1950. *Local Color*. New York: Random House.

———. 1956. *The Muses Are Heard*. New York: Random House.

———. 1965. *In Cold Blood: A True Account of a Multiple Murder and Its Consequences*. New York: Random House.

———. 1973. *The Dogs Bark: Public People and Private Places*. New York: Random House.

———. 1987. *A Capote Reader*. New York: Random House.

SECONDARY SOURCES

Clarke, Gerald. 1988. *Capote: A Biography*. New York: Simon and Schuster.

Hollowell, John W. 1977. *Fact and Fiction: The New Journalism and the Nonfiction Novel*. Chapel Hill: University of North Carolina Press.

Nance, William L. 1970. *The Worlds of Truman Capote*. New York: Stein and Day.

Plimpton, George. 1966, 16 Jan. "The Story Behind a Nonfiction Novel." *New York Times Book Review*: 38.

Reed, Kenneth T. 1981. *Truman Capote*. Boston: Twayne.

Tomkins, Philip K. 1966, June. "In Cold Fact." *Esquire* 65: 125, 127, 166–68, 170–71.

TOM WOLFE

Richard A. Kallan

His newspaper goes on strike, and so he decides to write an article on customized cars for *Esquire* magazine. He travels to California, gathers his facts, but then, as he says, just "couldn't pull the thing together." The managing editor, Byron Dobell, tells him to hand in his notes and another writer will be found. He stays up all night typing a personal, letterlike, forty-nine-page memorandum that so impresses Dobell that he decides to delete the "Dear Byron" and publish it virtually in its entirety: "There Goes (Varoom! Varoom!) That Kandy-Kolored Tangerine-Flake Streamline Baby."[1]

Thus began Tom Wolfe's embrace of literary journalism, or what he would later refer to as New Journalism. The now famous "Kandy" memorandum enabled Wolfe to recognize that feature journalism—in particular, magazine writing—could achieve added depth and realism by fusing the stylistic features of fiction and the reportorial obligations of journalism to form a "novelistic-sounding"—but still factually constrained—literature. This discovery would impel a receptive Wolfe to further cross traditional journalistic boundaries once the strike was settled at the New York *Herald Tribune* and he returned to work as a feature writer.

Part of Wolfe's motivation was to garner a readership he was otherwise unsure of securing. The problem, Wolfe wrote in *The New Journalism*, was simply that "most non-fiction writers, without knowing it, wrote in a century-old British tradition in which it was understood that the narrator shall assume a calm, cultivated and, in fact, genteel voice" (1973, 17). Its merits notwithstanding, the style was somewhat bland. "When they [readers] came upon that pale beige tone, it began to signal them, unconsciously, that a well-known bore was here again, 'the journalist,' a pedestrian mind, a phlegmatic spirit, a faded personality, and there was no way to get rid of the pallid little troll, short of ceasing to read" (17). Wolfe soon rejected the

traditional prescription that reportorial tone and perspective remain impersonal, and that any overt sense of the writer's presence be distilled.

Beyond capturing readers' interest, Wolfe sought to become something
more than just a "reporter." The dream of every journalist, he said, was to
become a novelist, the pinnacle of literary achievement and status.

The idea was to get a job on a newspaper, keep body and soul together, pay the
rent, get to know "the world," accumulate "experience," perhaps work some of the
fat off your style—then, at some point, quit cold, say goodbye to journalism, move
into a shack somewhere, work night and day for six months, and light up the sky
with the final triumph. The final triumph was known as The Novel. (1973, 5)

Wolfe, however, came to realize that *in the meantime* he could work within
the medium and produce a reporting with insight and execution resembling
fine literature. Before chancing the ultimate and going "into the shack," he
might safely experiment.

Not even the journalists who pioneered in this direction doubted for a moment that
the novelist was the reigning literary artist, now and forever. All they were asking
for was the privilege of dressing up like him . . . until the day when they themselves
would work up their nerve and go into the shack and try for real. (1973, 9; Wolfe's
ellipsis)

By trying to write "literature" as opposed to "mere journalism," Wolfe,
too, might experience the excitement and satisfaction of the higher, nobler
calling.

Finally, whereas the mission of conventional journalism was primarily to
inform and allow for informed judgment by dispensing a specific range of
facts, Wolfe was more interested in establishing the "larger," interpretive
truth.[2] Traditional journalism's limited conception of the "facts," he believed, often effected an inaccurate, incomplete story that precluded readers
from exercising informed judgment. In contrast, Wolfe (at his best) exercised
what Dan Wakefield has called "imaginative" reporting—imaginative

not because the author has distorted the facts, but because he has presented them
in a full instead of a naked manner, brought out the sights, sounds and feel surrounding those facts, and connected them by comparison with other facts of history,
society, and literature in an artistic manner that does not diminish but gives great
depth and dimension to the facts. (Wakefield 1966, 87)[3]

In the years following the "Kandy" memorandum, Wolfe produced a
colorful array of penetrating, stylistic reporting. In 1965, several of his
articles for *New York* and other publications were reprinted in *The Kandy-
Kolored Tangerine-Flake Streamline Baby. The Electric Kool-Aid Acid Test,*
a full-length nonfiction work about Ken Kesey and the acid-taking world,

was published in 1968; also appearing in the same year was *The Pump House Gang,* another collection of contemporary culture articles, most of which Wolfe had written for *New York* magazine, 1964 through 1966. *Radical Chic and Mau-Mauing the Flak Catchers* (1970) is comprised of two articles: "Radical Chic," a description of composer Leonard Bernstein's fund-raising party for imprisoned members of the Black Panther party, which appeared earlier in *New York*; and "Mau-Mauing the Flak Catchers," the recounting of interactions between militant blacks and the San Francisco Office of Economic Opportunity.

These four books exemplified what became known as the New Journalism, a school of reporting with which Wolfe became so closely linked that his writing often was viewed as symbolic of the entire class; one seemingly could not critique Wolfe without turning attention to New Journalism, and vice versa. Not surprisingly, Wolfe emerged in the early 1970s as New Journalism's major spokesperson and theorist. His forum included the *Bulletin of the American Society of Newspaper Editors, New York,* and *Esquire*; subsequently, most of these essays were revised to become the introductory chapters of *The New Journalism.*

Many, of course, questioned whether New Journalism was all that "new." The four literary devices Wolfe said were particularly prominent in New Journalism writing—reconstructing a scene-by-scene account of the story, as opposed to forging a conclusionary narrative; the use of extensive dialogue; providing the reader with multiple points of view, not just the author's; and the detailed describing of those verbal and nonverbal symbols depictive of a character's lifestyle (1973, 31–33)—had been used, albeit sporadically, by other journalists prior to Wolfe. Indeed, stylistic reporting has a long history that some say dates back centuries (e.g., Murphy 1974, 29; Berner 1986, 6). Still, New Journalism was more than style. It was also a method of data collection whereby subjects were researched less by the traditional direct interview than by "shadowing" and unobtrusively observing the verbal and nonverbal behaviors of the involved principals over an extended period. Through "saturation reporting," Wolfe maintained, one could more effectively determine genuine character (1970a, 22).

It seemed all-important to *be there* when dramatic scenes took place, to get the dialogue, the gestures, the facial expressions, the details of the environment. The idea was to give the full objective description, plus something that readers always had to go to novels and short stories for: namely, the subjective and emotional life of the characters. (1973, 21)

Stories were reconstructed from the subject's *and the writer's* memories and interpretations of experiences. As such, saturation reporting was not quite what has been called "depth" reporting. The latter generally implies an increased quantity of sources consulted and reportorial time spent; the former entails a more complex set of relationships wherein the journalist becomes an involved, more fully reactive witness, no longer distanced and detached from the people and events reported. What emerged was one's distinct and revealing thought processes. The journalist was unmasked.

It was this *imposition of personal sense-making* that inspired Wolfe's much noted stylistic flair. To be sure, a shy, inhibited narrator would not have championed exclamation points, italics, and ellipses; invented punctuation and sometimes used none at all; creatively experimented with typography and type fonts; written long, fact-stuffed sentences that celebrated the adjective and the adverb; and relished colloquial metaphor, contemporary slang, and the oral style in general.[4] Wolfe's tone was as bold as it was casual: his writings "read like personal letters—open, unassuming, intimate" (Kallan 1975, 109). One learned almost as much about Wolfe as about the subject described.

Most important, Wolfe's imposition of personal sense-making encouraged the artistic management of fact, the function of which is to render the author trustworthy and the analysis convincing. This becomes especially important in those areas in which readers lack knowledge and given that journalism operates from a standard of proof not requiring rigorous, logical demonstration.[5] Moreover, Wolfe's experientially based writings usually did not allow for external verification inasmuch as what was written was culled from a uniquely personal exposure to the individuals depicted, many of whom had neither the interest nor the means to provide corrective response.[6] To appreciate how Wolfe established the "logic" for message acceptance, one must consider Wolfe's portrayal of self and the means by which plausibility was fostered.

Wolfe, for instance, intimates his competence and trustworthiness through the frequent use of *historical analogy*, which, beyond illuminating the subject and strengthening the analysis presented (because it appears congruent with precedent), allows Wolfe to demonstrate knowledge of history, literature, science, and so forth in the nonsuspect process of appearing to present a logical argument.

[Record producer] Phil Spector is the bona-fide Genius of Teen. Every baroque period has a flowering genius who rises up as the most glorious expression of its style of life—in latter-day Rome, the Emperor Commodus; in Renaissance Italy, Benvenuto Cellini: in late Augustan England, the Earl of Chesterfield; in the sal volatile Victorian age, Dante Gabriel Rossetti; in late-fancy neo-Greek Federal America, Thomas Jefferson; and in Teen America Phil Spector is the bona-fide Genius of Teen. (1965a, 6)

The analogy does not really prove Spector's brilliance in the sense of showing that he possesses significant qualities in common with other geniuses. Rather, it reminds the reader of past geniuses, implying the plausibility that Spector could be the same. Perhaps the analogy's intent is only to show that every period has given rise to the genius spirit, but who would disagree that the analogy functions to embellish Wolfe's credibility by portraying him as someone more than just familiar with history, and that from this intimation of intellectual competence the reader's confidence in Wolfe begins to grow?[7] The very act of competent analogizing may convey the image of an omniscient speaker who grasps concepts so facilely that they can be structured and ordered in terms of yet other ideas.

Sometimes Wolfe uses historical analogy to enhance the importance of his writing by elevating his *subject's* credibility and significance. In his portrait of Las Vegas and Bugsy Siegel (1965a, 3–28), for example, he maintains that Siegel, who raised the Flamingo Hotel in the middle of a desert, may have represented the first post–World War II nonaristocrat to build a monument honoring himself. His lavish hotel set precedent for the construction of similar gambling skyscrapers; the Flamingo became the architectural style for all Las Vegas. Further, Wolfe contends that Siegel influenced the whole of America's architecture. "Las Vegas' neon sculpture, its fantastic fifteen-story-high display signs, parabolas, boomerangs, rhomboids, trapezoids and all the rest of it, are already the staple design of the American landscape outside of the oldest parts of the oldest cities" (1965a, xvi). Then, in a casually dropped, matter-of-fact comparison, Wolfe observes that "Siegel's aesthetic, psychological and cultural insights, like Cezanne's, Freud's, and Max Weber's, could not die" (11). That such a comparison is even attempted may suggest that it has some validity inasmuch as Wolfe simply could have said, "Siegel's aesthetic, psychological, and cultural insights would not die." Nor does Wolfe amplify what surely would be a difficult analogy to develop factually. Regardless, Siegel's image is enhanced by what Chaim Perelman and Lucie Olbrechts-Tyteca refer to as the mutual interaction and transference of credibility resulting from such a comparison.[8] Side by side, the credibility of Cezanne, Freud, and Weber interacts with gangster Siegel's, reforming the audience's views toward each. The images of Cezanne, Freud, and Weber may tarnish when placed in league with Siegel, but the lesser appreciated Siegel enjoys an ascendance in stature because of the comparison, and it is his credibility, not his counterparts', that most concerns Wolfe as a polemicist for Siegel.

Wolfe's suggestion that Siegel is great/significant only flirts with the idea, hinting but never developing similarities between Siegel and his supposed counterparts. As does the Spector analogy, the Siegel analogy serves to remind—in this case, to recall that some ideas do not die. Yet the implication, in light of Wolfe's reference to Cezanne, Freud, and Weber, is that great ideas do not die, and therefore Siegel was great because his did not. Too, there is the assumption that Siegel had aesthetic, psychological, and cultural *insights*—as opposed to simply having certain *tastes*. Yet, the analogy is seductive, perhaps because, like most of Wolfe's analyses, it is packaged without qualification. It is not "I think," "It would appear," "One might conclude." Nor do qualifiers such as "sometimes," "usually," or "perhaps" preface any of Wolfe's statements. The style connotes assuredness and promotes the sensation that everything described is obvious and absolute.

Wolfe's poised, confident tone is enhanced further by his use of *hyperbole* and its implication that the analysis is hilariously patent. A good illustration is Wolfe's two-part series, "Tiny Mummies! The True Story of the Ruler of 43rd Street's Land of the Walking Dead!" and "Lost in the Whicky Thicket: *The New Yorker*—II." Although written "as a lark, as a break in what to me were the serious articles I was doing," the series attests to Wolfe's skillful management of hyperbole. Authored in 1965, it "commemorated" the *New Yorker's* fortieth anniversary by contending that the magazine had become dull, predictable, and second-rate. In describing *New Yorker* editor William Shawn, Wolfe writes:

Shawn is a very quiet man. He has a soft, somewhat high voice. He seems to whisper all the time. The whole...*zone* around his office, a kind of horsehair-stuffing atmosphere of old carpeting, framed *New Yorker* covers, quiet cubicles and happy-shabby, baked-apple gentility, is a *Whisper Zone*. One gets within 40 feet of it and everybody...is whispering, all the secretaries and everybody. The *Shawn-whisper*, the whisper zone radiates out from Shawn himself. Shawn in the hallway slips along as soundlessly as humanly possible and—chooooo—he meets somebody right there in the hall. The nodding! The whispering! Shawn is 57 years old but still has a boyish face, a small, a plump man, round in the cheeks. He always seems to have on about 20 layers of clothes, about three button-up sweaters, four vests, a couple of shirts, two ties, it looks that way, a dark shapeless suit over the whole ensemble, and white cotton socks. (1965b, 9; Wolfe's ellipses)

Such dazzling and arresting hyperbole serves not only to enhance Wolfe's air of confidence but to insulate his analysis if readers become so engrossed with the minor details hyperbolically portrayed that attentions are consumed by materials thematically inconsequential; the reader may be distracted from assessing the writer's broader viewpoint.

The convincingness of Wolfe's analysis also stems in part from *selective detailing*. In one of his personally favorite works (cited in Overend 1979, 14), "Radical Chic," Wolfe offers *nostalgie de la boue* (social slumming) as the motive for celebrities and socialites who attend Leonard and Felicia Bernstein's fund-raising gathering for imprisoned members of the Black Panther party (Overend, 14). But surely some of the Bernsteins' guests could be sincere? And are not others motivated by *both* sincerity and *nostalgie de la boue*? And could there be those who attend because of curiosity and nothing more? Wolfe does not say that *nostalgie de la boue* is probably *a* motive of *many*, for it would weaken the strength and simplicity of his argument. Instead, he sets forth a categorical explanation the structural integrity of which mandates omission. To show that the Bernstein gathering represents a status exercise by white liberals wishing desperately to be fashionable, Wolfe must sculpture some of his evidence, beginning with the party list.

There seems to be a thousand stars above and a thousand stars below, a room full of stars, a penthouse duplex full of stars, a Manhattan tower full of stars, with marvelous people drifting through the heavens, Jason Robards, John and D. D. Ryan, Gian-Carlo Menotti, Schuyler Chapin, Goddard Lieberson, Mike Nichols, Lillian Hellman, Larry Rivers, Aaron Copland, Richard Avedon, Milton and Amy Green, Lukas Foss, Jennie Tourel, Samuel Barber, Jerome Robbins, Steve Sondheim, Adolf and Phyllis Green, Betty Comden, and the Patrick O'Neals.... There's Otto Preminger in the library and Jean vanden Heuvel in the hall, and Peter and Cheray Duchin in the living room, and Frank and Donna Stanton, Gail Lumet, Sheldon Harnick, Cynthia Phipps, Burton Lane, Mrs. August Heckscher, Roger Wilkins, Barbara Walters, Bob Silvers, Mrs. Richard Avedon, Mrs. Arthur Penn, Julie Belafonte, Harold Taylor, and scores more. (1970b, 6–7)

Wolfe admits that there are "others" in attendance, but they are not singled out. One Wolfe reviewer claims, "Personal friends of his [Wolfe's] who were at Bernsteins (like Gloria Steinem) go largely unscored, while old enemies are dragged incongruously from the wings to be nostalgie de la boue-ed" ("Tom Wolfe: Reactionary Chic" 1972, 61). The omission of Steinem could be seen as the protection of a friend inasmuch as the guests described do not fare well when scrutinized individually or when viewed collectively as symbolizing an ideology; but it is also evident that Steinem does not quite fit Wolfe's thesis of shallow, guilt-ridden, masochistic—but always chic—men and women being intimidated by knowing blacks. Whatever Wolfe's motivation, it is not to his rhetorical advantage to note Steinem's presence.

For their white audience, Wolfe argues, the Black Panthers symbolize romantic heroes: oppressed, alienated, militant, violent, they seem glamorously notorious. What with "shoot-outs, revolutions, pictures in *Life* magazine of policemen grabbing Black Panthers like they were Vietcong—somehow it all runs together in the head with the whole thing of how beautiful they are" (1970b, 8). According to Wolfe, it is radically chic—the ultimate status achievement—to know a Black Panther or two. They remain so poised, so stylish, so *black*.

These are no civil rights Negroes *wearing gray suits three sizes too big—*
—no more interminable Urban League banquets in hotel ballrooms where they try to alternate the blacks and whites around the tables as if they were stringing Arapaho Beads—
—*these are* real men! (1970b, 8)

The impression that the Panthers are the only blacks in the room and the only kind of blacks acceptable to the audience gathered is further insured

by Wolfe's not mentioning the presence of somewhat less militant blacks—
for example, Ray Innis, Floyd McKissick, Preston Wilcox, and Roy Wilkins
(Kuehl 1971, 214).

As the preceding examples demonstrate, Wolfe developed and enhanced
the credibility of his arguments through an array of strategies and devices,
most of which usually were not associated with conventional feature writing.
The result was a personalistic reporting that reflected the viewpoint of its
author *more rhetorically* than the older form. Indeed, Wolfe's earlier works
transformed what for years had been a structurally rigid magazine formula
into a bold, investigative literature having persuasive purpose and design.

Wolfe's journalism was new—a subset of the larger, established category
of literary journalism—to the extent that he engaged his subject "experientially," and the posture was hitherto uncommon. Because *his* sense-making
of the story was so integral to its presentation, Wolfe moved to the foreground of the reader's consciousness. Was this the appropriate neighborhood for the journalist? Whatever the answer, the debate following the
appearance of New Journalism at least prompted many reporters to recon-
sider the functional and ethical dimensions of their work. An increasingly
self-conscious journalist surfaced, one demonstrating greater interest in the
processes and meanings inhering within any written communication.

Wolfe's later, post–1970 writings reflect both a tempering of his vintage
stylistic tone and an even wider range of literary talent. He considered other
forms as he occasionally had done in the past,[9] and in 1975 he wrote *The
Painted Word*, which, while containing some stylistic traces of New Journalism, was basically a conventional literary essay, an "armchair" indictment of modern art. After a third anthology, *Mauve Gloves and Madmen,
Clutter and Vine* (1976), Wolfe focused his attentions on the American
space program and in 1979 wrote what has become his best known and
perhaps most enlightening piece of New Journalism, *The Right Stuff*.

His most commercially successful nonfiction work (eclipsed only by his
first novel), which was later made into a popular film of the same title, *The
Right Stuff* embraces a narrative structure wherein scene-by-scene construction and character dialogue are more limited, unlike Wolfe's other New
Journalism efforts. On the other hand, the detailing of status-life symbols
and the presentation of multiple points of view appear prominently and are
used effectively to endorse Wolfe's contentions. Too, while Wolfe exhibits
less of his customary stylistic flair, the bold strokes that do surface seem
more integral to the text, more elucidating of the point—rather than as
simple attention-securing devices.

But what remains most remarkable about *The Right Stuff* is what the
author discovers and the reader learns. The book elevated Wolfe's literary
status and name recognition as well as New Journalism's credibility because
it so exquisitely met the latter's charge of extrapolating the "larger truth."
The Right Stuff abounds with keen insights about the logic behind the choice

and training of the first astronauts; their mentality, drive, and lifestyle; and their public perception and symbolic national importance. All are scrupulously analyzed from a data base infused with the methodological essence of New Journalism: exhaustive and meticulous reporting. Indeed, when the book does falter it is on the side of excessive and repetitive description, a problem not uncommon to other Wolfe works, especially *The Electric Kool-Aid Acid Test*. By his own admission, Wolfe remains a "maximalist," someone dedicated to putting in everything—"that's what I am, a putter-inner" (quoted in "Master of His Universe" 1989, 92).

The Right Stuff, Wolfe's last full-length New Journalism effort to date, was followed in 1980 by *In Our Time*, a collection of previous drawings with commentary. A year later, Wolfe penned a stinging critique of contemporary American architecture, *From Bauhaus to Our House*. In 1987, years after having announced the literary supremacy of New Journalism in light of contemporary fiction's then abandonment of social realism, Wolfe authored his first novel, *The Bonfire of the Vanities*, an irony somewhat muted inasmuch as saturation reporting underscored the work.

Today, Tom Wolfe says of himself: "I'm a journalist at heart; even as a novelist, I'm first of all a journalist. I think all novels should be journalism to start, and if you can ascend from that plateau to some marvelous altitude, terrific. I really don't think it's possible to understand the individual without understanding the society" (quoted in "Master of His Universe" 1989, 92). Wolfe has done just that: his portraits of contemporary society detail a rich compendium of modern wants and desires. Whatever he is called—whatever genre of writing he chooses to practice—the result is likely to be another installment in an already illuminating social-psychological diary of American culture.

NOTES

1. The article first appeared in *Esquire* in November 1963 and was later reprinted in Wolfe's anthology. Wolfe's account of the "Kandy" memorandum appears in the book's introduction (xiii-xiv) and is confirmed by Hayes (1972, 12).

2. In *Public Opinion*, Walter Lippmann observed that news and truth were not the same: "The function of news is to signalize an event, the function of truth is to bring to light the hidden facts, to set them into relation with each other, and make a picture of reality on which men can act" (1965, 226). While Lippmann, however, believed that journalists should focus on delivering accurate news, Wolfe's major concern was portraying the "truth."

3. Put more precisely: "Whereas routing journalism focuses on the object of perception, 'the fact,' New Journalism describes the 'world view' which constitutes the facts. The reports focus not only on the signs and symbols which reveal reality but also on the communication codes which organize those signs and symbols" (Eason 1982, 146).

4. For a specific analysis of these features, see Kallan 1979.

5. Whereas at one extreme academic scholars must meet meticulous evidential criteria, the journalist is precluded from anything resembling a systematic presentation and referencing of supporting data by time and space limitations; professional conventions growing out of the need to simplify material for a large, diverse spectrum of readers; and the frequent practice of source confidentiality.

6. Macdonald notes that "the little people," because of their status, have no real power to object "if they think they have been misrepresented," while celebrities welcome any publicity, accurate or not (1965, 5).

7. The sheer volume of facts underscoring Wolfe's analogies easily can lead one to conclude, as did Vonnegut, that Wolfe "knows everything" (1965, 4).

8. Perelman and Olbrechts-Tyteca hold that in any analogy there is an interaction of terms, resulting in "transfers of value from phoros ('the terms that serve to buttress the argument') to theme ('the terms to which the conclusion relates') and vice versa." Phoros and theme interact, and the resulting mutual transference of meaning produces two mutated but similarly perceived terms; phoros and theme become one (1969, 381, 373).

9. Wolfe previously had taken time out while writing New Journalism to work on satirical editorials (e.g., "The Courts Must Curb Culture"); opinion pieces (e.g., "Pause, Now, and Consider Some Tentative Conclusions About the Meaning of This Mass Perversion Called Porno-Violence"); book reviews (e.g., "Son of *Crime and Punishment*"); and short stories (e.g., "The Commercial," in *Mauve Gloves*).

PRIMARY SOURCES

Wolfe, Tom. 1965a. *The Kandy-Kolored Tangerine-Flake Streamline Baby*. New York: Farrar, Straus and Giroux.

———. 1965b, Apr. 18. "Lost in the Whicky Thicket: *The New Yorker*—II." *New York*: 16 +.

———. 1965c, Mar. 14. "Son of *Crime and Punishment* or: How to Go Eight Fast Rounds with the Heavyweight Champ—and Lose." Review of *An American Dream*, by Norman Mailer. New York *Herald Tribune Book Review*: 1 +.

———. 1965d, Apr. 11. "Tiny Mummies! The True Story of the Ruler of 43rd Street's Land of the Walking Dead!" *New York*: 7 +.

———. 1966, Dec. 3. "The Courts Must Curb Culture." *Saturday Evening Post*: 10–12.

———. 1967, July. "Pause, Now, and Consider Some Tentative Conclusions About the Meaning of This Mass Perversion Called Porno-Violence: What It Is and Where It Came from and Who Put the Hair on the Walls." *Esquire*: 59 +.

———. 1968a. *The Electric Kool-Aid Acid Test*. New York: Farrar, Straus and Giroux.

———. 1968b. *The Pump House Gang*. New York: Farrar, Straus and Giroux.

———. 1970a, Sept. "The New Journalism." *Bulletin of the American Society of Newspaper Editors*: 1 +.

———. 1970b. *Radical Chic and Mau-Mauing the Flak Catchers*. New York: Farrar, Straus and Giroux.

———. 1973. *The New Journalism*. With an anthology edited by Tom Wolfe and E. W. Johnson. New York: Harper and Row.

———. 1975. *The Painted Word*. New York: Farrar, Straus and Giroux.

———. 1976. *Mauve Gloves and Madmen, Clutter and Vine*. New York: Farrar, Straus and Giroux.

———. 1979. *The Right Stuff*. New York: Farrar, Straus and Giroux.

———. 1980. *In Our Time*. New York: Farrar, Straus and Giroux.

———. 1981. *From Bauhaus to Our House*. New York: Farrar, Straus and Giroux.

———. 1987. *The Bonfire of the Vanities*. New York: Farrar, Straus and Giroux.

SECONDARY SOURCES

Berner, Thomas R. 1986. *Literary Newswriting: The Death of an Oxymoron*. Journalism Monographs 99. Columbia, S.C.: Association for Education in Journalism and Mass Communication.

Eason, David L. 1982. "New Journalism, Metaphor and Culture." *Journal of Popular Culture* 15: 142–49.

———. 1984. "The New Journalism and the Image-World: Two Modes of Organizing Experience." *Critical Studies in Mass Communication* 1: 51–65.

Edwards, Thomas R. 1969. "Electric Indian." *Partisan Review* 36: 535–44.

Grunwald, Lisa. 1990, Oct. "Tom Wolfe Aloft in the Status Sphere." *Esquire*: 146–60.

Hayes, Harold. 1972, Jan. "Editor's Notes." *Esquire*: 12.

Hellman, John. 1981. *Fables of Fact: The New Journalism as New Fiction*. Urbana: University of Illinois Press.

Kallan, Richard A. 1975. "Entrance." *Journal of Popular Culture* 9: 106–13.

———. 1979. "Style and the New Journalism: A Rhetorical Analysis of Tom Wolfe." *Communication Monographs* 46: 52–62.

Kuehl, Linda. 1971, May 7. "Dazzle-Dust: A Wolfe in Chic Clothing." *Commonweal*: 212–16.

Lippmann, Walter. 1922. *Public Opinion*. Rpt. 1965. New York: Free Press.

Macdonald, Dwight. 1965, Aug. 26. "Parajournalism, or Tom Wolfe and His Magic Writing Machine." *New York Review of Books* 26: 3–5.

"Master of His Universe." 1989, Feb. 13. *Time*: 90–92.

Murphy, James E. 1974. *The New Journalism: A Critical Perspective*. Journalism Monographs 34.

Overend, William. 1979, Oct. 19. "Down to Earth with Tom Wolfe." *Los Angeles Times* 4: 1+.

Perelman, Chaim, and Lucie Olbrechts-Tyteca. 1969. *The New Rhetoric: A Treatise on Argumentation*. Trans. John Wilkinson and Purcell Weaver. 1958. Notre Dame, Ind.: University of Notre Dame Press.

Rogoway, Rick. 1971. "Profile of an Electric Journalist." In *The Magic Writing Machine: Student Probes of the New Journalism*. Ed. Everette E. Dennis. Eugene: School of Journalism, University of Oregon, 17–23.

Scura, Dorothy, ed. 1990. *Conversations with Tom Wolfe*. Jackson: University Press of Mississippi.

"Tom Wolfe: Reactionary Chic." 1972, Jan. *Ramparts*: 58–61.

Vonnegut, Kurt. 1965, June 27. "Infarcted! Tabescent!" *New York Times Book Review*: 4+.

Wakefield, Dan. 1966, June. "The Personal Voice and the Impersonal Eye." *Atlantic*: 86–90.

Weber, Ronald. 1975. "Moon Talk." *Journal of Popular Culture* 9: 142–52.

GAY TALESE

Carol Polsgrove

Gay Talese flashed across the screen of *Esquire* in the 1960s—the Errol Flynn of New Journalism, sure-footed and suave, thrusting his way through the lives of the famous: Frank Sinatra, Joe DiMaggio, Joshua Logan, the *Paris Review* crowd. Tom Wolfe recalls the dramatic moment when he saw a 1962 *Esquire* piece by Talese and thought, "What inna namea christ is this." It didn't start out like an ordinary magazine piece at all.

"Hi, sweetheart! Joe Louis called to his wife..."

"*What the hell is going on?*" Tom Wolfe asked himself. "With a little reworking the whole article could have read like a short story." What struck Wolfe even more than the fictional feel was the reporting: How did Talese *get* this intimate moment between husband and wife (Wolfe 1973, 10–11)?

Later, Talese told the whole world of his readers how he got the story, not just this one but all his stories, including the three books: *The Kingdom and the Power, Honor Thy Father,* and *Thy Neighbor's Wife*—like the pieces in *Esquire,* journalistic biographies filled with intimate details. What he did, Talese explained in interviews, essays, and author's notes, was spend time with his subjects—not just a little time, but lots of time. He followed them golfing; risked his neck on long, drunken car trips; watched and listened. He saw how his subjects behaved, toward people close to them, toward people they barely knew. He heard what was said in unguarded moments. This was, to Talese, the essence of New Journalism—"this method of lingering and careful listening and describing scenes that offer insight into the individual's character and life" (1987, 166).

It is tempting, when we look at the product, to dwell on the scenes themselves—the finished construction—and to ascribe their impact to their fictional quality. But Wolfe had it right: what is at least as impressive in Talese's work is the reporting that went into the scenes. The two elements work in tandem: the scenic presentation and the reporting. Talese's work fascinates partly because the reader knows that these scenes, so minutely described, so textured, so *real,* really are real. The materials for making them were not, as in fiction, spun out of the writer's head. They had to be scrupulously gathered.

In a 1987 article for *Esquire,* "When Frank Sinatra Had a Cold," Talese looked back nostalgically to the days when magazines underwrote such research. Unable to interview Sinatra, Talese spent six weeks in Beverly Hills, interviewing people who knew Sinatra, and eventually following Sinatra around—but never able to talk to the man himself. The research cost *Esquire* nearly $5,000 in expenses, in 1965 dollars. Talese then spent six weeks organizing and writing a fifty-five-page article based on interviews with more than one hundred people, plus his observation of Sinatra. Such in-depth reporting is increasingly rare in magazines, Talese noted, because magazine editors simply will not put up the money for it.

Esquire was important to Talese in the sixties, not only because it underwrote his work, but also because it provided an appropriate forum for a kind of writing he turned out to be good at. *Esquire* encouraged a narrative voice—"an attitude" editor Harold Hayes like to call it—that seemed just right for the celebrity profiles.

Tom Wolfe recalled: "Harold often spoke of 'attitude'—a good ten years before that word became part of the hip patois. The attitude he had in mind was irony or, to use another of his words, the *raspberry,* or other forms of smiling through the apocalypse" (Eisenberg 1989, 22). David Newman and Robert Benton, both on the *Esquire* staff under Hayes, said that Hayes saw the staff "coming into editorial meetings with a slightly postcollegiate, wise-guy, smart-ass *attitude.* And he sensed that, with a little refining, that tone, that *attitude* could become the voice of this magazine" (Eisenberg 1989, 18).[1]

Attitude, tone, voice—whatever we call it, it was important to Talese from the start of his work for *Esquire.* In an early *Esquire* essay on obscurity in New York, Talese tried, he said later, "to somehow bring to reportage the tone that Irwin Shaw and John O'Hara had brought to the short story" (1971a, ix).

Tone is so important to Talese that as he moves through a project, he sits down every night at his typewriter before going to bed and describes what he has seen and heard during the day. His purpose is "self-clarification, reaffirming my own voice on paper after hours of concentrated listening to others" (1987, 163). In finished copy, he often eschews direct quotation for his own statement of the subject's feelings and thoughts. He does this, he says, partly because "you can give a kind of tone to your writing if you don't allow it to be broken into by a direct quote" (1974, 45).

Conventional newspaper journalists try to pretend that they have no voice at all—no individual identity: they are nothing, and they know nothing. All information they offer the reader they got from someone else. They are mere window panes, or conveyor belts, passing along facts, feelings, and ideas from "real" people—their sources. To the extent that conventional newspaper journalists have a voice at all, it is a borrowed, stereotypic voice: the voice of all newspaper journalism. It has a standardized vocabulary and cadence and an implied attitude about the world. But it is not, must not be (except in exceptional circumstances or under exceptional editors), distinctive.

Talese's voice, in the *Esquire* pieces, although not as original as Tom Wolfe's, *is* distinctive. Whether or not he personally appears in the stories, and he does, fleetingly, in some, there is an implied narrator. You can just see him—a man in a wilted tuxedo, leaning against a doorframe, or sitting slumped, his hands hanging down between his knees, listening without comment. Although he seems to be a particular person, occasionally even identified as "I," he also seems almost omniscient. In conventional journalism, journalists explain, however minimally, how they came by the facts: "According to X." Or "he said in a press conference." Or, more evocatively, "I arrived at his home in the late afternoon." Talese dropped those conventions and simply presented what he knew to be true, on his own authority. He comes through as a sophisticated observer: he knows a lot. He's been around.

Listen to the opening of "Frank Sinatra Has a Cold":

Frank Sinatra, holding a glass of bourbon in one hand and a cigarette in the other, stood in a dark corner of the bar between two attractive but fading blondes who sat waiting for him to say something. But he said nothing; he had been silent during much of the evening, except now in this private club in Beverly Hills he seemed even more distant, staring out through the smoke and semidarkness into a large room beyond the bar where dozens of young couples sat huddled around small tables or twisted in the center of the floor to the clamorous clang of folk-rock music blaring from the stereo. The two blondes knew, as did Sinatra's four male friends who stood nearby, that it was a bad idea to force conversation upon him when he was in this mood of sullen silence, a mood that had hardly been uncommon during this first week of November, a month before his fiftieth birthday. (1971a, 3)

How much this narrator knows: that the blondes are waiting for Sinatra to speak; that they know—as do Sinatra's male friends—that they had better not try talking if he isn't interested; that Sinatra has been silent for most of the evening; that Sinatra has been silent for most of the week.

The narrator might almost be the world-weary, cynical, sentimental detective of several generations of American detective fiction. And, in fact, he *is* a detective of sorts. The narrator of the celebrity pieces is out to uncover the dirt. His job is to find out all he can about these famous people, especially the dark, hidden sides of their lives: their weaknesses, their unacceptable passions, their humanity. For example, when Sinatra baited screenwriter Harlan Ellison, whom he did not know, in a poolroom:

"Hey," he yelled in his slightly harsh voice that still had a soft, sharp edge. "Those Italian boots?"

"No," Ellison said.

"Spanish?"

"No..."

"Are they *English* boots?"

"Look, I dunno, man," Ellison shot back, frowning at Sinatra, then turning away again.

Now the poolroom was suddenly silent. Leo Durocher who had been poised behind his cue stick and was bent low just froze in that position for a second. Nobody moved. Then Sinatra moved away from the stool and walked with that slow, arrogant swagger of his toward Ellison, the hard tap of Sinatra's shoes the only sound in the room. Then looking down at Ellison with a slightly raised eyebrow and a tricky little smile, Sinatra asked, "You expecting a *storm?*" (1971a, 10–11)

Anyone who writes celebrity journalism is likely to witness a scene like this at some time or another. What Talese did differently was actually to put these scenes into his stories. The high dramatic points of his celebrity pieces were less likely to be the interviews—although he does weave interviews into the narrative—than the scenes in which he has caught his subject off guard.

This was audacious journalism, breaking the unwritten pact between journalist and subject—the understanding that the journalist was an ally in creating the celebrity image.[2] Fame had turned sour in the sixties, at least for the editors and writers of *Esquire*. As Thomas B. Morgan recalled, they shared a sense that "image making in America was leading to a scary denial of reality." They knew that *Esquire* could not stop what was happening— was in fact "part of the deal." So they figured that "the next best thing was to expose self-creations and paraoccasions, to show the impact of the publicity process on personalities and causes." Morgan spoke of his own "impersonality" profiles of Sammy Davis, Jr., and David Susskind, published in 1959 and 1960, as "deconstructions" of their celebrity subjects (Eisenberg 1989, 23).

In the guise of writing celebrity journalism, Talese was, like Morgan, deconstructing celebrity journalism. He took on some of America's favorite celebrities and broke them down: found their flaws—sometimes petty, sometimes deeply sad. He was drawn to celebrities who had suffered defeats, spent time on life's downside:[3] Joshua Logan, retreating into his own private drama—returning, in 1953, to the old plantation where he grew up and "not quite realizing what he was doing," crawling back into the playhouse built by his grandfather, and then driving to New Orleans to sign himself into a psychiatric ward (1971a, 68).

Because the journalist-narrator was out to uncover celebrity secrets, his relationship with his subjects was inevitably ambiguous. He might present himself as a friend—and then betray them to the world. Talese himself suggests the ambiguity characteristic of the relationship in a piece on Joe DiMaggio. In that profile, Talese appears, Hitchcock-like, as "a man he [DiMaggio] did not wish to see." "The man" had told DiMaggio in New York that he was working on "some vague sociological project," but DiMaggio feared that he was really after information on his private life and that of his former wife, Marilyn Monroe. And so when "the man" entered DiMaggio's restaurant in San Francisco, DiMaggio abruptly disappeared.

Talese left angrily. Someone called him back. DiMaggio spoke to him on the phone.

> *"You are invading my rights. I did not ask you to come. I assume you have a lawyer, you must have a lawyer, get your lawyer!"*
> "I came as a friend," the man interrupted.
> "That's beside the point," DiMaggio said. "I have my privacy, I do not want it violated." (1971a, 77)

Talese ultimately gained access to DiMaggio and broke down his resistance, succeeded in invading his privacy; invaded it merely by reporting DiMaggio's protest of the act of invasion. In reporting DiMaggio's protest, Talese broke a code of journalistic manners, which dictates that the relationship between subject and journalist begins when the subject has agreed to a relationship (unless, of course, the journalist is attempting to uncover serious wrongdoing). Breaking the code made for bold, brash journalism: a shock effect.

But something else is going on here, too. Talese's minor deception—masking his own identity as "the man"—should set the reader on guard. The reader cannot help wondering if "the man" is Talese; from the story itself, the reader does not know for sure, although Talese confirms the suspicion in the introduction to *Fame and Obscurity* (1971a, x). The experienced reader of fiction begins to understand that Talese plays tricks with the narrative, just like some contemporary fiction writers. (In a *Playboy* interview, Talese said that his favorite English writer is John Fowles [1980b, 112].) Reading such writers, the reader must be active, not passive; must see the narrative as "story"—not a journalistic flow of facts.

In "The Loser," Talese again raises the question of journalistic invasion of privacy, and again focuses the reader's attention on the story as object. This time, the invasion takes a more central place in the piece, which has as its theme how and why one man tries to escape fame.

The story begins with the defeated fighter Floyd Patterson jogging up a mountain highway in upstate New York, where he is training for what he hopes will be a comeback. Motorists stop him and ask,

> "Say, aren't *you* Floyd Patterson?"
> "No," says Floyd Patterson. "I'm his brother, Raymond."

The motorists move on, but recently a man on foot, a disheveled man who seemed to have spent the night outdoors, staggered behind the runner along the road and yelled, "Hey, Floyd Patterson!"

"No, I'm his brother Raymond."

"Don't tell *me* you're not Floyd Patterson. I know what Floyd Patterson looks like."

"Okay," Patterson said, shrugging, "if you want me to be Floyd Patterson, I'll be Floyd Patterson."

"So let my have your autograph," said the man, handing him a rumpled piece of paper and a pencil.

He signed it—"Raymond Patterson." (1971a, 40)

Patterson carries his denial of his celebrity about as far as a man could. After suffering a disastrous defeat, he takes with him to later fights false whiskers and a mustache. Losing to Sonny Liston, he wears his disguise from Chicago to Madrid, where he checks in under the name "Aaron Watson." Then he goes to dinner at a restaurant and orders soup. "I hate soup," he tells Talese. "But I thought it was what old people would order. So I ate it. And after a week of this, I began to actually think I was somebody else. I began to believe it. And it is nice, every once in a while, being somebody else" (53).

What a journalist is at work here—getting Patterson to strip down to his bare soul. Patterson went all the way:

"You must wonder what makes a man do things like this. Well, I wonder, too... And I have figured out that part of the reason I do the things I do, and cannot seem to conquer that one word—*myself*—is because... is because... is because... I am a coward..."

He stopped. He stood very still in the middle of the room, thinking about what he had just said, probably wondering whether he should have said it. (53)

With that sentence, Talese draws a circle around his own story. The very piece he has written is part of the drama of fame that Patterson wants to escape. Patterson's feeling that they were just two men talking was an illusion. All this would end up on the printed page, for everyone to see. Thus Talese draws attention to his own narrative; he invites the reader's scrutiny. He almost dares the reader to ask: in reporting Patterson's confession, has the journalist-narrator overstepped a line?

Such self-questioning runs directly counter to conventional journalism. Conventional journalism—newspaper-style journalism—seeks above all ready acceptance of the stories offered. The very standardization of voice and form that characterizes conventional journalism has this partly as its purpose: to induce the reader to accept what is said, without question or quibbling. The conventional journalist does not want the reader to start noticing the frame; the conventional journalist wants an invisible frame, which will allow readers to accept "facts" as facts, delivered by an impersonal process.

In contrast, Talese suggests the drama inherent in journalism: the journalist's seduction and betrayal of his subject. In *The Journalist and the Murderer, New Yorker* writer Janet Malcolm has focused attention on this dynamic, in which the subject believes that the journalist will tell his—the subject's—story, only to discover later that the writer has his own story to tell.

Talese has shown some sensitivity to his subjects' vulnerability and his power over their lives. He was especially solicitous of his subjects in *Thy Neighbor's Wife*, a book that finally emerged in 1980, after nine years of work. The book took such a long time to write, he told *Playboy*, because "when you are asking people to open up to you about the most intimate moments of their lives, you have to spend weeks, months, sometimes years developing that relationship and building their trust. What is hard for critics—who don't know about the art of interview—is how much people will tell you about themselves if they really trust you" (1980b, 80).

So intimate were the details his subjects told him that he took the unusual precaution of sending them transcripts of taped interviews, and told them that they could delete, amend, or amplify what they had said. And when he had written one climactic episode, in which John Bullaro watches another man make love to his wife, Talese called Bullaro and read it to him. Bullaro had already signed a release. He could not legally stop Talese from publishing the passage. But Talese wanted him to hear it.

"There were no precedents for what I was doing," he explained to *Playboy*.

No book in nonfiction had ever described sex as explicitly as this, and I felt that there was a *chance* that the people I interviewed at great length, spent weeks or months with over five, six, even eight years, might not have realized that I was going to put into the book things they'd told me about themselves. They might have felt that since such things had never appeared in nonfiction books before, they would not appear in a nonfiction book now. (9180b, 100)

This fact supplies much of the interest of *Thy Neighbor's Wife*: it was an unprecedented expansion of journalism's boundaries, into a subject area long familiar in fiction. But the expansion also raised a sticky ethical issue, and one far more likely to be faced by the literary journalist than by the conventional journalist. To present real life in a fictional mode, especially a realistic fictional mode, the literary journalist must engage in "saturation reporting," spending hours, days, weeks in the lives of his subjects. Without this kind of reporting, he cannot hope to approach the texture of fiction—the subtlety of feeling and thought, of atmosphere and action.

And yet, in this kind of reporting, the distance between journalist and subject collapses. The subject easily forgets that all he says, all he does, is grist for the journalist's mill. The problem is especially worrisome if the subjects are *not* celebrities, and thus not accustomed to the ways of the press.

Why, in *Thy Neighbor's Wife,* did Talese not at least disguise the identities of those ordinary people like John Bullaro? Apparently, identifying his characters by name seemed to him essential to validating the book—giving it authority and significance. He also liked the idea that these people who had done such extraordinary things—breaking the bounds of convention— were, in his mind, "average" people (1980b, 86). During the days when he was writing about celebrities for *Esquire,* Talese was equally fascinated by ordinary lives: one of his finer works tells the story of building the Verrazano-Narrows Bridge, and of the lives affected by the bridge's construction. And the whole premise of *Honor Thy Father* is that even the Mafia live ordinary lives in their own homes.

An impulse to give full weight to his noncelebrity subjects may, then, have motivated him to name them. In order to get them to let him name them, he says in an author's note that he persuaded them that he would recount their stories accurately in a "non-judgmental tone." This nonjudgmental tone opened the door to heavy criticism. Reviewers and ordinary readers alike have turned away from the book puzzled, at least, and sometimes disturbed, by the narrator's bland acceptance of the lives he describes. Gone, it seemed, was the ironić detachment of the *Esquire* pieces, the sardonic raised eyebrow of *The Kingdom and the Power.* A reader reading *Thy Neighbor's Wife* as irony would read it wrong, according to Talese's own statements both inside and outside the book. Caught up in the idea of presenting his subjects' lives as they experienced them, he seems actually to admire the characters he portrays.

The distance between the sensibility behind the *Esquire* pieces and *Thy Neighbor's Wife* appears so great as to be baffling. It is hard to help wondering whether we owe the smart, sharp-eyed irony of the early pieces, and of *The Kingdom and the Power* (begun as an *Esquire* profile of Clifton Daniel) to the context in which they were written: as pieces for a magazine that, under Harold Hayes, encouraged that attitude.

It is difficult to tell how much magazine editors influence writers with whom they work over time, and how much writers influence magazine editors. Talese's own inclinations toward fictional scenes and a wry, fictional voice may have aroused or strengthened *Esquire* editors' interest in this new form of journalism. Hayes himself said as much, in a 1961 letter to Talese, in which he credits Talese and other writers with helping shape the "*Esquire* point of view."[4]

But Hayes also wrote about how magazines can help writers develop *their* point of view. In an unpublished manuscript on magazine editing, Hayes described *Esquire* editors' contribution to Talese's development—they took him seriously, gave him article ideas, offered him a national audience. "Magazines are an important factor in shaping the talented writer's work," Hayes wrote, "not in an institutional sense but in providing an occasion for the necessary symbiotic relationship to develop between himself and an editor." The editor "holds the writer's hand as he works on voice, structure, syntax and the more complex techniques of prose." The writer, in turn, "gives the magazine a very rich bonus indeed when his own voice comes to be received as an essential component of the magazine itself."[5]

No matter how much influence flowed which way, Talese's work for *Esquire* suggests a prime fact of the literary journalist's life. If the literary journalist writes regularly for a specific journal, whether *Esquire* or the *New Yorker*, the journal's identity, forged by the editors and other writers, will create boundaries within which the writer works. Perhaps when Harold Hayes left *Esquire* in 1973, Talese lost something important to him as a writer. True, his friendship with Hayes continued, and he has continued to publish in *Esquire*: excerpts from both *Thy Neighbor's Wife* and his newest book, a journalistic memoir of his Italian family, have appeared there. Still, the magazine is not what it was under Hayes, and Talese is no longer an *Esquire* writer.

On the other hand, perhaps we take too much to heart Talese's own statements about what he was doing in *Thy Neighbor's Wife*. Perhaps there is more *Esquire*-style irony here than he would have us believe. Perhaps Talese the private author is not quite as wide-eyed as Talese the narrator, or even Talese the public author. Talese opens the door to such a reading in his closing chapter, when he introduces himself as the last of his series of characters and tells his own story of writing the book.

Bringing himself into the narrative, he strikes the same low key that is characteristic of the book: describing a session at Sandstone, an institute for sexual experimentation, he says:

In addition to the speech by Alex Comfort, the audience heard briefly from Al Goldstein, the publisher of *Screw*, and Nat Lehrman, the associate publisher of *Playboy*; and they also were addressed at length by the second featured speaker of the day, a writer from New York named Gay Talese, who was researching a book about sex in America for Doubleday & Company.

A lean, dark-eyed man of forty-three whose brown hair was beginning to turn gray, Talese was not entirely a stranger to the people in the room. (1980a, 521)

He goes on to tell how, in pursuit of this book, he visited massage parlors, was masturbated by a masseuse, went to work as a nonsalaried manager at a massage parlor, watched a pornographic film being made, and met some of the book's characters, notably the key figures at Sandstone.

The climax of the passage comes when the leading lady of Sandstone, Barbara Williamson (who had once seduced the aforementioned Bullaro), seduced Talese. After they made love, she talked freely about her life and events at Sandstone. From her he heard, for the first time, the episode involving John Bullaro. Through her he met John Bullaro and his wife, Judith, and ultimately obtained permission to write their story, the most dramatic of the book.

Having confessed to "getting the story" in a way that some journalists would regard as unseemly (although not unprecedented), Talese then turns to the effect of the book on his own life. He narrates a telling event. He had returned home with a reporter who was writing a story for *New York* about Talese's sex research, and found there a note from his wife. She had left because his open discussion of his research (and sex life) had violated her own right of privacy.

Talese's response is revealing. He was "distressed by her departure." But he was also "eager to conceal the contents of the letter from the *New York* reporter who stood silently next to him" (543). However confessional he appears to have been about writing this book, he implies, he did not always tell all.

His wife returned without comment, and his work on the book continued. One weekend he visited a nudist camp near his old boyhood home and, taking his clothes off, joined the other nudists on the pier. Not far away, sailing vessels and motorboats had dropped anchor to watch the nudists.

There were also some catcalls coming from the boats, whistles and cheers; and after watching for a few moments, Talese stepped forward on the deck, separating himself from the other quiet nudists, and he faced the boats.... They were unabashed voyeurs looking at him; and Talese looked back. (546)

This ending, contrived as it may seem, suggests once again Talese's continuing fascination with the act of journalism. *Thy Neighbor's Wife* has been a book about sexual voyeurs; researching it, Talese has been a voyeur watching voyeurs. Now, at the end, he becomes the object of voyeurism, as he was outside the book, in interviews and articles on his research. And he *looks back.*

In *The Kingdom and the Power*, Talese spoke of the detachment required of conventional journalists:

For this detachment from the world they observe robs them of a deeper experience that springs from involvement, and they sometimes become merely voyeurs who see much, feel little. They take death and disaster as casually as a dock strike, and they take for granted their right to publicize the weakness in others but they never have to lay it on the line themselves. (1969, 51)

Talese's work, from the *Esquire* pieces in the sixties and *The Kingdom and the Power* through *Thy Neighbor's Wife,* suggests a fascination with journalism, which can turn celebrities into ordinary people and ordinary people into celebrities. He adopts the techniques of fiction not only to make journalism more vivid, more dramatic, but also to raise questions about journalism and those who practice it. The results of his effort have been uneven; his later journalism does not bear out the promise of the sixties. But he has at least provoked readers to ask, "*What the hell is going on?*"

NOTES

1. Harold Hayes has been credited with nurturing the New Journalism on the pages of *Esquire* (Obituary, "Harold Hayes, 62, *Esquire* Editor During Rise of New Journalism," *New York Times*, 7 Apr. 1989: D21).

2. Unpublished correspondence suggests a serious tug-of-war between *Esquire* and Sinatra's agent over control of the article, with *Esquire* resisting the agent's efforts to review the manuscript before publication. Although Hayes refused to allow prior review, he did agree to respect any designation the agent cared to make of any off-limits areas of Sinatra's life (unpublished letter, Harold Hayes to Jim Mahoney, 11 Nov. 1965, Rare Books Department, Z. Smith Reynolds Library, Wake Forest University, Winston-Salem, North Carolina).

3. Talese said as much at a *Writer's Digest* roundtable in 1970. Writing about his Joshua Logan piece, he said: "I was writing really about failure. It is a subject that intrigues me much more than success." He goes on to speak specifically of his interest in fame, as a subject, when he says that Frank Sinatra symbolized to him "fame and how a man lives with it" (see Robinson et al. 1970, 34).

4. Unpublished letter, 22 June 1961. Rare Books Department, Z. Smith Reynolds Library, Wake Forest University, Winston-Salem, North Carolina.

5. "Building the Magazine's Personality: Importance of the Writer," pp. 6–8. Unpublished manuscript, Rare Books Department Z. Smith Reynolds Library, Wake Forest University, Winston-Salem, North Carolina.

PRIMARY SOURCES

Talese, Gay. 1961. *New York: A Serendipiter's Journey*. New York: Harper and Brothers.

———. 1969. *The Kingdom and the Power*. New York: World.

———. 1971a. *Fame and Obscurity*. New York: Bantam Books. (Portions of this collection were published earlier as *The Bridge, New York: A Serendipiter's Journey,* and *The Overreachers*.)

———. 1971b. *Honor Thy Father*. New York: World.

———. 1974. "The Book as a Medium for Journalism." In *Liberating the Media: The New Journalism*. Ed. Charles C. Flippen. Washington, D.C.: Acropolis Books.

———. 1980a. *Thy Neighbor's Wife*. Garden City, N.Y.: Doubleday.

———. 1980b, May. "Playboy Interview: Gay Talese." *Playboy*: 75–116.

———. 1987, Nov. "When Frank Sinatra Had a Cold." *Esquire*: 161–66.

SECONDARY SOURCES

Eisenberg, Lee. 1989, Aug. "Harold Hayes Remembered." *Esquire*: 17–24. (This is a collection of statements by writers and *Esquire* staff members.)

Lounsberry, Barbara. 1990. *The Art of Fact.* Westport, Conn.: Greenwood Press.

Malcolm, Janet. 1990. *The Journalist and the Murderer.* New York: Knopf.

Robinson, L. W., Harold Hayes, Gay Talese, and Tom Wolfe. 1970, Jan. "The 'New' Journalism." *Writer's Digest*: 32–35.

Weber, Ronald. 1973. *The Reporter as Artist: A Look at the New Journalism Controversy.* New York: Hastings House.

————. 1980. *The Literature of Fact: Literary Nonfiction in American Writing.* Athens: Ohio University Press.

Wolfe, Tom. 1973. "The New Journalism." In *The New Journalism.* With an Anthology edited by Tom Wolfe and E. W. Johnson. New York: Harper and Row.

HUNTER S. THOMPSON

Arthur J. Kaul

gonzo (gan'zo) adj. [<?] [Slang] bizarre, unrestrained, extravagant, etc.; specif., designating a style of personal journalism so characterized.
(*Webster's New World Dictionary, Second College Edition*, 1980)

Playboy: What will you do? Do you have any projects on the fire other than the political stuff?

Thompson: Well, I think I may devote more time to my ministry, for one thing. All the hellish running around after politicians has taken great amounts of time from my responsibilities as a clergyman.

Playboy: You're not a real minister, are you?

Thompson: What? Of course I am. I'm an ordained doctor of divinity in the Church of the New Truth. I have a scroll with a big gold seal on it hanging on my wall at home. (1974, 246)

Hunter S. Thompson ended a self-imposed retirement from New Journalism in 1983, returning in the bizarre literary persona of a primitively vengeful deity. "I am Lono," Thompson proclaimed. "I am the one they've been waiting for all these years" (Thompson and Steadman 1983, 150). His comic transfiguration from free-lance writer to Hawaiian god in *The Curse of Lono*, ostensibly an account of the Honolulu Marathon, represents more than another installment of freelance Gonzo-style sports reporting. A character in Thompson's comic narrative recognized this with a warning: "You've gone too far this time. It's not funny anymore. You're fucking with their religion" (153).

Apocalyptic religious motifs resonate through Hunter Thompson's literary corpus, a more recent manifestation introducing *Generation of Swine: Tales of Shame and Degradation in the '80s*:

I have stolen more quotes and thoughts and purely elegant little starbursts of writing from the Book of Revelation than anything else in the English language ... because I love the wild power of the language and the purity of the madness that governs it and makes it music. (1988, 9)

The "fearful intensity" of Revelation, "a thunderhead mix of Bolero, Sam Coleridge and the ravings of Cato the Elder," Thompson wrote, is an inspirational "litany of doomsday gibberish" (1988, 36).

Language and madness—these terms signify Thompson's secularized style of literary prophecy. Like biblical prophecy, Thompson's reportage takes the form of volatile denunciatory literary jeremiads, challenging and reproving conventional morality, politics, and culture. "Most smart people tend to feel queasy when the conversation turns to things like 'certain death' and 'total failure' and the idea of a 'doomed generation,' " Thompson proclaimed. "But not me" (1988, 299). "I am comfortable with these themes.... Any conversation that can make smart people confront a mix of Death, Doom and Failure with a straight face is probably worth listening in on" (1988, 299). His Gonzo-style reporting in six books and other "major statements of our time" constitutes the "ravings" of a postmodern Jeremiah whose prophetic narrative discourse ranks him as the most brilliantly outspoken moralist to practice New Journalism.

His Gonzo brand of New Journalism, Thompson insists, transforms the writer into a performer. "True Gonzo reporting needs the talents of a master journalist, the eye of an artist/photographer and the heavy balls of an actor," he wrote.

Because the writer must be a participant in the scene, while he's writing it. Probably the closest analogy to the ideal would be a film director/producer who writes his own scripts, does his own camera work and somehow manages to film himself in action, as the protagonist or at least a main character. (1979, 120)

Playing a minor role in his first and somewhat conventionally written book, *Hell's Angels*, Thompson produced the account after a year's "close association" with the "outlaw motor-cycle gang"—"riding, loafing, plotting, and eventually being stomped" (1966, 279). His *Scanlan's Monthly* article (June 1970), "The Kentucky Derby Is Decadent and Depraved," set the stage for Thompson's distinctive first-person style in which he becomes the central dramatic figure. The story begins: "I got off the plane around midnight and no one spoke as I crossed the dark runway to the terminal" (1979, 23).

Fear and Loathing in Las Vegas radically broke with conventional reporting, going far beyond the "Kentucky Derby" performance to establish his own "outlaw journalist" reputation. In the drug-crazed persona of a pill-popping "Raoul Duke," Thompson stars in his outlandish coverage of a district attorneys' meeting convened to deal with "the drug menace." Thompson, alias Raoul Duke, traveled through his hallucinatory schizophrenic narrative using several guises: "Doctor of Journalism" ("Watch your language! You're talking to a doctor of journalism!" [1971, 19]) and "Doctor of Divinity, a certified minister of the Church of the New Truth" ("another fucked up cleric with a bad heart" [203–4]). His fractured multiple-identity persona was an actor's mask, a dramatic ploy to criticize the "Drug Culture of the Sixties" and the "American Dream" for being a "monster reincarnation of Horatio Alger," like Thompson as Duke, "just sick enough to be totally confident" (204).

Thompson was less confident about *Fear and Loathing in Las Vegas* as a literary work, describing it as a "gimped effort" at New Journalism, a "failed experiment in Gonzo Journalism," and "a victim of its own conceptual schizophrenia, caught & finally crippled in that vain, academic limbo between 'journalism' and 'fiction' " (1979, 122). Thompson later admitted that his Vegas saga was a "happy work of fiction"—"Only a goddam lunatic would write a thing like this and then claim it was true" (1979, 122–23). Yet, even "failed" Gonzo was not New Journalism to his way of thinking. Unlike Tom Wolfe and Gay Talese, Thompson told a *Playboy* interviewer, "I almost never try to *reconstruct* a story . . . They tend to go back and recreate stories that have already happened, while I like to get right in the middle of whatever I'm writing about—as personally involved as possible."[1] Indeed, Thompson bristled at the idea of even being a reporter: "I'm not a reporter. I'm a writer."

I've never tried to pose as a goddam reporter. I don't defend what I do in the context of straight journalism, and if some people regard me as a reporter who's gone bad rather than a writer who's just doing his job—well, they're probably the same dingbats who think John Chancellor's an acid freak and [Walter] Cronkite is a white slaver. (1974, 246)[2]

The Chancellor/Cronkite put-ons found their way into Thompson's *Fear and Loathing: On the Campaign Trail '72* as part of "an obvious heavy-handed joke," "a slash of weird humor" to relieve the monotony of politics (1974, 88).

Weird humor laced with strident invective is Thompson's Gonzo trademark, setting his work apart from conventional straight reporting and even New Journalism. Humor and satire are the moralist's weapons, and Thompson wields them with deadly and hilarious vengeance. A few examples from *Generation of Swine* make the point:

Ronald Reagan: "For the last 20 years he has functioned brilliantly as the flag-waving front man for a gang of fast-buck Southern California profit-takers who no longer need him." (186)

George Bush: "He has the instincts of a dung beetle. No living politician can match his talent for soiling himself in public. Bush will seek out filth wherever it lives... and when he finds a new heap he will fall down and wallow crazily in it, making snorting sounds out of his nose and rolling over on his back and kicking his legs up in the air like a wild hog coming to water." (228)

Oral Roberts: "Oral Roberts is a greed-crazed white trash lunatic who should have been hung upside down from a telephone pole on the outskirts of Tulsa 44 years ago before he somehow transmogrified into the money-sucking animal that he became when he discovered television." (229)

His admittedly "extremely harsh language" (1988, 227) used to denounce televangelists for being "the scum of the earth" and "acting like a gang of baboons" (229) was turned on television itself:

The TV business is uglier than most things. It is normally perceived as some kind of cruel and shallow money trench through the heart of the journalism industry, a long plastic hallway where thieves and pimps run free and good men die like dogs, for no good reason.... Mainly we are dealing with a profoundly degenerate world, a living web of foulness, greed and treachery ... which is also the biggest real business around and impossible to ignore. You can't get away from TV. It is everywhere. The hog is in the tunnel. (1988, 43–44)

Like televangelists and television, Thompson castigates journalism, "a low trade and habit worse than heroin, a strange seedy world full of misfits and drunkards and failures. A group photo of the top ten journalists in America on any given day would be a monument to human ugliness" (1988, 10).

Much of the rhetorical savagery of his satirical epithets possesses the tonality of a demonic doomsday oracle. Images of death, dismemberment, and destruction describe Washington, D.C., with "blood in the water," "human remains on the sidewalk," and "the hallways in the White House basement ... slick with human scum" (1988, 218). Thompson wreaks rhetorical vengeance upon White House officials for their deceptions and betrayals, his language a postmodern parody of the Old Testament prophets Amos and Jeremiah:

Valium sales will soar, and the stomach pumps at Bethesda will be kept cranked up at all times.... There will be uncontrolled howling and weeping, and many patients will be chained together like common criminals, with numbers inked on their foreheads and subpoenas attached to the backs of their gray pajamas with super glue and duct tape. (1988, 213)

Indeed, political corruption—Watergate in the 1970s and Iran-Contra in the 1980s—operates as a metaphor in Thompson's works for the degradation of American culture. Deception, fraud, greed, hubris, lying, and relentless perjury, among many others—all are indicted and condemned in an explosively prophetic moral rhetoric.

For instance, consider Thompson's "ravings" about the "generation that once embraced the Reagan Revolution"—"The Generation of Swine"—whose heroes stand publicly accused and mocked for "fraud, corruption and flagrant swindling" and who have been taught that "rain is poison," that "sex is death," and that "there is not much left except TV and relentless masturbation" (1988, 10–11). The "shame and degradation of the 1980s prompt Thompson's quasi-religious speculations about the ambivalences and contradictions of American culture in terms of Heaven and Hell. "Hell will be a viciously overcrowded version of Phoenix," Thompson wrote,

—a clean and well-lighted place full of sunshine and bromides and fast cars where almost everybody seems vaguely happy, except for the ones who know in their hearts what is missing. . . . And being driven slowly and quietly into the kind of terminal craziness that comes with finally understanding that the one thing you want is not there. Missing. Back ordered. (1988, 11)

In Thompson's scheme of things, Hell and its inhabitants look suspiciously like shoppers at a suburban American mall, hollow men and women whose "vaguely happy" mannequin like faces disguise their emptiness.

His attempt to describe Heaven unleashed a lengthy single-sentence Gonzo-style screed that ended in failure with the conclusion that "maybe there is no heaven."

Heaven will be a place where the swine will be sorted out at the gate and sent off like rats, with huge welts and lumps and puncture wounds all over their bodies—down the long black chute where ugliness rolls over you every 10 or 16 minutes like waves of boiling asphalt and poison scum, followed by sergeants and lawyers and crooked cops waving rule books; and where nobody laughs and everybody lies and the days drag by like dead animals and the nights are full of whores and junkies clawing at your windows and tax men jamming writs under your door and the screams of the doomed coming up through the air shaft along with white cockroaches and red stringworms full of AIDS and bursts of foul gas with no sunrise and the morning streets full of preachers begging for money and fondling themselves with gangs of fat young boys trailing after them. (1988, 11)

This is the "pure gibberish" of a self-confessed "demented imagination," a bizarre, unrestrained, and extravagant vision combining apocalyptic motifs of the Book of Revelation, the tortured, nightmarish iconography of Hieronymus Bosch, and the existential blasphemies of Samuel Beckett. Behind the mask of laughter and linguistic bravado, Thompson relentlessly confronts his great themes of Death, Doom, and Failure, telling us in often hilarious ways that American culture and institutions are absurd, a matrix of insanity that cannot be redeemed. No exit. No escape. No salvation.

Hunter S. Thompson emerges from his works as the practical joker of New Journalism, a clown whose comic antics—he's a character in Garry

Trudeau's "Doonesbury"—and satirical put-downs obscure the underlying moral seriousness of his cultural criticism. His Gonzo-style reporting speaks with a shrill, prophetic voice, warning readers that their quest for salvation and transcendence invariably leads to self-delusion in a culture in which "the yahoos never sleep" (1988, 32). Thompson performs with "An acrobat's sense of things, a higher and finer touch" and "a fatal compulsion to find a higher kind of sense in things that make no sense" (1988, 54). In a culture afflicted with terminal craziness, Thompson's demented ravings represent the voice of sanity.

"Take my word for it, folks," Thompson says. "I know how these things work" (1983, 32).

NOTES

1. Thompson's participatory reportage fits into the "cultural phenomenology" mode of New Journalism in which the act of observing is "a vital part of the story," according to David L. Eason (1984, 57). The phenomenological mode focuses on "observing as a form of lived experience ... that actor and spectator create in their interaction, the dynamics through which each is created in the reporting process" (57). His groundbreaking interpretive analysis of "New Journalism and the Image-World" represents an intelligent departure from professional journalism's commentaries. Popular criticism, largely contained in book reviews, reveals images of Thompson as "quintessential outlaw journalist" (Warren 1984), "loose gun on the deck of American journalism" (Clark 1988), and "literary lion of lunacy" (Finke 1987) whose vantage point is "perched on the fringe, where lunatics rave and sometimes the truth is told" (Montgomery 1988). These interpretive images tell us more about the professional identity and normative practices of conventional journalists than they do about their subject, John Pauly has observed of media mogul Rupert Murdoch, who also has been portrayed as a "demonic" journalistic "outlaw." Like Murdoch, Thompson "provides professional journalists with someone to be normal against. His incessant presence marks the darker border at which enlightened journalism imagines itself standing watch" (Pauly 1988, 247). Joseph Nocera's "How Hunter Thompson Killed New Journalism" (1981) is highly emblematic of the so-called enlightened journalist-as—border guard standing watch against the assaults of outlaw journalists. "The main purpose of Thompson's style," Nocera complained, "was to give its creator a persona" (46). Gonzo-style New Journalism was "purely a creature of the fashion of his day" (45), "a manifestation of an old and ignoble strain in American journalism" among "writers more interested in being fashionable, or snide, or above the fray than in understanding or enlightening" (49). New Journalism promised the possibility of "a new general form that would merge fact-writing and opinion-writing," Nocera wrote. "But more than anyone else, Hunter Thompson has damaged and discredited New Journalism's promise. Instead of being exhilarated by his freedom, he was corrupted by it. Instead of using it in the search for truth, he used it for trivial self-promotion" (50). Nocera concluded: "My guess is Thompson knew from the start what a literary fraud he was perpetrating" (48).

2. Thompson spent some time in the reportorial trenches. According to an "About the Author" blurb at the end of Hell's Angels (1966), Thompson "has worked on

newspapers and magazines in New York, San Juan, and Rio de Janeiro. His articles have appeared in *The Reporter, The Nation* and *Esquire.*" In the early 1960s, he was a Caribbean stringer for the *New York Herald Tribune,* later becoming a South American correspondent for the *National Observer.* He began writing as a sports columnist in Florida.

PRIMARY SOURCES

Thompson, Hunter S. 1966. *Hell's Angels: A Strange and Terrible Saga.* New York: Random House.

———. 1971. *Fear and Loathing in Las Vegas: A Savage Journey to the Heart of the American Dream.* New York: Random House.

———. 1973. *Fear and Loathing: On the Campaign Trail '72.* San Francisco: Straight Arrow Books.

———. 1974, Nov. "Playboy Interview: Hunter Thompson." *Playboy.*

———. 1979. *The Great Shark Hunt: Strange Tales from a Strange Time.* New York: Summit Books.

———. 1983, July 21-Aug. 4 "A Dog Took My Place." *Rolling Stone.*

———. 1988. *Generation of Swine: Tales of Shame and Degradation in the '80s.* New York: Summit Books.

———. 1990. *Songs of the Doomed: More Notes on the Death of the American Dream, Gonzo Papers Vol. 3.* New York: Summit Books.

Thompson, Hunter S., and Ralph Steadman. 1983. *The Curse of Lono.* New York: Bantam Books.

SECONDARY SOURCES

Clark, Tom. 1988, July 3. "Bashing the Swine: Hunter S. Thompson Trashes Venality, Greed and Hotel Rooms." *San Jose Mercury News.*

Eason, David L. 1984. "The New Journalism and the Image-World: Two Modes of Organizing Experience." *Critical Studies in Mass Communication* 1: 51–65.

Finke, Nikki. 1987, Oct. 18. "The New Hunter S. Thompson: A Doctor of Gonzo Journalism Turns Political Man." *Los Angeles Times.*

Montgomery, David. 1988, July 24. "Hunter Thompson Flails Away at the Foibles of Life in the '80s." *Buffalo News.*

Nocera, Joseph. 1981, Apr. "How Hunter Thompson Killed New Journalism." *Washington Monthly* 13, no. 2: 44–50.

Pauly, John J. 1988. "Rupert Murdoch and the Demonology of Professional Journalism." In *Media, Myths, and Narratives: Television and the Press.* Ed. James W. Carey. Newbury Park, Calif.: Sage Publications, 246–61.

Warren, Elaine. 1984, Mar. 1. "Fear and Loathing in Westwood." Los Angeles Herald-Examiner.

MICHAEL HERR

Donald Ringnalda

In a much-quoted passage from Joseph Conrad's *Heart of Darkness*, the external narrator, just as he is about "to hear about one of Marlow's inconclusive experiences" explains the difference between the way Marlow and other men of the sea tell stories:

The yarns of seamen have a direct simplicity, the whole meaning of which lies within the shell of a cracked nut. But Marlow was not typical (if his propensity to spin yarns be excepted), and to him the meaning of an episode was not inside like a kernel but outside, enveloping the tale which brought it out only as a glow brings out a haze, in the likeness of one of these misty halos that sometimes are made visible by the spectral illumination of moonshine. (Conrad 1950, 68)

This description sheds a great deal of "moonlight" on the story Marlow is about to tell; but it also sheds light on *Dispatches*, written by Michael Herr, the 1970s heir of Conrad's early-day literary journalism. Herr's reportage is as different from conventional journalism as Marlow's is different from conventional sea tales. Both men realized that what they had witnessed in the heart of darkness was simply beyond any kind of conventional storytelling, and perhaps beyond even unconventional storytelling. Their experiences had been altogether too dark. All "straight history" and straight anything became seriously compromised. The link between Herr and Marlow became secure in 1979 when Herr did the voice-over for Francis Ford Coppola's version of Marlow—Captain Willard— in *Apocalypse Now*. In one of Herr's great lines for Willard, we hear, "Charging a man with murder here is like handing out speeding tickets at the Indy 500." The only illumination Marlow and Herr did experience was the illumination of the disintegration of their confidently straight Western consciousnesses, like tracer rounds illuminating objects targeted for destruction. In *Dispatches*,

Herr suggests an analogue for this disintegration as he observes "the phosphorescence that gathered around rotting tree trunks and sent pulsing light over the ground from one damp spot to another" (1978, 269).

Instead of structuring episodes on a continuum, Herr moves pulsatingly from one "damp" critical mass to another. The episodes that Conrad's external narrator speaks of are like a tier of building blocks, coherent, self-contained parts of the larger structure. But for Marlow and Herr, all is *a-part*. Meaning is as elusive as the muddy serpentine Congo River or the ominous, unmappable Central Highlands of Vietnam. Instead of kernels, both stories are swirling strobes eerily illuminating the spooky shadows.

Thinking back on his experiences, some of which were "a translucent blur" (95), Herr says that everything stood in "a strange light; the light told the story, and it didn't end like any war story I'd ever imagined" (277). He says that the experience of horror leaves one "changed, enlarged and... *incomplete*" (260; emphasis added)—like a glow bringing out a haze. And as the participle "enveloping" suggests, this glowing haze is a process in which experience past and experience present are interwoven. Neither storyteller tells a story that already exists. It comes into being as it is being told. To a great extent the process is the content. Their past experiences are less things in themselves than they are catalysts for a future act. As Paul Fussell says in *The Great War and Modern Memory*, "it is only the ex post facto view of an action that generates coherence or makes irony possible" (1975, 310). *Heart of Darkness* and *Dispatches* are ex post facto collages that provide Marlow and Herr their only way of knowing their horrifying experiences. As Herr expresses it, "Plant you now, dig you later: information printed on the eye, stored in the brain" (1978, 268). Or:

The problem was that you didn't always know what you were seeing until later, maybe years later, that a lot of it never made it in at all, it just stayed stored there in your eyes. Time and information, rock and roll, life itself, the information isn't frozen, you are. (20)

Herr needed to immerse himself in time, memory, and the creative act in order to thaw himself out. "Immersion" would seem to be one of the primary earmarks of literary journalism. And both Marlow and Herr were immersed beyond their wildest imaginations. (Herr was so immersed that as he ends his book he says, "One last chopper revved it up, lifted off and flew out of my chest" [277].) But the really crucial kind of immersion is the secondary one, after the fact, when the writer does not recollect, nor even recreate, so much as *correlate*, *create*, and *image* the fragmentary raw material of the first immersion. So Herr is not really speaking hyperbolically when he says of this first immersion in Vietnam, "I hadn't been anywhere, I'd performed half an act" (268).

This brings up two paradoxes of literary journalism. First, the storyteller achieves immersion with distance—in both space and time. Herr wrote the greater share of *Dispatches* 12,000 miles from Hue and Khe Sahn, *years* after the fact. Marlow created his story aboard the *Nellie* more than 4,000 miles from the Congo, again, so one can infer, a number of years after the fact. (Conrad himself was thirty-two when he went to the Congo, forty-one when he wrote *Heart of Darkness*.)

The second paradox is that both Marlow and Herr scooped their stories by delaying the telling. By abjuring deadlines and wire services (literally, in the case of Herr), they assured themselves of an exclusive. A voice within them repeated the words that the *Commercial Advertiser*'s Lincoln Steffens said to his reporters: "Go on now, take your time" (1931, 317). To emphasize just how slow Herr was being in getting the "news" out, he calls his only in-country dispatch to *Esquire* "a lost dispatch from the Crimea" (1978, 226). Thus, it is paradoxically appropriate for Ward Just, a former reporter for the *Washington Post*, to call Herr the premier war correspondent from Vietnam, even though Herr rarely corresponded with anyone back in the States. He waited and struggled almost ten years before he did.

What do we call his belated response? Even if we label it "literary journalism," which I think we can, there are some nagging questions associated with that label. First of all, literally speaking, Herr's book is not *any* kind of "journalism" if we accept the root meaning of the word, namely, "daily." But there is a greater labeling problem: because of the fact/fiction tension that exists both in literary and journalistic circles, we have seen an awkwardness in deciding how to categorize certain books. This awkwardness is particularly acute in the field of Vietnam War writing. Thus, memoirs such as Ron Kovic's *Born on the Fourth of July* and Tim O'Brien's *If I Die in a Combat Zone* are often referred to as novels. Not surprisingly, for as Paul Fussell says, it is sometimes impossible to distinguish between a memoir and a first-person novel (1975, 310). And when it comes to *Dispatches* the lines separating fact, fiction, journalism, memoir, history, and autobiography become extremely blurred. Herr is the first to admit that his assignment in Vietnam was "vague" (1978, 227). The way Herr "wanders" (as in "vagabond") between categories is a clear manifestation of the word's literal meaning. And because "literary journalism" wanders between two perceived worlds, each of which is itself always evolving, it is a problematical appellation.

The most profound problem in Vietnam War studies is the stubborn assurance that fact and fiction are easily recognized opposites from two different worlds. Were it only so neat! War has a way of blurring such tidy categories. Notice the oxymoronic language of Tim O'Brien in "How to Tell a True War Story":

In a true war story nothing much is ever very true. A thing may happen and be a total lie; another thing may not happen and be truer than the truth. For example:

Four guys go down a trail. A grenade sails out. One guy jumps on it and takes the blast, but it's a killer grenade and everybody dies anyway. Before they die, though, one of the dead guys says, "The fuck you do *that* for?" and the jumper says, "Story of my life, man," and the other guy starts to smile but he's dead. That's a true war story that never happened. (1987, 213)

In this same vein, O'Brien's narrator in a recent *Esquire* short story says of a character given to hyperbole: "He wanted to heat up the truth, to make it burn so hot that you would feel exactly what he felt. For Rat Kiley, I think, facts were formed by sensation, not the other way around" (1989, 94). O'Brien simply is echoing the thoughts of Robert Graves, the British poet and essayist: "The memoirs of a man who went through some of the worst experiences of trench warfare [in World War I] are not truthful if they do not contain a high proportion of falsities" (1931, 32–33).

Finally, in a similar recognition of the slipperiness of the words "fact" and "fiction," William Eastlake, a former correspondent for *Nation*, has said that for the Vietnam War, history is the fiction and fiction is the history. Paul Fussell quotes a World War II RAF flier who expresses this same paradox. Having kept an accurate, detailed, truthful diary during the war, he now finds that

from all the quite detailed evidence of these diary entries I can't add up a very coherent picture of how it really was to be on a bomber squadron in those days. . . . No wonder the stuff slips away mercury-wise from proper historians. No wonder they have to erect rather artificial structures of one sort or another in its place. No wonder it is those artists who *re-create* life rather than try to *recapture* it who, in one way, prove the good historians in the end. (1975, 311; emphasis added)

There is something almost explicit in the language of this flier, O'Brien, Eastlake, and Graves—and most Vietnam War scholars and writers of all kinds seem afraid of going in after it. An analogy from Heller's *Catch–22* will help explain the source of this fear. Throughout the novel Heller flashes to a scene where Yossarian tends to the wound of Snowden, a fellow flier. The hip wound is not all that serious, and Yossarian carefully cleans it, packs it, and wraps it. He cannot figure out the relationship between such a minor wound and Snowden's deathly paleness. Finally he removes Snowden's flak jacket and his viscera come sliding out. Similarly, the wound suffered by America in Vietnam is far more serious—far more radical—than we have admitted.

Michael Herr is one of a very few writers who have removed the flak jacket. In his judgment, behind the sanitized columns of conventional print and the imperialistic sense-making stories on the six o'clock news was a "dripping, laughing death-face; it hid there in the newspapers and magazines and held to your television screens for hours after the set was turned off for the night, an afterimage that simply wanted to tell you at last what

somehow had not been told" (1978, 233). To this day conventional journalism and "kernelized" storytelling cover up a disemboweled epistemology.
Herr realized that most people could not even *see* the wound because they
were blinded by a habitual way of knowing. As a result, morality was
devitalized by an epistemological oil slick.

On the other hand, everyone has taken note of the hip wound. For example, everyone has pointed out the wounds that truth was subjected to at
the hands of Orwellian doublespeak, euphemisms, or what Herr calls "language fix" (43). But as John Hellmann says of Herr:

> He sees a deeper gulf between the consciousness of Americans and the actuality of
> the war that from the beginning produced an artificial, fictive "reality" conditioning
> the nature and course of experience.... He experienced ... an inability to compre
> hend the actuality before him as his consciousness seemed to protect him from the
> reality of the experience. Herr knows that if he is to capture the reality of the
> experience he must go beyond reporting, for the struggle is as much with his and
> the reader's consciousness as with the facts. (1980, 143–44)

Herr searches for a meaning, Hellmann goes on to say, "not available in
the fictive forms already imposed by one's culture upon the experiencing
mind" (146). Herr encountered the horror of a fictional world without an
exit. Those obsolescent, yet stubbornly kicking, fictive forms enable one to
make assumptions no longer available to a writer of Herr's insight. Because
the horror and the "hundred-channel panic" undermine everything—the
ability to distinguish between fact and fantasy, reason, logic, controlled
linear time—they also render inoperative those conventions that assume
such controls, whether literary realism, formula journalism, or even literary
journalism, as it is perceived by some. For when the subject is war, especially
one as insane and absurd as the Vietnam War, literary journalism, too, must
give up more control than perhaps it is used to.

So when Herr says, "I went to cover the war but the war covered me"
(1978, 20), he is admitting to the traumatic wound; he is admitting that
his assumptions were disemboweled, so the story he *did* get was that our
linguistic certainties no longer obtain. The story he got was that Vietnam
was a story. The term "nonfiction" lost its currency in a hurry.[1] Being
"covered" by the war does not simply mean that Herr was overwhelmed
by it; it means that he was *written* by it. The time-honored Western distinction between subject and object simply disintegrated. Herr says that he
was "debriefed by dreams" (277), and in Borgesian fashion he discovered
that the dreamer (writer) dreaming a dreamed man (the story) is in turn
being dreamed by another dreamer (the protean war itself and the myths
that sent us there to fight it). This leaves him in a terrifying hall of mirrors
where he must resort to gasping for ontological air and scrambling for an
epistemological footing (the very predicament suffered by Amlin Gray's

Reporter in the play *How I Got That Story*). So Herr carries literary journalism to new heights (or depths). After his many-year battle to write *Dispatches*, he came to understand that recognizing the conventions of hard journalism as just that is but one step. It *is* an important step to realize that the journalist needs to tap into the reservoirs of fiction and dream to get a truer story. But Herr makes two more steps, both of which will be elaborated on below: (1) he knows he is dreaming, and that "you could ask yourself whether you were sleeping even while you slept... cataloging the specifics ... without ever waking" (148). That is, he does something far more radical than merely *use* dream structures as a rhetorical device to make "facts" meaningful—he *experiences* them; (2) he knows *he* is being dreamed in turn.

In short, he knows that when the journalist's subject is the absurdity and bondage of an insane war, *all* linguistic structures are but provisional conventions, as unlike reality as maps are unlike the land they symbolize.[2] He knows that trying to fine-tune our habitual epistemology to make it dovetail with the reality of Vietnam is like trying to modify a pick-ax for use in brain surgery. Finally, he knows that instead of a solid kernel within a nut, he has liquids changing into gasses.

Taking the first step, Herr says, "Conventional journalism could no more reveal this war than conventional fire power could win it" (232). Earlier he says, "It would be as impossible to know what Vietnam looked like from reading most newspaper stories as it would be to know how it smelled" (98). Between Command, the Administration, and the conventional press, Herr saw a "cross fertilization of ignorance." As a result,

the spokesmen spoke in words that had no currency left as words, sentences with no hope of meaning in the sane world, and if much of it was sharply queried by the press, all of it got quoted. The press got all the facts (more or less); it got too many of them. But it never found a way to report meaningfully about death, which of course was really what it was all about. (229)

So Herr radically separated himself from those who were so enamored of their conventional symbols and interpretations that they ate the menu instead of the meal (to borrow a metaphor from Alan Watts). As David Eason points out, not even New Journalism is exempt from the practice of menu eating. The difference between Herr's mode of journalistic immersion and that of the menu eaters lies at the center of Eason's article "The New Journalism and the Image-World: Two Modes of Organizing Experience." Eason designates these two modes of New Journalism as "ethnographic realism" and "cultural phenomenology." Herr clearly operates in the second mode. Whereas the first mode assumes that the reporter can make sense of the world by putting new wine in old bottles, the second assumes a radical epistemological crisis. Whereas ethnographic realism is fine-tuning, cultural phenomenology is a total overhaul. Eason says:

Whereas ethnographic realism, like other forms of journalism, reveals the act of observing to be a *means* to get the story, cultural phenomenology reveals observing to be a vital part of the story. Observing is not merely a means to understand the world but an object of analysis. . . . Ethnographic realism represents style as a communicational *technique* whose function is to reveal a story that exists "out there" [like a kernel] in real life. Cultural phenomenology represents style as an epistemological strategy that constructs as well as reveals reality. (1984, 57, 59; emphasis added)

Herr's immersion in the Vietnam War forced him into the overhaul mode of cultural phenomenology.[3] In Eason's language, it did not take him long to experience "what it feels like to live in a world in which there is no consensus about a frame of reference to explain what it all means" (52). After hearing the much-quoted, inscrutable Lurp story early in *Dispatches* ("Patrol went up the mountain. One man came back. He died before he could tell us what happened" [4–5]), Herr comes to the conclusion that his epistemological training had ill prepared him for the wacky reality of Vietnam. He arrived in Vietnam believing that if something was inscrutable it simply needed to be restated. He was used to a language that had imperialistic control over the formless and the inconclusive. A language that insisted on order when there was none. A language that, like Agent Orange, obliterated any threat to our tidy, Euclidian, Newtonian epistemology. Herr discovered that the way Americans engaged in "language fix" found its perfect analogy in the motto of an Air Force defoliation outfit: "Only we can prevent forests" (163), an American mantra. America tried—all too "successfully"—to defoliate the image of Vietnam and replace it with our own. To borrow another metaphor from Alan Watts, it was as if by the convention of perspective America painted a doorway on an impenetrable wall. The Lurp story is but one instance where Herr banged his head against this illusory opening in the Vietnam labyrinthine landscape.

But he learned from his headache—he largely separated himself from those who insisted that the opening was real: "My ties with New York were as slight as my assignment was vague" (226–27). Rather than pledging allegiance to an illusory world of nonfiction, he plunges into a more promising world of self-conscious artifice—this is his second step. He calls *Dispatches* "my movie" (201). His many allusions to modern, existentialist writers such as Wallace Stevens, Stendhal, Proust, Graham Greene, Malraux, Camus, Conrad, and Heller are a tip-off that this book is *indeed* a new kind of journalism, one that ends up blurring all categories. *Dispatches* is a freewheeling collage of straightforward remembering, hallucination, irony, acid sarcasm, jump cuts, freeze frames, stream of consciousness, incongruous juxtaposition, realism, surrealism, Dadaism, and metafiction. It is a bulimic book that pigs out at the literary supermarket as it desperately tries to satisfy its appetite for a *real* opening in the wall. Finally, because Herr is acutely aware of "the fictive forms already imposed by one's culture upon the experiencing mind," his book is founded upon a paradox: *self-conscious* artificiality engenders authenticity.

The discovery of the illusory door and the search for a real opening into his and America's consciousness forms the foundation of Herr's counter-epistemology. The "painted" door is much like the maps that Americans were obsessed with in Vietnam. On the very first page of the book Herr talks about a map hanging on the wall of his room. He says: "That map was a marvel, especially now that it wasn't real anymore.... Even the most detailed maps didn't reveal much anymore" (1). Later he says that both language and our new maps of Vietnam were used as a cosmetic (98). If the maps "effectively obliterated even some of the most obvious geographical distinctions, [they] made for clear communication" (97–98). And there we have it. The maps and language may have satisfied America's hunger for order and clarity in the morass of the Vietnam War, but the result, once again, was that we ate the menu instead of the meal. Ignorance meticulously scripted. A carefully treated hip wound.

Herr's difficult time writing this book was caused by his search for a new map—a map that, instead of imposing order, truly followed the contours of Vietnam, the war, and America's complicity in the heart of darkness. *Dispatches* contains a number of analogies that serve as objective correlatives of Herr's search. Late in the book Herr offers us the analogy of his book's "contour flying." He goes up in a Loach (a wasplike, speedy, agile helicopter) with the First Cav's star flier:

We flew fast and close to the ground, contour flying, a couple of feet between the treads and the ground, treetops, hootch roofs. Then we came to the river where it ran through a twisting ravine, the sides very steep, almost a canyon, and he flew the river, taking us through blind turns like a master. When we cleared the ravine he sped straight toward the jungle, dipping where I'd been sure he would rise, and I felt the sharp freezing moment of certain death. Right in there under the canopy, a wild ship-shaking U-turn in the jungle, I couldn't even smile when we broke clear, I couldn't move, everything looked like images caught in a flash with all the hard shadows left in. (274)

This is part of the countermap that *Dispatches* offers us, and it is not one you can pin on your wall. In the words of James Gleick, this is the kind of map that "mirrors a universe that is rough, not rounded, scabrous, not smooth. It is a geometry of the pitted, pocked and broken up, the twisted, tangled, and intertwined" (1987, 94). At times the "language" of the map almost is like the Soldier's Prayer, not the standard one "printed on a plastic-coated card by the Defense Department," but the "Standard Revised, impossible to convey because it got translated outside of language" (60).

Conventional time also fails to survive Herr's contour flying. In his own words, "I was leaking time" (277). "It became possible to take a journey first and then make your departure" (68). In fact he arrives in Vietnam long after he got there—on page 177. Herr underscores a cyclical vortex on more than one occasion. He says, "There was the terrible possibility that a search for information there could become so exhausting that the exhaustion itself became the information" (68). And of fighting the VC: "It was us looking for him looking for us looking for him, war on a Cracker Jack box, repeated to diminishing returns" (64).

Everywhere, Herr denies himself the comfort of fixed-wing, linear flight. Early in the book he says, "It started out sound and straight but it formed a cone as it progressed, because the more you moved the more you saw, the more you saw the more besides death and mutilation you risked, and the more you risked of that the more you would have to let go of one day as a "survivor' " (7).

A second analogy has to do with where Herr spent his time in Vietnam. He eschewed the light of civilization in the official press clubs of the major cities and stepped outside, *way* outside, into the tangled geography of Vietnam and his imagination. Herr was afraid of the dark, but he knew that if he was to "report" this war, that is where he had to spend his time. He knew that "hiding under the fact-figure crossfire there was a secret history, and not a lot of people felt like running in there to bring it out" (51). Herr did not feel like it either, but he did it. And he did it by refusing to use what James William Gibson both figuratively and literally calls "the old trails" (1986, 11), which lead only to the destruction of serious intellectual and artistic inquiry, just as the literal trails ominously assured the likelihood of ambushes, claymore mines, and Bouncing Betties.

Like the Long Range Reconnaissance Patrols (known acronymically as Lurps), which spent many days at a time observing the enemy in the darkness of the far reaches of nowhere, so Herr's Lurp book pushes itself and the reader off the old trails and away from the artificially cleared landing zones of convention. *Dispatches* avoids what William Eastlake calls the classic American blunder—of giving the Indians the cover (1969, 22). The book is a deep "recon" probe (without fire support) into murky questions about who we are and how we know. Herr replaces the language-fixing, laundered narrative of old-trail realism and conventional journalism with a camera dropped in the bush that catches the weird, secret subtext of the war (224).

Someone once said that in Vietnam a grunt learned to live in the bush; a Lurp learned to *be* a bush, so thoroughly did he cut himself off and meld with his surroundings. Herr's book is a bush. It is not so much *about* Vietnam as it, in frightening ways, *is* Vietnam. In both form and content, *Dispatches* is serpentine, unpredictable, chaotic, hot, and as different from conventional war stories as the "purple haze" of Jimi Hendrix is different from the surfboards of the Beach Boys.

Both Herr and the Lurps realized that rather than throw the book at the enemy (which America did, both with its technological arsenal and with its "language fix"), they needed to throw the book away. It was obsolete, square pegs in amorphous holes. Conventional writing was as inappropriate as conventional fighting. It makes no sense to set up ambushes, as it were, to go out on sweeps and search and destroy missions when the enemy has in fact already tunneled beneath your base camp, shining your boots by day, satchel charging you by night.

Late in *Dispatches* (which appropriately occurs earlier in his Vietnam sojourn than previous parts of the book), a grisly experience provides us with another analogy of Herr's search for a new map:

They were bulldozing a junction into Route 22 near Tay Ninh and the old Iron Triangle when the plows ran into some kind of VC cemetery. The bones started flying up out of the ground and forming piles beside the furrows, like one of those films from the concentration camps running backward. (267)

Herr's "film" runs backwards. Like Marlow, he travels back in time to the debris of his first immersion. Both men needed to make a decision regarding what portion of their former idealistic selves needed to be exhumed from the dark center of their consciousness. Appropriately, Herr uses the term "triage" frequently. He is obviously fascinated by the concept. Like a doctor sifting through battlefield casualties, deciding who must be left to die and who must be saved, Herr sifts through language and epistemology, deciding which fictions of the American consciousness need to be saved by deconstruction. Like the city of Hue, which, according to what may be the most important sentence in *Dispatches*, "had been composed seemingly of destruction and debris" (259), Herr's book is composed of the fallout of a shattered epistemology.[4] And frankly, not much survives Herr's allocation operation. What is left is the same sobering, humbling truth discovered by Marlow, namely, that there is a horrible heart of darkness within the soul of all mankind. Herr expresses this in the famous concluding line of his literary journal: "Vietnam Vietnam Vietnam, we've *all* been there" (278; emphasis added). Just as Marlow realized that *all* of Europe went into making of Kurtz, so Herr discovered that *all* of America went into the making of the Vietnam quagmire.

In a sense, it was only by not corresponding in the conventional sense that Herr became a correspondent—the *premier radical* one of the war. I use these words in their literal sense: "first" "root." Herr's book is an archaeological dig that seeks correspondences between the historical strata of American consciousness. Herr finds them, and the "all" of "we've all been there" serves to take out of isolation the most recent stratum, namely, the war itself and those who found themselves physically in it. By taking his time, Herr discovered time in a much broader, more meaningful sense. To paraphrase and ruin the end of Yeats's poem "The Second Coming," Herr was able to see that America was *self*-vexed to nightmare by a rocking

"Captain America Complex" (Robert Jewett). And in his slow time he has seen the almost imperceptible movements of the rough beast, its hour come round at last, as it slouches toward Vietnam to be born.

In Herr's words, Vietnam was the place where America's "mythic tracks intersected" (19). Thus, when Herr dates the beginning of the war, he goes way back:

Mission intellectuals like 1954 [when the Vietminh captured Dien Bien Phu] as the reference date; if you saw as far back as War II and the Japanese occupation you were practically a historical visionary. "Realists" said that it began for us in 1961, and the common run of Mission flack insisted on 1965, post-Tonkin Resolution, as though all the killing that had gone before wasn't really war. Anyway, you couldn't use standard methods to date the doom; might as well say that Vietnam was where the Trail of Tears was headed all along, the turnaround point where it would touch and come back to form a containing perimeter; might just as well lay it on the proto-Gringos who found the New England woods too raw and empty for their peace and filled them up with their own imported devils. (51)

And finally, as he nears the end of his book, Herr underscores the correspondence between the American mythos and the war: "There's been nothing happening there [Vietnam] that hadn't already existed here, coiled up and waiting, back in the World" (268).

The admission that "we've all been there" is Herr's third step, the most disturbing step of the book, for it asserts that Herr's irony is inclusive, not selective. His archaeological dig discovers an entrenched, coiled complicity much too democratically pervasive for comfort. So when he says that you were responsible for what you *saw* (*not* just *did*) in Vietnam (20), he is acknowledging that Americans, including the reporters and photographers, were entangled in a script written long before the beast arrived in Vietnam.

Herr's confession of self and collective guilt may well have had its genesis in yet another analogy, the collage of Davies, a flipped-out door gunner that Herr met in Vietnam. The collage (as I have said elsewhere)[5] acts as an artistic analogue for *Dispatches* in that it sees around America's fictive consciousness and thereby also sees the incoherent coherence within the *officially* unrecognized chaos. Scrapping the Newtonian linear order that we brought with us to Vietnam, Davies's collage is a hip spatial emblem of cultural phenomenology, a nonlinear equation that lumps together grotesque "coefficients."

Herr says, "Years of media glut had made certain connections difficult" (223). Davies's collage is a microcosm of Herr's book in that it does make these difficult connections, connections that the military and political establishments would no doubt consider subversive junk. And they would be right! But this junk nonetheless is often a courageous, self-deprecating expression of Herr's and America's complicity. Among the collage's startling juxtapositions: a created-in-Hollywood Ronald Reagan and the narcotic cannabis; the procreative genitalia of machismo and the destruction of bombs; Cardinal Spellman and a Huey gunship; patriotism and money; the myth of the warrior hero and hog butchering; the beautiful ugliness—and again the sexuality of violence—of "one large, long figure that began at the bottom with shiny leather boots and rouged knees and ascended in a microskirt, bare breasts, graceful shoulders and a long neck, topped by the burned, blackened face of a dead Vietnamese woman" (187).

Obviously these *seemingly* disparate correlations are testimony that a whole lot more than containing communism was going on in Vietnam. And Herr engages in no self-righteous posturing. Indeed, he admits more than one wishes to the alluring correlation of eroticism and violence, being in a firefight and "undressing a girl for the first time" (144), or intensely hating and loving the war, almost simultaneously (66).

One feels uncomfortable with Herr's oxymoronic connections. But that is the whole point: the mythic die that stamped America's Vietnam into existence is so deeply rooted in what man loves to loathe that it is very hard to part with.

If the *content* of Davies's collage reveals a great deal about the counterepistemology of Herr's cultural phenomenology, so too does its *placement* within *Dispatches*. First of all, as I have said, it appears in a book that itself is a collage of colliding memories and free associations as he criss-crosses Vietnam in the omnipresent oxymoronic "saver-destroyer, provider-waster, right hand-left hand" collective meta-chopper (7). Second, it appears in the middle of a frenzied collage-like section called "Illumination Rounds." In it, in the space of twenty-one pages, "dipping where [we're] sure he would rise," Herr rapidly fires off sixteen vignettes that seemingly do not correspond with each other. The reader feels as if he were caught in an L-shaped ambush. Writers of straight history would likely deem this section poorly written, because it offers the reader no kernel, no hook, no linear progression, no angle—actually, far too many angles. But as Thomas Myers has said, these vignettes

bring momentarily darkened history into view. As the fading suggestion of each image hangs in the textual air, he launches a new one to bring the reader closer to the historian's problem of focusing on and correlating within individual imagination the plenitude of suggestions, of dealing aesthetically with the nonstop accumulation of quick glimpses and possible correspondence. (1988, 163)

Davies's collage is the heart of *Dispatches*. At this juncture of the book Herr gives us a collage within a collage within a collage, the very *center* of his map, and his way of insisting that we must stop looking for easy exits from the war. The war is too metastasized in the American "collage" to allow an "early out."

One final correlation in the collage needs to be looked at, for it not only brings us back to America's love of maps; it also goes a long way toward summing up what Herr discovered in his struggles as a cultural phenomenologist. In one part of the collage Davies has superimposed a reversed Vietnam over a map of California. Rather than continuing the mistake of seeing Vietnam in our own image, this cartographical gesture would have us see our image in our own Vietnam, an "East-West interface, a California corridor cut and bought and burned deep into Asia" (45). It would have us demystify the most recent progenitor of the mythic die: the fiction-making capital of the world—Hollywood—the respository of the male, frontier mythology, forever "facing west," as Richard Drinnon puts it, making "movies," defoliating and sanitizing whatever gets in the way.

To paraphrase David Eason, Davies's gesture would have us admit the disorienting truth that in America's $150 billion Vietnam movie, we all were actors, not audience. This is the spectral, hazy opening that Herr would have us develop the courage and humility to walk through.

NOTES

1. In his novel *DelCorso's Gallery* (New York: Dell, 1983), Philip Caputo explores this conflation of fiction and nonfiction in the field of photojournalism. Two photographers, DelCorso and Dunlop, have been at odds with each other for years, first in Vietnam, and later in the streets of Beirut. DelCorso accuses Dunlop of selling fraudulent photographs because he "doctors" them in all sorts of ways in the lab. Dunlop accuses DelCorso of being unartistic because he simply photographs the bald degradation of war. But Caputo would have us understand that both men change reality; it is just the means and timing that are different. Dunlop merely makes the changes later than DelCorso, who, on the *scene*, makes his modifications with shot selection, context, lighting, distance, lenses, and F-stops.

2. In "The New Journalism and Vietnam," John Hellmann elaborates on this map-territory/language-reality analogy, as I do in "Fighting and Writing: America's Vietnam War Literature."

3. Almost all other Vietnam writing partakes of the ethnographic mode. Irony in this writing remains selective, not radical. Hips remain the concern, not abdomens. Literary devices, such as shifts in point of view and disruptions of linear time, seem more tactical than strategic. Even in Ron Kovic's bitter memoir *Born on the Fourth of July* (New York: Pocket, 1976), the irony is directed solely outward. Guilt is largely imputed, not confessed. As an ethnographic realist, Kovic is angry over his disillusionment; as cultural phenomenologist, Herr uses this disillusionment as a terrifying opportunity radically to interrogate *all* of his and America's inherited belongings. As Peter Marin puts it, "All men, like all nations, are tested twice in the moral realm: first by what they do, then by what they make of what they do" (1980, 51). The power of *Dispatches* issues from Herr's unflagging willingness to take—and perhaps pass by failing—this second moral test.

4. This idea of composition from decomposition is a motif that "crops" up in the books of several Vietnam War writers, but the motif is particularly insistent in the work of Herr, Tim O'Brien, and Stephen Wright, three of the war's greatest

writers. We have already seen that Herr uses the word "furrows," which one can readily free-associate with farming, John Deere tractors, New Holland implements, fresh milk, and double-yolked eggs—all of which Herr puts in the context of mass slaughter. This same bizarre contextualization occurs in O'Brien's *Going After Cacciato*, where the title character earnestly fishes for walleyes in the putrid water of bomb craters. Similarly, Griffin, the main character in Wright's *Meditations in Green*, searches for the seeds that will sprout from the bomb craters. And while on an aerial recon mission he is intrigued with "a remarkable field of craters arranged in such neat nearly symmetrical rows as to resemble a bizarre species of farm crops" (202). All of these composition/decomposition motifs point to one thing: the construction of new fictions often involves the self-conscious destructive revision of old fictions, just as the Vietnam War forced destructive revisions of conventional journalistic credos.

5. For a fuller discussion of the role of collages as artistic analogues in Vietnam War literature, see John Clark Pratt, quoted in Lomperis 1987, 90–91. Also, by this author, see "Chlorophyll Overdose: Stephen Wright's *Meditations in Green*," *Western Humanities Review* (Summer 1986); and "Fighting and Writing: America's Vietnam War Literature," *Journal of American Studies* (Apr. 1988): 39–41.

PRIMARY SOURCE

Herr, Michael. 1978. *Dispatches*. New York: Avon.

SECONDARY SOURCES

Conrad, Joseph. 1950. *Heart of Darkness and The Secret Sharer*. New York: New American Library.

Drinnon, Richard. 1980. *Facing West: The Metaphysics of Indian-Hating and Empire-Building*. New York: New American Library.

Eason, David L. 1984. "The New Journalism and the Image-World: Two Modes of Organizing Experience." *Critical Studies in Mass Communication* 1: 51–65.

Eastlake, William. 1969. *The Bamboo Bed*. New York: Avon.

Fussell, Paul. 1975. *The Great War and Modern Memory*. London: Oxford University Press.

Gibson, James William. 1986. *The Perfect War*. New York: Random House.

Gleick, James. 1987. *Chaos*. New York: Viking.

Graves, Robert. 1931. *But It Still Goes On*. New York: J. Cape and H. Smith.

Hellmann, John. 1980. "The New Journalism and Vietnam: Memory as Structure in Michael Herr's *Dispatches*." *South Atlantic Quarterly* 79: 141–51.

Lomperis, Timothy J. 1987. *Reading the Wind: The Literature of the Vietnam War*. Durham: Duke University Press.

Marin, Peter. 1980, Dec. "Coming to Terms with Vietnam." *Harper's*: 41–56.

Myers, Thomas. 1988. *Walking Point: American Narratives of Vietnam*. Oxford. Oxford University Press.

O'Brien, Tim. 1987, Oct. "How to Tell a True War Story." *Esquire*: 208–12.

———. 1989, July. "Sweetheart of the Song Tra Bong." *Esquire*: 94–103.

Ringnalda, Donald. 1988. "Fighting and Writing: America's Vietnam War Litera-
    ture." *Journal of American Studies* 22, no. 1: 25–42.
Steffens, Lincoln. 1931. *The Autobiography of Lincoln Steffens.* New York: Har-
    court, Brace.

NORMAN MAILER

Anna Banks

"I keep thinking that if I study the contents of the kitchen long and hard enough, I will figure out some incongruous truth lurking beneath the chaotic surface of Mailer's venture." This is the reaction of Daphne Merkin who, seeking an interview with Mailer, walks into the set of the movie version of *Tough Guys Don't Dance*, which the author is directing (Merkin 1987, 44). Her reaction could just as well express the feelings experienced by a reader and critic of Mailer's vast body of literature. Seeking to understand Mailer's venture involves the careful scrutiny of his novels, nonfiction essays, poems, plays, social commentaries, and—now we must add—screenplays.

Mailer's latest creative venture, apparently, is in the realm of feature films, and the author's new role is as a director of films. Mailer likens being a director to being an "impresario" and states that while novel writing "is like having a difficult second wife," making a movie is "elegant work" (Merkin 1987, 47). Perhaps more accurately, Mailer's move into the visual realm of films is just a natural extension of his career-long search for central themes through which his experiences can best be conveyed. All his novels and nonfiction writing are evocative and visual in nature, a style that translates easily into the world of film.

Perusing Norman Mailer's literary works is frustrating to a critic trained in the twentieth-century Western traditions of a rational empiricism whose goal is usually to categorize and quantify. Mailer, perhaps intentionally, defies categorization. Each piece of work that Mailer produces represents a clear example of what the anthropologist Clifford Geertz calls "genre blurring." In his latest book, *Works and Lives: The Anthropologist as Author*, Geertz expands on his notion of genre blurring and takes as his central thesis the concept that awareness of the act of writing goes hand in hand with the analysis of a culture (using culture in the very broad sense of symbolic anthropology).

The collection of writings labeled literary journalism forms an explicitly recognizable case of a "blurred genre." Literary journalists have consciously combined the techniques and styles of fiction writing and journalism into the bisociation we call literary journalism. The themes of literary journalists tend to be concerned with social and political issues, usually examined within the context of contemporary culture. Most literary journalists were so-called straight journalists who found the boundaries of "objective" reporting too constrictive and inadequate to account for their content matter. Mailer is one of the few acknowledged members of this group who went over from the other side—the novelist-turned-journalist. Yet, even though Mailer is often labeled one of the core members of the literary journalism movement, his conversion from fiction writing was never accomplished completely. Furthermore, his role as a literary impresario, to use Mailer's own term, is more like that of a double-agent than of a zealous convert.

In *The Armies of the Night*, Mailer's first celebrated piece of literary journalism, published in 1968, Mailer describes a conversation between the poet Robert Lowell and himself as both were preparing their speeches to be delivered before the first mass rally and march on the Pentagon in October 1967:

"You know, Norman," said Lowell in his fondest voice, "Elizabeth and I really think you're the finest journalist in America."

... Lowell now made the mistake of repeating his remark. "Yes, Norman, I really think you are the best journalist in America."

The pen may be mightier than the sword, yet at their best each belong to extravagant men. "Well, Cal," said Mailer, using Lowell's nickname for the first time, "there are days when I think of myself as being the best writer in America." (1968a, 32–33).

Mailer continues to describe how Lowell, sensing the author's offense at his attempted compliment, tries to wriggle out of his faux pas while sinking himself deeper into the quagmire: "Oh, Norman, oh, certainly," he said, "I didn't mean to imply, heavens no, it's just that I have such *respect* for journalism."

"Well, I don't know that I do," said Mailer (33–34; emphasis in original).

Given that Mailer clearly expresses a distasteful and snobbish attitude toward journalistic writing, why did he publish a nonfictional account of the events surrounding the October 1967 march on the Pentagon, instead of a purely fictional account written in the form of a novel? Walter Benjamin, the German literary critic, stated emphatically that "the rigid isolated object (work, novel, book) is of no use whatsoever. It must be inserted into the context of living social relations" (1973, 87). This caveat is a useful guideline for critics of literary journalism, because their contents are inextricably linked to the social context that informs them. Less obvious, but equally significant, is the context surrounding the production of a given work in terms of the author's career and personal development. Before 1968 when Mailer published two well-acclaimed pieces of literary journalism—*The Armies of the Night* and *Miami and the Siege of Chicago*—he had published two relatively unsuccessful novels—*An American Dream* (1965) and *Why Are We in Vietnam?* (1967). Critically he was receiving much better reviews for his journalistic pieces (published primarily in *Esquire*) and was being categorized somewhat condescendingly as a journalist. As Tom Wolfe points out in *The New Journalism*, it was a commonly accepted axiom that "the novelist was the reigning literary artist, now and forever" (Wolfe 1973, 28).

Mailer's ego was made clearly apparent in his exchange with Lowell, and it seems natural that a writer with such an opinion of himself would prefer being listed in the ranks of the literary elites—the novelists—to being taken for a journalist. In a later article, Wolfe, paraphrasing Philip Roth, says, "We now live in an age in which the imagination of the novelist lies helpless before what he knows he will read in tomorrow morning's newspaper" (1989, 48). Wolfe continues in this vein to claim that by the 1960s, "American life was chaotic, fragmented, random, discontinuous; in a word *absurd*" (49).

Why Are We in Vietnam? was the closest Mailer came in purely fictional form to capturing the absurdity of the events he observed in American social and political life in the 1960s. Ostensibly, Mailer's 1967 novel relates a story told by D.J., an eighteen-year-old boy, as he sits "grassed out" at a dinner party given in his honor. The occasion for the dinner party is that it is the night before D.J. and his friend leave for Vietnam. While the title of the novel poses a crucial question—Why are we in Vietnam?—the story is not about Vietnam so much as about the narrator, D.J.: its information, themes, and effects are all filtered through his complex first-person narrative consciousness. The novel takes on the form of the inner consciousness and spontaneous outbursts of D.J., and beneath the surface structure action is the deep structure tale of the young man's "uncharted journey into the rebellious imperatives of the self" (a phrase used by Mailer in an earlier essay, "The White Negro"). Through D.J., Mailer examines the motives and actions behind U.S. foreign policy in terms of the American Dream, Manifest Destiny, and Western imperialism.

D.J.'s narrative function is to relate a "tall tale," a literary technique exemplified by Mark Twain. Mailer links his character directly to Twain's famous hero Huckleberry Finn in a chapter titled "Intro Beep One," where D.J. says, "Huckleberry Finn is here to set you straight" (1967, 7). But D.J. is more a perversion of ideal American boyhood. He is a schizophrenic character, a Jekyll and Hyde who is D.J. to the world, but Dr. Jekyll to his friend Tex Hyde. Insofar as D.J. takes on the characteristics of both an African American and a "white boy from Texas," the split is also racial. Thus D.J. is a perverted embodiment of the ideal Huck and the ideal Jim.

And when he is "grassed out" his relation to the world becomes transistorized and he is plugged into the mind of a Negro genius. Then, the white boy and the black boy speak simultaneously from the same mouth, "trapped in a Harlem Head" (41). As a narrator D.J. is more sophisticated than Huck, and as a character he is more complex. Indeed, D.J. is so complex that, unlike "normal" people, he is not ensnared by "inadequate and restrictively artificial modes of expression" (271).

The schizophrenic D.J. had a forerunner in the archetype described by Mailer in an earlier essay, "The White Negro," which is included in Mailer's collection *Advertisements for Myself* (1959). For Mailer, the African American man embodied what was "hip," he provided the language of "hip," he was the closest thing we had to an American existentialist. D.J. speaks in the language of hip. His is a King Lear character, the mad man who sees more clearly than the so-called sane ones, because he "suffers from one great American virtue—D.J. sees right through shit" (1967, 35).

The language of hip is key to Mailer's style of literary journalism. In *The New Journalism*, Tom Wolfe describes four devices that characterize new journalistic writing: scene by scene construction, recording the dialogue in full, "third-person point of view," and detailing everyday practices and styles (Wolfe 1973, 31–32). The language of hip and Mailer's concept of the American existentialist, described in great detail in "The White Negro," are informed by all four literary devices. Mailer describes the unique features of hip:

What makes "hip" a special language is that it cannot really be taught—if one shares none of the experiences of elation and exhaustion which it is equipped to describe, then it seems merely arch or vulgar or irritating. It is a pictorial language, but pictorial like non-objective art, imbued with the dialectic of small but intense change, a language of the microcosm, in this case, man, for it takes the immediate experiences of any passing man and magnifies the dynamic of his movements, not specifically but abstractly so that he is seen more as a vector in a network of forces than as a static character in a crystallized field. (1959, 348–49)

The language of hip is spoken by those who are aware of the absurdities inherent in modern life. For Mailer, writing his essay in 1957, the most aware are existentialists, psychopaths, and African Americans. These are the groups of individuals who are closest to their "inner consciousness" and, because of what Mailer views as their shared deviance from the norms of society, they are the ones who can most fully understand the absurd culture in which we live and "so submit that in a world of absurdities the existential absurdity is most coherent" (1959, 342).

The characteristics of hip as a language and a style and the personality of the existentialist, the psychopath, and the "White Negro" apply equally well to the schizophrenic fictional narrator D.J. and to the narrative persona of "Mailer" in *The Armies of the Night* and the reporter in *Miami and the Siege of Chicago*. These two books are the clearest and the most successful of Mailer's literary journalism. Both utilize the literary devices of realistic novels adopted by the new journalism described by Wolfe. Each book is comprised of a series of short chapters depicting, scene by scene, the author's observations and experiences of the context under scrutiny. The characters and the nature of the scenes are developed through careful and complete recording of the dialogue that the author overhears or in which he participates. Furthermore, the details of the characters' appearance and manner and the surroundings in which the author finds himself are described in almost obsessive detail. An example from *Miami and the Siege of Chicago* illustrates well the cumulative effect of these three devices a cappella, as well as Mailer's own brand of hip language:

At this party McCarthy looked weary beyond belief, his skin a used-up yellow, his tall body serving for no more than to keep his head up above the crowd at the cocktail party. Like feeder fish, smaller people were nibbling on his reluctant hulk with questions, idiotic questions, petulant inquiries he had heard a thousand times. "Why?" asked a young woman college instructor, horn-rimmed glasses, "Why don't we get out of Vietnam?" her voice near hysterical, ringing with the harsh electronics of cancer gulch, and McCarthy looked near to flinching with the question and the liverish demand on him to answer. "Well," he said in his determined mild and quiet voice, last drop of humor never voided—for if on occasion he might be surrounded by dolts, volts, and empty circuits, then nothing to do but send remarks up to the angel of laughter. "Well," said Senator McCarthy, "there seem to be a few obstacles in the way."

But his pale green eyes had that look somewhere between humor and misery which the Creation might offer when faced with the bulldozers of boredom. (1968b, 95–96)

The fourth technique described by Wolfe is the use by literary journalists of the third-person point of view. While the other three techniques are important elements of the Mailer style, it is his use of multiple narrative personae that distinguishes his literary journalistic works from those of others associated with the genre. In describing the style of hip, Mailer states: "Hip sees the context as generally dominating the man, dominating him because his character is less significant than the context in which he must function" (1959, 353). Mailer's response to the negatory powers of powerful social contexts is to develop a narrator with multifaceted qualities. Jennifer Bailey describes Mailer's approach in theatrical terms: "Like a good actor, the personae of Mailer's writing must be able to sift and select from the context of their acting in order to convey the truth of a situation" (1979, 88).

The acting qualities of Mailer's narrative style can best be illustrated by an examination of *The Armies of the Night*. In a review of *Armies*, Alvarez concluded that

[Mailer] has taken a fragment of contemporary history in which he played a part, presented it with all its attendant force, muddled argument and jostling power plays, and made it an internal scenario in which all the conflicting, deadening facts take on new consciousness as an artist. (1968, 362–63)

In "The Author as Producer," Walter Benjamin argues persuasively that the traditional dichotomy between form and content is sterile: "We are in the midst of a vast process in which literary forms are being melted down, a process in which many of the contrasts in terms of which we have been accustomed to think may lose their relevance" (1973, 89). The melting down of literary forms is an essential quality of the style of *The Armies of the Night*—the narrative voice is inextricably linked to the form of the book and, in Bailey's terms, the narrator is able to "sift and select" from the contexts in which he finds himself.

Armies is divided into two distinct parts: Book One, "History as a Novel: The Steps of the Pentagon" and the considerably shorter Book Two, "The Novel as History: The Battle of the Pentagon." Throughout the book, Mailer self-consciously analyzes the varying merits of the novelistic and historical forms of writing. Two sections are particularly revealing. In the final paragraph of Book One, Mailer discusses the problem with his historical account:

It insisted on becoming a history of himself over four days, and therefore was history in the costume of a novel. He labored in the aesthetic of *the problem* for weeks, discovering that his dimensions as a character were simple: blessed had been the novelist, for his protagonist was a simple of a hero and a marvel of a fool.... Yet in writing his personal history of these four days, he was delivered a discovery of what the March on the Pentagon had finally meant, and what had been won and what had been lost. (1968a, 241; emphasis added)

Later, in Book Two, Mailer elucidates on "the problem":

The mystery of the events at the Pentagon cannot be developed by the methods of history—only by the instincts of the novelist. The reasons are several, but reduce to one...the difficulty is that the history is interior—no documents can give sufficient intimation: the novel must replace history at precisely that point where experience is sufficiently emotional, spiritual, psychical, moral, existential, or supernatural to expose the fact that the historian in pursuing the experience would be obliged to quit the clearly demarcated limits of historical inquiry. (1968a, 284)

In Book One Mailer develops a narrator who functions both as an intrusive participant and as an observer. In Book Two, the narrator steps back and functions only as an observer whose goal is to record "the facts." To illustrate the change in his narrative voice, Mailer begins Book Two with an extended metaphorical image of a tower which must be erected in a dense forest if one is to "see the horizon," but of course "the tower is crooked, and the telescopes warped" (245). Mailer is attempting with this image to justify his abandonment of the historical form for the novelistic. Thus, in Book Two Mailer "zooms back" to give us a clearer vision (and version) of the events as they unfold and to step away from his own microscopic perspective.

Mailer's self-consciousness regarding the style and form of *Armies* and his protracted self-reflections regarding his narrative voice find a parallel in the works of contemporary anthropologists seeking to describe and explain the cultures they have journeyed to examine. From this perspective, Mailer's account of the events in October 1967 reads more like an ethnographic account of "that quintessentially American event" than a piece of either fiction or history as they are commonly known (241). In particular, Mailer's account is written in the style that John Van Maanen terms "confessional tales":

The confessional writings usually concern how the fieldworker's life was lived upriver among the natives. They are concerned primarily with how the fieldwork odyssey was accomplished by the researcher.... Often the ethnographer mentions personal biases, character flaws, or bad habits as a way of building an ironic self-portrait with which the readers can identify. The omnipotent tone of realism gives way to the modest, unassuming style of one struggling to piece together something reasonably coherent out of displays of initial disorder, doubt, and difficulty. (1988, 75)

Van Maanen stresses that the details that are important in confessional tales are not what happens to the "natives," but those that constitute the experiences of the author. In addition, the author tends to be a certain type:

Confessional writings rarely portray the author as a passive, unremarkable character who simply stands around waiting for something to happen or for the arrival of the white flash of discovery.... The narrator of the confessional is often a foxy character aware that others may be, intentionally or unintentionally, out to deceive him or withhold important information. (76)

Both Van Maanen's account of the typical style of a confessional and his description of the narrator of the tale characterize Mailer's brand of literary journalism. A further characteristic of the confessional links the mode more directly to journalism itself:

The confessional is apparently interesting only insofar as there is something of note to confess as well as something of note to situate the confession.... Authors of unknown studies will rarely find an audience who cares to read their confession. (81)

Not only will authors of unknown studies lack an audience, but Van Maanen suggests that unknown authors must first make their reputations as realist writers of ethnography before they can "sell" the more personal confessional works. Mailer himself only turned to nonfiction writing, and literary journalism in particular, after he had established a reputation as both a fine writer and a well-known public figure whose opinions were provocative and controversial.

Viewing Mailer as a confessional writer rather than as a journalist, novelist, or essayist also allows us to transcend the form and content dichotomy which forces us to focus on techniques rather than effects. Walter Benjamin regards technique as the dialectical starting point for an analysis which moves beyond this traditional dichotomy and forces us to look at the literary melting pot. This melting process, Benjamin argues, blurs the distinction not only between form and content, but also between author and reader (1973, 87–90).

Confessional tales allow the reader to relate to the event through the eyes of the author and from the perspective of others within the culture. A similar effect is produced in Mailer's literary journalism. The reader vicariously lives the events at the Republican and Democratic conventions in 1968 and participates in the march on the Pentagon in 1967. At the same time, Mailer's authorial narrative voice conveys his social reality. His is not an invisible narrator, but one who is intrusive, who insists on his view of the world. Other accounts of the events, whether from other participants or from the mass media, temper the author's opinions and allow the accounts to take the form of what Geertz calls "documentaries that read like confessionals"— a case of genre blurring (1983, 20). Yet, we are left in no doubt that, in Mailer's literary journalism, the issues that matter are those that affect the author. Mailer's account, like the confessional anthropologist's, is usually a tale that suggests that the activities he describes constitute a character-building conversion for him.

Mailer's literary journalism is characterized not just by a third-person point of view, but by a shifting point of view in which the author conveys an attitude of tacking back and forth between an insider's passionate perspective and an outsider's dispassionate one (Van Maanen 1988, 777). In other words, the author/narrator of Mailer's literary journalism moves between the roles of fictional hero and detached journalist, each with its own literary functions to perform. This narrative style is combined with the more clearly distinguishable techniques of realistic writing described by Wolfe— scene by scene construction, fully recorded dialogue, and detailing of incidentals.

In *The Executioner's Song* (1979), it would appear that Mailer has produced a work of literary journalism that is realist rather than confessional. The blurring of genres still applies, however. Although it won the Pulitzer Prize for *fiction* in 1980, the book is clearly in the literary journalistic tradition of Truman Capote's *In Cold Blood* and Joseph Wambaugh's *The Onion Field*. The real names of real people are used, as the book tells of the life and times of convicted murderer Gary Gilmore, who was executed in Utah in 1977. Mailer wrote the book after interviewing more than a hundred people and reviewing documents and court testimony. In addition, letters that Gilmore wrote play a central role in the narrative and in the development of Gilmore's character. Mailer admitted, however, in the book's Afterword that he had improved Gilmore's letters by trimming them and transposing certain words, sentences, and phrases. Mailer also explains in the Afterword that the book "does its best to be a factual account." He also says that his purpose was to write a *"true life story...* as if it were a novel." In the end, while the story is clearly Gilmore's, it is also Mailer's *version* of Gilmore and the West, and so bears some comparison to the concept of confessional writing. As one critic observed about the book: "He [Mailer] seems to have grafted an Eastern urban dream of the Wild West, complete with sixpacks, CBs, and pickup trucks, onto a conventional paradigm about poverty and child abuse eventuating in anomie and murder" (Johnson 1979, 3).

What distinguishes Mailer's writing on a more philosophical level is that he embodies Wolfe's claim that good writing will not come from accepting defeat at the absurdities of modern life, not to "leave the rude beast, the material known as life around us, to the journalists, but to do what journalists do, or are supposed to do, which is to wrestle the beast and bring it to terms" (Wolfe 1989, 55). Mailer's confessional anthropology is a direct challenge to the beast.

PRIMARY SOURCES

Mailer, Norman. 1959. "The White Negro." In *Advertisements for Myself.* New York: G. P. Putnam's Sons.

———. 1967. *Why Are We in Vietnam? New York:* G. P. Putnam's Sons.

———. 1968a. *The Armies of the Night.* New York: New American Library.

———. 1968b. *Miami and the Siege of Chicago.* New York: New American Library.

———. 1971. *The Long Patrol: Twenty-five Years of Writing from the Work of Norman Mailer.* Ed. Robert F. Lucid. New York: World.

———. 1974. *The Faith of Graffiti.* New York: Praeger.

———. 1979. *The Executioner's Song.* Boston: Little, Brown.

SECONDARY SOURCES

Alvarez, A. 1968, June 7. "Reflections in a Bloodshot Eye." *Commonweal.*

Bailey, Jennifer. 1970. *Norman Mailer: Quick Change Artist.* London: Macmillan.

Benjamin, Walter. 1973. "The Author as Producer." In *Understanding Brecht*. London: New Left Books.

Geertz, Clifford. 1983. *Local Knowledge*. New York: Basic Books.

————. 1988. *Works and Lives: The Anthropologist as Author*. Stanford, Calif.: Stanford University Press.

Johnson, Diane. 1979, Dec. 6. "Death for Sale." Review of *The Executioner's Song*, by Norman Mailer. *New York Review of Books*.

Merkin, Daphne. 1987, Oct. "His Brilliant (New) Career?" *American Film*: 44.

Van Maanen, John. 1979. "The Fact of Fiction in Organizational Ethnography." *Administrative Sciences Quarterly* 24: 539–50.

————. 1988. "Confessional Tales." In *Tales of the Field*. Chicago: University of Chicago Press.

Wolfe, Tom. 1973. *The New Journalism*. With an Anthology edited by Tom Wolfe and E. W. Johnson. New York: Harper and Row.

Wolfe, Tom. 1989, Nov. "Stalking the Billion-Footed Beast." *Harper's Magazine*: 45–56.

JOE ESZTERHAS

Jack Lule

The fire was roaring and Rise Risner's red Volkswagen, which had been pulled as close as possible, played Dylan, Hendrix, and, what the hell, Jose Feliciano. The people here were Charles Simpson's best friends. We were talking about a man who had killed three innocent people in cold blood. They were calling him a brother and telling me how much he loved people and how he believed in The Cause. . . .

It had been a long few days and I had scrutinized too many vivid details of four vicious killings and something in my mind flailed out now—Jesus Simpson, murderer, cold-blooded killer, compassionate, sensitive, sentimental. It could have been the fatigue or the Missouri weed or the beer mixed with wine, but I saw too many grotesqueries leaping about in that blazing bonfire. (Wolfe 1973, 158–59)

LANGUAGE AND POLITICS

The words above appear in the conclusion of Joe Eszterhas's "Charlie Simpson's Apocalypse." The scene brings to a close a searing story of rebellion in the heartland, a drama in which tensions between local youths and village elders of Harrisonville, Missouri, culminate with Charlie Simpson running amok through the village square, bearing a combat-regulation M-1 semi-automatic carbine with which he kills two policemen and a bystander before he puts the gun barrel in his mouth and blows his own head away.

The article is an extraordinary exemplar of what has come to be known as *literary* journalism. Certainly something about Eszterhas's prose differs from traditional journalism. The words violate rules of reporting; they ignore usual assumptions; they abuse canon; they cross conventions. The difference is a matter of . . . language.

Language gives meaning to the world, said the philosopher George Herbert Mead. Indeed, in his great book, Mead argued that mind, self, and society arise in and from language.[1] Without language, people would lack the common shared symbols that make understanding and meaning possible. Language gives meaning because it orders experience as it creates and provides shared symbolic forms.

Above all else, journalism is language—a shared symbolic form in which words and pictures are used to give meaning to the world. Journalism, though, is a distinctive kind of language, with styles, conventions, and traditions all its own. It orders experience, encourages particular events to be reported and in a particular way, and more broadly, helps shape certain ways of observing, portraying, and understanding the world.

Literary journalism challenges the traditional language of journalism. This is much more than a question of style or technique, however. *A change in language is a political act.* A change in language is an attempt to alter how the world is apprehended and understood. Sometimes it is the change of a single word, such as the change from "colored" to "black." Sometimes it is the change of an entire code and canon, such as the change embodied by literary journalism. By its very existence, literary journalism challenges the forms of experience, the ways in which traditional journalism observes, portrays, and understands the world. It is an act of revolt within language and within social life.

There is no way really to understand the writing of Joe Eszterhas without understanding literary journalism as a political act, one that confronts aspects of journalistic language as well as social tradition. Analysis of his work is an analysis of the ways that politically charged events are selected and portrayed through language which in itself is politically charged. The literary journalism of Joe Eszterhas can be studied as a means to understand in part how language gives meaning to social life; how the traditional language of journalism shapes and creates social life in a particular way; and how the language of literary journalism can be undertaken and understood as political action in the context of journalism and social life.

SOCIAL CONTEXT AND THE LIMINAL

Study of Eszterhas's work, and perhaps much of literary journalism, might usefully be grounded, then, in the contexts of society and language. First, Eszterhas used literary journalism to confront structures and processes of social life within a particular era: the late 1960s and early 1970s. His work reminds us that literary journalism first drew its subjects from those wrenching social rites of passage, something like what Arnold van Gennep called "the liminal," the intersections of time, struggle, conflict, drama, and sacrifice.[2] Literary journalism was the language of protest in those highly liminal times, the language of choice for the underground, alternative, and advocacy press. It arose amid an entire subculture—a *counterculture*—of question, protest, experimentation, and rebellion, and can most fruitfully be framed in the context of those times, a context that includes the music, dress, art, politics and hairstyles as well as the writing. The seeds of that writing might now be blossoming with concern over literary style and technique, but the roots of literary journalism are deep in the soil of passion, politics, and protest.

Politically charged topics of the era dominated Eszterhas's writing. He captured the battle in Harrisonville between long-haired youths and fearful town elders; he immersed himself in the use of informers in narcotics enforcement; he considered the bizarre cultural implications of Evel Knievel; he embraced the anguish and agony of a prisoner of war returned home.

Roots of Eszterhas's passion for politics can be found even in his early work. Indeed, he first attracted attention for his straight reporting on some of the galvanizing political incidents of the late 1960s and early 1970s. Born in Hungary and raised in East European refugee camps and the slums of Cleveland, Ohio, Eszterhas was a young reporter for the Cleveland *Plain Dealer* in the years of tumult and protest. His skills landed him a compelling national assignment. Through interviews with eyewitnesses, he put together *Life*'s ten-page account of the Mylai massacre in which U.S. servicemen deliberately slaughtered old men, women, and children.

The resulting article was gripping and skilled, traditional in structure and form. Eszterhas uncovered incredible details: a large pile of dead bodies; "a really tiny little boy" holding the hand of one of the dead; a GI dropping to his knees and killing the boy with a single shot; a black GI, who could not stomach the slaughter any longer, shooting himself in the foot so he could be flown, wounded, out of Mylai.[3]

Not long after the Mylai article, Eszterhas was on the scene of another cataclysmic event: the May 4, 1970, killing of four students by National Guardsmen at Kent State University. In the following weeks, Eszterhas and fellow reporter Michael Roberts interviewed hundreds of students, family members, and National Guardsmen and put together detailed accounts that eventually appeared in the book *13 Seconds*. Again, the subject was explosive, the style traditional, though descriptive. At times, though, the writing was colored by deep political conviction. "It was one thing to assemble all the known facts of what took place at the moment the National Guard lifted and fired their rifles," the final chapter stated, "it was another to attempt to trace the twisting circumstances that stretch deep into the very viscera of the society" (Eszterhas and Roberts 1970, 277).

Interestingly, the language of Eszterhas's straight journalism did bear hints of his literary journalism. There were detailed reporting; long quotations to reveal character and issues; unflinching acceptance of the complexity of human acts and honest attempts to discover and report motives and consequences for all parties; and, just beneath the surface of the reportorial hum, a real feeling of outrage, revulsion, and pain. Though neither the Mylai nor Kent State account contains the experiments and experience of literary journalism, both do betray the influence of social-political context on Eszterhas's work. Conventional journalism, too, is concerned with such context, but Eszterhas's literary journalism placed politics front and center. Social-political context was not simply a part of his literary journalism; it was tied to its very existence.[4]

In the early 1970s, as his work first started appearing regularly in *Rolling Stone*, Eszterhas began concentrating *exclusively* on political subjects.[5] And ultimately, his outrage was given voice in more expressive form.

USING LANGUAGE TO CONFRONT LANGUAGE

The traditional journalistic report is derived from language determinedly apolitical. Terms such as *facts, investigation, objectivity, bias, source,* and others buttress a language that strives for the supposed benefits of a dispassionate scientific approach.[6] Language orders experience—and the writers of literary journalism resist having experience ordered in traditional ways. Their work can be understood as a challenge to the benefit and possibility of objective, unbiased, apolitical reporting. Literary journalists celebrate passion, commitment, engagement. The things they want to talk about and the way they want to talk do not fit into the traditional report.

The second context in which to consider Eszterhas's work, then, is language itself. In his work for *Rolling Stone*, Eszterhas took up the style now called literary journalism and experimented with approaches and techniques usually found in fiction. Knowingly, purposefully, Eszterhas used the language of literary journalism to confront the language of traditional journalism. He broke free from the conventions and restrictions of a report and portrayed his subjects in a manner akin to that of a fairly modern novelist. He employed stream of consciousness, realistic dialogue, myriad points of view, scene by scene construction, first-person narration. He suddenly showed up in his own stories, ornery and obnoxious, causing events to occur. He took pains to point out differences between himself and other reporters.

In doing so, Eszterhas explicitly questioned journalistic claims to authority and objectivity; ignored or violated conventional practice; challenged the idea of a *report*; offered a very different kind of mediation and meditation upon social life. That was the point: to use language to confront language.

One mark of his literary journalism: he created scenes. In "Charlie Simpson's Apocalypse," Eszterhas reconstructed events from interviews and presented those events not with attributed quotations but as dramatic scenes as if he himself had observed them. The centerpiece of the story—the rampage by Simpson—was recreated with precision. For example, in the middle of the massacre, a bystander was killed in front of a laundry.

Charlie Simpson saw Orville Allen across the street, a man in faded khaki pants he had never seen before, and aimed his carbine. The burst caught Allen in the chest.

He dropped to the pavement, twisted on the ground, turned his bleeding chest to the sky, and clasped his hands in prayer. "God," he moaned. A trail of blood trickled across the street toward the sheriff's office. (1974d, 131)

"Death in the Wilderness: The Justice Department's Killer Nark Strike Force" opened with a young man waking from a nightmare about death by an execution squad (not long after, the young man was shot and killed by narcotics agents). The nightmare scene was recreated from the perspective of the man's lover

They were asleep in their cabin, at the edge of a woodline of sequoia and madrone, tucked safely into that vastitude of green darkness. Something woke her. He was staring at the ceiling, eyes large and unblinking. He was trembling. "Tell me," she said. (1973, 28)

Such finely rendered scenes, accomplished through extensive interviewing and observation, provided impact and immediacy. Yet Eszterhas did more than recreate scenes. Like a novelist, he told his story by stringing scene after scene together, often in a chronological, Faulkner-like order, until the reader sees, feels, *experiences* the story and its social significance.

Adding to the power and immediacy of Eszterhas's work was third-person point of view, presenting scenes through the eyes of individual characters. This technique has played an important role in literature but was used little in journalism, which limited itself to the unseen reporter or sometimes the first person. Eszterhas and other literary journalists pushed point of view to the limit. In "Death in the Wilderness," for example, immediately after describing the young woman watch her lover wake from a nightmare, Eszterhas switched to the nightmare itself, leaping inside the head of the doomed man (1973, 28).

Sometimes Eszterhas rode point of view all the way and gave over his articles to long—pages-long—first-person quotations. "The Prisons of War" was a compilation of first-person accounts by a former prisoner of war and his family. In other stories, Eszterhas even invented characters to carry his narrative. Sometimes the person was a minor stock character. The first paragraph of "Clawmen from the Outer Space," a story about a UFO sighting in Alabama, read:

You crazy, countryboy? Comin in heuh like a whinnyin nigguh glugged upon moon-shine cocktails...jabbering this rot about what you seen down by the rivuh in the devil's own pitchblack with them bloodfat blowflies stingin at yo eyes...these *Whatchamacallems* you says you seen. (1974a, 27)

In another piece, the created character was the primary narrator. Introducing "The Nature of Chief Perkins' Fury," Eszterhas wrote:

You might wonder as you read this story, about its narrator. I've spent a lot of time thinking about him too. I forget his name, but he is a man who's lived in McCall for many years. He can tell this story much better than I'd be able to. He knows the big country sky, he's more seasoned than I am. He's very human, realistic and mythical. (1975, 5)

Another important characteristic of Eszterhas's literary journalism was use of the first person. Like some traditional journalists, Eszterhas would appear in the story. Yet he usually used such occasions to confound journalistic canon. For example, at the end of the story on Charlie Simpson, Eszterhas suddenly showed up: "I got into Harrisonville about two weeks after the shooting," the concluding section began. And then Eszterhas told how he deceived the older townspeople to get the story, how he slicked back his long hair with "a bottle of gooey hair-oil," donned a tie and blue blazer, walked around "with a fat Special Corona 77 cigar sticking out" of his mouth, and bought the people beer and malt liquor to get them to talk. "When I was finished talking to the townspeople I drove back to my motel and washed my hair and changed. I put my jeans on and let my hair fall down over my ears and put on my leather jacket and drove back into town (1974d, 158)"[7] Eszterhas went on in the first person to commit another nontraditional act: he confessed his own mixed feelings about the story, the confusion he felt over events, "the grotesqueries leaping about in that blazing bonfire," the aching ambiguity (1974d, 159). In philosophical terms, the story became *reflexive* as Eszterhas exposed the creation of meaning and its influence on him.

Eszterhas again used the first person to confound journalistic canon in "King of the Goons: Deliver Us from Evel." In this scathing portrait, self-proclaimed daredevil Evel Knievel was portrayed as a bullying fraud who beat up a press cameraman and took money in golf bets from the ailing boxer Joe Louis. After having watched Knievel assault the NBC cameraman, Eszterhas attended a press conference the next day with dozens of other reporters—none of whom mentioned the assault. Eszterhas finally asked promoter Bob Arum if Knievel planned to apologize. He wrote: "As the words tumble from my mouth most of my colleagues hush and blink their eyes at me and shake their heads. I am a killjoy. I am a freak. I don't belong here. I am some kind of asshole, you can bet. Just who the hell do I think I am?" (1974c, 57).

His appearance in the story served to make explicit the opposition between him and the traditional reporters.[8] Better than any academic treatise on differences and distinctions, the episode dramatized the rebellion of literary journalism against the tradition and canon of journalism.

CONCLUSION: LANGUAGE AS POLITICAL ACTION

The language of conventional journalism has been a potent force in social life. Its conventions and traditions provide order for reporter, editor, reader, and viewer, influence what events are reported and in what ways, and, in doing so, shape an important part of social experience. Literary journalism challenges the force of that language. It challenges that way of observing, portraying, and understanding the world. At heart, then, literary journalism has been political expression.

The writing of Joe Eszterhas makes the political edge of literary journalism difficult to ignore. Politics were placed in sharp relief by his lightning rod topics, his precise rendering of scenes, his experimentation with point of view, his dramatization of differences with journalism convention and practice. Eszterhas's writing challenged not only journalism's conventions but the society served by those conventions.

Ironically, Eszterhas's abandonment of literary journalism emphasizes further his political stance. Since the late 1970s, he has forsaken journalism and taken up a career as a highly successful writer and producer of movie screenplays. Many of his projects, though certainly mainstream in approach, continue to at least touch upon political issues. *F.I.S.T.* was one of his first efforts, dramatizing the rise and fall of an American union leader. Eszterhas wrote the original story and coauthored the screenplay with Sylvester Stallone in a less than amicable, highly publicized arrangement.[9] Other efforts include the terribly successful *Flashdance*, with its blue-collar concern providing some gritty counterpoint to the soundtrack; *Jagged Edge*, about a murderous, hugely rich publisher; *Big Shots*, in which two boys, black and white, overcome prejudice and fear; *Betrayed*, which considered the rise of white supremacist groups in the heartland; and *Music Box*, which focused on former Nazis living new lives in America.

Rather than a radical departure from his early work, Eszterhas's film career helps drive home the point: literary journalism, for Eszterhas, was a political vehicle, a political act. His use of language challenged journalism's conventions and how those conventions shape and create social tradition.[10] And readers and researchers of literary journalism can find much of its power and meaning through attention to and study of the language through which it understands the world.

NOTES

1. See George Herbert Mead, *Mind, Self, and Society* (Chicago: University of Chicago Press, 1934); also see Kenneth Burke, *Language as Symbolic Action* (Berkeley: University of California Press, 1966).

2. Discussions and extensions of van Gennep's concept can be found in Victor Turner, *The Ritual Process: Structure and Anti-Structure* (Ithaca, N.Y.: Cornell University Press, 1967), and Victor Turner, *Dramas, Fields and Metaphors: Symbolic Action in Human Society* (Ithaca, N.Y.: Cornell University Press, 1974).

3. Joe Eszterhas, "The Massacre at Mylai," *Life* 67 (5 Dec. 1969): 43. Evidence that the report successfully communicated its outrage: two weeks later, *Life* filled two pages with a special section of letters and interviews devoted to the Mylai

article. "Americans Speak Out on the Massacre at Mylai," *Life* 67 (19 Dec. 1969): 46–47.

4. Indeed, one anthology of new journalism organized its contents by political subjects, such as race relations, the Vietnam War, student protest, assassinations, the women's movement, and others. See Nicolaus Mills, ed., *The New Journalism: A Historical Anthology* (New York: McGraw-Hill, 1974).

5. Eszterhas eventually served as associate editor and senior editor for *Rolling Stone*, even sharing space for a time at the infamous National Affairs Desk with Hunter Thompson and Timothy Crouse.

6. It is of interest to note that the conventional language of journalism arose partly out of attempts by the press to shuck its partisan, passionate past. See Michael Schudson, *Discovering the News* (New York: Basic Books, 1978), and Daniel Schiller, *Objectivity and the News* (Philadelphia: University of Pennsylvania Press, 1981).

7. In an introduction, Tom Wolfe made note of Eszterhas's presence in the story. He contrasts Eszterhas to Truman Capote, "who was determined above all to write nonfiction according to the conventions of the twentieth-century novel." By suddenly introducing himself, Wolfe writes, Eszterhas "decides to tell you how he put the story together. Far from being like an epilogue or anticlimax, however, the device leads to a denouement of considerable power." See Wolfe and Johnson 1973, 127.

8. This opposition is a common theme in the work of Hunter Thompson: see especially *Fear and Loathing: On the Campaign Trail '72* (New York: Popular Library, 1973).

9. See Jean Vallely, "Stallone's Latest Fight," *Esquire* 89 (8 May 1978): 79–82. The story begins with two quotations. Joe Eszterhas: "I could go ten or fifteen rounds with him and win. I've been in more barroom brawls and won most of them." Sylvester Stallone: "He just has to name the time and the place. He couldn't last three rounds with me."

10. Current articles about Eszterhas's incredibly successful film career include Eszterhas 1990; Harmetz 1990; "Carolco Pays $4 Million" 1990.

PRIMARY SOURCES

Eszterhas, Joe. 1969, Dec. 5. "The Massacre at Mylai." *Life*.
———. 1973, May 24. "Death in the Wilderness: The Justice Department's Killer Nark Strike Force." *Rolling Stone*.
———. 1974a, Jan. 17. "The Clawmen from the Outer Space." *Rolling Stone*.
———. 1974b, Mar. 28. "The Prisons of War." *Rolling Stone*.
———. 1974c, Nov. 7. "King of the Goons: Deliver Us from Evel." *Rolling Stone*.
———. 1974d. *Charlie Simpson's Apocalypse*. New York: Random House.
———. 1974e. *Nark!* San Francisco: Straight Arrow Books.
———. 1975, May 8. "The Nature of Chief Perkins' Fury." *Rolling Stone*.
———. 1990, July 8. "From a Writer's Standpoint, Rewards Are Worth the Risks." *New York Times*: H11.
Eszterhas, Joe, and Michael D. Roberts. 1970. *13 Seconds: Confrontation at Kent State*. New York: Cornwall Press.

SECONDARY SOURCES

Burke, Kenneth. 1966. *Language as Symbolic Action*. Berkeley: University of California Press.

"Carolco Pays $4 Million for Original Screenplay." 1990, June 26. *Wall Street Journal*: B7.

Harmetz, Aljean. 1990, July 8. "Thrills? Millions? 'Spec' Scripts Bring Big Bids." *New York Times*: H11.

Mead, George Herbert. 1934. *Mind. Self, and Society*. Chicago: University of Chicago Press.

Mills, Nicolaus, Ed. 1974. *The New Journalism: A Historical Anthology*. New York: McGraw-Hill.

Schiller, Daniel. 1981. *Objectivity and the News*. Philadelphia: University of Pennsylvania Press.

Schudson, Michael. 1978. *Discovering the News*. New York: Basic Books.

Vallely, Jean. 1978, May 9. "Stallone's Latest Fight." *Esquire*: 79–82.

Wolfe, Tom. 1973. *The New Journalism*. With an Anthology edited by Tom Wolfe and E. W. Johnson. New York: Harper and Row.

C.D.B. BRYAN

R. Thomas Berner

Late in *Friendly Fire*, its author, C.D.B. Bryan,[1] issues this disclaimer: "I never wanted to be in this book. I had intended to be a journalist: unbiased, dispassionate, receptive to all sides" (1977, 77). Instead, he confesses, he adopted the technique not of the journalist but of the novelist, and it led him to participate and include himself in a piece of writing that he had intended to be "unbiased, dispassionate, receptive to all sides." Whether or not Bryan should feel that he was remiss about this is one of the matters under discussion in this essay.

Friendly Fire is the story of a couple from Iowa whose eldest son is killed in the Vietnam War under conditions that make them suspicious. The story traces their lives, with some flashbacks, from the point their son leaves for Vietnam in September 1969, through April 1972, when Bryan meets with the couple to tell them what his investigation has revealed about the death of their son.

The story is a complex one. The couple, Peg and Gene Mullen, seem far from the "typical" antiwar protesters they become. Their doubt arises when initial questions about the death of their son Michael by "friendly fire"— in this case, artillery fire by U.S. troops—cannot be explained to their satisfaction. They begin a quest to learn the truth, and it is their quest that Bryan sets down.

As one reviewer observes:

He soon found himself recording not the neat political morality play he thought he had discovered but a frantic and unsettling psychodrama. The Mullens' obsession is not a pretty one, and Bryan does little to soften it in this overstuffed, melodramatic account, full of unlikely third-person omniscience. But Peg and Gene Mullen were casualties of the Vietnam War as surely as their son was. (Heller 1976, 93)

Friendly Fire's twenty-five chapters can be divided into three parts. The first two-thirds of the book tells the story of the Mullens' quest for truth. Bryan appears in Chapter 20, which begins the second part. The third part of the book—actually a separate section—is Bryan's reconstruction of the mission on which Michael Mullen died.

What makes this book literary journalism?

Bryan's reconstructive technique, for one thing, although technique is not the only defining characteristic of literary journalism, and reconstruction is typical of many "straight" journalistic accounts as well. In the book's first sentence, in an author's note, Bryan explains his technique:

All material in this book not derived from my own firsthand observation of the events is taken from historical texts, public or official records, original correspondence, journals kept by a participant or extended interviews with those persons directly involved. All interviews with the major participants were tape recorded. Transcripts of these interviews were then submitted to those individuals to provide them an opportunity to make corrections. In those few instances of disparate recollections or failing memory, I have had to rely upon the majority opinion and my own judgment in determining what actually took place. (1977, ix)

Bryan goes on to explain how he confirmed conversations and thus felt comfortable reconstructing dialogue. He relied on third-party corroboration to reconstruct the Mullens' conversations. He also relied on notes by Peg Mullen and the "consistency of details as recalled."

Another mark of literary journalism is the way in which subject matter is approached. In standard journalism, Norman Sims argues, journalists wait near the centers of power for scraps of information, whereas literary journalists, "rather than hanging around the edges of powerful institutions ...attempt to penetrate the cultures that make institutions work" (1984, 3). That is clearly one aspect of *Friendly Fire*. Bryan uses the story of a single family to look at how our government—perhaps more specifically, the Department of Defense—operates.

The author's intention must also count. Recall that Bryan feels that he ultimately adopted the techniques of the novelist rather than the journalist. As noted, Bryan felt the need to render not direct quotations but dialogue and conversations, to show people interacting. In this regard, Bryan acknowledges the influence of his late stepfather, the novelist John O'Hara. "I don't think anybody has put conversations on a page as well as O'Hara. ...O'Hara, I think, helped me know what to say" (Metzger 1984, 83).

Bryan's intention goes beyond using dialogue and conversation. In explaining his approach, Bryan says that he gave away the story immediately (Metzger 1984, 84). By the end of *Friendly Fire*'s first chapter, the reader knows two of the major facts of the story—that Michael Eugene Mullen had been killed in Vietnam and "one year after that, his mother was under surveillance by the FBI" (Bryan 1977, 6). Bryan says that the book was not about Michael Mullen's death but about what happened to his parents and the impact of the war on America.

But nobody would want to read that book, so the way to handle it was to create the sense that it was a mystery. How did Michael die? And it isn't until you're about two-thirds of the way through *Friendly Fire* that you realize this isn't what the book's about at all. But by that time you're hooked. The characters, Peg and Gene, are so strong that you have to find out what happened to them, so you have to keep reading it. (Metzger 1984, 85)

Bryan is talking about pacing and tension. In effect, he uses Chapter 1 to establish the broad outline of the book, then sets about to tell the story. The approach invites comparison with *In Cold Blood* by Truman Capote, in which the murder of the four members of the Clutter family is revealed on the third page, although Capote does not reveal their names at that time. One reads on to learn what the story is about. In both instances, and in many other examples, the storyteller imposes himself or herself on the material.

Bryan's imposition gives the material a theme and, in doing so, Bryan goes beyond the facts of the situation to provide a feel for those facts. This is an essential element in defining a story as literary. By definition, routine journalism provides only facts; and whereas a journalist does impose a theme on any story, that theme is told outright rather than developed.

One of *Friendly Fire*'s major themes is the obsessiveness—especially of Peg Mullen—to learn what really happened to Michael Mullen. In showing the Mullens' increasing doubt about their son's death and their growing impatience with the behavior of various government officials, Bryan tells the story of how Peg and Gene Mullen refused to be reconciled to the ambiguities of Michael's death and how this changes them. A related theme is the change both in Bryan's attitude regarding the circumstances of Michael Mullen's death and in his feelings toward Michael's parents. Just as he shows the evolving change in the Mullens, so, too, does Bryan gradually reveal the change in himself. Christopher Lehmann-Haupt, a reviewer, praises Bryan for not only deftly presenting two opposing points of view chronologically but for doing it in a way that "gradually weans us from one attitude to the other by showing us how the Mullens grew increasingly obsessed with their antiwar mission and how they eventually lost touch with reality" (1976, 39)

What makes the book journalism?

Bryan's disclaimer aside, he did behave as a journalist might by seeking out the many sides of a dispute. "He tended himself to be more tolerant, to see both sides," writes Robert Sherrill (1976, 2). Lehmann-Haupt makes a similar point in commending Bryan for dealing with two points of view "with the utmost sensitivity and precision" (1976, 39).

Bryan's journalistic side shows when he enters the story and attempts to resolve the question of how Michael Mullen died. As he says both in the author's note at the book's beginning and in Chapter 25, where he tells the Mullens what he believes is the truth, Bryan interviewed as many of the participants as possible and even read the transcript of a court-martial for one of them. (The court-martial was unrelated to Michael Mullen's death.)

Bryan interviewed Michael's battalion commander, his company commander, the senior medic, the assistant machine gunner and one of Michael's friends, the court-martialed soldier, the rifleman who lost his leg in the explosion from the same shell that killed Michael. "Each separately confirmed the details of the incident which had brought about Michael's death. Each of them had been on that hill that night; each of them furthered my conviction that Schwarzkopf (the battalion commander) had told the Mullens the truth."

The next sentence captures both the "literary" and the "journalistic": "I felt, therefore, that I had come to the end of the story" (1977, 365). Novelists and journalists tell stories, impose themselves on the material according to their own medium.

The phrase "literary journalism" is paradoxical and oxymoronic on its face. One of the initially jolting aspects of *Friendly Fire* is the appearance of Bryan in the story. He shifts from Bryan-the-author to Bryan-the-investigator as he attempts to learn how Michael Mullen died. The narrative also shifts from the third person, and the voices of Peg and Gene Mullen, to the first person of Bryan, and the mixed voices of Bryan and the Mullens.

But once the initial jolt is over, the reader comes to appreciate what Bryan has done. He has refused—like a good journalist—to let the story rest until he can ferret out his best notion of the truth. Bryan's intrusion into the story effectively ends the literary aspects of *Friendly Fire*.[2] It is almost as if he has used the opening two-thirds of the book as a device to get the reader to the last third. As noted, he admits that he structured the story as a mystery in order to hook the reader.

Some of the reviews of *Friendly Fire* also reflect the paradox. For example while Sherrill sees the journalist in Bryan, he also notes the change that occurred in Bryan in his attitude toward the Mullens. "Suddenly, he became fed up with them" (1976, 2). That is not the behavior of a supposedly disinterested and objective journalist.

Whereas Sherrill is mostly approving of Bryan's overall effort, Diane Johnson is less satisfied. She tells of having read the book in its original three-part appearance in the *New Yorker*. Writing about the point where Bryan enters the story, she says: "It was as if the Sinister Force had come in and finished Bryan's book for him in the night. Qualified, now, was the generous sympathetic tone. A note of condescension had crept into his voice when he came to explain to the Mullens the 'truth' of what he had discovered about Michael's death" (1976, 42).

Johnson also raises questions about Bryan's technique. She feels that readers will find themselves dissatisfied, even though they will accept Bryan's conclusions.

The problem may lie in part in the nature of New Journalistic accounts, in which truth is attested to, verified by third parties, taken from tapes, and so on, but dramatized like fiction. The reader experiences such accounts as both truth and fiction, that is, as adequate accounts of the real world, but also as having certain formal qualities we expect in art. If we complain that somehow coherence, integrity, unity have been violated in the work, the journalist can protest, like the student in a beginning creative writing class, "but that's the way it really happened," and to a certain extent we have indeed contracted to believe him. (1976, 42)

Among the eight reviews examined for this essay,[3] only two reviewers—Sherrill and Johnson—challenge Bryan's conclusion that he had done everything he could to learn the truth. Sherrill expresses dismay that Bryan changed heroes, from the Mullens to Michael Mullen's battalion commander, and Johnson wonders if Bryan pursued every document he could have and points out the self-interest of some of those interviewed. But by Bryan's own account, he had interviewed various people present during the night of Michael's death and had received separate confirmation of the events of that night. Perhaps Bryan could be faulted for not pursuing yet one more document, for not asking to see more Army records, maybe even classified ones. But given that Sherrill and Johnson are both skeptical of Bryan's official sources to begin with, one wonders how another official document would ease their doubts.

At some point, a story—to be a story—must be put down on paper. Bryan reached that point and wrote *Friendly Fire*. It is a story that is both literary and journalistic. It is the story of how a couple comes to terms with the senseless death of their son in Vietnam and how the writer who chose to tell their story comes to terms with the material.

NOTES

1. C.D.B. Bryan's full name is Courtlandt Dixon Barnes Bryan.
2. A colleague of mine, Jeffrey Rush, a film professor at Penn State, suggests another way of looking at this. He offers the insight that Bryan's intrusion is a fictional construct rather than straight reportage. Rush argues that Bryan goes from Bryan-the-narrator to Bryan-the-character-and-Bryan-the-narrator.
3. The remaining three: Walter Clemons, "A Mother's Rage," *Newsweek*, 17 May 1976: 107–8; Marcel Pittet, *Library Journal*, 1 May 1976: 1103; R. Z. Sheppard, "Prairie Protest," *Time*, 19 Apr. 1976: 93.

PRIMARY SOURCE

Bryan, C.D.B. 1976. *Friendly Fire.* New York: G. P. Putnam's Sons. Rpt. 1977. New York: Bantam Books.

SECONDARY SOURCES

Heller, Amanda. 1976. June 1. Review of *Friendly Fire,* by C.D.B. Bryan. *Atlantic* 1: 93.

Johnson, Diane. 1976, Aug. "True Patriots." *New York Review of Books* 5: 42.

Lehmann-Haupt, Christopher. 1976, May 12. "Why We're out of Vietnam." *New York Times*: 39.

Metzger, Linda, ed. 1984. *Contemporary Authors.* New Rev. Series. Vol. 13. Detroit: Gale Research.

Sherrill, Robert. 1976. May 9. Review of *Friendly Fire,* by C.D.B. Bryan. *New York Times Book Review.*

Sims, Norman, ed. 1984.. *The Literary Journalists.* New York: Ballantine Books.

JANE KRAMER

Steve Jones

Jane Kramer's writing for the *New Yorker* and *Village Voice* (collected and augmented in her several books) features her reports from countries around the world. Morocco, Sweden, Uganda—dozens of exotic locations have been the backdrop for her explorations inside the lives and cultures of individuals who seem to be always on the move. Kramer sometimes writes about famous and well-known people such as Kurt Waldheim and Klaus Barbie, whose portrayals figure prominently in *Europeans*, or the simulta-neously pointed and flattering characterization of poet Allen Ginsberg in her first widely reviewed book, *Allen Ginsberg in America*.

But it is Kramer's depictions of ordinary people and their traditions, rituals, and everyday lives that allow her to delve deeply into the psyche of the culture she is examining. The four families she writes about in *Unsettling Europe*, for instance, represent a class of citizens that has fallen through the gaps in Europe's post–World War II restructuring. Modernization, the sweeping economic, political, and ideological reorganization that acceler-ated almost exponentially, and whose effects have been most visible in 1980s Poland, is Kramer's topic. But she approaches it by observing the people modernization has set adrift, people uprooted physically and culturally.

Predrag Ilic, for instance, lives in Sweden, one of 10 million foreign workers living in Western Europe, struggling to make enough money to support his family in Sweden and build a house in his hometown. Ilic is from Yugoslavia, but millions like him come from Greece, Italy, Albania, Hungary, Turkey, and Spain as well. Kramer captures his homesickness by watching his actions and interpreting his moods. Ilic himself speaks very little; there is little dialogue, a smattering of monologue, and overall the narrative closely resembles fiction. On the journalistic level, it is an article about foreign workers in Europe; on the literary plane it is a story about a lonely, displaced man. Instead of dialogue, passages such as the following illustrate his state of mind:

In August of a good year, Predrag comes home with 10,000 kronor. Augusts, he *is* somebody, a gentleman on holiday with his family, a gentleman with a wallet full of cash and a 1967 Peugeot. But in a month the money is gone, and he flees—with barely enough to pay for the food and gas on the long drive north to Sodertalje—before the confidence he has shored up over a month of spending is gone, too....

Winters in Sodertalje, Predrag lives a kind of half-life. He says that in his mind he does not live there at all, that in his mind he is always home. He sits by the kitchen window in his little flat, listening to Serbian music on a secondhand short-wave radio, staring at snapshots in a family album that by now is entirely given over to the villa under construction, nibbling on chunks of Yugoslavian cheese and sausage that he buys, Saturdays, at the Haymarket in downtown Stockholm, drinking the slivovitz he smuggles into Sweden each September in empty beer bottles. (1981, 82–83)

Ultimately, Kramer breaks down the lines between sociology and journalism by engaging in a form of social history that meshes the individual and myth. Ilic and the millions like him scattered about Europe are deeply connected, and Kramer implicitly makes a social representation that implicates her own feeling and judgments, by way of the graphic, select details she reports and by her choice of subject. She reveals much about her intention (and her journalistic sensibilities) in the introduction to *Unsettling Europe*:

I wrote about the particular people in this book because I liked them (or at least most of them), because they moved me, because they had what seems to me more and more to have been a remarkable kind of courage. A professor of the genre that usually refers to itself as "neo-Marxist" pleased me the other day by complaining that my "sociology" of Italian Communism fell away (he meant apart) when the Communists themselves took over the narrative of "The San Vincenzo Cell" and distracted me with their rich and eccentric histories as "people." I do not believe much in sociologies. In a way, the people in this book are my analogue to what my friend would probably call "alienation." And the often ordinary details of their lives, the dramas that absorb them, would be *their* answer, I imagine, to the hypocrites of armchair class analysis....

It is the triumph of these private people over their public "sociology" that interested me. (1981, xvii-xviii)

Honor to the Bride, Kramer's third book (portions of which appeared in the *New Yorker*), marks the expansion of her sociological interests. Written during a stay in Morocco, the story is an Arabian fable about Khadija, the thirteen-year-old daughter (and only valuable, convertible asset) of Omar ben Allel. Khadija, while taking a walk, is kidnapped and taken to a brothel, where she loses her virginity—the very thing that made her valuable to Omar.

Honor to the Bride is an important development in Kramer's writing. It shows her skill as a journal-keeper (and, by extension, as a journalist), and it is very entertaining. What it offers is an extraordinary look into Arab values, via Kramer's extensive use of dialogue and a narrative that propels the reader into an exotic world of mosques, seers, and whitewashed huts:

Monday, June 19th: This morning, Omar told Dawia that he was of many minds on the subject of their daughter. Now that she had been stolen, he said, he could not help thinking that perhaps she should stay stolen forever and spare him a reconciliation which would bring great hshuma [shame] to everyone. Still, yesterday the blind seer claimed to have "seen" Khadija in a white hut near a lemon tree somewhere south of the city, and *he* was insisting that it was Allah's will that Omar go looking for her there. (Like most of the men in Sidi Yussef, Omar often said that the seer, the shuwwaf, had no power—"If he is blind, tell me, how can he see?" Omar would ask whenever Dawia slipped a dirham from the mint money into her pocket and paid the seer a visit—but already, since Khadija's disappearance, he had sent Dawia down the road for a consultation five times.)

Finally, Omar came to the conclusion that he could not abandon Khadija entirely. Dawia had been refusing food as a mark of grief, and Sidi Mohammed had been bawling all morning for his sister, who had always been next to him at night on the family's sleeping carpet. (1970, 32)

Essentially, *Honor to the Bride* reads like a folk tale, or, as Kramer calls it in the book's introduction, a love story. As with all good journalism, it is astounding that Kramer was at the scene of such revealing moments. But it is likely that she is better able than most to understand which moments are revealing and which are not. It is also likely that she is able to understand which people are most revealing of their culture, and it is by way of that understanding that she allows her subjects to interpret society.

Generally, Kramer's writing can be divided into two categories. *Honor to the Bride* is an indication of the intimate style of personality profile that Kramer would bring to fruition in *The Last Cowboy*. *Europeans*, along with many of Kramer's *New Yorker* pieces, is evidence of her interest in political and intellectual trends, though she rarely abandons writing about people. In a revealing interview in *Contemporary Authors*, Kramer said:

I enjoy switching back and forth between two types of pieces, because each allows me to learn about a country and its people in different ways. . . . While I enjoy the challenge of the theoretical pieces, I find it equally important to come back to the personal. In truth, I prefer the profiles. When I write them I am consciously creating; they are about real people, but I structure them as novels. (May 1983, 312–13)

In due time it becomes apparent that Kramer is celebrating the idiosyncratic expressiveness of the people she writes about. That she treats her books as novels is a clue to her contempt for sociology; it does not account for the distinctive resilience she finds among people such as Omar ben Allel and Predrag Ilic.

In these terms Kramer's greatest success is her book *The Last Cowboy*. Having spent several years in Europe, Kramer returned to New York and embarked on a search for America. Her journey mirrored the traditional journalistic adventure that attracted writers from Kerouac to Capote. Kramer decided to go west, to find cowboys, the quintessential American character. Instead she discovered Henry Blanton, the "last cowboy," a man caught between his desire to live in the mythological "old West" and his life as a *modern*, professional cowboy.

Blanton, who had just turned forty when Kramer met him in Texas, manages a 90,000 acre ranch—for someone else. He seems all too aware that he will never manage a ranch of his own. And, it seems, he understands that his life will remain forever mundane, untouched by the cowboy myth he so desperately wishes to live and whose evanescence frustrates him.

Though it is unlikely that prior to researching *The Last Cowboy* Kramer had been any further west than New Jersey, she maintains a familiarity with Texas, a familiarity based on the common American myths and traditions that guide her (despite ill-chosen cowboy boots). Her American heritage serves her well—she knows what questions to ask Blanton. But it is her skill as a journalist that allows her to formulate and ask those questions. And what makes this book her best is precisely that she finds the answers mysterious, and each new question she asks belies the wonder of her discovery—but still her questioning never intrudes. She scans the myth:

It took ... the imagination of Easterners to produce a proper cowboy—a cowboy whom children could idolize, and grown men, chafing at their own domesticated competence, hold as a model of some profoundly masculine truth.... The proper cowboy was a fiction appropriate to a frontier so wild and inhospitable that most Easterners regarded it as a landscape of Manichaean possibilities. He became for those Easterners the frontier's custodian. They made him Rousseau's Emile with a six-gun. They turned man-in-nature into a myth of natural man, and added natural justice to ease the menace of a place that lay beyond their hegemony and their institutions. (1977, 6–7)

Then she probes it:

There was not much room in the cowboy myth for the real cowboys of the nineteenth century—range bums and drifters and failed outlaws, freed slaves and impoverished half-breeds, ruined farmers from the Reconstruction South and the tough, wild boys from all over who were the frontier's dropouts, boys who had no appetite for the ties of land or family, who could make a four-month cattle drive across a thousand miles and not be missed by anyone.... Henry Blanton's grandfather Abel was one of the ruined farmers. (9)

Finally, Kramer observes Henry Blanton's legacy, and weighs myth against Blanton's experience. Chronically underpaid by the ranch owner, Blanton strikes a deal with him for some calves—but is warned by friends that he should sign a contract. His responses illustrate the intersection of myth and reality and are the highlight of Kramer's exploration of American values:

"Seems to me a man's handshake ought to be enough. My Granddaddy Abel never signed no contract. My granddaddy always said a man's word should be his contract, and that's what I do believe, and that's what any cowboy believes, and"—he took a long drink—"that's how I'm going to live." (85)

The connection to the unsettled *Europeans* is obvious: alienation is the link. Kramer's expression of the myth to which Henry Blanton clings is as telling of America's cultural underpinnings as it is of Blanton's situation. But the American imagination which constructed the West is of little help to Blanton. The fact that he shares in that construction only serves to alienate him from the social organization of his surroundings. He knows what it is like to be a cowboy (movies provide the evidence), he knows what he wants cowboys to be like, but he also instinctively knows that it is difficult to mesh myth and reality.

The Last Cowboy is an account of the rituals and social structures of the mythic West as they intersect with the real world—it just so happens that the intersection takes place in the person of Henry Blanton. And that is what makes *The Last Cowboy* so like a novel. The scenes Kramer depicts are as evocative as those in a Louis L'amour book or a John Wayne movie. And Blanton himself draws most of his inspiration from countless viewings of Glenn Ford and Gary Cooper movies:

Henry valued his authority.... He liked to sit on the wagon, waiting, with his scratch pad in his hand and a pencil behind his ear, and he made it a point to be properly dressed for the morning's work in his black boots, a pair of clean black jeans, and his old black hat and jacket. Henry liked wearing black. The Virginian, he had heard, wore black, and so had Gary Cooper in the movie "High Noon," and now Henry wore it with a kind of innocent pride, as if the color carried respect and a hero's stern, elegant qualities. Once, Betsy discovered him at the bathroom mirror dressed in his black gear, his eyes narrowed and his right hand poised over an imaginary holster. (17)

Blanton, though, knows in his heart that he is not Gary Cooper, is not at all like him, and the knowledge erodes his belief in himself and his circumstances; he grew up with the mythical West much the way boys in New York did, by way of the movies:

Henry's Granddaddy Wesley took him to the movies. Every other Sunday...they drove in Wesley's jeep a hundred and five miles to Amarillo and made the rounds of the movie theaters, watching one Western after another, with the old man poking and pointing and guffawing, and sometimes even shouting at the screen. Afterward, at the soda fountain, they went over the day's movies, one by one, discussing what was accurate and appropriate and what was not. . . . Henry and Tom started playing hooky on weekdays and hitching rides to Amarillo alone. They took up brooding like Joel McCrea. They practiced staring into sunsets. They tried on John Wayne's wise, squinty looks and Gary Cooper's virile silences. They lit campfires in the back yard and sat there after supper, alert to all sorts of danger in the darkness past the shed. They rode their horses as if rustlers were after them, or wild Indians. They longed for six-guns. They kept the girls in town giggling as they trotted down Main Street with their empty holsters. tipping big black hats to everyone they saw. (97–98)

A boy in New York may see a John Wayne western and play cowboys and Indians; Blanton, due to his upbringing and his environment, wished to live the cowboy life he saw in the movies. But, like most of the figures Kramer writes about throughout her books and articles, Blanton cannot make his dreams and reality mesh. Blanton's sadness and alienation are felt by the reader as it becomes plain that Blanton's reality is wonderful in and of itself. It is only by comparison to myth that it pales. To quote singer/songwriter Lynn Canfield, "the mundane can be beautiful, too." Kramer's ability to show the beauty and wonder of everyday people, who are nonetheless authentic and substantive, is her real strength.

Her talent at conveying the displacement such people feel in a society that rigidly segments dreams and reality is social commentary of the most powerful order. Kramer's settings, plots, and characters are not only *based* in reality, they *are* real. Perhaps the names have been changed to protect the characters. But where does one draw the line between fiction and nonfiction? Such distinctions can be made easily in a library. Kramer's approach, to write about real people in real situations as candidly as possible, is not much different from a novelist's—or a journalist's. Possibly the main feature that distinguishes *The Last Cowboy* as nonfiction is Kramer's inclusion of facts and details about the cattle industry and ranching. Her writing in these sections is so influenced by the *New Yorker*'s reporting style that one cannot help being aware of the reality of the cattle industry. In chapters that divide Henry Blanton's narrative from Kramer's reporting, she explores the political and economic history of "the new ranching":

There are parts of America where ranching has kept its character. Up in Montana, the ranchers still run herds of their favorite cows, and their cows calve every spring, and their yearlings pasture in the summer on mountains that the state preserves as open range. But the Panhandle is not one of those places. West Texans live on the frontier of money. They believe in luck and high stakes and big killings—in oil splashing up suddenly from a neighbor's pasture, in feedyards that in ten years' time are servicing a million steers. . . . Memory is short in west Texas, and only the cowboys and the rich widows talk much anymore about the good old days of ranching. (76–77)

Such passages provide an alternate narrative that helps explain Blanton's fractured existence. On the one hand he is attracted to the cowboy legend. On the other hand he is relentlessly buffeted by the pecuniary nature of modern ranching. It is Kramer's weaving together of the two narratives that causes *The Last Cowboy* to fall between the cracks of the standard definitions of fiction and nonfiction. Blanton's story, as he tells it and as real as it may be, is rooted in romantic ideals of the old West. But his circumstances are structured by the market forces that define the cattleman's usefulness. It may very well be that Blanton would have been better off watching episodes of "Dallas" instead of westerns.

The end of *The Last Cowboy* brings the narrative strands together and provides a much different view of the West than any fiction might. Instead of saddling up for a shootout with a rancher whose prize bulls have worked over a cow, Blanton settles for getting drunk and castrating the bulls. The myth of the West is not exploded—it still lives in Blanton and his friend Sam, who will pass their ideas on to their children. Ironically, the conversations Kramer records throughout the book seem like a parody of life on the range and undermine the cowboys' intentions. For instance: "I'd say here's four men what don't like working with these chutes." Blanton's friend Sam says. The image of John Wayne (with Walter Brennan teetering behind him) is irrepressibly evoked. The question, then, is not whether their children will learn the skills necessary to be cowboys, but how and from whom they will acquire the mythology (and reality) of the American West. Kramer exposes the *reality* of the West, in scenes that elicit anger, sadness, and pity. A novelist couldn't ask for more.

PRIMARY SOURCES

Kramer, Jane. 1968. *Allen Ginsberg in America*. New York: Random House.
———. 1970. *Honor to the Bride*. New York: Farrar, Straus and Giroux.
———. 1977. *The Last Cowboy*. New York: Harper and Row.
———. 1981. *Unsettling Europe*. New York: Vintage Books.
———. 1988. *Europeans*. New York: Farrar, Straus and Giroux.

SECONDARY SOURCE

May, Hal, ed. 1983. *Contemporary Authors 102*. Detroit: Gale Research.

RICHARD BEN CRAMER

Robert Schmuhl

Richard Ben Cramer first received national recognition as a journalist and writer for his newspaper reporting from the Middle East. As a foreign correspondent for the *Philadelphia Inquirer* during 1978, he covered the strife of life in Israel, Lebanon, and Egypt, and won both the 1979 Pulitzer Prize in international reporting and the 1979 American Society of Newspaper Editors newswriting competition in the deadline category. The announcement statements for these awards focused on Cramer's ability to portray people—how they look, what they say, why they act a certain way—as a distinctive hallmark of his work. This concern for rendering people as they actually are and not as stereotypes or image-oriented personalities pervades Cramer's literary journalism, contributing to its appeal and enduring merit.

Discussing his approach when he began his foreign reporting, Cramer said that he wanted to avoid the conventional methods of presenting news—in his phrase "the casualty figure school of reporting"—so that he could concentrate on the impact political and social affairs had on individuals without titles or elite status. "I must confess I was never a great reader of foreign news," Cramer told an interviewer. "I figured out . . . that I never read it because I never got a sense of the people who were caught in it" (Clark 1980, 36).[1] Keeping people rather than policies or personages at the forefront of his work, Cramer emphasizes the human dimension of decisions and disputes. Instead of providing the institutional viewpoint (facts and statements from elevated public figures), he looks at Middle Eastern life from a common person's eye level. Viewed this way, territorial, ideological, and religious differences and dilemmas assume a concrete, human context. Faces replace abstract forces.

One dispatch, published by the *Inquirer* October 11, 1978, illustrates Cramer's method of presenting news from the perspective of ordinary people involved in the bloody, complex power struggle in Lebanon. The first three paragraphs of the report focus on (1) a little girl, "with freckles on her nose and a startling red rim of blood under the iris of her left eye," searching for her sister; (2) a fifty-five-year-old woman "crying like a schoolgirl" because for a third day she has been unable to get any water; and (3) a family in adjoining beds in a hospital corridor; the mother and two children are seriously injured, while the father has died the day before. These are some of the victims of the over "10,000 rounds from mortars, heavy cannon, rockets and grenade launchers" that Syrian forces used in the assault on the Christian section of East Beirut. A cease-fire is the news peg for the story, and it allows Cramer to get around the city to describe the effects of nine days of fighting.

After the brief, imagistic treatment of the people at the opening and four explanatory paragraphs about the fighting that led to the cease-fire, Cramer takes a reader closer to this urban war zone by tracing the destructive power of a single mortar shell. Through in-depth reporting and writing that is both precise and poignant, he makes one shell's consequences symbolic of what takes place in this civil war.

One shell from a 240-millimeter mortar hit the apartment house at 33 Rue Antoine Khoor, in the Asherafiye section, at 11 A.M. Saturday, just nine hours before the cease-fire took hold.

A 240-millimeter mortar shell is a missile of steel almost five feet long. It weighs 233 pounds. When the shell came in the front of the 10-year-old concrete building, it shattered the front wall of the first floor entryway, where a couple with the family name of Saier were sitting against an interior wall.

The woman, whose age was estimated to be 60, was thrown into a corner and partially buried by a hail of plaster and glass shards. Her neck was broken and she died.

The man, said to be slightly older, suffered a crushed arm and a broken leg. Doctors will check for spinal damage when there is time.

The shell continued through the entryway into a rear basement, where it smashed into the roof of a makeshift concrete-block shelter erected by the family of Abi Saad. George and Joseph Abi Saad, their wives and their children, 14 people in all, had lived in the shelter for a week.

The roof and walls of the shelter caved in on the family when the shell hit. Two dead members of the family were discovered five minutes later, when neighbors burrowed in and found them. Ten others died later. George Abi Saad and Joseph's eldest daughter, Josephine, are still alive in hospitals.

When the shell hit the shelter, it flew apart, scattering bits of steel jagged enough to cut through a man like a knife through soft cheese. Of the 70 to 80 persons in the basement, about 20 were hurt badly enough by shell fragments or debris to require hospitalization. Some, like Nicola Emteini, were lucky enough to escape with something minor: a cement chunk that flew into his face, scraping it raw and breaking his nose but sparing his eyes and skull. Luckier still, Emteini, 13, blacked out when the shell came through.

"I just saw the shelter explode in my eyes. I don't know, I'm trying to remember," he said.

"I hope he never remembers," said a neighbor who was there. (Clark 1980, 27–29)

In this passage and elsewhere in his work, Cramer relies on telling facts to help a reader see and understand a situation. There is restraint, similar to Hemingway's, in the presentation—"Her neck was broken and she died." However, the factual details and how they are rendered create a compelling human account of innocent people who are victims of war. The quotation at the end, "I hope he never remembers," underlines the anguish caused by the solitary shell. Cramer concludes his dispatch by making a tour of East Beirut hospitals, which received not only hundreds of casualties but heavy shelling before the cease-fire. The last paragraph ends with a young woman telling her seriously injured boyfriend, "Tony, it's not over, Tony, Tony, it's not over, do you hear?" (Clark 1980, 33). A reader not only hears but comes to realize that the civil strife will continue, with the human toll mounting. A specific person concludes this story, just as one began it. Through them and the article's other elements, we become witnesses to the vicious spiral of violence in Lebanon and look beyond statistics of those injured and dead at individuals intimately affected by the fighting.

Seeking to portray representative people who illuminate larger problems or issues is a fundamental characteristic of the work Cramer did for the *Philadelphia Inquirer* between 1976 and 1984, when he became a freelance writer.[2] For most of the stories he wrote for the *Inquirer*, Cramer assumes the role of detached observer. He refers to himself in some articles as a "visitor," a "wanderer," an "outsider," or a "strange young man." But even in these instances he strategically remains in the background. The people he chooses to write about are his principal concern. He deviates from the third-person point of view rarely; however, when he does, the effect is dramatic and, in most cases, indicative of the lengths to which he will go in covering a story.

The most striking example of Cramer's being a participant in the experience he is describing occurs in his reports for the *Inquirer* during 1980 about the fighting between Russian troops and Afghan guerrilla fighters. In these accounts Cramer explains the dangers and hardships facing the people of Afghanistan. To illustrate how arduous the life of the Afghan rebel is, he discusses some of his reactions to traveling with the fervently religious and nationalistic mujaheddin. In one particularly effective scene as part of a lengthy profile of "one family's own holy war" with the Russians, Cramer relates how he and some guerrillas reach the house of a rebel leader, Azim Khan, in Konar Province of Afghanistan. The language is concrete and compelling. The staccato style conforms to the quick movements of a dangerous situation. The description is immediate as well as intensely personal;

however, the reader knows that what is happening occurs for some people every day.

The Konar River, gray and swift, is difficult in the best of times. Now, it is a menace.

Russians watch the river. They blast anything that tries to move. The raft is the lifeline between Pakistan and the Afghan villages on the west bank.

The raftmen are pumping, sweat flying off them. They push and pull at small goatskins—leather pumps to inflate the buffalo hides that help float the raft.

Two MiGs fly up the gorge. Low, gray darts, they grow in seconds to steel monsters and their roar shakes the rocks.

Everyone jumps. Helicopters will follow, they know. That is always the way.

The raft rocks and wallows. The skins are still too soft. The rowers jump back on. They pull for their lives. The veins stand out in their necks. Ten passengers, a babble of prayer. Everyone watches the sky.

We touch the bank on the other side. We run; the raftmen hide. A minute, two minutes—we have scaled the gorge—we race in a sweaty panic through open terrace land.

The moan of the helicopters grows to a crazy organ chord. No cover, nowhere to run. We lie in balls, swaddled in blankets. We pray the blankets look like rocks.

The helicopters hover. It seems like hours, must be minutes. Through an opening in the blanket, I see only a sliver of blue. The helicopters do not pass. Their noise seems to pound like the blood inside me. I am afraid to move.

I wonder, how many days before the raftmen misjudge and the rockets catch them in the river? One hit, the end of the lifeline, the end of everybody aboard. How many days? Maybe a morning like this?

Up and running. The helicopters are gone. We see them as specks, north toward Chigal. We hear them smash the hills with rockets. Run, they will return soon.

Sweat stings the eyes, the dry earth cracks, dry throat rasps. No water, no cover, no shade, no rest. Then, a stream bed below. A mile ahead, dark delicious green.

Shade and a whoosh of water falling. We scramble up the rocks. Collapse on a patch of smooth, cool mud. Adrenaline ebbs; my hands are shaking.

But, oh, what water! A white foaming cascade free-falls 10 feet from beneath a bush of pink wild rose.

The helicopters moan by. But we are covered. We laugh crazily. A little boy peers through the rose bush. He smiles and runs for his father.

The father comes at a trot. He carries bread, fresh cheese, cool yogurt in a bowl. He says, "I believe in God. Whatever I have to eat, my Muslim brothers will have it too." He wants us to lie down in his house. We have met Azim Khan. (Cramer 1980, 9)

By using the present tense and by relying on phrases instead of sentences, Cramer conveys both immediacy and urgency. Through his words and style, he involves the reader in the perilous experience. He and the others reach safety, yet they seem more vulnerable than heroic.

From 1978 until leaving the *Inquirer* in 1984, Cramer was primarily a foreign correspondent, filing dispatches not only from the Middle East but Europe and Africa as well. In 1979, however, he returned to Philadelphia to do a profile of one family's effort "to stay one step ahead of hard times." He spent a month living with a West Philadelphia family of seven, and the result was a novella-length account, "Portrait of a Family," which took up almost an entire issue of the *Inquirer*'s Sunday magazine on October 21, 1979. In this extraordinary piece of journalism, Cramer explores the lives of people existing on "the edge of the American economic system." The portrait is starkly realistic. The members of the Monroe family are symbolic of individuals confronting the "routine of poverty"; however, they are rendered in such dimension that they are not stereotypes of the urban poor. Russell and Connie Monroe sincerely want to improve the lot of their family. But their opportunities for employment are limited, and they realize that if they work they will sacrifice a substantial portion of the governmental aid they depend on to get by.

Through deft use of quotations and effective arrangement of telling scenes and details, Cramer shows how the Monroes are squeezed from every direction. Outbursts of genuine anger punctuate their existence. Their only real source of amusement or relief is a rented color television that plays throughout the day and night. Despite their situation, the Monroes scrimp along. Near the end of the article, Connie says: We're living. I feel good about today, And if the Lord wakes me up tomorrow, I'll feel good" (Cramer 1979, 46). Cramer renders the portrait of this family with such faithfulness and depth that a reader feels compassion.

Explaining why he left daily journalism, Cramer remarked that he wanted "to write things you can't write in newspapers" (Eisenberg 1984, 7). The twelve-year apprenticeship—besides his years at the *Inquirer*, he had been a reporter for the *Baltimore Sun* from 1972 to 1976—had been valuable in learning reporting methods and in working out some of his techniques as a literary journalist. Cramer, however, sought the latitude that comes from writing for such magazines as *Rolling Stone* and *Esquire*. Being a freelance writer meant that he no longer had to worry as much about standard journalistic conventions. He could consistently probe subjects at length (as he had in "Portrait of a Family"), and he could be freer in integrating his judgments into articles. Moreover, his audience changed dramatically: from the general circulation of a metropolitan newspaper to the younger, trendier national readership of *Rolling Stone* and *Esquire*.

Cramer's first two magazine articles, "The Strange and Mysterious Death of Mrs. Jerry Lee Lewis" for *Rolling Stone* and "Can the Best Mayor Win?" for *Esquire*, are examples of in-depth reporting and engaging writing. Both explore their subjects from different facets, but the writer's viewpoint presides, as he shapes and dramatizes the material. This authorial voice, however, is secondary to the wealth of facts and quotations he presents. Cramer's first article for *Esquire* prompted the magazine to do a full-page biographical sketch about him. In it he recalls his days on the *Baltimore Sun* and the importance of thorough reporting: "A reporter got points for *details*. Details made a story worth writing. Accuracy was important, but in detail there's *truth*" (Eisenberg 1984, 7; emphasis in original).

"The Strange and Mysterious Death of Mrs. Jerry Lee Lewis," which ran in *Rolling Stone* on March 1, 1984, is an 18,000-word chronicle of the details and questions surrounding the suspicious passing away of twenty-five-year-old Shawn Michelle Lewis in August of 1983. The first sentence of the article establishes Cramer's viewpoint and approach: "The Killer was in his bedroom, behind the door of iron bars, as Sonny Daniels, the first ambulance man, moved down the long hall to the guest bedroom to check the report: 'Unconscious party at the Jerry Lee Lewis residence' " (Cramer 1984a, 22). Lewis's nickname is, in fact, "The Killer," but Cramer's methodical reconstruction and investigation of what happened add a literal quality to repeated usage of the sobriquet. At one point Shawn's sister, Shelley, tells of an encounter she had with Lewis the day after she became his sister-in-law: " 'You scared of me? You should be. Why do you think they call me the Killer? How'd I get that name, huh?' Then he slapped my face" (33).

Cramer establishes a pattern of behavior for Lewis. Unanswered questions also surround the death of his fourth wife shortly before the divorce settlement. Throughout the article, the DeSoto County, Tennessee, authorities seem more interested in protecting their resident celebrity than in investigating potentially criminal matters. (J. W. Whitten, Lewis's manager, was the largest contributor to Sheriff James Riley's campaign. The autopsy of Shawn Lewis was conducted by a doctor paid by Lewis rather than the county.) Cramer ends with a quotation from Whitten: "They'll never bust him [Lewis] in DeSoto County. That's like bustin' Elvis in Memphis. Never. Never. And you can quote me on that" (56). Whitten's statement drives home Cramer's doubts that "no foul play" was involved in the death. The volume of incriminating evidence Cramer stunningly presents is too great to think otherwise.

"The Strange and Mysterious Death of Mrs. Jerry Lee Lewis" is the first of several magazine articles by Cramer about well-known people. Other pieces focus on William Donald Schaefer, then-mayor of Baltimore; baseball Hall-of-Famer Ted Williams; and Peter Ueberroth, the Commissioner of Major League Baseball at the time. Personal prominence, however, does not lead to the conventional personality profile so common in today's print journalism. Using techniques he developed as a newspaper reporter, Cramer takes a reader closer to the figure he is writing about by specifically explaining what the person says and does. The ordinary people portrayed in his foreign dispatches were never stereotypes. The well-known people of the magazine articles are never the self-created images these people try to maintain. Cramer's literary journalism probes beyond the superficial impressions to capture the public figures with greater human dimension—quirks, warts, and all.

"What Do You Think of Ted Williams Now?," which appeared in *Esquire* in June 1986, is an example of Cramer's abiding attention to detail and his increasing willingness to be more personal in rendering a subject. The involvement of the narrator and the offering of opinions are so pronounced that the article is included in *The Best American Essays 1987*. There is a first-person presence from the start, as he dramatizes a revealing anecdote about Williams. The aptly chosen story highlights his subject's remarkable athletic abilities and his monumental self-regard.

Few men try for best ever, and Ted Williams is one of those. There's a story about him I think of now. This is not about baseball but fishing. He meant to be the best there, too. One day he says to a Boston writer: "Ain't no one in heaven or earth ever knew more about fishing."
    "Sure there is," says the scribe.
    "Oh, yeah? Who?"
    "Well, God made the fish."
    "Yeah, awright," Ted says. "But you had to go pretty far back." (Cramer 1986, 74)

Cramer shifts back and forth between extensive biographical sections about Williams's past (on and off the baseball field) and a detailed look at the former star in retirement. There is admiration for the accomplishment; however, Cramer attempts to provide more perspective (more truth, if you will) to his portrait. Williams lives life on *his* terms—avoiding people and phones and wanting tattered underwear ironed "just so." Cramer is able to enter "The Kid's" world for a couple of days. How he shapes and presents what he sees and hears is critical to the literary success of the article.

Cramer describes the difficulty of getting access to Williams in his home in the Florida Keys and the even more difficult job of getting beyond the carefully constructed personal facade his subject projects. Cramer integrates exchanges from their conversations to show Williams's preoccupation with privacy. En route to a hospital to check on tests that were done on Lou, the woman with whom he lives, we hear:

"How long have you and Lou been together?"
    "Oh, I've known Lou for thirty-five years. You shouldn't put any of that shit in there. Say I have a wonderful friend, that's all."
    "Yeah, but it makes a difference in how a man lives, Ted, whether he's got a woman or not—"
    "Boy, that Sylvester Stallone, he's really made something out of that Rocky, hasn't he?..."
    "So Ted, let me ask you what—"
    "LOOK, I don't wanta go through my personal life with YOU, for Christ's sake. I won't talk to you about Lou, I won't talk to you about any of it. You came down here and you're talkin' about me, as I'm supposed to be different and all that..."
    "Do you think you're different?"

"NO, not a damn bit. I'm in a little bit different POSITION. I mean, I've had things happen to me that have, uh, made it possible for me to be different. DAMN DIFFERENT in some ways. Everybody's not a big league ballplayer, everybody doesn't have, uh, coupla hitches in the service, everybody hasn't had, uh, as much notoriety about 'em as I had ALL MY LIFE, so..." (Cramer 1986, 83)

Cramer uses capital letters throughout the quotations to indicate the volume of Williams's voice. Although a loner with only a few friends, when Ted Williams has something to say he does so with force and profane gusto. The end of the article is a compelling conclusion, highlighting the human complexity of Williams. Cramer reports that Williams might buy a car for his college-bound son and establish rules for its use. Thinking about the son, who doesn't live with him, triggers his memory about his daughter and what she did years ago:

Something has turned in his gut, and his face is working, growing harder. There's a mean glitter in his eye, and he's thinking of his elder daughter, walking away from him.
"SLAM OUT. LIKE MY DAUGHTER USED TO..."
His teeth are clenched and the words are spat. It's like he's turned inward to face something we cannot see. It is a fearsome sight, this big man, forward, stiff in his chair, hurling ugly words at his vision of pain. I feel I should leave the room but too late.
"...THAT BURNED ME..."
The switch is on. Lou calls it the Devil in him.
"...A PAIN IN MY HAIRY RECTUM!"
"Nice," says Lou. She is fighting for him. She has not flinched.
"Well, DID," he says through clenched teeth, "AND MAKES YOU HATE BROADS!..."
"Ted. Stop." But Ted is gone.
"...HATE GOD!..."
"TED!"
"...HATE LIFE!"
"TED!...JUST...STOP!"
"DON'T YOU TELL ME TO STOP. DON'T YOU EVER TELL ME TO STOP."
Lou's mouth twists up slightly, and she snorts: "HAH!"
And that does it. They've beaten it, or Lou has, or it's just gone away. Ted sinks back in his chair. His jaw is unclenched. He grins shyly. "You know, I love this girl like I never..."
Lou sits back, too, and laughs.
"SHE'S IN TRAINING," Ted says, "I'M TEACHIN' HER..."
"He sure is," Lou says, like it's banter, but her voice is limp. She heads back to the kitchen, and Ted follows her with his eyes.
Then he finds me on the couch, and he tries to sneer through his grin: "WHEN ARE YOU LEAVING? HUH?
"...JESUS, YOU'RE LIKE THE GODDAMN RUSSIAN SECRET POLICE!"
"...OKAY, BYE! YEAH, SURE, GOODBYE!"

Ted walks me out to the driveway. As I start the car, Lou's face is a smile in the window, and Ted is bent at his belly, grabbing their new dalmatian puppy, tickling it with his big hands while the dog rolls and paws the air. And as I ease the car into gear, I hear Ted's voice behind, cooing, very quiet now: "Do I love this little dog, huh?... Yes, this little shittin' dog. Yes, yes I love you... Yes, I do." (1986, 92)

The outburst, so faithfully rendered, reveals a father's fiery rage. The cool kid has strong personal feelings about both the past and the present. Cramer captures the interplay of competing emotions, ending with a human touch. Authorial authority comes from close transcription and description. Ted Williams *is* different, but he is considerably more than a standoffish, self-absorbed sports hero now in retirement. Cramer's reporting and writing show his subject as he is, with the mask of image down.

Two contributions to *Esquire* in 1987 represent further movement by Cramer away from a third-person point of view. In "Citizen Ueberroth" and "Fore Play: A Celebration of Golf the Glorious," the writer is center stage from the first sentence. "Fore Play," in fact, begins with heavy emphasis on the first person: "I play golf, I recommend golf, I celebrate golf—for the exercise. For this I am roundly derided by friends. God knows what my enemies say" (Cramer 1987b, 99). The essay continues in this self-absorbed vein. "Citizen Ueberroth" is different from either a profile or an essay. It is primarily the rendering of the questions and answers from several interviews between Cramer and then-Baseball Commissioner Peter Ueberroth. Cramer, however, introduces each section with boldface headnotes, reporting his observations and opinions. These passages are snidely critical, the writer's attempt to portray the power and control Ueberroth seems to demand, whatever the situation. The opening paragraph establishes Cramer's tone:

Before we go nose to nose, as he says, I want to tell a story behind the commissioner's back. This might seem cowardly. But after five interviews with Mr. Ueberroth, I am in possession of these facts: when he turns his face to the matter at hand and fixes it with the crooked grin and eyes that crinkle but do not smile, we are going to talk about what he wants to talk about, in a way he wants it talked about. And we'll talk in a place he has chosen for our talk. Over a span of three weeks last fall, I talked to Peter Ueberroth in seven states spread over half the continent, but always in one of his places—in New York, a pricey hotel coffee shop; in Boston and Houston, presidential suites a la Sheraton and Hyatt; twenty thousand feet above Louisiana, in the white-leather cocoon of a *USA Today* jet. After a while, they all seemed to be one place—clean, neutral, and well padded, somewhere in the middle of corporate America. All the interview tapes hum with the background noise of climate control. But to make any study of the man himself (a topic that has no place on his agendas), it's best to catch the commissioner off his turf, from behind. (1987a, 69)

Each boldface digression has a smug, at times hostile, quality. Cramer even halts the conversation at one place to say: "I think I can save a lot of time here by summarizing the rest of this dance" (1987a, 76). Ueberroth is quoted at length, but his statements seem secondary to the more sharply worded introductory passages. As with his earlier work, Cramer wants to get to the heart of a subject—in this case beyond the persona of a very public (and self-conscious) figure. In the execution, however, genuine questions of fairness arise. Does Cramer's frustration at being kept at a deliberate distance lead to unduly harsh judgments? Is he shaping the material to conform to his personal bias? The gifted reporter and prose stylist seems shrilly subjective and out of character.

Despite the variety of Cramer's literary journalism, his abiding concern is the portrayal of people—whether unknown or well-known—in their human complexity. His apprenticeship of writing for newspapers established techniques and approaches he subsequently developed as a freelance magazine writer. The next step in the evolution of his literary career is a book about seven political figures who sought the presidency in 1988. Cramer began his reporting in 1986, and he is focusing on the seven

as lives, not as candidacies.... The two questions I'm trying to answer about them are these: Number one, what kind of person can be president? How does this guy develop the will, the focus, the energy, the discipline and the faith in himself to say, "Yes, I ought to be president"? And number two... what happens to him? Not in the sense of how does he win and how does he lose, but in the sense of what the process does to him. (Williams 1988, 36)

This book, to be published by Random House in 1991, offers Cramer the challenge of capturing in words the human lives of people for whom the media-transmitted image is a central preoccupation. He is devoting four years to the project. Whether he succeeds in rendering these public figures as genuine people will be critical to his development and standing as a literary journalist.

NOTES

1. See "Interview with Roy Clark and Richard Ben Cramer," in *Best Newspaper Writing*, ed. Roy Peter Clark, 36. In addition to the interview, this volume contains five of Cramer's articles.

2. During Cramer's years as a foreign correspondent, the *Philadelphia Inquirer* collected his dispatches into several special supplements that were distributed to journalists and educators across the country. Supplements included "Report from the Mideast: A Human Drama" (1978), "Inside the Afghan Rebellion" (1980), and "Feeding on the Hungry" (1981).

PRIMARY SOURCES

Cramer, Richard Ben. 1978. "Report from the Mideast: A Human Drama." *Philadelphia Inquirer* special supplement.

———. 1979, Oct. 21. "Portrait of a Family." *Philadelphia Inquirer Sunday Magazine.*

———. 1980. "Inside the Afghan Rebellion." *Philadelphia Inquirer* special supplement.

———. 1981. "Feeding on the Hungry." *Philadelphia Inquirer* special supplement.

———. 1984a, Mar. 1. "The Strange and Mysterious Death of Mrs. Jerry Lee Lewis." *Rolling Stone*: 22–56.

———. 1984b, Oct. "Can the Best Mayor Win?" *Esquire*: 57–72.

———. 1985a, Feb. 14. "Olympic Cheating." *Rolling Stone*: 25–30.

———. 1985b, Oct. "The Ballad of Johnny France." *Esquire* 110–20.

———. 1985c, Oct. 24. "The Valley of Death." *Rolling Stone*: 29–86.

———. 1985d, Nov. 21. "Beyond Mengele." *Rolling Stone*: 67–120.

———. 1986, June. "What Do You Think of Ted Williams Now?" *Esquire*: 74–92.

———. 1987a, Feb. "Citizen Ueberroth." *Esquire*: 69–81.

———. 1987b, June. "Fore Play: A Celebration of Golf the Glorious." *Esquire*: 99–101.

SECONDARY SOURCES

Berner, R. Thomas. 1988. *Writing Literary Features.* Hillsdale, N.J.: Lawrence Erlbaum Associates.

Clark, Roy Peter, ed. 1980. *Best Newspaper Writing.* St. Petersburg, Fla.: Modern Media Institute.

Eisenberg, Lee. 1984, Oct. "Backstage with *Esquire*: Our Man in Baltimore." *Esquire.*

Fry, Donald K. 1982, Fall. "The Presence of Richard Ben Cramer." *Style* 16: 437–43.

Schmuhl, Robert. 1982. Fall. "Richard Ben Cramer and 'People Journalism.' " *Style* 16: 444–47.

Talese, Gay, ed. 1987. *The Best American Essays 1987.* New York:: Ticknor and Fields.

Williams, Marjorie. 1988, Aug. 15. "The Publishing of the President, 1988." *Washington Post National Weekly ... Edition.*

JOHN MCPHEE

Sharon Bass

John McPhee's name inevitably comes up in any discussion of literary journalism. He gets mentioned, but the focus quickly shifts to the newspaper-men-novelists, a rather larger, more cacophonous group. McPhee makes a cameo appearance, and then he's gone. Although McPhee has published more books and articles than most of the literary journalists, writers and critics cannot seem to agree on how to classify him. To some he is not a journalist because he is not a newsman, and to others, he is not enough of a novelist to be literary.

One reason McPhee is so hard to classify when the discussion turns to literary journalism may be that he simply does not fall along the newspaperman-novelist continuum.[1] Although he was not a newsman, he is a great reporter; few people so thoroughly immerse themselves in their subject. He has been writing up his reports all his life, from high school on, and he has learned some lessons along the way. To make a report fascinating, the writer has to tell a story and have a good character or two to throw in. As does any good storyteller, McPhee leaves his reader with memorable characters: Bill Bradley, the basketball player; Arthur Ashe, the black tennis player; Donald Gibbie, the crofter; Floyd Dominy, the builder of mammoth dams; Ted Taylor, the nuclear scientist; and Dave Brower, the archdruid of conservationists, to mention only a few. But McPhee's place in literature has been developed on a road less traveled. McPhee has spent a lifetime in a corner of literature left for dead, the personal essay, but with a twist. The twist is that these essays are heavily reported and extensively researched, and rely on the personal in only the most unobtrusive manner imaginable. McPhee's literary device as a new journalist was his own vibrant redefinition of the essay.

Robert Atwan in his introduction to *The Best American Essays 1987* says that the essay as literature was "permanently flattened by the one-two punch of news journalism and New Journalism" (ix-xii). More precisely, what was flattened or what died was the old-fashioned essay. McPhee has specialized in what Atwan describes as the new personal essay: tougher minded, more candid, less polite, and taking greater emotional risks. The hallmarks of McPhee's works are thorough reporting, a clear sense of voice, and the ability to create memorable characters despite the limitations of nonfiction writing, all accomplished with a highly developed but nonintrusive sense of craftsmanship and design in the writing.

These characteristics clearly place McPhee beyond the realm of the traditional essayist and squarely at the center of the emerging literary journalistic tradition.

In almost everyone's book, McPhee is an artful, creative, and comprehensive reporter. Ronald Weber sees McPhee as a journalist working at a higher level of the game, although he does not consider him a literary journalist as he defines it. In *The Literature of Fact*, Weber acknowledges a certain amount of fussiness in making such distinctions. He goes on, however, to discuss McPhee's *Coming into the Country* as one work that stands apart from his earlier work.[2] It is, Weber says, a "distinguished work of literary nonfiction which nonetheless retains the broad form of the journalistic report" (1980, 116).

What makes McPhee's work so rich is that it is so informed. It is clear that this writer has done the research and done it with a passion. He works to understand the subject—whether it is the chain of events in a nuclear reactor or the physical history of the American West. McPhee has said that he tries to go into his subject as a blank page. It has never seemed to bother him that his subjects might think him slow or ignorant (Howarth 1976).

His research has taken him all over: the Northern Cascades, the American Southwest, Maine, his home state of New Jersey, Florida, Scotland, and Switzerland. No matter the place, after he has heard the same answer at least three times, he knows that the research and reporting are done. He heads home to type up his notes and get on with what he calls the hard work of this business: the writing itself.

The thoroughness pays dividends. Every passage delivers something of interest, something new. In this passage from *Encounters with the Archdruid*, the reader learns the exact meridian that separates the drylands from the wetlands, the date of the Homestead Act, the size of a land grant, and the consequences of uninformed planning:

East of the hundredth meridian, there is enough rain to support agriculture, and west of it there generally is not. The Homestead Act of 1862, in all its promise, did not take into account this ineluctable fact. East of the hundredth meridian, homesteaders on the hundred and sixty acres of land were usually able to fulfill the dream that had been legislated for them. To the west, the odds against them were high. With local exceptions, there just was not enough water. The whole region between the hundredth meridian and the Rocky Mountains was at that time known as the Great American Desert. Still beyond the imagination were the ultramontane basins where almost no rain fell at all. (1971, 154)

His research fills notebooks with typewritten notes. And then there are the maps. McPhee has never met a map he didn't like. He describes one map in *Encounters with the Archdruid*. In this book, McPhee positions his protagonist, Dave Brower, the militant conservationist and archdruid, in various settings with three antagonists, Charles Park, a mineral engineer and miner; Charles Fraser, a resort developer; and Floyd Dominy, a builder of great dams and Commissioner of the Bureau of Reclamation. In one encounter Dominy and Brower rafted down the Colorado River. They had a map.

We have a map that is seven inches high and fifty feet long. It is rolled in a scroll and is a meticulously hand-done contemporary and historical portrait of the Colorado River in the Grand Canyon. River miles are measured from the point, just south of the Utah line, where the Paria River flows into the Colorado—the place geologists regard as the beginning of the Grand Canyon. As the map rolls by, it records who died where. "Peter Hansbrough, one of the two men drowned, Mile 24, Tanner Wash Rapids, 1889 . . . Bert Loper upset, not seen again, Mile 24, 1949 . . . Scout found and buried in talus, Mile 43, 1951 . . . Roemer drowned in Mile 89, 1948." (1971, 179)

His voice within the work is the soft voice of the BBC commentator at Wimbledon, or on the eighteenth green when the leader faces a difficult chip onto the green. Just so, McPhee's voice provides the insights and background on the key players, probing the nature and history of the game or the field itself. The relentless massing of detail, delivered in an engaging manner, without any mannered intrusion of the writer or writer-ego, leaves the reader satisfied and secure: this is information one can trust. The reader has spent this little time in expert company, taken along to witness vicariously great events, critical games, or serious debates.

McPhee usually relies on a deceptively simple language and vocabulary, even in the most technical of subjects. He makes Ted Taylor so compelling a character that the problem of controlling nuclear materials becomes quite clear in *The Curve of Binding Energy*, even to the nonscientist:

Because the fissioning plutonium puts out many extra neutrons and because there is a high proportion of fertile U–238 in the reactor core, the breeder makes more plutonium than it uses up. Theoretically, the breeder can make more than fifty times better use of uranium than present-day reactors. Moreover, it could use as fertile material the two hundred thousand tons or so of leftover U–238 that has been separated from U–235 since the military weapons program began. (1974, 47–48)

On the other hand, McPhee makes simple subjects, like oranges, more interesting, less taken for granted. "Most citrus trees consist of two parts. The upper framework, called the scion, is one kind of citrus, and the roots and trunk, called the rootstock, are another" (1967, 22).

He gives the reader their history and provenance. Plain building blocks, common words have been his stock in trade. He introduces the reader to the jargon of the trade, but carefully lays the groundwork so that the reader understands—more than understands, feels brought into—the brotherhood of science or agriculture or military strategy. Only in his recent works on geology does he seem to deviate from the plainness of speaking. In the geological books, he seems to have settled into the very mystery and magic of the dense material of geologic vocabulary.

But McPhee does not simply translate the language of experts. He also gathers the kind of observed detail that yields rich, evocative scenes that establish a sense of place and immediacy. For example, here is the opening to "Giving Good Weight":

You people come into the market—the Greenmarket, in the open air under the downpouring sun—and you slit the tomatoes with your fingernails. With your thumbs, you excavate the cheese. You choose your stringbeans one at a time. You pulp the nectarines and rape the sweet corn. You are something wonderful, you are—people of the city—and we, who are almost without exception strangers here, are as absorbed with you as you seem to be with the numbers on our hanging scales.

"Does every sink grow on your farm?"

"Yes, Ma'am."

"It's marvellous. Absolutely every sink?"

"Some things we get from neighbors up the road."

"You don't have no avocados, do you?"

"Avocados don't grow in New York State."

"Butter beans?"

They're a Southern crop."

"Who baked this bread?"

"My mother. A dollar twenty-five for the cinnamon. Ninety-five cents for the rye."

"I can't eat rye bread anymore. I like it very much, but it gives me a headache."

Short, born abroad, and with dark hair and quick eyes, the woman who likes rye bread comes regularly to the Brooklyn Greenmarket, at Flatbush and Atlantic. I have seen her as well at the Fifty-ninth Street Greenmarket, in Manhattan. There is abundant evidence that she likes to eat. She must have endured some spectacular hangovers from all that rye. (1979, 3–4)

That concrete, specific beginning thus establishes a point of view, that of a seller behind the counter at a farmer's market in New York City, and begins an article that on one level is a highly informative and factual insider's view of running such a market. But in McPhee's hands, the piece also becomes a story of contrasts and subcultures, as city and country meet and cautiously define and try to understand one another.

When necessary, McPhee's prose and detail become as lush and sensual as the moment requires. Here, for instance, is his description of what he felt after working hard loading crates of onions in "Giving Good Weight":

After thirty minutes of filling boxes, my arms feel as if they have gone eighteen innings each. I scarcely notice, though, under the dictates of the action, the complete concentration on the shifting of the crates, the hypnotic effect—veiling everything else in this black-surfaced hill-bordered surreally level world—of the cascade of golden onions. Onions. Onions. Multilayered, multilevelled, ovate, imbricated, white-fleshed, orange-scaled onions. Native to Asia. Aromatic when bruised. When my turn is over and a break comes for me, I am so crazed with lust for these bulbous herbs—these enlarged, compressed buds—that I run to an unharvested row and pull from the earth a one-pound onion, rip off the membranous bulb coat, bare the flesh, and sink my teeth through leaf after leaf after savory mouth-needling sweet-sharp water-bearing leaf to the flowering stalk that is the center and the secret of the onion. Yash at the end of the day will give me three hundred pounds of onions to take home, and well past the fall they will stand in their sacks in a corner of the kitchen—the pluperfect preservers of sweet, fresh moisture—holding in winter the rains of summer. (1979, 61)

With so much material and with the rich characters and full, detailed descriptions that populate his works, the great strength McPhee brings to his material is an ability to find the perfect structure for the telling of the story.[3] In this phase of his work McPhee operates as a designer, an architect, perhaps an engineer, so that ultimately the immense amount of facts and information is transformed into a more meaningful piece of prose. Sometimes the design is apparent, as in *Levels of the Game*, which reads the way a tennis match looks and sounds. The action as the story opens moves cross-court, from one paragraph on Arthur Ashe to the next paragraph on Clark Graebner.

Some designs are less noticeable, as in the article "Travels in Georgia." Norman Sims, in his discussion of this piece in *The Literary Journalists*, refers to the "architecture of the piece." He calls it one that "depends on a skillfully designed looping flashback, entered through a smooth, nearly invisible transition" (1984, 27). In the introduction to this book, Sims describes a diagram for the article seen in McPhee's book of notes. The diagram "looked like a lowercase 'e.' " Sims quotes McPhee on the approach taken in this story:

It's a simple structure, a reassembled chronology. I went there to write about a woman who, among other things, picks up dead animals off the road and eats them. There's an immediate problem when you begin to consider such material. The editor of *The New Yorker* is practically a vegetarian. I knew I was going to be presenting this story to William Shawn and that it would be pretty difficult to do so. That served a purpose, pondering what a general reader's reaction would be. When people think of animals killed on the road, there's an immediate putrid whiff that goes by them. The image is pretty automatic—smelly and repulsive. These animals we were picking up off the road were not repulsive. They had not been mangled up. They were not bloody. They'd been freshly killed. So I had to get this story off the ground without offending the sensibilities of the reader and the editor. (Sims 1984, 13)

When McPhee wrote about Bill Bradley, the basketball star with extraordinary peripheral vision, the piece had a similar viewpoint, a wide-angle on Bradley. It is as if the reader sees through a fish-eye lens—covering the widest possible angle, probing relentlessly into one man's game and trying to freeze frames of excellence. The story and the writing give the reader a way to see clearly what would otherwise be blurred or lacking clear resolution.

In 1983, McPhee revisited Bradley, but this time *Senator* Bradley, not basketball player Bradley. The piece, "Open Man," is a slice of life: one day with the politician in his home state of New Jersey. It is crisply written, but reads more like a report from the stump. The design is less complex and less compelling and therefore the work is much less memorable than *A Sense of Where You Are*.

Nowhere is there more a sense of design than in McPhee's selection of subjects. His subjects are not the usual newsmakers, nor are they celebrities in the usual sense of the word. All of them, however, are experts. And all of them are archetypes of excellence. It is no accident that in *Levels of the Game* Arthur Ashe faces Clark Graebner. Graebner is the epitome of the privileged middle-class, country club set. He grew up in a WASP world, supported by his family and his society. He is strong and steady in his approach to the game. Ashe is the opposite. He is black, a product of an America where country club tennis courts are not available. Ashe is unpredictable, even flashy in his risk taking.

While it is clear that McPhee values and admires the excellence in his subjects' expertise, he is unsentimental in his introduction of his characters to his readers. He does not hype their heroics or hide their blemishes. In *Encounters with the Archdruid*, Charles Park, the mining expert, gets blisters on his feet as a result of wearing brand new boots on a backcountry trip. Dave Brower bails out of the raft just before Upset Rapids, one of the more treacherous runs on the Colorado.

We got back on the raft and moved out into the river. The raft turned slightly and began to move toward the rapid.

"Hey," Dominy said. "Where's Dave? Hey! We left behind one of our party. We're separated now. Isn't he going to ride?"

Brower has stayed on shore. We were forty feet out.

"Well, I swear, I swear, I swear," Dominy continued slowly. "He isn't coming with us.... The great outdoorsman!" Dominy said in a low voice... "The Great outdoorsman standing safely on dry land wearing a God-damned life jacket!" (1971, 231)

Through it all, McPhee brings his reader characters that last, that impress, that inspire. They are whole and vivid and complex. But unlike the novelist, McPhee cannot "imagine" his characters. He has to take them as they come. And unlike the journalist, he does not reduce his characters to a categorical entry: male/female, title/occupation, age, and place of residence. And unlike many literary journalists, he does not make them interchangeable cultural types. McPhee fully shapes them. His characters come alive on paper. Consider this memorable description of Floyd Dominy, the builder of the Hoover Dam:

Floyd Elgin Dominy raises beef cattle in the Shenandoah Valley. Observed there, hand on a fence, his eyes surveying his pastures, he does not look particularly Virginian. Of middle height, thickset, somewhat bandy-legged, he appears to have been lifted off a horse with a block and tackle. He wears bluejeans, a white-and-black striped shirt, and leather boots with heels two inches high. His belt buckle is silver and could not be covered over with a playing card. He wears a string tie that is secured with a piece of petrified dinosaur bone. On his head is a white Stetson. (1971, 153)

A few readers might even recall the John Steinbeck piece, "How to Tell Good Guys from Bad Guys." Among other things, the good guys, says Steinbeck, always wore a white hat (1958). Thus, McPhee nicely suggests either that it is no longer so easy to tell the good guys from the bad guys, or that the bad guys are not as bad as they seem.

McPhee's characters do not all wear white hats, but he treats all of them with respect. His *Encounters with the Archdruid* reveals as well as any of his works just how character and design work together to produce an original work, a fresh perspective. *Archdruid* seems to have a deceptively simple, straightforward construction. To some observers it is merely a package of profiles bound together in book form: David Brower, the environmentalist, and his enemies, Charles Park the mining geologist, Charles Fraser the real estate developer, and Floyd Dominy, the Commissioner of the U.S. Bureau of Reclamation.

But like all McPhee's work, *Archdruid* is carefully plotted and conceived. McPhee's use of the very word "archdruid" and his names for the book's three distinct parts reveal a grander design: "A Mountain," "An Island," "A River." And Brower is not merely a personality in a journalistic feature. Rather he is the warp thread of the book, a powerful and complicated protagonist who is thoroughly human and a great American individualist, but somewhat of a visionary as well. McPhee presents him as a high priest of environmental conservation pitted against each of the other characters but also fighting his very human self. Through McPhee's organic design, the reader is presented with a tale of two forces clashing in American culture, development and conservation, a variation of the theme of the machine in the garden.[4] The tensions and conflicts that arise from these forces and the book's characters cannot be easily reconciled. As with good fiction, the reader sees and understands, but some ambiguity remains.

No matter which side they might identify with at the outset, the readers come away, like the characters in *Encounters with the Archdruid*, perhaps not agreeing one bit, but genuinely liking and respecting one another. It may be McPhee's ability to respect his reader that keeps the readers coming back for more reports. McPhee was quoted in *Fame* magazine:

The writer stands somewhere behind the book, not the other way around. The reader is the more creative partner in the writer-reader relationship. The reader creates many things, including the author figure. When a writer steps into the foreground, he denies the reader an important part of his experience. (Streitfeld 1989, 26–30)

With a writer so determined to stay in the background, with a writer whose books are scattered so widely by topic throughout the libraries, it is no wonder the critics have had a hard time identifying his place in literature or journalism. In part because of the trend toward professionalization,[5] and in part because of the new journalism controversy, McPhee's form of writing is discouraged in contemporary journalism. It may be that it is only because a publication like the *New Yorker* exists that a writer like John McPhee has been able to thrive.

NOTES

1. Literary journalists in this century have their roots primarily in magazines, but Wolfe and Talese, two of the principal architects and practitioners of the new journalism, started in newspapers. Capote and Mailer, two of the other central figures in new journalism, came to new journalism from writing novels and short stories. Thus the newspaperman-novelist continuum. In addition, much of the discussion over the impact of the new journalism tended to come from defenders of the novel or defenders of newspaper journalism's objective approach.

2. Lounsberry specifically disagrees with Weber's view and calls all of McPhee's works "highly ambitious—and artful" (1990, n.8, 194–95).

3. It would be difficult to discuss McPhee's writing without discussing how he structures his work. For a detailed account of how McPhee determines an overall design for a work, see Roundy (1989). Roundy analyzes the devices McPhee uses to organize his material, playing off the ideas of Kenneth Burke in *Counter-Statement* (1931). Lounsberry is also concerned with structure in McPhee, with his use of geometric figures and abstract forms and specifically his use of circles and levels. Lounsberry provides more of a traditional literary analysis than Roundy, presenting McPhee as a son of Thoreau and Emerson.

4. Lounsberry goes so far as to demonstrate how Brower can be viewed as somewhat of a Christ figure, while Dominy can be seen as a false god (1990, 94).

5. James Fallows ("The Case Against Credentialism," *Atlantic*, Dec. 1985) referred to the rise to professional status as "one of the most familiar and cherished parts of the American achievement ideal." Joseph McKerns, Arthur Kaul, and John Pauly discussed various concerns about the professionalism of journalism at the 1984 meeting of the American Journalism Historians Association. McKerns outlined the pathways to professionalism in American journalism, stating that professional journalism is a twentieth-century institution born of the Progressive Era and resting on a set of shared values. Professional journalists, according to McKerns, "like other professionals, seek to enhance their social prestige and status while serving the social order with their acquired skills and expertise." Arthur Kaul concluded that professionalism was a cover for the exploitation of journalists *and* the public to protect the property interests of capitalist mass media. John Pauly discussed the news itself as having become professionalized, a "privileged form of knowledge." He has argued that journalists since the 1920s have not only joined the professional ranks, but have "proposed to teach citizens how to read the news more carefully." The significance of these efforts, according to Pauly, is that they have established in newspaper reading "a new conception of citizenship, democracy and public discourse."

PRIMARY SOURCES

McPhee, John. 1965. *A Sense of Where You Are: A Profile of William Warren Bradley.* New York: Farrar, Straus and Giroux.
———. 1967. *Oranges.* New York: Farrar, Straus and Giroux.
———. 1968. *A Roomful of Hovings.* New York: Farrar, Straus and Giroux.
———. 1969a. *The Crofter and the Laird.* New York: Farrar, Straus and Giroux.
———. 1969b. *Levels of the Game.* New York: Farrar, Straus and Giroux.
———. 1971. *Encounters with the Archdruid: Narratives About a Conservationist and Three of His Natural Enemies.* New York: Farrar, Straus and Giroux.
———. 1974. *The Curve of Binding Energy: A Journey into the Awesome and Alarming World of Theodore B. Taylor.* New York: Farrar, Straus and Giroux.
——— 1976. *The John McPhee Reader.* Ed. William L. Howarth. New York: Random House.
———. 1979. *Giving Good Weight.* New York: Farrar, Straus and Giroux.
———. 1985. "Open Man." In *Table of Contents.* New York: Farrar, Straus and Giroux.

SECONDARY SOURCES

Atwan, Robert. 1987. *The Best American Essays 1987.* New York: Ticknor and Fields.
Howarth, William L. 1976. Introduction to *The John McPhee Reader.* Ed. William L. Howarth. New York: Random House.
Lemann, Nicolas. 1983, Mar. "Today's Best Journalism: Better Than Fiction." *Washington Monthly.*

Lounsberry, Barbara. 1990. "John McPhee's Levels of Earth." In *The Art of Fact: Contemporary Artists of Nonfiction*. Westport, Conn.: Greenwood Press.

Roundy, Jack. 1989. "Crafting Fact: Formal Devices in the Prose of John McPhee." In *Literary Nonfiction: Theory, Criticism, Pedagogy*. Ed. Chris Anderson. Carbondale: Southern Illinois University Press.

Sims, Norman, ed. 1984. *The Literary Journalists: The New Art of Personal Reportage*. New York: Ballantine Books.

Singular, Stephen. 1977, Nov. 27. "Talk with John McPhee." *New York Times Book Review*: 1, 50–51.

Steinbeck, John. 1958. "How to Tell Good Guys from Bad Guys." In *Ideas in Context*. Ed. Joseph Satin. Boston: Houghton Mifflin.

Streitfeld, David. 1989, Apr. "Pulling the Plug." *Fame*.

Weber, Ronald. 1980. *The Literature of Fact*. Athens: Ohio University Press.

JOAN DIDION

Sandra Braman

The reportage of Joan Didion always tells us about the same thing—la situacion, the situation—whether she is reporting from San Salvador or Miami or Los Angeles, whether the subject is the water supply or a presidential campaign.

Her writing is powerful in several ways: aesthetically, journalistically, psychologically, morally, and politically. Though typically considered a journalist, Didion can also be read as an existentialist. She differs from writers like Beckett or Sartre, however, in her detail. Insistently concrete, Didion focuses always on the specificities that both mask and reveal the universal. Dense stories about unique individuals and circumstances are, for her, tales of "triumph over nothingness" (1979a, 66), what Davenport calls "a desperation of purposelessness" (1970, 903).

She also sets herself apart by the millennial tone of her writing, the flat-voiced recounting of the most horrible of tales. Millennial events are not teleological for Didion; rather, they appear within a constantly shifting environment in which meaning is ominous but unclear. As we build toward the year 2000, Didion's tone is spreading throughout the culture.

Technically, Didion is immaculate and original. As early as 1963, literary critic Guy Davenport could say, "Her prose is her servant" (371). She understands grammar as a source of "infinite power":

To shift the structure of a sentence alters the meaning of that sentence, as definitely and inflexibly as the position of a camera alters the meaning of the object photographed. . . . The arrangement of the words matters, and the arrangement you want can be found in the picture in your mind. . . . The picture tells you how to arrange the words and the arrangement of the words tells you, or tells me, what's going on in the picture. (Didion 1986, 7)

The particularities of writing style, then, are meant to have utility and to enlighten. In *Democracy*, for example, she explains the use of certain techniques in writing about Latin America: "It seemed constantly necessary to remind the reader to make certain connections. Technically it's almost a chant. You could read it as an attempt to cast a spell or come to terms with certain contemporary demons" (1984, 14).

The process by which the grammar of a situation is perceived is, for Didion, a Dostoyevskian web of migraine pain and visions:

When I talk about pictures in my mind I am talking, quite specifically, about images that shimmer around the edges.... You can't think too much about these pictures that shimmer. You just lie low and keep your nervous system from shorting out and you try to locate...the grammar in the picture. (1986, 7)

Critics consider her an accurate and sophisticated reporter and praise the quality of her intellect, the powers of her perception, and the astonishing coherence of her vision. Though she is sometimes faulted for her overuse of certain signature techniques that cloy over time and for the resonance of certain themes,[1] Dan Wakefield considers her among the best writers of the era.

In reviewing a work by Mailer in 1965, Didion wrote of her admiration of his technical skill and the way in which he says "the right things" (1965, 329). She has also claimed Hemingway as an influence, and she used a Conrad epigraph to open *Salvador*.

Like most literary journalists, Didion thoroughly researches the subjects about which she writes. (*Miami*, for example, includes bibliographic notes.) The combination of careful research, a perceptive eye, and a belief that it is the media that tell us how to live makes Didion a particularly valuable observer of journalists themselves. A number of passages describe the activities of those around her, from the time in the 1960s when Didion, along with a *Los Angeles Times* man and a radio newscaster, interviewed black activist Huey Newton in prison, to the 1980s press conference of a Cuban candidate for mayor of Miami, or the cluster of reporters in George Bush's entourage.

Her persistence of vision and the cohesiveness of her growing oeuvre make her a good model for comparing the genres of "new journalism" and "objective journalism" (as typified by the *New York Times*). A comparison of the procedures each used in collecting and reporting facts on El Salvador in June 1982 reveals that radically different realities were ultimately portrayed, though each reported on the same place and the same time, often about the same events, affairs, and individuals. The *New York Times* is bureaucratic in orientation and Washington-centered, while Didion reported local Salvadoran chaos and terror (Braman 1985, 75–96).

Didion's own artery of short reportage was first demonstrated in book form in her collection on the 1960s, *Slouching Towards Bethlehem*, which explored the lives of rock stars, hippies, and other California characters of the time. *The White Album* collects her reportage about the 1970s, covering the ground from the California water supply, to the governor's mansion, to the questioning of all premises endemic to the time. The pieces of the 1980s appear in the *New York Review of Books* (which serialized *Miami*) and *Esquire*. She writes regular "Letters from Los Angeles" for the *New Yorker*. (Didion's narrator in *A Book of Common Prayer* tried to sell the same magazine "Letter from Central America.")

There are certain recurring themes and characters. The Pentecostal minister of *Slouching Towards Bethlehem* shows up again in a 1988 *New Yorker* piece about earthquakes; the emeralds of her 1973 reportage about Bogota appear later on the hand of a novel's character. The gun runners of *Salvador* walk the streets of *Miami*.

Didion rejects the canon of objectivity that still, at least rhetorically, drives conventional journalism. "The point," she says, is to *"remember what it was to be me"* (1979a, 134–35). Her subjectivity is a deliberate stance understood to be a position of strength, the source of her credibility. Identification of the speaking voice is critical, she argues, for people are "uneasy about a story until we know who is telling it" (1977, 21). She also uses a medieval argument for the existence of God to defend subjectivity: her referents must exist, says Didion, or they would not be in her mind.

This insistence that certain images remain in her mind over time is critical to her understanding of the purpose of the writing act. The pictures in one's mind are of importance in contradistinction to dreams generated by the mass media. Didion believes that much of the world is living in a somnambulistic state created and sustained by the media. Thus, she sees communicating the evidence of one's own senses as a radical and central human effort.

The millennial connection is spelled out in *Slouching Towards Bethlehem* and *The White Album*. Both resonate with pentecostal modes of thought, starting with Yeats's poem "The Second Coming." The mood this writing generates is perceived by some critics as pessimistic or anxious, while others find it realistic. Eason sees Didion's position as that of a realist at a point in history "when events are ambiguous, the imposition of narrative self-consciously arbitrary and the meanings not satisfactory" (1977, 126).

Latin American themes (or the theme that is Latin America) run throughout Didion's work. Writing autobiographically in *The White Album*, she commented on her belief that writing about a place to some extent *creates* that place both by bringing it to life and by replacing impressions readers may have received elsewhere (1979b, 147).

She calls California the nerve center of the world, the perfect place from which (and about which) to report, with its many sites of the other, Hispanic, culture within our midst. She is certainly telling us what is seen from one of the strands of early and continuing Hispanic penetration north. Hollywood lives surrounded by Latin pueblos, and Latin angels carry her sets and still pick her fields. Didion tells us about the Hispanic colorations at the center of America's image machine, which she believes is so powerful.

Didion's work on the interactions of Hispanic cultures with others in the Americas must therefore include those pieces about California, as well as "In Bogota," describing a 1973 trip to that city; *A Book of Common Prayer*, a novel set in an unidentified Central American country; *Salvador*, which reports on San Salvador during June 1982; and *Miami*, 1987 reportage focusing on the Latin American forces that shape that city.

In this group of writings, in particular, Didion's need to "remember what it was to be me" takes on the character of witness, a term in use for at least 1,500 years to mean "attestation of a fact," a bringing of evidence, as to a courtroom. While she does not ask for judgment, one is helpless not to judge. It is significant that Didion always brings her characters back to the United States, for it is here that the effects are felt, the facts are accumulated.

This lineage reveals a counter-hegemonic tracery in her work—rather than working from the center out, Didion travels from the periphery in, back toward the center. Her most powerful writing about Latin America is in her book about a U.S. city. In Miami she sees arms deals. Contras. People's lives bought and sold. Training. Cubans—rich, powerful, and insistently monolingual in a language that is not our own.

Toward the close of *Miami*, Didion reminds us of the Santa Fe document, a 1980 policy paper on Central America generally seen as a blueprint for Reagan Administration activities. This document portrays Central America as the World War III battlefront, in a war largely ideological (and therefore image-driven).[2]

Didion, the journalist, tracked down the resulting White House Outreach Working Group on Central America—a group not at all friendly to the media—and heard it asked why Central American countries should be needed as surrogates for the United States in its battle against communism. The Administration's response was to point to the enemy within—the media, liberals in general, a number of individuals by name.

Though Didion's work drives one against U.S. policy in Central America, her politics are not to be simply taken. She admits to voting for Goldwater and voting in few presidential elections thereafter. She wrote in *Morning After the Sixties*: "If I could believe that going to a barricade would affect man's fate in the slightest I would go to that barricade, and quite often I wish that I could, but it would be less than honest to say that I expect to happen upon such a happy ending" (1979b, 208).

Perhaps the closest she comes to such barricades is in the close of a *New Yorker* "Letter from Los Angeles" of 1988. These letters are elegantly segued reportage on a number of subjects that have caught her attention. This one opens by noting, "People brought up to believe that the phrase 'terra firma' has real meaning often find it hard to understand the apparent equanimity with which earthquakes are accommodated in California" (80). She describes the wait for the earthquakes expected to destroy San Francisco: "At odd moments...people would suddenly clutch at tables or walls. 'Is it going?' they would say, or 'I think it's moving,' They almost always said 'it,' and what they meant by 'it' was not just the ground but the world as they knew it" (80).

This same letter goes on to discuss the Los Angeles real estate market, the new house of Candy and Aaron Spelling, and the strike by the Writers Guild of America, a group that includes screenwriters who work for people like Spelling and others in Hollywood. Didion's fury is finally triggered by the refusal of producer/director Paul Mazursky to cross Hollywood class lines and loan her his floor pass at the 1988 Democratic National Convention.

Here Didion finds her barricade, and it turns, as might be expected from her work, on style and manner. (Style, she notes in a piece on painter Georgia O'Keeffe, is character.) It is in these social forms that Didion comes closest to locating moral order. Narrative is among those social forms; she sees a decline of literacy, a loss of understanding of the sentence.

It is here, at the conjuncture of the sentence, of the construction of meaning and social coherence through style, one's own experience as expressed in personal manner rather than mass media-provided facts and behaviors, that the convergence of vision and narrative form that characterize the mid-twentieth-century genre of "new journalism" is so exquisitely realized in the work of Joan Didion.

Though the sensitivity to the issues of the 1960s and seventies has died down, all "new journalists" walk political ground to some degree through the simple but radical choice to adhere to their own version of the facts, their own experience, in a traditional Lockean sense. Although today the dogma resisted is not of the Church, but of the mass media, the doctrine has political consequences just as it did when first enunciated.

Didion, however, walks a finer line, or a sharper edge, than most. It cannot be said that Didion is documenting the impact of by now decades-long war in Central America on U.S. society. She is simply reporting on what she remembers in a time when helicopters float slowly past apartment windows in Brooklyn, cars are randomly stopped and searched on Nebraska roads, and the color of our television models' skin slowly darkens, the bones beginning to widen.

NOTES

1. See Duffy 1979, 43–44, Friedman 1984, Johnson 1971, Weber 1974, and Winchell 1989.

2. In the mid-1980s, dancing and singing guerrillas with machine guns introduced the Clio awards, the annual prizes for the best television advertising.

PRIMARY SOURCES

Didion, Joan. 1965. "A Social Eye." Review of *An American Dream*, by Norman Mailer. *National Review* 17:329–30.

———. 1977. *A Book of Common Prayer*. New York: Simon and Schuster.

———. 1979a. *Slouching Towards Bethlehem*. New York: Simon and Schuster.

———. 1979b. *The White Album*. New York: Simon and Schuster.

———. 1983. *Salvador*. New York: Simon and Schuster.

———. 1984. *Democracy*. New York: Simon and Schuster.

———. 1986. *Miami*. New York: Simon and Schuster.

———. 1988, Sept 5. "Letter from Los Angeles." *New Yorker* 64: 80–88.

———. 1989, Sept. "Unforgettable Women: The Startling Vision of Robert Mapplethorpe." *Esquire* 112: 214–23.

SECONDARY SOURCES

Anderson, Chris. 1987. "The Cat in the Shimmer." In *Style as Argument*. Carbondale: Southern Illinois University Press.

Braman, Sandra. 1985. "The 'Facts' of El Salvador According to Objective and New Journalism." *Journal of Communication Inquiry* 9: 75–96.

Davenport, Guy. 1963. "Midas' Grandchildren." Review of *Play It as It Lays*, by Joan Didion. *National Review* 14: 371.

———. 1970. "On the Edge of Being." Review of *Play It as It Lays*, by Joan Didion. *National Review* 22: 903.

Diamonstein, Barbaralee. 1972. *Open Secrets: Ninety-Four Women in Touch with Our Time*. New York: Viking Press.

Duffy, Martha. 1979. Review of *The White Album*, by Joan Didion. *New York Review of Books* 26: 43–44.

Eason, David L. 1977. "Metajournalism: The Problem of Reporting in the Nonfiction Novel." *Dissertation Abstracts International* 38: 2387-A (University Microfilms #77–24459). See also Eason, David L. 1990. "The New Journalism and the Image-World." In *Literary Journalism in the Twentieth Century*. Ed. Norman Sims. New York: Oxford University Press.

Friedman, Ellen G. 1984. *Joan Didion: Essays and Conversations*. Princeton, N.J.: Ontario Review Press.

Johnson, Michael L. 1971. *The New Journalism*. Lawrence: University Press of Kansas.

Lounsberry, Barbara. 1990. "Joan Didion's Lambent Light." In *The Art of Fact: Contemporary Artists of Nonfiction*. Westport, Conn.: Greenwood Press, 107–37.

Wakefield, Dan. 1968, July 21. Review of *Slouching Towards Bethlehem*, by Joan Didion. *New York Times Book Review*, 8.

Weber, Ronald, ed. 1974. *The Reporter as Artist: A Look at the New Journalism Controversy*. New York: Hastings House.

Winchell, Mark Royden. 1989. *Joan Didion*. Rev. ed. Boston: G. K. Hall.

BOB GREENE

Steve Jones

Bob Greene's work is deceptively simple. Like the hook from a Beatles' song that goes in one ear and, instead of going out the other, reverberates inside one's mind for days, Greene's writing arouses the senses. His columns for *Esquire*, the *Chicago Sun-Times*, and the *Chicago Tribune* and his books about subjects such as life on the Alice Cooper rock 'n' roll tour and the Nixon-McGovern campaign combine plain but well-crafted writing, keen observation, and even sharper sifting of details and impressions to tell good stories.

Though Greene is unquestionably a fine writer, perhaps his greatest skill is in finding those stories. His *American Beat* collection brings together some of his finest columns, including "Kathy's Abortion," the story of a young woman's few hours in an abortion clinic; "Speck," an interview with mass murderer Richard Speck; and "Michael Testifies," the story of a boy paralyzed from an attack in a Chicago housing project.

Greene's stories are about America and the American dream—gone wrong and gone right. Piece them together and the picture is as comprehensive and satisfying as a cross-country drive along Route 66.

But for each American dream he describes, a price is paid, and nowhere is this more evident than in *Billion Dollar Baby*, Greene's unmasking of the image manipulation that lies at the heart of the popular music industry.

Elvis Presley's first appearance on the Ed Sullivan show affected Greene's life as it did the lives of millions of others—it made him a devout rock 'n' roll fan. It also reoriented the American dream. Once, most kids wanted to be like Babe Ruth, Joe DiMaggio, or their favorite movie star. Rock 'n' roll soon became the touchstone for America's fantasy life. Once, most kids had baseball gloves or Barbie dolls in their bedrooms. Now they have Casios.

Rock music was a part of everyday life for Greene, too, and he sought to discover what it is really like to be a rock star. Having recently completed

Running: A Nixon-McGovern Campaign Journal, Greene was dissatisfied with playing the role of outsider, covering stories as an observer and not a participant. His introduction to *Billion Dollar Baby* not only reveals his motives for researching and writing the book, but gives insight into his adoption of a form of participatory journalism.

The giant rock and roll tours represented a fantasy life that millions of people all over the world thought about and, at least during wistful moments, longed to be a part of, if only to affirm that someone really was living that way. If, in the 1920s and '30s and '40s, the dream of a kid growing up was to be a member of the New York Yankees or the Brooklyn Dodgers, then by the '70s the dream of America's young was the rock and roll dream, and the heroes were the rock and roll heroes. The cross-country tours—with their daily jet flights and lavish hotel suites and packed concert halls and astonishing profits and beautiful young girls and loud, throbbing music every night—embodied all the facets of that dream.

On a number of occasions I had been out on tour briefly with big-money bands, working on magazine and newspaper stories. It had always been exciting and fast and fun to watch—but every time I finished one of those road trips, I felt, in the end, frustrated, wondering why it was that I still was not satisfied that I knew what it felt like to live in the rock and roll world. And the conclusion was always the same: I didn't know because I wasn't really living in that world, I was only a visitor from the real world on a three-day pass. (1974, 4)

Greene's solution? Become a performer on Alice Cooper's 1973 Holiday Tour.

Billion Dollar Baby thus chronicles the ups and downs of the daily routine that comprises major league rock 'n' roll. Greene is with the group every step of the way, from recording background vocals in a New York studio for a new Alice Cooper album, to playing the part of Santa Claus during the closing of the Cooper stage show (during which Santa is kicked, beaten, and stomped to death by the band).

As a performer he becomes part of the inner circle of musicians, treated much the same as they are, and his observations of their world simultaneously evoke envy and pity. On the one hand there were the perks that have physical evidence of the rock star's life. Greene describes the Alice Cooper tour jet:

The outside of the airplane was painted brown and gold. I got out of the lead limousine and walked up the portable stairway and into the plane, and I burst out laughing. It was ridiculous; it was a dream. The first section of the airplane had the look of an elegant private club. Red wall-to-wall carpeting covered the floor. Against one wall was a long, multi-section couch, covered with an expensive patterned fabric. There were card tables and leather swivel chairs in this compartment; against the wall opposite the couch was a television set; complete with a cabinet full of videotape cassettes featuring movies from *Deep Throat* to *The Maltese Falcon.* Farther back in this compartment were more couches, and a second television set.

The next compartment back was dominated by a long, brass-topped bar. Behind the bar was a butler, who had already laid out a steak-and-salad buffet for us. Beneath the bar, the butler had arranged every conceivable kind of liquor.... At the rear of the plane there was a short hallway, with framed paintings hung on the walls. Two rooms opened off this hallway: a library-study, complete with easy chairs and work tables, and a master bedroom, with a king-size bed and an adjoining bathroom complete with full-size shower. (1974, 1480)

The extravagance of the tour corresponds to the stereotypical image of big-time rock 'n' roll life, and Greene illustrates it in detail. There are parties, trashed hotel rooms, limousines, groupies, and on and on.

The power of the book, and indeed of virtually all Greene's writing, is that he sees and describes the scenes he encounters as would the average person. Though he is obviously a part of the story, he is primarily a recorder of events, and as such he remains largely *out* of the story. Never mind that he includes his reactions—they are as much *our* reactions as his. Though he is not in the background, one does not get the sense that he intrudes on the story in any way.

Greene's weaving of dialogue and observation is noteworthy. He faithfully records dialogue but uses it as another form of illustration rather than a documentary device. That is, quotes do not explain; they unfold a setting or situation just as the details of a room or a person's character traits tell part of the story. In a particularly evocative passage from *Billion Dollar Baby*, Greene exposes Alice Cooper's true self:

Montreal was full of clothes shops that featured the freaky, outlandish, glittery fashions that Alice Cooper had first made popular on stage, and which had since become acceptable street attire for the young and the hip. There were tiny spangled shrink tee shirts, and see-through blouses for men, and rainbow-colored boots with six-inch heels, and denim jackets covered with sequined stars and stripes. All of the stores seemed to be doing a brisk business, and judging from the attire of the young people around town, the sleazo fop look was very much in vogue.

When I got back to the hotel, I stopped by Alice's suite. He and Norm were watching television, and I told them about the clothing stores.

"Yeah, I know," Alice said."I bought some clothes today."

"What did you get?" I asked him.

He smiled at Norm. "Should I?" Alice said.

"Sure," Norm said. "Go ahead."

"Okay," Alice said. "But don't tell the others."

He went up to his bedroom, which was at the top of a winding staircase. He was gone for about five minutes. Then I heard him call, "Okay."

I looked at the stairs. He came down wearing his purchase of the day. It was a gray flannel suit, cut very conservatively and severely. "It was the only thing I saw that I could stand," he said. (1974, 327–28)

Though he made a point of conducting lengthy interviews with each of the principal members of the group and tour managers (and deftly wove them into the book), Greene observes the dialogue around him as he beholds the physical reality surrounding him. It is all part of the story, part of the life that becomes evident to him only after he *processes* his observations by checking his reactions against those of the others on the tour.

What makes his observations especially insightful is his ability to relate the slightly skewed, the lightly troubling. As an episode of "The Twilight Zone" relinquishes its off-balance sensibility only gradually, Greene's stories surrender their vision a little at a time. *Billion Dollar Baby*, piece by piece, reveals the down side of rock 'n' roll, in penetrating passages such as the one describing Greene's last performance on stage:

It was supposed to be a joyous, unbridled, happy bit of slapstick, a final public blast of communal energy for everyone in the tour party. The pie plates and the shaving cream flew, and we all tumbled over one another and slid across the slick stage floor, and it seemed to go on and on. But then, at one point, I stood up and looked out at the audience. They were out of their minds with frenzy. . . . And then I looked back, and I saw Alice. He was standing near the rear of the stage, detached from the lunacy. His arms were hanging limply by his sides. He was not moving. He was just staring out into the shrieking, churning audience, as if hypnotized by what he was seeing. . . when our eyes met I saw as dejected and empty a look in his face as I ever hope to witness. He shook his head from side to side, once. Then, without waiting for the others, he turned and walked off the stage. (1974, 359–60)

Cooper had become trapped by the image that made him famous. Not only did he become inaccessible and slightly paranoid (he drank only from sealed bottles for fear of being poisoned), but he traded part of his personality for that of the public image presented each night on stage.

Much of Greene's writing carries through that theme of something lost, or someone disappointed. Greene himself, in the autobiographical *Be True to Your School*, longs for his early sixties high school days. In particular, Greene's reconstructed diary of high school circa 1964 is a nostalgic reliving of early sixties teenage life in the Midwest. It is suggestive in a way that invokes the timeliness of growing up:

We went to the Bexley basketball game tonight, and afterward we went over to Steve Pariser's house to hang out with the seniors. The seniors were all smoking pipes.

We cruised in Gary Robins's car, and they lent us their pipes. I smoked one with some cherry-flavored tobacco. I didn't know you weren't supposed to inhale it, so I just kept sucking it in and not saying anything, and I felt my head getting dizzier and dizzier. No one else seemed to be affected by it, though, so I just kept it up. Everyone in the car had pipes in their mouths, and the whole inside of the car was filled with smoke. You could hardly breathe.

By the time they dropped me at home I felt like I was about to pass out. All I could feel was that burning cherry flavor in my throat and this hot sickness in my stomach. I've just thrown up twice; Mom knocked on the door to ask if I was all right—I guess she heard me in the bathroom. Never again. (1987, 54)

It is in his short pieces, though, that Greene best evokes the themes of disappointment and loneliness—perhaps because the shorter format forces him to reach quickly for the heart of the matter. Among the most evocative is a story in *American Beat* titled "Night Callers," about Audrey Loehr, a woman who approves credit card charges for a gas company. Greene writes:

Most of the time they are straightforward business calls—gas dealers dialing to confirm a charge card.

But on weekends...late at night, the obscene calls will begin....

She has it figured out: "At that time of the night, most gas stations are manned by only one person," she said. "It's usually a young man who has been assigned to work all night. He's alone there, and it's dark, and there's no one to talk to."

"I just answer the calls," she said. "When I find out that it's one of those calls, I hang up. But I always silently wish that the men find inner peace, and that they somehow get better." (1983, 24–25)

In Greene's work generally, as in this story, there is no social analysis. He is a reporter, and telling stories is what he does best. But the social commentary is there, in the understanding and consideration given to everyday lives. It is in the expression Greene finds by giving voice to the decisions, the trade-offs, that are made daily.

Indeed, much of Greene's work carries through a theme of exchange. In *Good Morning, Merry Sunshine*, Greene's journal of his daughter's first year, the focus shifts—this time it is on Greene himself, and the changes brought about it in his life by his daughter. He has traded in barhopping for going home to be with her, traded his study for a nursery, and we see him balancing his professional drive with the happiness he derives from being at home:

A sixteen-year-old high school girl came to see me at the newspaper late this afternoon. She has been coming around for about three years; she will disappear for months on end, and then show up with news about her life...in the middle of listening to her I realized that I don't necessarily want to be in Chicago anymore. I have a little girl who has to grow up in this world; I'm not sure I want her to grow up with the same diversions that this girl was talking about. Maybe you can't run away from the changes that have overtaken the world; but there must be a way to do your work and yet avoid an environment that offers readily available dope and booze and gang membership and one-night stands with famous young television stars. There must be a place where sixteen-year-old girls don't automatically turn for companionship to thirty-five-year-old men whom they've seen in their newspapers. (1984, 146–47)

And though *Good Morning, Merry Sunshine* is a book about Bob Greene, his hopes and fears, he still does not get in the way of presenting a slice of life that is interesting without being sloppily sentimental or corny. True, one has to wonder how the most banal events in his daughter's life can maintain any poignancy. But they do, and therein lies Greene's strength. He lacks pretentiousness and does not aim at being profound. Instead it is most ordinary events that he reports on, be it in ordinary situations like *Good Morning, Merry Sunshine*, extraordinary ones like *Billion Dollar Baby*, or some combination such as that found in his columns.

Perhaps that is the key to Greene's ability to keep from drying up despite writing hundreds of daily columns. It is the smaller, everyday events that he covers that make his work interesting and worthwhile and that keep Greene squarely within the ranks of journalists. Indeed, such events are the bread and butter of journalism. They are the points at which the news intersects with human life, and Greene expresses this human, emotional face of the news in a manner that betrays no bias, only thoughtfulness.

"Kathy's Abortion," for instance, *American Beat*'s powerful account of a young woman's abortion, is neither an argument for or against abortion nor a report of the facts surrounding the issue. It is, instead, Kathy's story, but Greene gives it a distinct focus and a specific shape by choosing how to tell it and what to tell. For instance, he begins this way:

"Oh Jesus," she moaned softly. She squeezed my hand. The vacuum machine purred steadily and the fetus that was her unborn child was sucked through a clear plastic hose and into a large glass bottle.

"Oh," she said again, and scratched my forearm.

"We're almost done," the doctor said. "I just have to check and make sure you're all clean and empty."

She squeezed my hand harder.

He then switches from that dramatic moment to the previous afternoon, and Kathy describes how she "felt guilty about not feeling guilty." She talks about the growth inside her not being a baby, and Greene writes: "That night Kathy went to see a play at the Goodman Theatre. The production was *Much Ado About Nothing.*"

He regularly provides this type of ironic contrasting in the piece, at one point allowing the word "Catholic" to stand as its own single-word sentence and a paragraph's conclusion, or noting that the song "Stayin' Alive" plays as Kathy lies on her back in the operating room, and that the emotionally wrought and culturally significant process takes only two and a half minutes. The article's controlling irony comes from the peculiar shared intimacy between Greene, the narrator, and Kathy, who met Greene only twenty-four hours before the abortion. "Kathy's Abortion" ends with just a hint of ambiguous tension, which has been running through the piece from the start:

At 10:15 A.M. Kathy and I walked out of the Concord Medical Center and into the sunlight. The counselor had told her to eat some lunch and then to rest for the remainder of the day.

"I don't want to think about it now," Kathy said. "I was on the bed in the recovery room...and all of a sudden I wanted to burst out and cry a whole lot. I looked at the ceiling and...I tried to think about Miami. I didn't want to think about what had happened. I looked up at the ceiling and I tried to pretend I was in Miami." (1983, 50–54)

Greene is, ultimately, keeping journals, be they his own (*Good Morning, Merry Sunshine*) or someone else's (*Billion Dollar Baby*, "Kathy's Abortion"), long or short. Yet the bits and pieces he chooses to reveal shape a complete and coherent narrative unlike the fractured tales one usually finds in a diary. Greene is simultaneously journal keeper and editor, keeping a record of what goes on around him, finding meaning in the events and conversations he records, and organizing that meaning into a comprehensible tale.

It is the struggle between the timeliness of journalism and the timelessness of literature that makes Greene's work absorbing, particularly in the case of *Good Morning, Merry Sunshine*, based as it is on the matter-of-fact chronicle of his daughter's first year of life. Greene writes quintessential "human interest" stories, peopled with immediately memorable characters and resonant narratives. While he seems well aware of journalism's emphasis on timeliness, on newsworthiness, Greene also seeks to illuminate what is timeless about the stories he tells, and that is what makes Bob Greene more a storyteller and less a traditional journalist.

PRIMARY SOURCES

Greene, Bob. 1974. *Billion Dollar Baby*. New York: Atheneum.
———. 1983. *American Beat*. New York: Atheneum.
———. 1984. *Good Morning, Merry Sunshine*. New York: Atheneum.
———. 1987. *Be True to Your School*. New York: Atheneum.

JOE MCGINNISS

Linda Steiner

Joe McGinniss created considerable controversy, as well as a reputation for himself, from the beginning of his journalism career, with his critical examination of the marketing successes of media advisors during Richard Nixon's 1968 campaign. McGinniss's topics, his professional techniques, methods, styles, and commitments since then, place him in the literary journalism camp. Unlike most other literary journalists, however, McGinniss tends not to develop or sustain affection for the people and cultures he describes. His intense negativism, if not hostility, brings him closer to the bleak worldview of some modern novelists and separates him from the more tolerant or even enthusiastic sensibility of literary journalists. It may be that, as Mark Kramer said of McGinniss's *Going to Extremes*, "with an elegant journalistic jujitsu, McGinniss has his people do themselves in, announce their own poignancy, crassness, lostness, and now and then, nobility" (1980, 290). But whether he chooses topics that he is bound to find repulsive or whether his disdain emerges over time, the familiarity and close contact demanded by literary journalism breed, in McGinniss's case, contempt.

McGinniss does not explain in *The Selling of the President 1968* how he managed to convince Nixon's advisors to allow him to spend five months on the campaign trail, attending strategy meetings, speeches, and tapings. Apparently predicting the repercussions of such close observation, Hubert Humphrey's staff refused to cooperate. Presumably the Republicans anticipated neither what might happen with such a book nor what McGinniss was thinking while conducting his research. McGinniss certainly was not going to warn them. But he announces his position to his readers at the start, making no pretense that he is objectively reporting facts. First declaring that politics and advertising have always been "con games" (1969, 26, 27), he goes on to assert that television, with its emphasis on style and disinterest in substance, is particularly useful to politicians without ideas. *Selling* shows how the image of Richard Nixon—initially grumpy, aloof, and fearful of television—was transformed and promoted through television to audiences. McGinniss minimizes references to himself, not wanting to position himself as a member of Nixon's cast. For all his repugnance for the techniques used to sell Nixon, however, McGinniss at least once attempted to help out the campaign by suggesting names of people to participate in a pseudo-panel interview being staged for, with, and by Nixon.

Despite his studious avoidance of overstatement, some critics saw *Selling* as a hatchet job by a young know-it-all. Others claimed to be neither surprised nor frightened by his revelations. But it was the fame attending his rise to the top of the best-seller list that caused McGinniss, then twenty-six, considerable trauma. The critical failure of *The Dream Team*, his presumably autobiographical novel about an author on a book tour, compounded his bafflement at having been displaced from "the center of things (1976, 55). Thus, in *Heroes*, his second nonfiction book, he grapples with his own success and lack of it at the same time he searches for the American hero.

In *Heroes*, McGinniss experiments with subjectivity and autobiography, fully willing to make personal despair the theme and the focus of his journalism. He intermingles maudlin confessions about his girlfriend Nancy (their fragile relationship apparently complicated and often compromised by guilt feelings about his first wife and their children) among pedantic reviews of scholarly literature on hero worship and sodden interviews with a number of famous men, including authors, military leaders, and politicians.

McGinniss is unembarrassed about inserting his professional/personal angst into the story; consistently McGinniss is as willing to disclose his own personal and professional errors as those of others. For example, *Heroes* opens with the fact that in 1967, when he was, at twenty-four, the youngest columnist in the country writing for a major newspaper (the *Philadelphia Inquirer*), he wanted to meet Robert Kennedy for one reason: "To have him know who I was" (1976, 1). Later McGinniss mocks his own pride that he had been "there, on the inside," when Kennedy died (8).[1] McGinniss also describes the great pains he took to interview Edward Kennedy, who was advised not to cooperate because McGinniss played "by a different set of rules" (148). Noting that other reporters might be trusted not to print carelessly made damaging remarks, Kennedy's press secretary tells McGinniss, "With a guy like you, we can't be sure" (148). Eventually the aide allowed the interview, and even warned McGinniss what not to say, so as not to alienate Kennedy. McGinniss coolly admits that he said precisely that wrong thing, and Kennedy "froze" (148).[2]

Eugene McCarthy, William Westmoreland, and his other sources cannot tell him whether they will ever recover their lost glory. They say nothing illuminating about heroes. Close up, they do not appear particularly heroic. And nearly all of them are struck dumb by McGinniss's questions. The only exception to this is Daniel Berrigan, but the morning after their discussion, McGinniss found in his notes only drunken, nonsensical scrawls instead of accurate transcriptions of Berrigan's insights. Again, including this incident seems to exemplify McGinniss's commitment to honesty. He admits his emotional and intellectual pretensions and errors, forgoing the assumed power and authority of mainstream journalists.

But he ignores both the circularity of his gloomy outlook and the extent to which his literary invitation to readers to judge his experiences and his interpretations undercuts his goals. With predictable disappointment, McGinniss concludes that America lacks genuine heroes because the values that heroes once personified are obsolete and because "there were no heroic acts left to be performed" (21). Having entered the critical space opened up by McGinniss's acknowledgment of his own private failings, however, readers may conclude merely that it is McGinniss who has no heroes, has no heroic energy, is no hero.

McGinniss is analogously disillusioned by Alaska, where he spent eighteen months researching *Going to Extremes*. If he had embarked on his Alaskan adventure with joy and enthusiasm for producing a richly detailed literary portrait, he soon came to regard Alaska—its cultures and styles of life—as dismal and depressing. McGinniss met natives, newcomers, short-term workers, long-term immigrants. As he sees it, nearly all of them are overwhelmed by encounters with harsh weather and physical elements, with modernity and encroaching city life, or both. They are bored, cynical; they abuse drink, drugs, each other. McGinniss refuses to become intimate with any of them. Consequently, his vignettes are precise but cursory. His writing is informed by his moral position, but not by any high degree of intensity or sense of spiritual possibility.

McGinniss's major personal achievement in Alaska, which translates into his more fluid and lyrical reportage, comes with a dangerous climbing expedition into a remote mountain range. McGinniss is invigorated, challenged, dazzled; this lovely place has never been seen by humans. Here he respects Alaska; we respect McGinniss not only for his graceful account of the trek but also for surviving it. After all, born in New York City, McGinniss was raised in Rye, an only child who compensated for being "skinny, awkward, weak and physically uncourageous" through a "splendid fantasy life" involving invented games (1976, 43–44).[3]

In some sense, the intense emotional lightning generated by that expedition and ripping through the otherwise monochromatic grayness of his book underscores how *Going to Extremes* fails and succeeds as literary journalism. One does not doubt the accuracy of his reportage. Presumably the quotes are correct. Still, one also suspects that much of the sheer thrill and mystique of Alaska eluded him. As a self-portraitist, however, McGinniss is more "truthful"; we learn quite a bit about the author as a man.

After completing *Going to Extremes*, McGinniss lived in California, writing a column for the *Los Angeles Herald*. There he became interested in the story of Jeffrey MacDonald, an Army doctor under indictment for the 1970 murder of his pregnant wife and their two pre-school-age daughters. Hoping that a book would generate favorable publicity and royalties to be used to defray defense expenses, and assuming that he would be portrayed as innocent, MacDonald had invited McGinniss to write a book about the case. Instead, *Fatal Vision* paints a damning picture of MacDonald, despite—or perhaps because of—its persistent attention to his charm, good looks, and sex appeal. The book portrays MacDonald as a "pathological narcissist" rightly convicted (1983, 656).

Fatal Vision became a best-seller and was made into a for-TV movie. But MacDonald accused McGinniss of violating a written agreement to maintain "the essential integrity of [MacDonald's] life story." Claiming betrayal, MacDonald sued McGinniss. (McGinniss's publisher apparently agreed to pay MacDonald $325,000 after the judge declared a mistrial.) That lawsuit became grounds for a controversial two-part *New Yorker* article attacking McGinniss and his methods.[4] Furthermore, taking the MacDonald-McGinniss encounter as "a grotesquely magnified version of the normal journalistic encounter" (Malcolm 1989a, 46), Janet Malcolm's article questions the general methods of literary journalists (although that term is not used). Ultimately, Malcolm challenges all journalism, beginning with her much-quoted introduction:

Every journalist who is not too stupid or too full of himself to notice what is going on knows that what he does is morally indefensible. He is a kind of confidence man, preying on people's vanity, ignorance, or loneliness, gaining their trust and betraying them without remorse. (1989a, 38)

Malcolm's vocabulary list also includes "perfidy," "treachery," and "bad faith."

As critics see it, one of the primary issues is the ostensibly mutual friendship that developed between author and subject. McGinniss's All-American male bonding approach (involving tough talk and late-night drinking) had proven to be self-defeating for *Heroes*, but it worked well with MacDonald. MacDonald invited McGinniss to live with him and his defense team during the seven-week murder trial. MacDonald authorized access to letters and files and sent McGinniss letters and tapes after his conviction and imprisonment. In turn—and this apparently turned several jurors against McGinniss during the civil trial—McGinniss wrote MacDonald a series of friendly, encouraging, supportive letters; this correspondence never hints that McGinniss had come to believe the prosecutors, not MacDonald. The book itself ignores these letters, although McGinniss notes in his conclusion: "MacDonald never came right out and asked me what I thought. And I never came right out and said. . . . it was easier to let him go right on believing whatever he cared to believe" (596–97).

In his defense (for example, he wrote a column for the *New York Times* and an epilogue for a book reprint) McGinniss claims that MacDonald breached the contract—by lying to him; that MacDonald manipulated and tried to con him; that MacDonald is a public figure who, after all, used a club, knife, and icepick to kill his family. McGinniss agrees with Tom Wolfe that reporters and subject may gradually develop friendships. But he denies that reporters ought to issue Miranda-type warnings that people won't like how they appear in print.

Literary journalists, given their commitment to extensive and intensive immersion with their subjects/objects, certainly are likely to become involved in people's lives, even as they generate their own versions of truth. McGinniss quotes a 1975 letter by Joseph Wambaugh in which he rebuffs MacDonald's invitation to write a book about MacDonald's story, since "it would be *my* story" (McGinniss 1983, 597). Justifiably, the implication is that *Fatal Vision* is McGinniss's story, faithful to his interpretation of the truth, both of the case and of its cultural and social meaning.

With its 659 pages, its selected bibliography of medical textbooks, its quotations from the Bible as well as *Macbeth* (for the title), its judicious alternating between the stories of the characters and transparently self-serving first-person recollections by MacDonald, *Fatal Vision* seems to aim at more than a supermarket-rack "true crime story." McGinniss's methods for getting the story—spending immense amounts of time with the major characters, participating in both the intimate and dramatic moments of their lives—testify to his artistic intentions. But its writing and organization are clumsy, in part because, until the concluding chapters, McGinniss is determined to submerge his own voice, his "authorship." To avoid his potential "authority" or reponsibility for his interpretation, he eschews elaborate literary devices, relying on exhaustive attention to detail and forcing readers to work through the material, although it could also be said that he resembles the Victorian novelist more than the modern journalist in using sheer bulk to slow down the reading process and to prevent scanning for highlights. For example, readers learn that when, nine years after the murder, McGinniss visited the MacDonalds' Fort Bragg home, he found cranberry sauce and ginger ale still in the refrigerator. Other details can be oppressive or even tedious, especially the gory facts of the crime itself. The entire bloody set is repeated several times in the course of recounting different versions of what happened on February 17, 1970, what investigators found and how they interpreted their findings, and what was said during various investigations, prosecutions, and appeals. But again, if McGinniss intended to protect—or limit—himself by awkward repetition and lengthy report, he failed.

The problem of getting bogged down in sordid details is solved in *Blind Faith*, again a best-seller and the basis for a television mini-series. *Blind Faith* tells the 1984 story of a successful New Jersey businessman convicted of conspiring to murder his wife so that he could collect on a $1.5 million insurance policy and marry his girlfriend. Here, confronted with conflicting testimony, McGinniss boldly takes the lead in offering the version that he believes is "the most plausible." He thereby produces a seamless, straight-forward, linear narrative. *Blind Faith* is McGinniss's most novelistic work, given its organization around fully developed and fully motivated characters who act out their roles in a plot so as to dramatize a particular theme. Rather than expose readers equally to all sides and viewpoints, McGinniss sets out what he alone decides is the truth. An "explanatory note" adds that McGinniss reconstructed dialogue and dramatically recreated scenes "in order to portray more effectively the personalities of those most inti-mately involved" (McGinniss 1989a, 9). McGinniss is essentially taking literary license in order, again, to write a more compelling story. He also changed certain names, as he had in *Fatal Vision* and *Going to Extremes*, to protect individuals' privacy. Nonetheless, this fictionalization presents certain problems; it has made effective complaint more difficult for indi-viduals who feel that they have been falsely depicted by McGinniss.[5]

Well before the plot is "enacted," each major cast member is introduced in his or her own chapter by a narrator who is technically implicit but nonetheless unambiguously judgmental. This same narrator leisurely con-structs the scenes and evaluates the setting: Toms River, New Jersey, with its appalling (to McGinniss's mind) shallowness and snobbery. The author clearly marks out his larger anticonsumerist, antisuburban theme; the Mar-shall case is the "quintessential symbol of the consequences" (257) of the money- and status-hungry but ultimately value-impoverished lifestyle of Toms River and places like it. McGinniss is generous in his pity for Robert and Maria Marshall's three sons (only one of whom begins with the epon-ymous faith in his father). His sensitivity to their pain is reflected in both his methods and his writing.[6] But it lacks any sort of moral complexity or ambivalence. There is surface horror but no mystery; if it is dramatic, it certainly is not poetic. The writing is not flashy or pretentious, but neither is it particularly sophisticated. When clichés fail, McGinniss resorts to italics or exclamation points to underscore his personal disgust. Ultimately, McGinniss fails to persuade readers of the significance of his topic. Readers won't care.

While much of the power of literary journalism depends on writers' per-sonal integrity, questions about McGinniss's methods appear to have dam-aged neither McGinniss's credibility nor the status of other literary journalists. Even McGinniss's detractors generally do not challenge his "facts or his commitment to total immersion in his subject matter."[7] Furthermore, despite his flat, wry style, he never entirely erases himself. He does not pretend detachment and objectivity, and he concedes that his presence inevitably has some impact on his subjects, as much as he wishes it would not (he associates himself with the fly-on-the-wall school). But his anxiety about his position can undermine his effectiveness. More critically, readers may dispute either his larger (that is, bleaker) truth or simply reject it as trivial.

In 1991 McGinniss returned again to grisly family murder in a small town, and once more did so at the request of an interested party. McGinniss was asked by Bonnie Von Stein to tell the story of her son, who had failed to kill her but succeeded in stabbing to death his stepfather as part of a plot to inherit $2 million. McGinniss, who sold the television rights to *Cruel Doubt* before the book was even finished, received full authorization from the mother to interview not only her and her son and daughter but also their lawyers and doctors. McGinniss's engaging boyish charm as well as his reputation as a writer continue to work in his favor when he is interviewing sources, but, again, some minor figures in his newest piece of journalism have complained about McGinniss's negative treatment.

McGinniss graduated from the College of the Holy Cross in 1964. Rejected by the Columbia Graduate School of Journalism, he briefly worked for several newspapers before getting the high-status *Inquirer* job; he has also freelanced for a number of magazines. McGinniss compares himself to a surfer, compulsively seeking to write that perfect book. Yet he calls writing "lonely, awful, terrible, frustrating and depressing." He lives with his wife Nancy and their children in Williamstown, Massachusetts, where "there is nothing else to do but write" (*Current Bio.* 1984, 269).

NOTES

1. He wrote an *Inquirer* column that blamed violence generally inherent in society for Robert Kennedy's assassination—a column that the paper's own publisher, Walter Annenberg, publicly attacked.

2. McGinnis later began researching a book about Edward Kennedy, but abandoned the project when the Senator and his family erected what McGinnis saw as too many "barricades."

3. Later he did some sports writing, and for ten years ran marathons.

4. Janet Malcolm's *New Yorker* article was later published as a book.

5. One state senator, for example, denies the implication that he intervened in (or obstructed) the murder investigation; but since he is called by another name in the book, he told a *New York Times* reporter. "it's like fighting a ghost."

6. He showed a pre-publication draft of *Blind Faith* to the sons. It is interesting to note that one of them, Roby Marshall, actively served as a consultant to the mini-series based on the book.

7. Both Malcolm and a recent TV documentary hint that MacDonald may be

innocent; at least one review of that documentary maintains that *Fatal Vision* is no longer authoritative.

PRIMARY SOURCES

McGinniss, Joe. 1969. *The Selling of the President 1968*. New York: Trident Press.
————. 1972. *The Dream Team*. New York: Random House.
————. 1976. *Heroes*. New York: Viking Press.
————. 1980. *Going to Extremes*. New York: Knopf.
————. 1983. *Fatal Vision*. New York: G. P. Putnam's Sons.
————. 1989a. *Blind Faith*. New York: G. P. Putnam's Sons.
————. 1989b, Apr. 3. "My Critic's Cloudy Vision." *New York Times*: 23.
————. 1989c, Apr. 7. "The Art of Non-fiction: The Creation of Everyday Life." Panel discussion, University of Massachusetts, Amherst.
————. 1991. *Cruel Doubt*. New York: Simon & Schuster.

SECONDARY SOURCES

Gottlieb, Martin. 1989, July-Aug. "Dangerous Liaisons? Journalists and Their Sources." *Columbia Journalism Review*: 21–36.
"Joe McGinniss." 1984. In *Current Biography Yearbook*: 268–71.
King, Wayne. 1989, Mar. 29. "It's Not Us, Toms River Says of Portrayal in Book." *New York Times*: B1–2.
Kramer, Mark. 1980, Sept. 27. Review of *Going to Extremes*, by Joe McGinniss. *Nation* 231: 290.
Malcolm, Janet. 1989a, Mar. 13. "Reflections: The Journalist and the Murderer." Part 1. *New Yorker*: 38–73.
————. 1989b, Mar. 20, "Reflections: The Journalist and the Murderer." Part 2. *New Yorker*: 49–82.
Ruth, Daniel. 1989, July 12. "Convicted Murderer Pins New Hopes on 'False Witness' Show." *Chicago Sun-Times*: 35.

TRACY KIDDER

John M. Coward

The jacket photo on Tracy Kidder's 1974 book, *The Road to Yuba City*, shows the twenty-eight-year-old author lounging happily on a porch in jeans and a denim jacket. With wire-rim glasses, sporting a mustache and long hair, Kidder is the very image of the journalist-adventurer circa 1970: intelligent, street-wise, and fashionably bohemian. It was a fitting image too, given that Kidder traveled to California by boxcar and tramped along skid row as he researched the grisly topic of his first book: the life and times of Juan Corona, the labor contractor convicted of murdering twenty-five migrant workers.

The photo on Kidder's 1989 book, *Among Schoolchildren*, reveals a different man. His hair is shorter and his wire-rims have given way to traditional tortoise-shell frames. But there are more substantial differences too. The newer photo shows a man in a classroom staring pensively into the camera. Kidder's intelligence still comes through, but his face seems wiser. Maybe the years have added character. Or perhaps the newer picture simply reveals a man completely at ease with himself and his achievements: three books in the 1980s, all best-sellers, all critical successes, and one of them, *The Soul of a New Machine*, honored with an American Book Award and a Pulitzer Prize.

Tracy Kidder's journey to the front rank of American literary journalists can be traced back to his undergraduate years at Harvard, where he began writing short stories. After graduation and a stint as an army intelligence officer in Vietnam, Kidder continued his literary studies at the University of Iowa, where he completed a creative writing degree. Along the way, Kidder made friends with Dan Wakefield, then a contributing editor at the *Atlantic Monthly*. Wakefield recommended Kidder to the *Atlantic*, which launched his career in journalism by sending him in pursuit of Juan Corona.

Unfortunately, Kidder was unable to solve all the mysteries of the Corona case. *The Road to Yuba City* was the work of a literary apprentice, and it was neither a popular nor a critical success. The book's failure, however, was not for lack of trying. Kidder immersed himself in the project, hopping trains to California, sleeping in flophouses, eating in storefront missions, and hiring out to thin peach trees, a job held by some of Juan Corona's victims. This is Kidder's—and the reader's—introduction to the subculture of migrant farm workers, a world of rootlessness, exploitation, and despair, all qualities Kidder emphasizes in *Yuba City*. Nevertheless, Kidder, a Harvard man, after all, remains an outsider in this world. Migrant workers are a suspicious lot, and few of Kidder's sources are helpful. As a result, *The Road to Yuba City* rarely achieves the depth or emotional intensity needed to tell the Corona story effectively.

Kidder is more successful explaining the legal gamesmanship and courthouse characters surrounding the Corona trial. Kidder, whose father was a lawyer, carefully explains the inconsistencies in the state's case and provides illuminating portraits of the prosecutors, men so ill-prepared to prove Corona's guilt that they nearly cause the judge to drop the charges. But the book's central force is Corona's flamboyant attorney, Richard Hawk, a "short, chubby man with a missing thumb" (1974a, 57). Hawk opens up to Kidder, using him as a sounding board for his legal strategies, walking him through the evidence and, eventually, introducing him to Juan Corona. Although dedicated and energetic, Hawk is driven by something more than a desire to help his client: "Yeah, if I win this one, it'll propel me past Bailey. Lee hasn't done that much" (63). Moreover, Hawk, as Kidder shows, is as much hot air as he is legal strategist, effectively impeaching many of the state's witnesses, but unable to explain away the mounting evidence against his client. In fact, when it comes time to actually mount his much-ballyhooed defense, Hawk simply rests the case. This is a major blunder, and the jury, as Kidder later discovers, seizes on Hawk's failure when it votes to convict.

One of the book's most powerful chapters comes from Kidder's visit with the family of Donald Dale Smith, or "Boogy Red," as he called himself. Smith grew up in Frankfort, Kansas, drifted through the Depression, and was drafted during World War II. He was in his thirties then, Kidder notes, and the army was his first steady job. From England, Smith wrote home about coming back to Kansas and raising a family. It didn't work out that way. He returned home in 1945, but left abruptly after a week. The last letter the family received was posted from Caliente, Nevada, in 1949. "Maybe he was just born with wanderlust," a family member told Kidder. "Maybe really inside him he had a love for the outdoors" (175). This is one of the book's most poignant scenes, moving the reader to the emotional center of the story by recreating the life of Boogy Red.

Despite such successes, *Yuba City* suffers from Kidder's shifting point of view. The book is written in first person and organized around Kidder's investigation—"I took the sheriff's advice. I called up Hawk that evening" (56)—but that narrative is more effective when Kidder slips into the background and lets his sources tell the story. Thus Kidder's prominence in *Yuba City*—an attempt, apparently, to explain his feelings and motives as he worked the Corona case—results in a narrative so transparent that it undermines much of the story's inherent interest and emotional power. In addition, the conflicting evidence and other uncertainties of the case lead Kidder to equivocate too often. Meanwhile, some of the most important aspects of the story, such as the personality of the mysterious Juan Corona, go wanting. In a jailhouse interview, for example, Kidder agrees to Hawk's request not to ask Corona about the crimes. Instead, they talk about television, and Kidder learns that Corona's favorite show is "The Big Valley," which he can get in Spanish. Even when Kidder tells Corona that he believes in his innocence, Corona says merely, "sure" and "fine" (79). Given such answers, Kidder is never able to make Corona a vivid character in his own story.

In the end, Kidder's book is a sad one, both thematically and stylistically. In spite of Corona's successful prosecution, the murders were so bizarre, the evidence so disputed, and the major figures so disappointing that the book was bound to leave readers unsatisfied. Kidder apparently thought so too. In 1982, an interviewer for *Contemporary Authors* asked Kidder about his intentions in *The Road to Yuba City*. Kidder replied: I didn't know what I was doing. That was the first piece of journalism I ever did" (May 1983, 251).

If Kidder was disappointed with the reception of *Yuba City*, he did not let it slow down his writing career. Even before *Yuba City* appeared, the *Atlantic* published Kidder's Vietnam short story, "The Death of Major Great," in which a group of jaded GIs murder and dismember their despised commanding officer in the opening paragraph. But Kidder soon returned to journalism and, in a series of *Atlantic* articles, he refined his reporting skills, sketching his characters more distinctly and exercising greater authority over his prose. He wrote about life in the Caribbean ("Winter in St. Lucia") and contributed two pieces on American railroading ("Trains in Trouble" and "Railroads: Aboard the Ghost Trains"). Kidder also developed a particular interest in the environment, investigating such topics as water pollution ("Sludge"), solar energy ("Tinkering with Sunshine"), and nuclear power ("The Nonviolent War Against Nuclear Power").

Kidder returned to the Vietnam experience for one of his best *Atlantic* pieces, a study of Vietnam veterans that later won a Sidney Hillman Foundation Prize. In "Soldiers of Misfortune," Kidder describes the postwar tribulations of a variety of veterans, starting with Max Cleland, who lost an arm and two legs in the war before serving as the first Vietnam veteran to lead the Veterans Administration (VA). Kidder compares the stereotypical Vietnam vet—"an angry, confused young man who has brought the war

home in a duffel bag full of heroin and automatic weapons" (1978a, 43)—
with the reality of Marion Tyson, a thirty-two-year-old combat veteran
from Birmingham who cannot get a job, despite continuing Congressional
promises and a host of GI programs. The article closes with the story of
Bobby Muller, a paralyzed veteran who, Kidder writes, represents "a paradigm of what was worst about the war and best about many of the men
who had to fight it" (89). Muller's spinal cord was severed by a bullet when
he was twenty-two. He woke up on a hospital ship, glad to be alive. But
his treatment at the hands of the VA left him embittered. After a year in
the rat-infested Kingsbridge VA Hospital in the Bronx, Muller enrolled in
law school with one goal in mind: to sue the VA. At the end of the article,
Kidder departs from the straightforward style of the piece to recreate one
of Muller's recurrent dreams, a Vietnam nightmare in which Muller, restored to a healthy body, foresees the outcome of the battle, the very battle
in which he was wounded. In the dream, Muller tries to explain this vision
to his men. Kidder puts this scene in italics:

*[Muller] tries to warn them about the coming fire fight, attempting to frighten the
ones he knows are going to die that afternoon. He shouts at them that this battle
will leave him, their lieutenant, three-quarters paralyzed. . . . They are saddling up,
shrugging into knapsacks, picking up their weapons. He has to follow them. He is
weeping, because he knows that it is going to happen all over again.* (90)

Kidder's success with such reporting—his growing ability to clarify complex issues and to infuse his journalism with emotional power—prepared
him well for his next writing project: documenting the eighteen-month
struggle of a group of Data General engineers to create a speedy new mini-
computer. In *The Soul of a New Machine*, Kidder succeeded admirably,
turning workaday computer engineering into high drama, filling out the
story with stress-driven managers, manipulated recruits fresh from grade
school, and the near-magical presence of computer technology.

Unlike *The Road to Yuba City*, *The Soul of a New Machine* was an
immediate success, climbing the best-seller lists and commanding reviews
in publications as diverse as the *New York Review of Books*, *English Journal*, *Nature*, *Business Week*, and *Technology Review*. In fact, the differences
between *Yuba City* and *The Soul of a New Machine* provide a number of
insights into Kidder's growth as a literary journalist. *Yuba City* involved
the bizarre murders of farm workers in California, a territory both physically
and psychologically foreign to an educated easterner like Kidder. Moreover,
the Corona case was largely inexplicable; even the trial had produced no
fully convincing version of the murders. Kidder, like the police, was forced
to reconstruct the case from bits and pieces of circumstantial evidence. *The
Soul of a New Machine* involved no such difficulties, reflecting Kidder's
new care in selecting subjects for his writing. In addition, Kidder was literally

and figuratively close to home in this book. Data General's main office was in Westborough, Massachusetts, home turf for Kidder. More important, *The Soul of a New Machine* was created from the lives of articulate and energetic engineers to which Kidder enjoyed complete access. *The Soul of a New Machine* succeeds, in large measure, because Kidder enters the minds of Data General managers and engineers so thoroughly that their work habits, office politicking, technical prowess, and midnight ramblings are rendered in convincing detail. And this time Kidder's first-person voice is limited, placing the book's emphasis on the engineers, where it belongs. If *Yuba City* was the work of a beginner, *The Soul of a New Machine* demonstrated Kidder's new mastery of the nonfiction form.

Kidder is clearly enthusiastic about his task here—explaining the art and science of computer design in a way that ordinary readers can follow. In fact, Kidder's explanations are among the principal strengths of *The Soul of a New Machine*. Faced with the intricacies of computer architecture as well as abstract programming concepts, Kidder uses analogies to bring the technology into everyday understanding. A translator, as Kidder explains it, can be thought of as "a newfangled, automatic barnyard gate in an electrical fence" (1981, 93). Kidder also tackles the complexities of the new computer's thirty-two-bit architecture, the electronic plan for storing and managing data. The thirty-two-bit design problem fell to a Brooklyn-born engineer named Steve Wallach. "If you imagine the computer's storage—its memory—to be a large collection of telephones," Kidder writes, "then what Wallach was doing might be described as designing a logical system by which phones and groups of phones could be easily identified—a system of area codes, for instance" (76). But this was the easy part. The hard part was devising a system to protect stored information. Wallach solved this problem by adapting a system of "rings," an image that inspires one of Kidder's strongest analogies:

Picture an Army encampment in which all the tents are arranged in several concentric rings. The general's tent lies at the center, and he can move freely from one ring of tents to another. In the next ring out from the center live the colonels, say, and they can move from their ring into any outer ring as they please, but they can't intrude on the general's ring without his dispensation. The same rules apply all the way to the outermost ring, where the privates reside. They have no special privileges; they can't move into any ring inside their own without permission. (79)

The Soul of a New Machine hit the bookstores in 1981, when public interest in the "computer revolution" was dawning. Timing, perhaps, accounts for some of the book's enormous popularity. But *The Soul of a New Machine* works because it goes beyond the machine to the people who are struggling to build it. From his months in the catacombs of Data General,

Kidder comes to know both the personalities and the dynamics of this world. In fact, Kidder's portraits of the Data General engineers hold the book together and make computer-building a compelling and very human endeavor. At the center of this process is Tom West, project manager for the new machine. Sometimes mysterious, sometimes angry, West is the central force in the book, a former folksinger and self-taught engineer whose nickname is "Prince of Darkness." Kidder opens *The Soul of a New Machine* by recalling a sailing trip that West took with a group of other men. Most of the others got seasick. West did not; he would not let himself go queasy. Other men needed sleep; West stayed awake for days, much of that time at the tiller. As Kidder explains, this was typical Tom West:

The people who shared that journey remembered West. The following winter, describing the nasty northeaster over dinner, the captain remarked, "That fellow West is a good man in a storm." The psychologist did not see West again, but remained curious about him. "He didn't sleep for four whole nights. *Four whole nights.*" And if that trip had been his idea of a vacation, where, the psychologist wanted to know, did he work? (7)

In Tom West, Kidder finds a personality strong enough to unify and drive his narrative. As project manager, West is the link between a host of technical problems and the engineers who must solve them. As the new computer takes shape, Kidder reveals an increasingly driven West and then expands his story outward to describe key members of West's team. Carl Alsing, for example, is one of West's top lieutenants. As a child, Kidder says, Alsing disassembled the family telephone. These days, Alsing has a habit of disabling all the television sets in his home, "on the theory that his sons would learn more from trying to repair a TV than from watching one" (163). Kidder also profiles Neal Firth, a twenty-two-year-old "Microkid," one of the new engineers pegged to write the language that controls the machine. Firth has degrees in computer science and electrical engineering, Kidder notes, and likes to program. This makes him Alsing's natural choice to develop a complex computer program that will simulate the workings of the new machine, a task vital to the project's success, but one that Alsing thinks could take an experienced programmer a year and a half. Alsing wants it sooner—much sooner. How do you get an engineer to do the near-impossible? Kidder provides this scene:

Shortly after Firth arrived, Alsing sat down with him and discussed ideas for a simulator. "There are a number of things you have to do to write one," said Alsing, drawing a grossly oversimplified picture of the task.

"Yeah, I could do that," Firth replied.

They talked about simulators with growing enthusiasm, until Alsing felt they had a "nice little fire going." Then casually, Alsing popped the question: "How long do you think it would take to write this simulator?"

"Six weeks or two months?" said Firth.
"Oh, good," said Alsing. (164)

Firth is wrong; it takes him over three months to write the simulator, and another two months to refine it. But Alsing gets his simulator, and the new machine gets one step closer to reality. In *The Soul of a New Machine*, Kidder sketches dozens of these engineering encounters, reconstructing the actions as well as the motives of those involved and supporting his apparent clairvoyance with quotations, daydreams, memories, and other details mined from his sources. The ultimate effect of this technique is credibility. Kidder knows so much, and tells it so well, that *The Soul of a New Machine* seems unassailably true. And if Kidder has neither the stylistic flair of Tom Wolfe nor the lyricism of Truman Capote, his prose is nonetheless effective. Kidder is a master of detail and nuance, describing the everyday experiences of Tom West and the other Data General engineers with such clarity that their lives and their computer take on heightened significance. In the end, *The Soul of a New Machine* succeeds not because of its innovative technique or its stylistic excellence but because of Kidder's skill as a storyteller: *The Soul of a New Machine* is a thickly woven, intelligent, and illuminating story, filled with fascinating characters and a wide range of knowledge and emotions. Kidder closes the book, in fact, by noting both the success of the new machine and the bitterness of the engineers who built it. Having invested extraordinary amounts of time and energy in the project, the engineers suddenly face the prospect of mere eight-hour days without pressure. They feel empty and unappreciated. Steve Wallach and Carl Alsing leave the company, while the rest of the team moves on to other projects. Tom West stays with Data General, taking a marketing job. He is philosophical about the end of the project: "It was a summer romance. But that's all right. Summer romances are some of the best things that ever happen" (287).

The formula for *The Soul of a New Machine*—profiling a group of talented people involved in a high-stress project—was highly successful, which may explain why Kidder employed it again in his next book. *House*, published in 1985, involved none of the high-tech explanations that distinguished *The Soul of a New Machine*, but the people, the pressure, and the psychological situations of the two stories are similar. Like the engineers at Data General, the carpenters of Apple Corps are creative people with complex problems to solve and a deadline to meet. And even though house-building is far less glamorous than computer-building, Kidder demonstrates that building a beautiful house is every bit as rewarding and frustrating.

The house in question is the Souweine house, designed by a Yale-educated architect named Bill Rawn for Jonathan and Judith Souweine of Amherst, Massachusetts. He is a Harvard-educated lawyer with a liberal, activist past. She has a master's and a doctorate in education and runs the preschool program for "special needs" children in Amherst. Their new house will sit on a pretty hillside near the edge of a woods. The opening scene in the book describes the groundbreaking for the new house, a happy occasion attended by Jonathan and Judith, architect Rawn, and Jim Locke, one of the Apple Corps builders, who directs the bulldozer as it carves out the Souweine's new foundation.

It sounds like an ideal situation: well-to-do owners, a gifted architect, and four skilled, sensitive "New Age" carpenters, all working together to create the perfect house. That is not the case. Architect Rawn has been practicing for several years, but this is his first house, a fact that the builders rarely forget. They do not trust him; confrontations are inevitable. The house itself is ambitious. Rawn draws a Greek Revival house so elegant that it overtakes the Souweines' budget. To get the price below $160,000, in fact, the Souweines drop a garage and other features of Rawn's original design. There is also a running battle between the Souweines and the builders, mostly about money. As an attorney, Jonathan is an aggressive negotiator, and he insists that Apple Corps agree to a contract price, a move the builders think will lock them into a no-profit deal. In the end, Apple Corps grudgingly agrees to Jonathan's price—$142,000—but Jonathan's attitude remains a sore point to the carpenters.

House is divided into five sections, starting with "The Contract" and moving chronologically through the seasons of house-building: "Architecture," "Wood," "In a Workmanlike Manner," and the conclusion, "Returns." As in *The Soul of a New Machine*, Kidder is a keen observer, keeping close watch on the progress of the house and the personalities involved in it. Jim Locke, Apple Corps' carpenter and principal negotiator, is a study in contradictions. Son of an eminent lawyer, Jim is guarded and insecure around Jonathan. Locke want to prep school but never succeeded at college. "It's funny," he says, "because I love learning things and I got some real highs in there, and even now I get purely intellectual joy out of things" (1985, 25). One of the other carpenters, Richard, has a working-class background. His father was a farmer and a repairman, which explains how Richard learned to build things. Less high-strung than Jim, Richard is the group's best cabinetmaker and an emotional anchor for the Apple Corps partners.

Once again, Kidder is at home in this world—in Massachusetts, among interesting people. Caught up in the details of house-building and the hundreds of decisions that go with it, Kidder narrates the contest of wills between architect, owner, and builder in an even-handed manner. Rawn is pursuing his vision of the perfect house, but the Souweines, strapped for cash and unwilling to live in a pretentious Greek temple, are caught between the architect's ideals and the builders' reality. By the end, the carpenters are sniping at each other and all the parties seem exhausted. But the house gets built, to the final delight of Rawn and the Souweines. "For Judith," Kidder writes, "living in her new house is like a treasure hunt. She keeps finding little acts of genius in the design, and she calls Bill often to report her discoveries" (316). Apple Corps, however, has less to smile about. After taking out their wages and paying off the final bills, the partners calculate a profit of $3,000, far below their expectations. " 'It's always the same,' says Jim. 'When you're done, the work's gone, and you focus on money. That's when you think, they have a house and you don't have very much to show for it' " (326). There is one consolation, however; in 1985, the Souweine house won a prestigious award from the Boston Society of Architects.

Like *The Soul of a New Machine*, *House* demonstrates Kidder's ability to draw vivid and memorable characters. Early in the book, for example, architect Rawn is introduced by his height: "The top of a standard door frame is six-feet-eight-inches from the floor. Bill Rawn's head just misses tops of doorways, like a trailer truck going under highway bridges" (14). Here is a man, Kidder writes, who can speak fluently on many subjects, though "it can be nerve-racking to hear him talk about designs of houses and buildings. When he begins a sentence, you worry that he may not find his way to the end of it" (15). Later, Kidder reveals more about Rawn's love of architecture: "Bill Rawn's heart raced when he first saw the old buildings of Venice. In Barcelona he once climbed over a rooftop, recklessly breaking the law in Franco's Spain, horrifying his Catalonian friends, just to get a close look at some of Gaudi's work" (51).

House brims with details of this sort. It is graceful work, perhaps the most elegant and richly textured book Kidder has written. In a sketch about the architecture of Western Massachusetts, for example, Kidder describes the nineteenth-century heritage of Northfield, a village "that belongs in an old lithograph." "Northfield," Kidder continues, "has houses with hipped roofs and center chimneys, ones with pediments and columned porticoes, ones with the pointy-topped windows of the prototypical American haunted house. The late Georgian, the Federalist, the Greek Revival and the Gothic, all are represented in the old houses on Northfield's streets." Typically, Kidder sees these houses in human terms: "The curious fact about them is that most were designed and built, for about five hundred dollars apiece, by a carpenter named Calvin Stearns and by his sons and brother." Stearns's houses, Kidder concludes, "look straighter and squarer than most things 150 years old. An elderly man who lives in a Stearns Federalist likes to say that someone once put a cable around another Stearns house and tried to pull it over, and the cable broke" (109).

House is also enriched by Kidder's more formal approach to research. Unlike his previous two books, *House* contains a two-page explanation of building terms and a seven-page list of people, books, articles, and even dissertations that Kidder used in researching the book. This new approach contrasts sharply with the personal, impressionistic approach Kidder took in *The Road to Yuba City*. Even *The Soul of a New Machine* was not as thoroughly documented as *House*, and the book benefits from Kidder's informed digressions into the history of architecture and New England building customs and the like. Moreover, Kidder finally solves his point of view problems in *House* by disappearing entirely from the text. Once a participant in his reporting, Kidder is only a listener here, but he is a wise and knowing listener, and his observations consistently ring true. By the end, the reader may very well long to follow Bill Rawn back to the house and to sit, as he does, in the living room he designed: "Morning light really does stream in just as he dreamed it would" (317).

Among Schoolchildren, Kidder's fourth book, opens with the words of its primary subject, a fifth grade teacher in Holyoke, Massachusetts, named Chris Zajac:

Mrs. Zajac wasn't born yesterday. She knows you didn't do your best work, Clarence. Don't you remember Mrs. Zajac saying that if you didn't do your best she'd make you do it over? As for you Claude, God forbid that you should ever need brain surgery. But Mrs. Zajac hopes that if you do, the doctor won't open up your head and walk off saying he's almost done, as you said when Mrs. Zajac asked you for your penmanship. (1989, 1)

Chris Zajac does more than scold her pupils. An energetic thirty-four-year-old, she constantly encourages and cajoles her students, pushing them to do better, never satisfied. In a classroom of twenty fifth-graders—about half of them Puerto Rican—Kidder discovers Chris Zajac's true calling: teaching, yes, but much more. Chris Zajac, like so many other public school teachers, works to inspire confidence, to instill curiosity, to offer hope.

Kidder's method here is familiar. By immersing himself in Chris Zajac's routine and shadowing her and her pupils as they plod through the school year, Kidder again highlights the extraordinary textures of ordinary life. And by focusing so intensely for so long on one teacher, Kidder's portrait of Chris Zajac reaches a level of psychological truth unmatched in his other books; Chris Zajac's *thoughts* are important parts of this story. The story also works because Kidder describes the schoolchildren and their families in considerable detail. There is Judith, for example, a Puerto Rican child whose father runs a storefront ministry and whose academic gifts never fail to impress. Then there's Clarence, the class troublemaker, also Puerto Rican, whose disciplinary file is as thick as the Boston phonebook. Clarence is bright and charming and utterly uninterested in anything to do with school. Try as she might—and it is abundantly clear that she does—Mrs. Zajac cannot keep Clarence interested in learning. Yet she tries, again and again, fretting over her frequent confrontations with Clarence, even dreaming about them. Chris Zajac is consumed with her job, doing all she can to save her children from the easy slide into mischief, drugs, teenage pregnancy, and life at the bottom of the socioeconomic ladder.

As in *House*, Kidder is the hidden but nearly omniscient observer, emphasizing the small but important lessons that take place daily in Mrs. Zajac's classroom. Kidder also provides a larger context for her classroom, offering informative asides on the continuing efforts to reform public education as well as the social and economic history of Holyoke, once a prosperous industrial city, now racked by unemployment, poverty, and racial tension. But Kidder's effort here is less revolutionary than descriptive. He advances no prescriptions for classroom reform. Kidder's achievement in this book is to show the near-impossible tasks placed on Chris Zajac and, by extension, every public school teacher in America. And by rooting *Among Schoolchildren* in one classroom, Kidder celebrates the particular and frames the debate over public education in human terms, a refreshing change from the doublespeak that frequently overtakes this topic.

Tracy Kidder started his journalism career covering a mass murder, a topic all too familiar in American journalism. But Kidder, whose original ambition was to write fiction, seemed ill-suited to the Juan Corona story, an elusive tale that would have stumped even seasoned reporters. Thus the Corona case, Kidder's most traditionally newsworthy topic, resulted in his least successful book. Kidder became successful, in fact, investigating more subtle matters: the design of computers, the psychology of house-building, and the challenges of teaching. Kidder's ability to transform these routine topics into readable and revealing character studies is one of his greatest strengths as a literary journalist.

One measure of Kidder's growth as a nonfiction writer is the increased authority of his voice. In *The Road to Yuba City* Kidder was a novice reporter and a participant in his own investigation, following the example of his friend Dan Wakefield, who once argued that reporters are individuals, "not all-knowing, all-seeing Eyes but separate, complex, limited, particular 'I's' " (Weber 1980, 23). Yet Kidder's prose has been more effective when his personality has been submerged in the story, becoming, in contrast to Wakefield, more authoritative by virtue of being (apparently) all-knowing. *House* and *Among Schoolchildren* are thus enriched by Kidder's wide range of reading and his careful and refined explorations of his subjects. This stance—this scholarly approach to journalism—seems to suit Kidder, who has no overt personal or ideological agenda to advance in his writings. Kidder is more interested in the story—the complete and living story—and he uses his descriptive skills to bring his characters to life in vivid and memorable ways. For this reason, Kidder's technique as a literary journalist is deceptively simple, as if his characters carry the narrative by themselves. But such simplicity is clearly an illusion. Kidder's stories look easy, but this is the ease and grace that comes only after months of research and thousands of pages of notes. What makes Kidder's work effective is his consistent ability to sift through his materials and come up with the telling details and critical moments that move and inspire the reader.

PRIMARY SOURCES

Kidder, Tracy. 1974a. *The Road to Yuba City: A Journey into the Juan Corona Murders.* Garden City. N.Y.: Doubleday.

———. 1974b, Jan. "The Death of Major Great." *Atlantic*: 82–84.

———. 1975, Apr. "Sludge." *Atlantic*: 62–70.

———. 1976a, Jan. "Winter in St. Lucia." *Atlantic*: 92–94.

———. 1976b, Aug. "Trains in Trouble." *Atlantic*: 29–39.

———. 1977, Oct. "Tinkering with Sunshine." *Atlantic*: 70–83.

———. 1978a, Mar. "Soldiers of Misfortune." *Atlantic*: 41–52, 87–90.

———. 1978b, June. "Railroads: Abroad the Ghost Trains." *Atlantic* 14–22.

———. 1978c, Sept. "The Nonviolent War Against Nuclear Power." *Atlantic*: 70–76.

———. 1980, Sept. "In Quarantine." *Atlantic*: 92–100.

———. 1981. *The Soul of a New Machine.* Boston: Little, Brown.

———. 1985. *House.* Boston: Houghton Mifflin.

———. 1989. *Among Schoolchildren.* Boston: Houghton Mifflin.

SECONDARY SOURCES

May, Hal, ed. 1983. *Contemporary Authors 109.* Detroit: Gale Research.

Weber, Ronald. 1980. *The Literature of Fact.* Athens: Ohio University Press.

SELECTED BIBLIOGRAPHY

The following works are either cited in the preface and introduction or are significant works on literary journalism and the new journalism. Works pertaining to the writers discussed in the essays in this book appear at the conclusion of each essay. Other related works are mentioned in the Introduction under Other Literary Journalists and in the Introduction's notes section.

Ade, George. 1941. *Stories of the Streets and of the Town from the Chicago Record, 1893–1900*. Ed. Franklin J. Meine. Chicago: The Claxton Club.

Agee, James. 1937, Sept. "Havana Cruise." *Fortune*: 117. Rpt. in *James Agee: Selected Journalism*. Ed.Paul Ashdown.

Agee, James, and Walker Evans. 1939. *Let Us Now Praise Famous Men*. Boston: Houghton Mifflin.

Anderson, Chris. 1987. *Style as Argument: Contemporary American Nonfiction*. Carbondale: Southern Illinois University Press.

———, ed. 1989. *Literary Nonfiction: Theory, Criticism, Pedagogy*. Carbondale: Southern Illinois University Press.

Anderson, Frederick, ed. 1971. *Mark Twain: The Critical Heritage.* New York: Barnes and Noble.

Ashdown, Paul, ed. 1985. *James Agee: Selected Journalism*. Knoxville: University of Tennessee Press.

Berner, R. Thomas. 1982, Fall. "Literary Notions and Utilitarian Reality." *Style* 16: 452–57. This issue of *Style* is devoted to "Newspaper Writing as Art."

———. 1986, Oct. *Literary Newswriting: The Death of an Oxymoron*. Journalism Monographs 99. Columbia, S.C.: Association for Education in Journalism and Mass Communication.

———. 1988. *Writing Literary Features*. Hillsdale, N.J.: Lawrence Erlbaum Associates.

Best Newspaper Writing. St. Petersburg, Fla.: Poynter Institute for Media Studies.

Boylan, James. 1984. "Publicity for the Great Depression: Newspaper Default and Literary Reportage." In *Mass Media Between the Wars: Perceptions of Cul-*

tural Tension, 1917–1941. Ed. Catherine Covert and John Stevens. Syracuse: Syracuse University Press.

Boyton, H. W. 1904, June. "The Literary Aspect of Journalism." *Atlantic* 93: 845–51.

Brown, Charles H. 1972a, Mar. "New Art Journalism Revisited." *Quill*: 31–38.

———. 1972b, June. "The Rise of the New Journalism." *Current*: 31–38.

Carey, John. 1987. *Eyewitness to History*. Cambridge, Mass.: Harvard University Press.

Carlson, Oliver. 1942. *The Man Who Made the News*. New York: Duell, Sloan and Pearce.

Chase, Dennis. 1972, Aug. "From Lippman to Irving to New Journalism." *Quill*: 19–21.

Cheney, Theodore A. Rees. 1987. *Writing Creative Nonfiction*. Cincinnati: Writer's Digest Books.

"Confessions of a Literary Journalist." 1907, Dec. *Bookman* 26: 370–76.

Crane, Stephen. 1960. *Stephen Crane: Letters*. Ed. Lillian Gilkes and R. W. Stallman. New York: New York University Press.

———. 1970. "War Memories." *Tales of War*, vol. 6 of *The University of Virginia Edition of the Works of Stephen Crane*: 222–63. Charlottesville: University Press of Virginia.

———. 1973a. "The Broken-Down Van." In *Tales, Sketches, and Reports*, vol. 8 of *The University of Virginia Edition of the Works of Stephen Crane*: 275–80.

———. 1973b. "When Man Falls, a Crowd Gathers." In *Tales, Sketches, and Reports*.

Davis, Lennard. 1983. *Factual Fictions: The Origins of the English Novel*. New York: Columbia University Press.

Dennis, Everette E. 1971. *The Magic Writing Machine*. Eugene: University of Oregon Press.

Dennis, Everette E., and William L. Rivers. 1974. *Other Voices: The New Journalism in America*. San Francisco: Canfield Press.

Didion, Joan. 1968. "Dreamers of the Golden Dream." In *Slouching Towards Bethlehem*. New York: Farrar, Straus and Giroux.

———. 1979. *The White Album*. New York: Simon and Schuster.

———. 1984. "Why I Write." In *Joan Didion: Essays and Conversations*. Ed. Ellen G. Friedman. Princeton: Ontario Review Press.

Eason, David. 1981, Fall. "Telling Stories and Making Sense." *Journal of Popular Culture* 15: 125–29.

———. 1982, Spring. "New Journalism, Metaphor and Culture." *Journal of Popular Culture* 15: 142–49.

———. 1990. "The New Journalism and the Image-World." In *Literary Journalism in the Twentieth Century*. Ed. Norman Sims. New York: Oxford University Press. This is a new version of Eason, "The New Journalism and the Image-World: Two Modes of Organizing Experience," *Critical Studies in Mass Communication* 1 (Mar. 1984): 51–65.

Fishkin, Shelley Fisher. 1985. *From Fact to Fiction: Journalism and Imaginative Writing in America*. Baltimore: Johns Hopkins University Press.

Flippen, Charles C., ed. 1974. *Liberating the Media: The New Journalism*. Washington, D.C.: Acropolis Books.

Fontaine, Andre. 1974. *The Art of Writing Nonfiction*. New York: Thomas Y. Crowell.

Ford, Edwin H. 1937. *A Bibliography of Literary Journalism*. Minneapolis: Burgess Publishing.

———. 1950. "The Art and Craft of the Literary Journalist." In *New Survey of Journalism*. Ed. George Fox Mott. New York: Barnes and Noble. Orig. pub. as *Journalism Outline* in 1937.

Franke, Warren T. 1974, Summer. "W. T. Stead: The First New Journalist?" *Journalism History* 1, no. 2: 36, 63–66.

Franklin, Jon. 1986. *Writing for Story: Craft Secrets of Dramatic Nonfiction by a Two-Time Pulitzer Prize Winner*. New York: Atheneum.

———. 1987, Autumn. "Myths of Literary Journalism: A Practitioner's Perspective." *Journalism Educator*: 8–13.

Goldstein, Richard. 1989. *Reporting the Counterculture*. Boston: Unwin Hyman.

Grant, Gerald. 1970, Spring. "The 'New Journalism' We Need." *Columbia Journalism Review* 9: 12–16.

Greene, Bob. 1983. *American Beat*. New York: Penguin.

Hapgood, Hutchins. 1905. "A New Form of Literature." *Bookman* 21: 424–47.

———. 1939. *A Victorian in the Modern World*. New York: Harcourt, Brace.

Hayes, Harold. 1972, Jan. "Editor's Notes." *Esquire*: 12. Rpt. in Weber 1974.

———. ed. 1969. *Smiling Through the Apocalypse: Esquire's History of the Sixties*. New York: McCall. Introduction reprinted in Weber 1974.

Hellman, John. 1981. *Fables of Fact: The New Journalism as New Fiction*. Urbana: University of Illinois Press.

Hernadi, Paul. 1972. *Beyond Genre: New Directions in Literary Classification*. Ithaca, N.Y.: Cornell University Press.

Hersey, John. 1949, Nov. "The Novel of Contemporary History." *Atlantic Monthly*.

———. 1980, Autumn. "The Legend on the License." *Yale Review* 70: 1–25.

Hollowell, John. 1977. *Fact and Fiction: The New Journalism and the Nonfiction Novel*. Chapel Hill: University of North Carolina Press.

Hough, George A., III. 1975, Summer. "How 'New'?" *Journal of Popular Culture* 9: 114–21.

Howe, Quentin. 1967, May 20. "The Age of the Journalist-Historian." *Saturday Review*: 25–27.

Jensen, Jay. 1974, Summer. "The New Journalism in Historical Perspective." *Journalism History* 1, no. 2: 37, 66. Taken from Flippen 1974, 18–28.

Johnson, Michael L. 1971. *The New Journalism: The Underground Press, the Artists of Nonfiction, and Changes in the Established Media*. Lawrence: University of Kansas Press.

———. 1975, Summer. "Wherein Lies the Value?" *Journal of Popular Culture* 9: 135–41.

Journal of Popular Culture 9. 1975, Summer. Contains eighteen articles on "The New Journalism": 99–249.

Landreth, Elizabeth. 1975, Summer. "There Shall Be No Light: Las Vegas." *Journal of Popular Culture* 9: 197–203.

Lapham, Lewis H. 1981, July. "Gilding the News." *Harper's*: 31–39.

Lee, Gerald Stanley. 1900, Feb. "Journalism as a Basis for Literature." *Atlantic*: 231–37.

"Literature and Journalism." 1897, Jan. 1. Editorial in *New York Commercial Advertiser*, 4.

Lounsberry, Barbara. 1990. *The Art of Fact: Contemporary Artists of Nonfiction.* Westport, Conn.: Greenwood Press.

Macdonald, Dwight. 1965, Aug. 26. "Parajournalism, or Tom Wolfe and His Magic Writing Machine." *New York Review of Books*: 3–5. Rpt. in Weber 1974.

MacLeish, Archibald. 1958. "Poetry and Journalism." Gideon Seymour Lecture. Minneapolis: University of Minnesota Press. See also MacLeish, "The Poet and the Press," *Atlantic Monthly* 205 (Mar. 1959): 40–46.

Markel, Lester. 1972, Jan. "So What's New?" *Bulletin of the American Society of Newspaper Editors*: 1, 7–9. Rpt. in Weber 1974.

Masterson, Mark. 1971, Feb. "The New Journalism." *Quill*: 15–17.

Mills, Nicolaus, ed. 1974. *The New Journalism: An Historical Anthology*. New York: McGraw-Hill.

Murphy, James E. 1974, May. *The New Journalism: A Critical Perspective*. Journalism Monographs 34.

Murray, Donald M. 1982, Fall. "From *What* to *Why*: The Changing Style of Newswriting." *Style* 16: 448–51.

Newfield, Jack. 1972, July-Aug. "Is There a New Journalism?" *Columbia Journalism Review* 11: 45–47. Rpt. in Weber 1974.

"Newspaper and Fiction." 1906, July. "The Point of View," *Scribner's Magazine* 40: 122–24.

"Plea for Literary Journalism." 1902, Oct. 25. *Harper's Weekly* 46: 1558.

Podhoretz, Norman. 1958, July. "The Article as Art." *Harper's*: 74–79. Rpt. in Weber 1974.

Ridgeway, James. 1971, June. "The New Journalism." *American Libraries* 2: 585–92.

Robinson, L. W., Harold Hayes, Gay Talese, and Tom Wolfe. 1970, Jan. "The New Journalism: A Panel Discussion." *Writer's Digest*: 32–35. Rpt. in Weber 1974.

Ruehlmann, William. 1977. *Stalking the Feature Story*. Cincinnati: Writer's Digest.

Scanlon, Paul, ed. 1977. *Reporting: The Rolling Stone Style*. New York: Anchor Press/Doubleday.

Schudson, Michael. 1978. *Discovering the News: A Social History of American Newspapers*. New York: Basic Books.

Sims, Norman. 1982, July-Aug. "A New Generation of 'New' Journalists." *Quill*: 9–14.

———, ed. 1984. *The Literary Journalists*. New York: Ballantine Books.

———, ed. 1990. *Literary Journalism in the Twentieth Century*. New York: Oxford University Press.

Snyder, L. L. 1962. *A Treasury of Great Reporting*. 2nd ed. New York: Simon and Schuster.

Steffens, Lincoln. 1931. *The Autobiography of Lincoln Steffens*. New York: Harcourt, Brace.

Stott, William. 1973. *Documentary Expression and Thirties America*. New York: Oxford University Press.

Tebbel, John W. 1971, Mar. 13. "The 'Old' New Journalism." *Saturday Review*:
    86–90.
Trachtenberg, Alan. 1974a. "Experiments in Another Country: Stephen Crane's
    City Sketches." *Southern Review* 10: 278.
———. 1974b. "What's New." Review of *The New Journalism*, by Tom Wolfe.
    Partisan Review 41: 296–302.
Wakefield, Dan. 1966, June. "The Personal Voice and the Impersonal Eye." *Atlantic*:
    86–90. Rpt. in Weber 1974.
Warnock, John Ed. 1989. *Representing Reality: Readings in Literary Nonfiction*.
    New York: St. Martin's Press.
Webb, Joseph M. 1974, Summer. "Historical Perspective on the New Journalism."
    Journalism History 1, no. 2: 38–42, 60.
Weber, Ronald. 1975. "Moon Talk." *Journal of Popular Culture* 9: 142–52.
———. 1980. *The Literature of Fact: Literary Nonfiction in American Writing*.
    Athens: Ohio University Press.
———, ed. 1974. *The Reporter as Artist: A Look at the New Journalism Contro-
    versy*. New York: Hastings House.
Wolfe, Tom. 1973. *The New Journalism*. With an Anthology edited by Tom Wolfe
    and E. W. Johnson. New York: Harper and Row.
Zavarzadeh, Mas'ud. 1976. *The Mythopoeic Reality: The Postwar American Non-
    fiction Novel*. Urbana: University of Illinois Press.

INDEX

Page numbers in *italic* indicate main entries.

ABOUT THE EDITOR AND CONTRIBUTORS

PAUL ASHDOWN is a professor of journalism at the University of Tennessee and a former wire service and newspaper journalist. He edited a collection of James Agee's magazine articles, *James Agee: Selected Journalism* (1985), and has done research on such topics as medical news, Irish media, television editorials, newspaper economics, and popular culture.

ANNA BANKS is an assistant professor of communication at the University of Idaho. Her research interests include the use of social iconography in films (fictional and documentary) and in photographs. She is working on a study of the portrayal of journalists in Hollywood films of the 1980s.

SHARON BASS is an associate professor of journalism at the University of Kansas, where she teaches magazine publishing, design, and writing. She has done research and writing on the New Journalism, documentary photography, editorial management, and forestry and land management. She has written a book on the Ozark–St. Francis National Forest, coordinates two annual competitions for city and regional magazines, and directs the City and Regional Magazine Education Fund.

R. THOMAS BERNER is a professor of journalism and American Studies at the Pennsylvania State University. He is the author of four books, including *Writing Literary Features*, which was derived from the Journalism Monograph *Literary Newswriting: The Death of an Oxymoron*. His articles include "The Narrative and the Headline," which was published in *Newspaper Research Journal*.

PATRICIA BRADLEY has a Ph.D. in American Studies from the University of Texas and is an associate professor of journalism at Temple University. She is a former newspaper reporter and editor, magazine writer, and television journalist. She has published in the area of early American journalism and is currently writing on the philosophical underpinnings of nineteenth-century American journalism.

SANDRA BRAMAN is Research Assistant Professor at the Institute of Communication Research, University of Illinois. Her research focuses on law and policy, including the impact of the legal environment on the development of narrative form in general, and the nature, use, and impact of facticity in particular.

THOMAS B. CONNERY is an associate professor of journalism and chair of the Department of Journalism and Mass Communication at the University of St. Thomas, where he teaches a course in literary journalism. His writing on literary journalism has appeared in the journals *American Journalism* and *Journalism History* and in the book *Literary Journalism in the Twentieth Century*, ed. Norman Sims. He is a former president of the American Journalism Historians Association.

JOHN M. COWARD is an assistant professor of communication at the University of Tulsa. His research and writing have explored the image of Native Americans in the nineteenth-century press and other aspects of journalism history. His articles have appeared in *Grassroots Editor*, *Newspaper Research Journal*, and *Journalism Quarterly*. He is a former newspaper editor, reporter, and freelance writer.

BRUCE J. EVENSEN is an assistant professor in the Department of Communication at DePaul University. His work in journalism history has been published in *American Journalism*, *Journalism Quarterly*, and *Journalism History*. His work on the relationship of the American press to public opinion and foreign policy has been published in *Diplomatic History*, *Presidential Studies Quarterly*, and *Middle Eastern Studies*. His forthcoming book on the press and the origins of the Cold War will be published by Greenwood.

GILES FOWLER is an associate professor of journalism at Iowa State University, where he teaches a course in journalism and literature. He is a former staff member of the *Kansas City Star*, where he was a reporter, theater critic, feature writer, and editor of the Sunday magazine. He also spent a year writing for the *Times* of London.

HOWARD GOOD is associate professor in the Journalism Program at the

State University of New York at New Paltz. He is the author of *Acquainted with the Night: The Image of Journalists in American Fiction, 1890–1930* (1986) and the forthcoming *Yesterday's News: Journalists as Autobiographers*. He has also published articles on war correspondence, the portrayal of the press in American poetry, and journalism education. He teaches a course called "The Literature of Journalism."

DONALD R. HETTINGA is a professor of English at Calvin College, where he teaches journalism and literature, including a course on literary journalism. He is the author of *In the World: Reading and Writing as a Christian* and is a contributing editor of the *Heath Anthology of American Literature*. He is currently working on two books on children's literature.

ROBERT E. HUMPHREY is a professor of journalism at the University of California, Sacramento. Humphrey has a Ph.D. in history and a master's degree in communication studies. He is the author of *Children of Fantasy: The First of Greenwich Village*.

DAN R. JONES is an associate professor of English at the University of Houston-Downtown where he teaches journalism and nonfiction writing in the Professional Writing Program. He has a doctorate in American Studies, and his primary research interest is the theory of nonfiction writing. He has worked as a freelance writer and editor and as a professional writing consultant to business.

STEVE JONES is an assistant professor of communication at the University of Tulsa. He writes and teaches on mass communication and society, technology, popular culture, and popular music. He is the editor of *Tracking*, a quarterly journal of popular music studies. He has a doctorate from the Institute of Communication Research, University of Illinois.

RICHARD A. KALLAN teaches courses in media history, ethics, and criticism at California Lutheran University. His work has been published in *Communication Monographs, Journalism Quarterly, Federal Communications Law Journal*, and *Journal of Popular Culture*. His research interest in Tom Wolfe began during graduate study at Northwestern University, where he received a doctorate in rhetorical theory and criticism.

ARTHUR J. KAUL is an associate professor of journalism and Chair of the Department of Journalism, School of Communication, University of Southern Mississippi. His scholarly interests include literary journalism, mass media ethics and history, and the integration of history and social theory. His work has appeared in *Critical Studies in Mass Communication, Journal of Mass Media Ethics*, and other publications.

JACK LULE is an assistant professor of journalism at Lehigh University with a specialization in media studies and criticism. A former contributing writer for the *Philadelphia Inquirer*, he received a Ph.D. in mass communication and the Certificate in Global Policy Studies from the University of Georgia. His work has appeared in *Journalism Quarterly*, the *International Communication Bulletin, Political Communication and Persuasion*, and other journals.

RONALD S. MARMARELLI teaches journalism at Central Michigan University. A former newspaper reporter, Marmarelli has a master's degree in journalism and has done doctoral work in American Studies. His primary research interest is William Hard and the Progressive Era. His research and writing have been published in various biographical and magazine histories and guides.

MARILYN ANN MOSS, a doctoral candidate at the University of California, Riverside, is working on a psychoanalytic study of autobiography in late nineteenth-century American fiction. The author of articles on Paul Bowles and film director Francis Ford Coppola, she also is a book reviewer for the *Review of Contemporary Fiction* and a film writer for a Los Angeles film magazine, and has written textual annotations for *The Norton Anthology of American Literature*.

JACK A. NELSON is director of the magazine journalism program at Brigham Young University. A primary area of interest has been the frontier press, including the writing of Mark Twain. Nelson has a master's degree in English and a doctorate in journalism.

PETER PARISI, an assistant professor of humanities and communication at Penn State, Harrisburg, teaches journalistic writing, popular culture, and literary journalism. His primary research focus has been the development of newswriting style and the human-interest story. He has worked as a newspaper reporter and editor and has a Ph.D. in English from Indiana University.

JOHN J. PAULY is an associate professor of communication at the University of Tulsa. His research on the history and sociology of the mass media has appeared in *Communication, Communication Research, Critical Studies in Mass Communication, Journalism Monographs, American Quarterly*, and other journals and books. In 1989 he began a six-year term as editor of *American Journalism*, the quarterly journal of the American Journalism Historians Association.

CAROL POLSGROVE is an associate professor of journalism at Indiana

University. She has been an editor at *Mother Jones* and the *Progressive* and has published articles and reviews in the *Nation, Atlantic, Sierra,* and other magazines. She has a Ph.D. in English from the University of Louisville.

DONALD RINGNALDA is an associate professor of English at the University of St. Thomas. He has published widely in the field of Vietnam War literary studies. His articles have appeared in *Western Humanities Review, Journal of American Studies,* a Modern Language Association anthology on teaching the Vietnam War, and two books of literary criticism.

ARTHUR W. ROBERTS is professor of English at State University of New York College at Morrisville, where he has taught since 1966. Recently named a Distinguished S.U.N.Y. Teaching Professor, he is the coeditor of *"As Ever, Gene": The Letters of Eugene O'Neill to George Jean Nathan* (1987).

NANCY ROBERTS is an associate professor in the School of Journalism and Mass Communication at the University of Minnesota. Her publications include *Dorothy Day and the "Catholic Worker"* and *"As Ever, Gene": The Letters of Eugene O'Neill to George Jean Nathan* (coeditor), as well as articles for *Christian Century,* the *Boston Globe,* the *Philadelphia Inquirer, Americana, U.S. Catholic,* and other publications. She has a master's degree in American civilization from Brown and a doctorate in mass communication from the University of Minnesota.

MICHAEL ROBERTSON teaches American literature and American Studies at Lafayette College. He has published work in *Columbia Journalism Review, American Quarterly,* and *American Studies.* He received a National Endowment for the Humanities Fellowship for his book in progress on Stephen Crane's journalism.

ROBERT SCHMUHL is an associate professor in American Studies and Director of the Program on Ethics and the Media at the University of Notre Dame. Schmuhl's *Statecraft and Stagecraft: American Political Life in the Age of Personality* was published in 1990. He is the editor of *The Classroom and the Newsroom* and *The Responsibilities of Journalism,* and the author of *The University of Notre Dame: A Contemporary Portrait.* His articles have appeared in several journals, including *Critical Studies in Mass Communication,* the *Review of Politics,* and the *Annals of the Academy of Political and Social Science.* His features, columns, and reviews have appeared in a number of newspapers and magazines, including the *Washington Post* and *Sports Illustrated.* He is currently working with Max Lerner on a collection of statements about American civilization called *The Soul of America.*

NORMAN SIMS is associate professor and chair of the Journalism Department at the University of Massachusetts. He edited and contributed to *Literary Journalism in the Twentieth Century* (1990) and edited and wrote the introduction to *The Literary Journalists* (1984). His articles have appeared in *Journalism History, The Quill, Critical Studies in Mass Communication, Gannett Center Journal,* and *The Dictionary of Literary Biography.*

LINDA STEINER teaches in the Department of Journalism and Mass Media at Rutgers University. She has published articles and chapters in several scholarly journals and books. Her research interests include ethics, feminist theorizing and feminist communication, and journalism history, especially the woman's suffrage press. She coauthored *And Baby Makes Two: Motherhood Without Marriage* and is writing a book about feminist ethics.

GARY L. WHITBY is chair of the Division of Communication and Fine Arts at Spring Hill College in Mobile, Alabama. He holds the MFA in creative writing from the Iowa Writers Workshop and the Ph.D. in mass communication from the University of Iowa. He is the founding editor of *American Journalism,* the publication of the American Journalism Historians Association, and former editor of the *Journal of Communication Inquiry.*